HARCOURT BRACE COLLEGE OUTLINE SERIES

SPANISH GRAMMAR

Bridget Aldaraca

Edward Baker

Department of Romance Languages
University of Florida

Harcourt Brace College Publishers
Fort Worth   Philadelphia   San Diego
New York   Orlando   Austin   San Antonio
Toronto   Montreal   London   Sydney   Tokyo

Printed in the United States of America

LIBRARY OF CONGRESS CATALOGING IN PUBLICATION DATA

Aldaraca, Bridget.
    Spanish grammar.

    (Harcourt Brace Jovanovich college outline
series)   (Books for professionals)
    Includes index.
    1. Spanish language—Text-books for foreign
speakers—English.   2. Spanish language—Grammar—
1950–   . I. Baker, Edward.   II. Title.
III. Series.   IV. Series: Books for professionals.
PC4129.E5B35   1986   468.2.'421   85-14162
ISBN 0-15-601689-3

9 0 1 2 3 4   145   16 15 14 13 12

CONTENTS

PREFACE

The purpose of this book is to present a complete introductory course in Spanish grammar in the clear, concise format of an outline. It is comprehensive enough to be used by itself for independent study, or as a supplement to college courses and textbooks on the subject. In the case of independent study, regular features of the book are specially designed to build your skills in a logical sequence of study. If used as a supplement to your course work, these regular features are easily located and structured to give extra practice in all areas of Spanish grammar.

ORGANIZATION The book is organized according to the parts of speech; that is, nouns and articles, adverbs and adjectives, verbs, and so forth. Each rule of grammar and of syntax (word order) is explained, and each explanation is followed by one or more examples. All examples are translated into English so that you do not need to look up vocabulary. If you have difficulty understanding a grammar explanation, study the example.

EXERCISES Once you understand each grammar explanation and the corresponding examples, do the exercise or exercises relating to that section. *Do not skip the exercises and go to the next point of grammar.* Each exercise should be completed immediately following the corresponding grammar point for reinforcement of learning. Try to finish the exercise before you turn to the answers. If you are unable to complete an item within the exercise, go to the next item, completing as many as you can.

SUMMARY This feature consists of a brief restatement of the main grammatical points in each chapter. A brief example is included with most points. Because it is presented in the efficient form of a numbered list, you can use the summary to refresh your memory quickly before an exam.

RAISE YOUR GRADES This feature is located at the end of the chapter and consists of more exercises offering comprehensive application of or extra practice in the major grammatical points covered in the chapter. Should you have trouble completing any of these exercises, section references are provided so that you can locate and review the relevant information.

ANSWERS The answers to all of the exercises, including the Raise Your Grades exercises, are provided at the end of each chapter and translated into English. Because the answers are translated, the vocabulary of the exercises is slightly more varied than is usual in a book of this kind. This enables you to use the answers as a tool in building vocabulary. Once you have completed and checked the exercises, you can use the English translations to further reinforce your vocabulary by translating them back into Spanish and checking them against the completed exercises.

The authors owe a debt of gratitude to a number of people whose knowledge and hard work made this book possible. Special thanks, however, go to Susan Wiseman, for her expert editing throughout.

1 NOUNS AND ARTICLES

1-1. Forms of the Definite Article

In English, the definite article *the* has only one form and can be used to modify any noun regardless of whether that noun is singular or plural. In Spanish, however, the form of the definite article changes according to the *number* and *gender* of the noun it precedes.

A. The definite article has four forms.

Study the following chart and examples.

	Singular	Plural
Masculine	el	los
Feminine	la	las

el libro	*the book*	los libros	*the books*
la ventana	*the window*	las ventanas	*the windows*

EXERCISE 1-1: Look at the article that precedes the noun. Write in the gender (masculine or feminine) and the number (singular or plural) of the article and the noun. Answers are at the end of the chapter.

Example: el libro   *M-sing*

        las ventanas   *F-pl*

1. el dibujo _____
2. las sillas _____
3. los muebles _____
4. la lámpara _____
5. el maestro _____
6. la maestra _____
7. los hijos _____
8. las manos _____
9. la ciudad _____
10. los panaderos _____
11. el poeta _____
12. la cantante _____
13. las paredes _____
14. los Estados Unidos _____
15. la española _____
16. el español _____
17. el pizarrón _____
18. la tumba _____
19. la Argentina _____
20. el país _____
21. las canciones _____
22. el partido _____
23. el papa _____
24. la papa _____

B. **The masculine singular article *el* is used before feminine nouns beginning with a stressed *a*.**

Feminine nouns such as **agua**, **álgebra**, and **águila**, are preceded by the masculine **el** instead of the feminine **la** in order to avoid the awkward sound of **la . . . a**. For the plurals of these feminine nouns, however, the feminine plural form **las** is used. Nouns that begin with a silent **h** followed by a stressed **a** follow the same pattern.

Stressed **a**		Unstressed **a**	
Singular	Plural	Singular	Plural
el agua	**las** aguas	**la** albóndiga	**las** albóndigas
el alma	**las** almas	**la** arteria	**las** arterias
el hacha	**las** hachas	**la** habitación	**las** habitaciones

> **REMEMBER:** The noun ending is *not* the most reliable indicator of noun gender. The article that precedes the noun always indicates the noun gender *except* in the case of nouns beginning with a stressed **a** or **ha**.

EXERCISE 1-2: Choose the correct article: **el**, **la**, **los**, or **las**. Watch for words beginning with a stressed **a** or **ha**. If you are not sure whether the noun is masculine or feminine, look it up in your dictionary. Don't guess. Answers are at the end of the chapter.

1. _____ campana
2. _____ sombrero
3. _____ voto
4. _____ álgebra
5. _____ abuela
6. _____ hijos
7. _____ disco
8. _____ ajo
9. _____ sopa
10. _____ anuncio
11. _____ sábana
12. _____ alfombra
13. _____ haba
14. _____ sandalia
15. _____ mesas
16. _____ estado
17. _____ besos
18. _____ máquinas
19. _____ armas
20. _____ armario

1-2. Gender of Nouns

A. **All nouns in Spanish are either masculine or feminine.**

Nouns like *table* or *chair*, which are genderless in English, are either masculine or feminine in Spanish. As a general rule, most nouns ending in **o** are masculine and most ending in **a** are feminine, but there are some exceptions. Study the following examples of masculine nouns ending in **o** and feminine nouns ending in **a**.

Masculine		Feminine	
el mach**o**	*male*	**la** hembra	*female*
el muchach**o**	*boy*	**la** muchacha	*girl*
el maestr**o**	*teacher*	**la** maestra	*teacher*
el teléfon**o**	*telephone*	**la** casa	*house*
el trabaj**o**	*work*	**la** mesa	*table*

B. **Some nouns ending in *a* are masculine.**

The following is a list of some frequently used nouns belonging to this group.

el día	*day*	**el** programa	*program*
el mapa	*map*	**el** sistema	*system*
el planeta	*planet*	**el** tema	*theme, subject*
el poema	*poem*	**el** telegrama	*telegram*
el problema	*problem*	**el** teorema	*theorem*

> **NOTE:** There are two commonly used nouns ending in **o** that are feminine: **la mano**, *hand*, and **la foto**, *photo* (an abbreviation of the longer word *fotografía*).

C. **Nouns ending in *-tad*, *-dad*, and *-tud*, are always feminine.**

Study the following list of nouns. Note the frequent correspondence between **-dad** in Spanish and *-ty* in English.

la bon**dad**	*goodness*	**la** mal**dad**	*wickedness*
la cari**dad**	*charity*	**la** pleni**tud**	*abundance*
la ciu**dad**	*city*	**la** sani**dad**	*health*
la dificul**tad**	*difficulty*	**la** santi**dad**	*holiness*
la igual**dad**	*equality*	**la** sole**dad**	*solitude*
la juven**tud**	*youth*	**la** universi**dad**	*university*
la liber**tad**	*liberty*	**la** vani**dad**	*vanity*

D. **Nouns ending in *-ción* and *-umbre* are always feminine.**

Study the following list of nouns. Note the correspondence between **-ción** in Spanish and *-tion* in English.

-ción		umbre	
la ac**ción**	*action*	**la** c**umbre**	*peak*
la bendi**ción**	*blessing*	**la** l**umbre**	*fire*
la constitu**ción**	*constitution*	**la** muched**umbre**	*crowd*
la fun**ción**	*function*	**la** pesad**umbre**	*burden, worry*
la libera**ción**	*liberation*	**la** podred**umbre**	*rot*
la legisla**ción**	*legislation*		
la medita**ción**	*meditation*		
la motiva**ción**	*motivation*		
la revolu**ción**	*revolution*		

E. **Nouns referring to persons and animals can be masculine or feminine.**

The masculine and feminine forms of the nouns are usually distinguished by the addition of **o** or **a** to a common stem.

el novi**o**	*bridegroom*	**la** novi**a**	*bride*
el prim**o**	*cousin (m)*	**la** prim**a**	*cousin (f)*
el gat**o**	*cat (m)*	**la** gat**a**	*cat (f)*

Sometimes, however, the **o** or **a** ending that indicates a masculine or feminine noun is absent.

el rey	*king*	**la** reina	*queen*
el conde	*count*	**la** condesa	*countess*
el señor	*gentleman (Mr.)*	**la** señora	*lady (Mrs.)*
el tigre	*tiger*	**la** tigresa	*tigress*
el león	*lion*	**la** leona	*lioness*

F. **Nouns referring to a person's profession or social position often end in *-ista*, *-ante*, or *-ente*.**

These noun endings do not change according to gender. The difference in gender is indicated by the masculine or feminine article preceding the noun.

Masculine		Feminine	
el estudiante	*student*	**la** estudiante	*student*
el presidente	*president*	**la** presidente	*president*
el artista	*artist, performer*	**la** artista	*artist, performer*
el dentista	*dentist*	**la** dentista	*dentist*
el poeta	*poet*	**la** poeta	*poet*

G. **Some nouns have a common stem to which both *o* and *a* endings are added.**

The meanings of common-stem nouns may or may not be related. Study the following lists of common-stem nouns and compare their meanings.

Related Pairs of Common-Stem Nouns

el manzano	*apple tree*	la manzana	*apple*
el político	*politician*	la política	*politics, policy*
el músico	*musician*	la música	*music*
el pimiento	*red or green pepper*	la pimienta	*black pepper*

Unrelated Pairs of Common-Stem Nouns

el puerto	*port*	la puerta	*door*
el caso	*case*	la casa	*house*
el cuento	*story*	la cuenta	*bill*
el preso	*prisoner*	la presa	*dam*

H. Some common-stem nouns do not change their endings to indicate a change in gender.
Only the article preceding these nouns signals a change in gender and, consequently, a change in meaning. These pairs of common-stem nouns do not always have related meanings.

Masculine		Feminine	
el papa	*pope*	**la** papa	*potato*
el cura	*priest*	**la** cura	*cure*
el capital	*capital (money)*	**la** capital	*capital city*
el radio	*radio set*	**la** radio	*radio broadcasting system*
el guía	*guide*	**la** guía	*guidebook*
el orden	*order (opposite of disorder)*	**la** orden	*religious order; command*
el frente	*military front*	**la** frente	*forehead*

NOTE: If the common-stem noun signifies a person rather than a thing, the gender is masculine: **el papa, el guía.**

EXERCISE 1-3: Look up the noun stem in your dictionary and add the correct ending. Then write in the corresponding definite article. Answers are at the end of the chapter.

1. ____ maestr____ *teacher (m)*
   ____ maestr____ *teacher (f)*
2. ____ bailar____ *dancer (m)*
   ____ bailar____ *dancer (f)*
3. ____ estudi____ *student (m)*
   ____ estudi____ *student (f)*
4. ____ obrer____ *worker (m)*
   ____ obrer____ *worker (f)*
5. ____ cond____ *count*
   ____ cond____ *countess*
6. ____ tigr____ *tiger*
   ____ tigr____ *tigress*

7. ____ novi____ *bridegroom, boyfriend*
   ____ novi____ *bride, girlfriend*
8. ____ escrit____ *writer (m)*
   ____ escrit____ *writer (f)*
9. ____ cociner____ *chef (m)*
   ____ cociner____ *chef (f)*
10. ____ pian____ *pianist (m)*
    ____ pian____ *pianist (f)*
11. ____ cant____ *singer (m)*
    ____ cant____ *singer (f)*
12. ____ tax____ *taxi driver (m)*
    ____ tax____ *taxi driver (f)*

1-3. Plural of Nouns

The plural is formed by adding either **-s** or **-es** to nouns. The formation of the plural can affect the accenting and spelling of the word.

A. Add *-s* to nouns ending in a vowel to form the plural.

Singular		Plural	
el gato	*cat*	los gatos	*cats*
la silla	*chair*	las sillas	*chairs*
la tribu	*tribe*	las tribus	*tribes*
el puente	*bridge*	los puentes	*bridges*

NOTE: Most nouns ending in a vowel end in **o**, **a**, or **e**. A few nouns end in an accented vowel: **neblí, tisú,** and **muftí** are some examples. They form the plural by adding -es: **neblíes, tisúes, muftíes.**

B. **Add -es to nouns ending in a consonant to form the plural.**

Singular		Plural	
el árbol	*tree*	los árbol**es**	*trees*
el pintor	*painter*	los pintor**es**	*painters*
la verdad	*truth*	las verdad**es**	*truths*
el rey	*king*	los rey**es**	*kings; king and queen*
el mes	*month*	los mes**es**	*months*

NOTE: If a noun is more than one syllable long, ends in an **-n** or an **-s**, and there is an accent on the last syllable, the accent is dropped in the plural form.

Singular		Plural	
el atún	*tuna*	los atun**es**	*tunas*
el avión	*airplane*	los avi**ones**	*airplanes*
la misión	*mission*	las misi**ones**	*missions*
el compás	*beat (measure)*	los compas**es**	*beats (measures)*

NOTE: If a noun is more than one syllable long, ends in **-n**, and the last syllable is *not* stressed, the stressed syllable retains its stress and a written accent is added in the plural form.

Singular		Plural	
el crimen	*crime*	los crím**enes**	*crimes*
el examen	*examination*	los exám**enes**	*examinations*
la orden	*religious order; command*	las órd**enes**	*religious orders; commands*

C. **If a noun ends in -z, change the z to c and add -es to form the plural.**

Singular		Plural	
la matriz	*matrix*	las matri**ces**	*matrices*
la voz	*voice*	las vo**ces**	*voices*
el avestruz	*ostrich*	los avestru**ces**	*ostriches*
la luz	*light*	las lu**ces**	*lights*
la vez	*time, instance*	las ve**ces**	*times, instances*
la cicatriz	*scar*	las cicatri**ces**	*scars*
el lápiz	*pencil*	los lápi**ces**	*pencils*

D. **The masculine plural form of Spanish nouns can include the female members of a group as well as the males.**

Study the following possible translations.

los hijos	*sons*	*son and daughter (children)*	*sons and daughters*
los reyes	*kings*	*king and queen*	*kings and queens*
los padres	*fathers*	*father and mother (parents)*	*fathers and mothers*
los señores	*gentlemen*	*Mr. and Mrs.*	
los niños	*boys*	*boy and girl (children)*	*boys and girls*

E. **Compound nouns are formed by combining the plural form of a noun with a verb or preposition.**

The article preceding compound nouns changes from singular to plural to indicate a change in number, but the noun itself does not change its ending. Compound nouns are *always* masculine.

	Singular		Plural	
el tocadiscos	*record player*	**los** tocadiscos	*record players*	
el rompecabezas	*jigsaw puzzle*	**los** rompecabezas	*jigsaw puzzles*	
el lavaplatos	*dishwasher*	**los** lavaplatos	*dishwashers*	
el rascacielos	*skyscraper*	**los** rascacielos	*skyscrapers*	
el cumpleaños	*birthday*	**los** cumpleaños	*birthdays*	
el paraguas	*umbrella*	**los** paraguas	*umbrellas*	
el pararrayos	*lightening rod*	**los** pararrayos	*lightening rods*	
el paracaídas	*parachute*	**los** paracaídas	*parachutes*	
el parabrisas	*windshield*	**los** parabrisas	*windshields*	

EXERCISE 1-4: Change the plural form of the noun to its singular form and write in the correct translation. Don't forget to change the definite article from plural to singular. Answers are at the end of the chapter.

Example: los árboles   *el árbol, tree*

1. los novios _____
2. las mujeres _____
3. las instituciones _____
4. los albañiles _____
5. los teléfonos _____
6. los lápices _____
7. los niños _____
8. los paraguas _____
9. las luces _____
10. los elefantes _____
11. los amores _____
12. las naciones _____
13. los cumpleaños _____
14. los reyes _____
15. los hombres _____
16. las leonas _____
17. los gigantes _____
18. las sociedades _____
19. los deportes _____
20. las calles _____
21. los mapas _____
22. las águilas _____
23. las aguas _____
24. las actitudes _____
25. las funciones _____
26. los exámenes _____
27. los muebles _____
28. los abrelatas _____
29. las niñas _____
30. los bailarines _____
31. los crímenes _____
32. los días _____
33. las democracias _____
34. los meses _____
35. los lunes _____
36. las hachas _____

1-4. Use of the Definite Article

The definite article is generally used more frequently in Spanish than it is in English. In both languages, the definite article is used with specific nouns: **la casa blanca**, *the white house*. In Spanish, however, the definite article is also used with collective or abstract nouns, names of languages, days of the week, certain geographic locations, measures of value and weight, parts of the body, and articles of clothing.

A. **The definite article is used with specific nouns.**

La sal está en **la** cocina.	*The salt is in the kitchen.*
Dame **los** platos rojos primero.	*Give me the red plates first.*
¿Dónde están **los** niños?	*Where are the children?*
Necesito **las** tazas y **los** platillos.	*I need the cups and saucers.*

> **NOTE:** Unlike English, the Spanish definite article is generally used before each noun in a series, rather than before the first noun only.
>
> Quiero **la** sal y **la** pimienta, por favor.
> *I want the salt and pepper, please.*

B. **The definite article is used with collective or generic nouns and with nouns conveying an abstract sense.**

Collective nouns

Me gusta **el** pan.	*I like bread (all bread).*
La política es un negocio sucio.	*Politics is a dirty business.*
Los amigos son necesarios.	*Friends are necessary.*
Las blusas de seda son mejores que las de nylon.	*Silk blouses are better than nylon ones.*

> **NOTE:** Spanish often uses a singular noun to convey a collective sense:
>
> | | |
> |---|---|
> | **El** caballo es un animal hermoso. | *Horses are beautiful animals.* |
> | | OR |
> | | *The horse is a beautiful animal.* |

Abstract nouns

Dame **la** libertad o dame **la** muerte.	*Give me liberty or give me death.*
Necesitamos **la** paz y **la** justicia.	*We need peace and justice.*

C. **The *absence* of the definite article before a collective or abstract noun conveys the sense of a whole.**

This "partitive" sense is usually expressed in English as *some* or *any*. Compare the following Spanish and English examples.

¿No queda pan?	*Isn't there any bread left?*
Quiero galletas.	*I want some crackers.*
No hay huevos, pero hay carne.	*There aren't any eggs, but there's some meat.*
No hay justicia.	*There's not any justice.*

D. **The definite article is used instead of the possessive pronoun with parts of the body and articles of clothing.**

Dame **la** mano, José.	*Give me your hand, José.*
No quiero llevarme **la** bolsa.	*I don't want to take my purse.*
Me corto **el** pelo una vez al mes.	*I cut my hair once a month.*
Los niños se lavaron **las** manos.	*The children washed their hands.*
Miguel nunca se pone **el** traje azul.	*Miguel never wears his blue suit.*
Dejé **la** cartera en casa.	*I left my briefcase at home.*

E. **The definite article is used with the days of the week.**

An exception to this rule occurs when the day or days follow the verb **ser**. The definite article is not used with the months of the year. Study the following examples carefully.

Llegaré **el** lunes.	*I will arrive on Monday.*
Todos odiamos **los** lunes.	*We all hate Mondays.*
Los trabajadores descansan **los** domingos.	*The workers have a day off (rest) on Sunday (every Sunday).*
Los bancos no están abiertos **los** sábados y **los** domingos.	*The banks aren't open on Saturday and Sunday (all Saturdays and Sundays).*
No hay clase **el** jueves.	*There's no class this Thursday.*

> **NOTE:** Spanish uses the singular rather than the plural article to distinguish between an event happening on one day (**el jueves**) and a customary event (**los jueves**). English is more likely to use the demonstrative adjective.
>
> | | |
> |---|---|
> | No hay clase **el** jueves. | *There's no class this Thursday.* |

NOTE: The articles **el** and **los** take the place of the English preposition *on.*

Now study the use of the definite article with **ser** and the days of the week.

When the day of the week precedes the verb **ser***:*

Los lunes son horribles.	*Mondays are horrible.*
El sábado es mi cumpleaños.	*This Saturday is my birthday.*

But when the day of the week follows the verb **ser***:*

Hoy es lunes.	*Today is Monday.*
Los días de la semana laboral son lunes a viernes.	*The days of the work week are Monday through Friday.*

> **REMEMBER:** Only **sábado(s)** and **domingo(s)** have a separate plural ending. The remaining days of the week end in **s**, and the singular and plural are distinguished by a change of the definite article from **el** to **los**.

F. **The definite article is used with the names of languages.**

An exception to this rule occurs when the names of languages follow the verb **hablar** and the prepositions **en** and **de**. The definite article may or may not be used after the verb **entender**.

Quiero estudiar **el** japonés.	*I want to study Japanese.*
Dicen que **el** ruso es difícil.	*They say Russian is difficult.*
No entienden inglés.	*They don't understand English.*

OR

No entienden **el** inglés.

BUT

Los niños hablan español en casa.	*The children speak Spanish at home.*
Nosotros hablamos inglés en la escuela.	*We speak English at school.*
Soy maestra de francés.	*I am a French teacher.*
¿La película está en francés o en inglés?	*Is the movie in French or English?*

G. **The definite article is used with certain geographical names but not with others.**

Study the following list:

el Afganistán	**el** Paraguay
la Argentina	**el** Perú
el Brasil	**la** Unión Soviética
el Canadá	**el** Uruguay
la China	**la** América del Norte (Norteamérica)
los Estados Unidos	**la** América del Sur (Sudamérica)
la India	**la** América Central (Centroamérica)
el Japón	*BUT* Sudáfrica

> **NOTE:** Except for **la Unión Soviética**, European countries do not take the definite article.

H. **The definite article is used with titles of people except in forms of direct address.**

Los señores López han salido ya.	*Mr. and Mrs. López have already left.*
El doctor Méndez tiene cuarenta años.	*Dr. Méndez is forty years old.*

BUT

Señores López, ¡qué gusto verles!	*Mr. and Mrs. López, how nice to see you!*
Señor Presidente, haga el favor de sentarse.	*Mr. President, please sit down.*

I. **The definite article is used with expressions of quantity.**

In English, the indefinite articles *a* or *an* are usually used with expressions of quantity. Compare the following examples.

Los huevos cuestan noventa centavos **la** docena.　*Eggs cost ninety cents a dozen.*

La ternera cuesta setecientas pesetas **el** kilo.　*Veal costs seven hundred pesetas a kilo.*

EXERCISE 1-5: Fill in the blank with the correct form of the definite article, if one is required. Answers are at the end of the chapter.

1. _____ muchacha se pone _____ vestido rojo.
2. Dejé _____ paraguas en casa.
3. _____ leche cuesta noventa centavos _____ litro.
4. Hay _____ cerveza en _____ nevera.
5. _____ Señorita Brown, ¿quiere usted _____ café o _____ té?
6. ¿Dónde están _____ señores Smith?
7. _____ presidente vive en _____ Casa Blanca.
8. Trabajo todos _____ lunes.
9. Fui a _____ México _____ año pasado.
10. _____ sopa está en _____ mesa.
11. ¿Dónde están _____ libros nuevos?
12. _____ agua es mejor que _____ cerveza.
13. Mi hermano vive en _____ Japón.
14. Me gusta _____ deporte.
15. Me gustan _____ música y _____ pintura.
16. Quiero _____ carne.

EXERCISE 1-6: Translate the following sentences into Spanish. Answers are at the end of the chapter.

1. I don't want any bread.

2. He gets up early on Mondays.

3. She speaks Italian.

4. The children are going to China.

5. Miss García isn't here.

6. The children washed their hands.

7. Houses are expensive nowadays.

8. Tomatoes cost forty cents a pound.

9. I like baseball.

10. He writes in English.

11. There is no justice without compassion.

12. Do you want some coffee, Mr. Moreno?

13. I forgot my overcoat.

14. Today is Thursday.

15. Truth is relative.

1-5. Personal *a* and Contractions of the Definite Article

A. **The preposition *a* precedes the direct object when the object is either a person or a personalized animal or thing.**

The purpose of the personal **a** is to make it clear that the noun following it is the object, not the subject, of the verb.

1. The personal **a** may precede either a noun or an object pronoun, such as **quien**, **nadie**, or **alguien**.

Person Object		Nonperson Object	
Vi **a** María.	*I saw María.*	Vi la mesa.	*I saw the table.*
¿**A** quién viste?	*Whom did you see?*	¿Qué viste?	*What did you see?*
No conozco **a** nadie.	*I don't know anyone.*	No conozco la ciudad.	*I don't know the city.*
Encontré **a** Roberto.	*I found Roberto.*	Encontré un anillo.	*I found a ring.*

2. The personal **a** always implies a personal relationship.

Necesito jardinero.   *I need a (any) gardener.*
Necesito **al** jardinero.   *I need the gardener (because I have to give him instructions).*

3. The personal **a** ordinarily is not used with the verb **tener**, except to express a very close or emotional relationship.

| Tengo dos hijos y tres hijas. | *I have two sons and three daughters.* |
| No tengo ni madre ni padre. | *I have neither mother nor father.* |

BUT

| Aunque estoy solo, tengo **a** mi perro. | *Although I'm alone, I have my dog.* |
| Yo no tengo **a** nadie. | *I don't have anybody.* |

EXERCISE 1-7:   Use the personal **a** if required. Answers are at the end of the chapter.

1. ¿Conoce usted _____ Juan?
2. Yo no conozco _____ Los Angeles.
3. ¿ _____ quién viste?
4. ¿ _____ qué quieres hacer?
5. Vine solo, no traje _____ nadie.
6. María no vio _____ la película.
7. Vimos _____ la maestra de francés.
8. Tengo _____ un carro nuevo.
9. No estoy sola, tengo _____ mis hijos conmigo.
10. ¿Vieron _____ Tomás ayer?

B. **When *a* or *de* precedes the masculine singular definite article *el*, the two words form a contraction.**

a + el = al, *to the*
de + el = del, *of the, from the*

There are no contractions with the other forms of the definite article.

Vi **al** hermano de Juan.   *I saw Juan's brother.*

BUT

Vi **a la** hermana de Juan.   *I saw Juan's sister.*
Voy **al** cine mañana.   *I'm going to the movies tomorrow.*

BUT

Voy **a la** plaza mañana.	*I'm going to the plaza tomorrow.*
Es la casa **del** presidente.	*It's the president's house.*

BUT

Es la bolsa **de la** francesa.	*It's the French woman's purse.*
Háblame **del** poeta Pablo Neruda.	*Talk to me about the poet Pablo Neruda.*

BUT

Háblame **de los** problemas mundiales.	*Talk to me about world problems.*

> **REMEMBER:** The definite article is used before proper names that include a title, but not before proper names that do *not* include a title. Therefore, the use of **al** or **del** before a proper name depends on whether or not the definite article **el** must be used.

Quiero ver **al** señor Machado.	*I want to see Mr. Machado.*

BUT

Quiero ver **a** Antonio.	*I want to see Antonio.*
El libro es **del** profesor Hernández.	*The book is Professor Hernández's.*

BUT

El libro es **de** Juan Hernández.	*The book is Juan Hernández's.*

EXERCISE 1-8: Write in the definite article and **a** or **de** when they are required. Use the contraction **al** or **del** when necessary. Answers are at the end of the chapter.

1. Vengo _____ escuela.
2. Vi _____ hermano de Leopoldo hoy.
3. Tengo que ir _____ centro.
4. Hablamos _____ libro nuevo.
5. Dale la leche _____ vecina.
6. Iremos _____ plaza mañana.
7. Volvimos _____ parque temprano.
8. Mañana hablaremos _____ tema.
9. Visité _____ señores Moreno ayer.
10. Fui _____ Argentina el año pasado.

1-6. Forms of the Indefinite Article

The indefinite article changes according to the number and gender of the noun it modifies.

	Singular	Plural
Masculine	**un**	**unos**
Feminine	**una**	**unas**

un libro	*a book*	**unos** libros	*some (a few) books*
una silla	*a chair*	**unas** sillas	*some (a few) chairs*

EXERCISE 1-9: Translate the definite article and noun into English in the first column. Then change the definite article to the indefinite article in the second column, and translate into English. If necessary, use your dictionary to look up the correct translation of the nouns. Answers are at the end of the chapter.

Examples:				
la pluma	*the pen*	una pluma	*a pen*
las plumas	*the pens*	unas plumas	*some (a few) pens*
el libro	*the book*	un libro	*a book*
los libros	*the books*	unos libros	*some (a few) books*

1. los zapatos＿＿＿＿＿＿＿＿ ＿＿＿＿zapatos＿＿＿＿＿＿＿
2. el pastel＿＿＿＿＿＿＿＿＿ ＿＿＿＿pastel＿＿＿＿＿＿＿＿
3. la ciudad＿＿＿＿＿＿＿＿＿ ＿＿＿＿ciudad＿＿＿＿＿＿＿＿
4. las ideas＿＿＿＿＿＿＿＿＿ ＿＿＿＿ideas＿＿＿＿＿＿＿＿＿
5. los estudiantes＿＿＿＿＿＿ ＿＿＿＿estudiantes＿＿＿＿＿
6. el vaso＿＿＿＿＿＿＿＿＿＿ ＿＿＿＿vaso＿＿＿＿＿＿＿＿＿
7. los maestros＿＿＿＿＿＿＿＿ ＿＿＿＿maestros＿＿＿＿＿＿＿
8. las madres＿＿＿＿＿＿＿＿＿ ＿＿＿＿madres＿＿＿＿＿＿＿＿
9. las primas＿＿＿＿＿＿＿＿＿ ＿＿＿＿primas＿＿＿＿＿＿＿＿
10. el árbol＿＿＿＿＿＿＿＿＿ ＿＿＿＿árbol＿＿＿＿＿＿＿＿＿
11. el tiovivo＿＿＿＿＿＿＿＿＿ ＿＿＿＿tiovivo＿＿＿＿＿＿＿＿
12. las estrellas＿＿＿＿＿＿＿＿ ＿＿＿＿estrellas＿＿＿＿＿＿＿
13. el dentista＿＿＿＿＿＿＿＿＿ ＿＿＿＿dentista＿＿＿＿＿＿＿＿
14. el cantante＿＿＿＿＿＿＿＿ ＿＿＿＿cantante＿＿＿＿＿＿＿

1-7. Use of the Indefinite Article

A. In its singular forms, *un* and *una*, the indefinite article may mean either *one* or *a*.
The context of the sentence will clarify the meaning.

Tengo **una** casa bonita.　　*I have a pretty house.*
Tengo solamente **una** casa.　*I have only one house.*

B. In its plural forms, *unos* and *unas*, the indefinite article may mean either *some* or *a few*.

Tengo **unos** discos estupendos en casa.　*I have some terrific records at home.*

> **NOTE:** **Unos** may also be used with **cuantos** or **pocos** to mean *a few*.
>
> ¿Tienes **unos** discos nuevos?　　　*Do you have some new records?*
> Sí, tengo **unos cuantos** en casa.　*Yes, I have a few (quite a few) at home.*
> OR
> Sí, tengo **unos pocos** en casa.　　*Yes, I have a few (not many) at home.*

C. The indefinite article is frequently omitted in Spanish.
Unlike English, the indefinite article is omitted before an unmodified noun that follows the verb **ser**, *to be*.

Unmodified Noun		Modified Noun	
Soy escritora.	*I'm a writer.*	Soy **una** buena escritora.	*I'm a good writer.*
Es médico.	*He's a doctor.*	Es **un** médico inteligente.	*He's an intelligent doctor.*
Es francés.	*He's French.*	Es **un** francés muy educado.	*He's a very well-bred Frenchman.*

> **NOTE:** The indefinite article is frequently omitted before certain nouns when they are used in a generic or unspecific sense.
>
> No tengo casa.　　*I don't have a house (any house).*
> Necesito trabajo.　*I need work (any kind).*

D. The indefinite article is omitted before certain words.
Study the following list of words and examples.

Otro(a)
Quiero **otra** copa.　　*I want another drink.*
Necesito **otro** coche.　*I need another car.*

Cien, mil

Gané **cien** dólares.	*I made a hundred dollars.*
Quiero vivir **mil** años.	*I want to live a thousand years.*

Medio(a)

Quiero **medio** vaso de leche.	*I want half a glass of milk.*
Dame **media** libra de café.	*Give me half a pound of coffee.*

E. **The indefinite article is omitted in the exclamation ¡qué plus a noun.**

Qué plus a noun translates as "*What a(n)* _____!*" Study the following examples.

¡**Qué** idiota!	*What an idiot!*
¡**Qué** lástima!	*What a pity!*
¡**Qué** mundo!	*What a world!*
¡**Qué** muchacha más bonita!	*What a pretty girl!*

> **NOTE:** **Qué** plus an adjective translates as "*How_____ ____!"*
>
> | | |
> |---|---|
> | ¡**Qué** triste! | *How sad!* |
> | ¡**Qué** difícil! | *How difficult!* |
> | ¡**Qué** bonito! | *How pretty!* |

F. **The indefinite article is used before each noun in a series.**

Quiero **una** hamburguesa y **unas** patatas fritas.	*I want a hamburger and some french fries.*
Compré **una** blusa y **un** pantalón.	*I bought a blouse and a pair of pants.*

G. **The feminine *una* is shortened to *un* before feminine nouns beginning with a stressed *a* or *ha*.**

Tiene **un** águila viva en casa.	*He has a live eagle at home.*
Compré **un** hacha.	*I bought an ax.*

> **NOTE:** For a review of words beginning with a stressed **a** or **ha**, see Section 1-1B.

EXERCISE 1-10: Translate the following sentences into Spanish. Answers are at the end of the chapter.

1. I'm not a sailor.

2. I want a big plate, please.

3. I want another drink, please.

4. He's an Englishman.

5. What a pity!

6. He needs another pair of shoes.

7. I need a new car.

8. I don't have a house.

9. I have a hundred dollars.

10. She's a lawyer.

11. I want some new shoes.

12. I only have one car.

13. She has six sons but only one daughter.

14. She wants a hamburger, please.

15. She needs some bread, half a pound of meat, and a bottle of milk.

1-8. Use of *lo* as a Definite Article

Since there are no neuter nouns in Spanish, **lo** never precedes a noun. **Lo** precedes adjectives, such as **bueno**, **malo**, and **triste**, that are being used as nouns. Study the following Spanish sentences and their English meanings.

Lo bueno es que estás aquí.	*The good thing (what's good) is that you're here.*
Lo gracioso de la película es el final.	*The funny part of the movie is the ending.*
Lo mejor es que iremos en tren.	*The best part is that we'll go by train.*
Lo inglés me gusta.	*I like English things.*

NOTE: The English translation must supply a noun to convey the sense of the Spanish. Note the use of the words *thing* and *part* in the English translations above.

EXERCISE 1-11: Translate the English expressions given in parentheses into Spanish. Answers are at the end of the chapter.

1. Tú no sabes (the best part) del asunto. _____
2. (The dangerous thing) de la caza son los cazadores. _____
3. El huyó de (what is beautiful) de la vida. _____
4. (The worst thing) es que tenemos que madrugar. _____
5. Me interesa (ethical matters). _____
6. (What is mine) es mío. _____
7. (The only thing) es que no tengo dinero. _____
8. Me gusta mucho (Mexican things). _____
9. Su novela subraya (the strange aspects) de la psicología humana.
   _____
10. (The interesting thing) es que no quiso hablar él. _____

1-9. Diminutive and Augmentative Forms of Nouns

The meaning of Spanish nouns can change by adding a diminutive or augmentative ending to the noun stem.

A. **The diminutive form refers to a smaller size of the original noun or is used to express endearment.**

The most common diminutive endings are **-ito(a)**, **-cito(a)**, **-illo(a)**, and **-cillo(a)**.

1. If the noun ends in **a** or **o**, the **-ito(a)** ending is added to the noun stem after removal of the **a** or **o**.

rosa	rosita	*little rose*
gato	gatito	*little cat (kitty)*

2. If the noun ends in **l**, the **-ito(a)** ending is added to the complete noun.

animal	animalito	*little animal*
chaval	chavalito	*little boy (kid)*

3. If the noun ends in **e**, **r**, or **n**, the **-cito(a)** or **-cillo(a)** ending is added directly to the noun.

amor	amor**cito**	*dear little love*
puente	puente**cito**	*little bridge*
rat**ón**	raton**cito**	*little mouse*

4. Some words change the spelling of the noun stem in order to accommodate the diminutive ending.

chi**co**	chi**quito**	*little boy*
peda**zo**	peda**cito**	*little piece*

EXERCISE 1-12: Change the following nouns to their diminutive form. Answers are at the end of the chapter.

1. la palabra _____
2. el libro _____
3. el beso _____
4. la leche _____
5. el cajón _____
6. el coche _____
7. la mujer _____
8. el hogar _____
9. el agua _____
10. el vaso _____
11. el árbol _____
12. el ratón _____
13. el pájaro _____
14. el corazón _____
15. el tambor _____
16. la mesa _____
17. la silla _____
18. el sombrero _____
19. el pollo _____
20. el hermano _____
21. el león _____
22. el hombre _____
23. la nube _____
24. la mañana _____
25. el cielo _____
26. la casa _____

B. The augmentative form refers to a larger size of the original noun and it can convey a sense of disrespect or scorn.

The most common augmentative endings are **-ote(a)**, **-ón(a)**, and **-azo(a)**. Unlike the diminutive form, which is used with great frequency, the augmentative form is used only occasionally. Study the following examples.

mujer	mujer**ona**	*big (tough) woman*
hombre	hombr**ón**	*tough guy*
árbol	arbol**ote**	*large tree*
muchacho	muchach**ote**	*big kid*
cara	car**ota**	*wise guy*
perro	perra**zo**	*big scary dog*

NOTE: The **-azo** ending may also be added to the name of an object to convey the idea of a blow from that object. The derived noun is always masculine regardless of the gender of the original noun.

el hacha	*ax*	el hachazo	*blow from an ax*
la estaca	*big stick*	el estacazo	*blow from a big stick*
el martillo	*hammer*	el martillazo	*blow from a hammer*

SUMMARY

1. The definite articles **el**, **la**, **los**, and **las** must agree with the noun they modify in number and gender. All forms translate as **the**.

2. The masculine singular article **el** precedes feminine nouns that begin with a stressed **a** or **ha**, such as el **agua**, el **hacha**, and el **álgebra**.

3. Almost all nouns ending in **o** are masculine. **La mano** and **la foto** are important exceptions to this rule.

4. Most nouns ending in **a** are feminine. There are some exceptions to this rule, including nouns ending in **-ema**, such as el **problema**, el **tema**, and el **poema**.

5. Nouns ending in **-tad**, **-dad**, **-tud**, **-ción**, and **-umbre** are always feminine.
6. Form the plural of nouns by adding **s** to nouns ending in a vowel, and **es** to nouns ending in a consonant.
7. The definite article is used more frequently in Spanish than in English. It is used before abstract nouns and nouns having a collective or generic meaning.
8. The definite article is also used (a) in place of the possessive pronoun with parts of the body or clothing, (b) with the days of the week, except following the verb **ser**, (c) with the names of languages, except after the verb **hablar** and the prepositions **en** and **de**, (d) with the names of certain countries, (e) with titles, except in forms of direct address, and (f) with expressions of quantity.
9. The absence of the definite article before a noun often conveys a partitive sense that translates as *some* or *any*.
10. The preposition **a** is used before direct objects that are persons or personalized things.
11. The prepositions **a** and **de** combine with the masculine singular form of the definite article **el** to create two contractions: **al**, *to the*, and **del**, *of the* or *from the*.
12. The indefinite articles **un**, **una**, **unos**, and **unas** must agree with the noun they modify in number and gender. The singular forms translate as *one* or *a*. The plural forms translate as *some* or *a few*.
13. The indefinite article is not used as frequently in Spanish as it is in English. It is omitted (a) before unmodified nouns following the verb **ser**, (b) before certain words such as **otro**, **cien**, **mil**, and **medio**, and (c) after **qué** in exclamatory expressions.
14. **Lo** is used as a definite article to introduce adjectives functioning as nouns. Expressions such as **lo bueno** and **lo malo** translate as *the good thing* and *the bad part*.
15. Diminutive noun endings are added to nouns to refer to a smaller size of the original noun or to express fondness. Augmentative noun endings refer to a larger size of the original noun and may also express a lack of respect.

RAISE YOUR GRADES

✓ Use of the definite article [Section 1-4]

Write in the correct form of the definite article if it is necessary. If it is *not* necessary, omit it. Then choose the reason for its use or omission from the list on the right, and write in the correct letter in the space provided to the left of each sentence. You may use the same letter more than once. Answers are at the end of the chapter.

_____ 1. Voy a _____ Argentina.	*Definite article required*
_____ 2. Voy a _____ Inglaterra.	a. abstract noun
_____ 3. Hablo _____ español.	b. collective/generic noun
_____ 4. Doy la clase en _____ francés.	c. body or wearing apparel
_____ 5. Me lavé _____ pelo ayer.	d. day of the week
_____ 6. _____ verdad es hermosa.	e. language
_____ 7. Mañana es _____ domingo.	f. certain countries require definite article
_____ 8. _____ viernes llegará pronto.	g. title
_____ 9. ____ señores Brown están aquí.	h. quantity
_____ 10. No hay ____ leche en la nevera.	
_____ 11. Dejé _____ abrigo en casa.	*Definite article omitted*
_____ 12. Buscamos _____ felicidad.	i. partitive (*some* or *a few*)
_____ 13. Soy maestra de _____ inglés.	j. day following **ser**
_____ 14. _____ miércoles son libres.	k. language following **hablar**, **en**, or **de**
_____ 15. Quiero _____ pastel.	l. certain countries do not require definite article
_____ 16. Nunca trabajo _____ jueves.	
_____ 17. Llegó ____ profesor Moreno ayer.	m. title in direct address
_____ 18. _____ niños son inteligentes.	
_____ 19. _____ hombre necesita _____ paz.	
_____ 20. _____ huevos cuestan noventa centavos _____ docena.	
_____ 21. Soy de _____ India.	
_____ 22. _____ pavo cuesta treinta centavos _____ libra.	

_____ 23. Tengo que lavarme _____ manos.
_____ 24. Siéntese usted, _____ señorita Brown.
_____ 25. Me gustan _____ caballos.

☑ **Use of the indefinite article** [Section 1-7]

Write in the correct form of the indefinite article if it is necessary. If it is *not* necessary, select the reason for its omission from the list on the right, and write the correct letter in the space provided to the left of each sentence. You may use the same letter more than once. Answers are at the end of the chapter.

_____ 1. Necesito _____ otra cuchara.

_____ 2. Dame _____ vaso, por favor.

_____ 3. Compré _____ nuevo vestido.

_____ 4. ¡Qué _____ lástima!

_____ 5. Tengo _____ media libra de café.

_____ 6. Tengo _____ discos nuevos.

_____ 7. Ella es _____ maestra.

_____ 8. Ella es _____ maestra buena.

_____ 9. Quiero _____ coca cola y _____ cerveza.

_____ 10. Me va a costar _____ millón de pesetas.

_____ 11. Quiero _____ cien dólares más.

_____ 12. Ellos tienen _____ caballo y _____ motocicleta.

_____ 13. Mi hijo es _____ médico.

_____ 14. Jaime es _____ estudiante muy bueno.

_____ 15. Tengo _____ mil cosas que hacer.

Indefinite article omitted

a. unmodified noun following ser
b. before **otro**
c. before **cien** or **mil**
d. before **medio(a)**
e. after ¡**qué** plus a noun

☑ **Personal *a*** [Section 1-5]

Write in the preposition **a** if it is needed and the correct form of the definite article. Use the contraction **al** where necessary. Answers are at the end of the chapter.

1. Vi _____ Universidad de México ayer.
2. Vi _____ profesor Moreno el otro día.
3. He visto _____ maestra de francés.
4. Vi _____ Rafael ayer.
5. Fui _____ médico el martes.
6. Fui _____ plaza ayer.
7. He ido _____ Argentina.
8. Fui _____ Japón.
9. Fuimos _____ Estados Unidos.
10. Busco _____ María.
11. Busco _____ maestro.
12. Buscamos _____ calle Sexta.
13. Busco _____ señorita Hernández.
14. Busco _____ Paseo de la Reforma.
15. Busco _____ alguien diferente.

☑ **Number and gender of nouns** [Sections 1-2 and 1-3]

Identify the noun as masculine or feminine and write *m* or *f* in the space provided to the left of each number. If you are not sure, look it up in the dictionary. Next, write the correct form of the singular definite article (**el** or **la**) in the space provided between the number and each noun. Finally, write in the correct plural form of the definite article (**los** or **las**) and noun in the spaces provided to the right of the noun. Watch out for nouns that begin with a stressed **a** or **ha**. Answers are at the end of the chapter.

_m_ 1. _el_ libro _los_ _libros_

_____ 2. _____ habitación _____ _____

_____ 3. _____ corazón _____ _____

_____ 4. _____ estrella _____ _____

_____ 5. _____ tocadiscos _____ _____

_____ 6. _____ fuente _____ _____

_____ 7. _____ crimen _____ _____

_____ 8. _____ teléfono _____ _____

_____ 9. _____ mano _____ _____

_____ 10. _____ dinero _____ _____

_____ 11. _____ águila _____ _____

_____ 12. _____ padre _____ _____

_____ 13. _____ lunes

_____ 14. _____ mueble _____ _____

_____ 15. _____ dentista _____ _____

_____ 16. _____ diente _____ _____

_____ 17. _____ universidad _____ _____

_____ 18. _____ paraguas _____ _____

_____ 19. _____ álgebra _____ _____

_____ 20. _____ alma _____ _____

_____ 21. _____ albóndiga _____ _____

_____ 22. _____ alimento _____ _____

_____ 23. _____ muchedumbre _____ _____

_____ 24. _____ bailarín _____ _____

_____ 25. _____ obrero _____ _____

_____ 26. _____ elección _____ _____

CHAPTER ANSWERS

EXERCISE 1-1

1. m-sing *drawing*
2. f-pl *chairs*
3. m-pl *furniture*
4. f-sing *lamp*
5. m-sing *teacher*
6. f-sing *teacher*
7. m-pl *sons, children*
8. f-pl *hands*
9. f-sing *city*
10. m-pl *bakers*
11. m-sing *poet*
12. f-sing *singer*
13. f-pl *walls*
14. m-pl *the United States*
15. f-sing *Spaniard*
16. m-sing *Spaniard*
17. m-sing *blackboard*
18. f-sing *tomb*
19. f-sing *Argentina*
20. m-sing *country*
21. f-pl *songs*
22. m-sing *political party, game*
23. m-sing *pope*
24. f-sing *potato*

EXERCISE 1-2

1. la (f) *bell*
2. el (m) *hat*
3. el (m) *vote*
4. el (f) *algebra*
5. la (f) *grandmother*
6. los (m) *sons, children*
7. el (m) *record*
8. el (m) *garlic*
9. la (f) *soup*
10. el (m) *advertisement*
11. la (f) *sheet*
12. la (f) *rug*
13. el (f) *lima bean*
14. la (f) *sandal*
15. las (f) *tables*
16. el (m) *state*
17. los (m) *kisses*
18. las (f) *machines*
19. las (f) *weapons*
20. el (m) *clothes closet*

EXERCISE 1-3

1. el maestro, la maestra
2. el bailarín, la bailarina
3. el estudiante, la estudiante
4. el obrero, la obrera
5. el conde, la condesa
6. el tigre, la tigresa
7. el novio, la novia

8. el escritor, la escritora
9. el cocinero, la cocinera
10. el pianista, la pianista
11. el cantante, la cantante
12. el taxista, la taxista

EXERCISE 1-4

1. el novio *boyfriend, bridegroom*
2. la mujer *woman*
3. la institución *institution*
4. el albañil *construction worker*
5. el teléfono *telephone*
6. el lápiz *pencil*
7. el niño *little boy*
8. el paraguas *umbrella*
9. la luz *light*
10. el elefante *elephant*
11. el amor *love*
12. la nación *nation*
13. el cumpleaños *birthday*
14. el rey *king*
15. el hombre *man*
16. la leona *lioness*
17. el gigante *giant*
18. la sociedad *society*
19. el deporte *sport*
20. la calle *street*
21. el mapa *map*
22. el águila *eagle*
23. el agua *water*
24. la actitud *attitude*
25. la función *function*
26. el examen *exam*
27. el mueble *piece of furniture*
28. el abrelatas *can opener*
29. la niña *little girl*
30. el bailarín *dancer*
31. el crimen *crime*
32. el día *day*
33. la democracia *democracy*
34. el mes *month*
35. el lunes *Monday*
36. el hacha *ax*

EXERCISE 1-5

1. La, el *The girl puts on her red dress.*
2. el *I left my umbrella at home.*
3. La, el *Milk costs ninety cents a liter.*
4. No def. article, la *There's some beer in the refrigerator.*
5. No def. article *Miss Brown, do you want coffee or tea?*
6. los *Where are Mr. and Mrs. Smith?*
7. El, la *The president lives in the White House.*
8. los *I work every Monday.*

9. No def. article, el *I went to Mexico last year.*
10. La, la *The soup is on the table.*
11. los *Where are the new books?*
12. El, la *Water is better than beer.*
13. el *My brother lives in Japan.*
14. el *I like sports.*
15. la, la *I like music and painting.*
16. No def. article *I want some meat.*

EXERCISE 1-6
1. No quiero pan.
2. El se levanta temprano los lunes.
3. Ella habla italiano.
4. Los niños van a la China.
5. La señorita García no está.
6. Los niños se lavaron las manos.
7. Las casas son caras hoy día.
8. Los tomates cuestan cuarenta centavos la libra.
9. Me gusta el béisbol.
10. El escribe en inglés.
11. No hay justicia sin compasión.
12. ¿Quiere usted café, señor Moreno?
13. Olvidé el abrigo.
14. Hoy es jueves.
15. La verdad es relativa.

EXERCISE 1-7
1. a *Do you know Juan?*
2. *I don't know Los Angeles.*
3. A *Who did you see?*
4. *What do you want to do?*
5. a *I came alone; I didn't bring anyone.*
6. *María didn't see the movie.*
7. a *We saw the French teacher.*
8. *I have a new car.*
9. a *I'm not alone; I have my children with me.*
10. a *Did they see Tomás yesterday?*

EXERCISE 1-8
1. de la *I'm coming from school.*
2. al *I saw Leopoldo's brother today.*
3. al *I have to go downtown.*
4. del *We talked about the new book.*
5. a la *Give the milk to the neighbor.*
6. a la *We'll go to the plaza tomorrow.*
7. del *We came back from the park early.*
8. del *Tomorrow we'll talk about the matter.*
9. a los *I visited Mr. and Mrs. Moreno yesterday.*
10. a la *I went to Argentina last year.*

EXERCISE 1-9
1. *the shoes,* unos zapatos, *some shoes*
2. *the cake,* un pastel, *a cake*
3. *the city,* una ciudad, *a city*
4. *the ideas,* unas ideas, *some ideas*
5. *the students,* unos estudiantes, *some students*

6. *the glass,* un vaso, *a glass*
7. *the teachers,* unos maestros, *some teachers*
8. *the mothers,* unas madres, *some mothers*
9. *the cousins* (f), unas primas, *some cousins* (f)
10. *the tree,* un árbol, *a tree*
11. *the merry-go-round,* un tiovivo, *a merry-go-round*
12. *the stars,* unas estrellas, *some stars*
13. *the dentist,* un dentista, *a dentist*
14. *the singer,* un cantante, *a singer*

EXERCISE 1-10
1. Yo no soy marinero.
2. Quiero un plato grande, por favor.
3. Quiero otra copa, por favor.
4. Es inglés.
5. ¡Qué lástima!
6. Necesita otro par de zapatos.
7. Necesito un carro nuevo.
8. Yo no tengo casa.
9. Tengo cien dólares.
10. Es abogada.
11. Quiero unos zapatos nuevos.
12. Sólo tengo un carro.
13. Ella tiene seis hijos, pero sólo una hija.
14. Ella quiere una hamburguesa, por favor.
15. Ella necesita pan, media libra de carne, y una botella de leche.

EXERCISE 1-11
1. lo mejor *You don't know the best of it.*
2. Lo peligroso *The dangerous thing about hunting is hunters.*
3. lo bello *He fled from the beautiful part of life.*
4. Lo peor *The worst thing is that we have to get up early.*
5. lo ético *I'm interested in ethical matters.*
6. Lo mío *What's mine is mine.*
7. Lo único *The only thing is that I don't have any money.*
8. lo mexicano *I like Mexican things very much.*
9. lo extraño *His novel stresses the strange part of human psychology.*
10. Lo interesante *The interesting thing is that he didn't want to speak.*

EXERCISE 1-12
1. la palabrita *little word*
2. el librito *little book*
3. el besito *little kiss*
4. la lechecita *little bit of milk*
5. el cajoncito *little box*
6. el cochecito *little car*
7. la mujercita *little woman*
8. el hogarcito *little home, household*
9. el aguita *little bit of water*
10. el vasito *little glass*
11. el arbolito *little tree*

12. el ratoncito   *little mouse*
13. el pajarito   *little bird*
14. el corazoncito   *little heart*
15. el tamborcito   *little drum*
16. la mesita   *little table*
17. la sillita   *little chair*
18. el sombrerito   *little hat*
19. el pollito   *little chicken, chick*
20. el hermanito   *little brother*
21. el leoncito,   *little lion, cub*
22. el hombrecito   *little man*
23. la nubecita   *little cloud*
24. la mañanita   *(nice) little morning*
25. el cielito   *(nice) little sky*
26. la casita   *little house*

RAISE YOUR GRADES

Use of the definite article

1. f, la   *I'm going to Argentina.*
2. l   *I'm going to England.*
3. k   *I speak Spanish.*
4. k   *I'm giving the class in French.*
5. c, el   *I washed my hair yesterday.*
6. a, La   *Truth is beautiful.*
7. j   *Tomorrow is Sunday.*
8. d, El   *Friday will come soon.*
9. g, Los   *Mr. and Mrs. Brown are here.*
10. i   *There isn't any milk in the refrigerator.*
11. c, el   *I left my overcoat at home.*
12. a, la   *We're looking for happiness.*
13. k   *I'm an English teacher.*
14. d, Los   *Wednesdays are free.*
15. i   *I want some cake.*
16. d, los   *I never work on Thursdays.*
17. g, el   *Professor Moreno arrived yesterday.*
18. b, Los   *Children are intelligent.*
19. b, a, El, la   *Man needs peace.*
20. b, h, Los, la   *Eggs cost ninety cents a dozen.*
21. f, la   *I'm from India.*
22. b, h, El, la   *Turkey costs thirty cents a pound.*
23. c, las   *I have to wash my hands.*
24. m   *Sit down, Miss Brown.*
25. b, los   *I like horses.*

Use of the indefinite article

1. b   *I need another spoon.*
2. un   *Give me a glass, please.*
3. un   *I bought a new dress.*
4. e   *What a pity!*
5. d   *I have half a pound of coffee.*
6. unos   *I have some new records.*
7. a   *She is a teacher.*
8. una   *She is a good teacher.*
9. una, una   *I want a coke and a beer.*
10. un   *It's going to cost me a million pesetas.*
11. c   *I want one hundred dollars more.*
12. un, una   *They have a horse and a motorcycle.*
13. a   *My son is a doctor.*
14. un   *Jaime is a very good student.*
15. c   *I have a thousand things to do.*

Personal *a*

1. la   *I saw the University of Mexico yesterday.*
2. al   *I saw Professor Moreno the other day.*
3. a la   *I've seen the French teacher.*
4. a   *I saw Rafael yesterday.*
5. al   *I went to the doctor on Tuesday.*
6. a la   *I went to the plaza yesterday.*
7. a la   *I've gone to Argentina.*
8. al   *I went to Japan.*
9. a los   *We went to the United States.*
10. a   *I'm looking for María.*
11. al   *I'm looking for the teacher.*
12. la   *We're looking for Sixth Street.*
13. a la   *I'm looking for Miss Hernández.*
14. el   *I'm looking for the Paseo de la Reforma.*
15. a   *I'm looking for someone different.*

Number and gender of nouns

1. m, el, los libros   *books*
2. f, la, las habitaciones   *houses*
3. m, el, los corazones   *hearts*
4. f, la, las estrellas   *stars*
5. m, el, los tocadiscos   *record players*
6. f, la, las fuentes   *fountains*
7. m, el, los crímenes   *crimes*
8. m, el, los teléfonos   *telephones*
9. f, la, las manos   *hands*
10. m, el, los dineros   *monies*
11. f, el, las águilas   *eagles*
12. m, el, los padres   *fathers, parents*
13. m, el, los lunes   *Mondays*
14. m, el, los muebles   *furniture*
15. m (f), el (la) dentista, los (las) dentistas   *dentists*
16. m, el, los dientes   *teeth*
17. f, la, las universidades   *universities*
18. m, el, los paraguas   *umbrellas*
19. f, el, las álgebras   *algebra*
20. f, el, las almas   *souls*
21. f, la, las albóndigas   *meatballs*
22. m, el, los alimentos   *food*
23. f, la, las muchedumbres   *crowds*
24. m, el, los bailarines   *dancers*
25. m, el, los obreros   *workers*
26. f, la, las elecciones   *elections*

2 ADJECTIVES AND ADVERBS

THIS CHAPTER IS ABOUT

☑ **Forms of Descriptive Adjectives**
☑ **Use of Descriptive Adjectives**
☑ **Adjectives of Quantity**
☑ **Possessive Adjectives**
☑ **Demonstrative Adjectives**
☑ **Comparison of Adjectives**
☑ **Comparison of Equalities**
☑ **Forms of Adverbs**
☑ **Use of Adverbs**

2-1. Forms of Descriptive Adjectives

In Spanish, all adjectives must agree in number with the nouns they modify. Thus, all adjectives have a singular and a plural form. Follow the same rules as apply to nouns to form the plural of adjectives.

• If the adjective ends in a vowel, add **-s**.
• If the adjective ends in a consonant, add **-es**.
• If the adjective ends in **-z**, change the **z** to **c** and add **-es**.

A. Gendered adjectives

Some adjectives must agree in gender with the nouns they modify. There are three classes of adjectives that change their form to indicate a difference between masculine and feminine gender.

1. Adjectives ending in **-o** change to a feminine form by replacing the **-o** with an **-a** ending.
2. Adjectives ending in **-or**, **-án**, **-ón**, or **-ín** change to a feminine form by adding **-a** to the final consonant. Accented masculine endings drop the accent in the feminine form.
3. Adjectives of nationality ending in a consonant change to a feminine form by adding **-a** to the final consonant. Adjectives of nationality ending in **-o** follow the same rules as for all adjectives ending in **-o**.

Study the examples of gendered adjectives in the chart below. Note that the plural is formed according to the rules given at the beginning of the chapter.

M-Sing	F-Sing	M-Pl	F-Pl	
-o endings				
gord**o**	gord**a**	gord**os**	gord**as**	*fat*
flac**o**	flac**a**	flac**os**	flac**as**	*thin*
roj**o**	roj**a**	roj**os**	roj**as**	*red*
pequeñ**o**	pequeñ**a**	pequeñ**os**	pequeñ**as**	*small*

M-Sing	F-Sing	M-Pl	F-Pl	
-or, -án, -ón, -ín endings				
trabajad**or**	trabajad**ora**	trabajad**ores**	trabajad**oras**	*industrious, hard-working*
holgaz**án**	holgaz**ana**	holgaz**anes**	holgaz**anas**	*idle, lazy*
pregunt**ón**	pregunt**ona**	pregunt**ones**	pregunt**onas**	*inquisitive*
pequeñ**ín**	pequeñ**ina**	pequeñ**ines**	pequeñ**inas**	*tiny*
Nationality				
inglé**s**	ingle**sa**	ingle**ses**	ingle**sas**	*English*
alem**án**	alem**ana**	alem**anes**	alem**anas**	*German*

EXERCISE 2-1: Fill in the blank with the correct form of the adjective given in parentheses. Be sure that the adjective agrees in number and, if necessary, in gender with the noun it modifies. Answers are at the end of the chapter.

1. (mexicano) Mis primos son _____.
2. (japonés) Las muchachas _____ vienen pronto.
3. (hermoso) Las rosas son _____ ahora.
4. (portugués) Me gusta la literatura _____.
5. (alto) Quiero ver el edificio _____.
6. (chillón) Los niños _____ me despertaron.
7. (calculador) Los gatos son muy _____.
8. (hablador) Mis primas son muy _____.
9. (encantador) Tu tía es _____.
10. (amarillo) Compré un vestido _____ ayer.
11. (estrecho) Es una calle bastante _____.
12. (burlón) Los estudiantes son muy _____.
13. (español) Nos gusta la comida _____.
14. (sucio) Mi camisa está _____.
15. (suizo) El chocolate _____ es el mejor.
16. (folklórico) Me interesa el arte _____.
17. (catalán) Estudiamos la poesía _____.
18. (puro) Preferimos el agua _____.
19. (negro) Vi un águila _____.
20. (fresco) El aire está _____.

B. Ungendered adjectives

All adjectives ending in **-e** have only singular and plural forms. Adjectives ending in a consonant have only singular and plural forms (except for those discussed in Section 2-1A). Study the examples in the following chart.

-e Ending			Consonant Ending		
Sing	Pl		Sing	Pl	
verde	verd**es**	*green*	fácil	fácil**es**	*easy*
pobre	pobre**s**	*poor*	difícil	difícil**es**	*difficult*
alegre	alegre**s**	*cheerful*	feliz	feli**ces**	*happy*
triste	triste**s**	*sad*	gris	gris**es**	*gray*

EXERCISE 2-2: Change the following phrases from the singular to the plural. Be sure to indicate gender agreement where necessary. Then write in the correct translation of the plural form. Answers are at the end of the chapter.

Example: el árbol verde   *los árboles verdes*   *the green trees*

1. el deporte difícil   _____   _____
2. la iglesia española   _____   _____
3. la lección fácil   _____   _____
4. el agua sucia   _____   _____

5. la historia verdadera _____ _____
6. el hombre rico _____ _____
7. la muchacha mexicana _____ _____
8. la mujer alta _____ _____
9. el hacha aguda _____ _____
10. el muchacho trabajador _____ _____
11. el español triste _____ _____
12. el maestro criticón _____ _____
13. el niño holgazán _____ _____
14. el castillo inglés _____ _____
15. el zapato blanco _____ _____
16. la habitación vieja _____ _____
17. el águila negra _____ _____
18. la conversación frustrante _____ _____
19. la escalera grande _____ _____
20. el crimen violento _____ _____
21. la nube gorda _____ _____
22. el mantel blanco _____ _____
23. el día gris _____ _____
24. la mano blanca _____ _____
25. la hoja verde _____ _____

REMEMBER: Feminine nouns such as **águila** and **hacha** that begin with a stressed **a** or **ha** are preceded by the masculine article **el** in the singular form, but are always preceded by the feminine article **las** in the plural form. Since these nouns are feminine, they must be modified by a feminine form of the adjective if one exists. Check your answers in Exercise 2-2.

C. Shortened form of some adjectives

1. Some adjectives drop the final **-o** in the masculine singular form when they precede the noun they modify. Study the following list of adjectives.

				BUT	
prime**ro**	(*first*)	prime**r** libro	BUT	prime**ra** persona	
terce**ro**	(*third*)	terce**r** libro	BUT	terce**ra** persona	
ma**lo**	(*bad*)	ma**l** libro	BUT	ma**la** persona	
bue**no**	(*good*)	bue**n** libro	BUT	bue**na** persona	
algu**no**	(*some*)	alg**ún** libro	BUT	algu**na** persona	
ningu**no**	(*none*)	ning**ún** libro	BUT	ningu**na** persona	

2. The adjective **grande** changes to the shortened form **gran** before both masculine and feminine singular nouns.

un **gran** hombre   *a great man*   una **gran** mujer   *a great woman*

EXERCISE 2-3: Fill in the blank with the correct form of the adjective given in parentheses. Answers are at the end of the chapter.

1. (ninguno) No hay _____ ventana abierta.
2. (tercero) Quiero el _____ cuadro.
3. (primero) Necesito leer las _____ páginas.
4. (grande) Es un _____ atleta.
5. (malo) Es una _____ persona.
6. (alguno) Hay _____ servilletas en la mesa.
7. (bueno) Es una _____ idea.
8. (bueno) Es un _____ médico.
9. (bueno) Son _____ maestras.
10. (grande) Voy a estudiar las _____ obras de arte.

2-2. Use of Descriptive Adjectives

The meaning of an adjective can change depending on its position within a sentence. It is therefore important to be aware of the position of an adjective in relation to the noun it modifies.

A. Placement of descriptive adjectives

Descriptive adjectives generally follow the noun they modify.

| la casa **vieja** | *the old house* | las casas **viejas** | *the old houses* |
| la libro **rojo** | *the red book* | los libros **rojos** | *the red books* |

Descriptive adjectives may also precede the noun they modify. The meanings of some adjectives change depending on whether they precede or follow the noun. Study the following chart.

Adjective	Before Noun	After Noun
cierto	*a certain*	*definite, sure*
grande, gran	*great*	*big, large*
medio	*half*	*average*
pobre	*miserable, pitiful*	*poor, needy*
puro	*total, complete*	*pure, unadulterated*
único	*only*	*unique*
viejo	*of long duration, long-time*	*old*

EXERCISE 2-4: Translate the English phrases given in parentheses into Spanish. Answers are at the end of the chapter.

1. Roberto tiene (a unique personality). _____
2. No quiero más que (half a glass). _____
3. (The average man) no es muy alto. _____
4. Einstein fue (a great man). _____
5. Roberta no tiene dinero; ella es (a poor woman). _____
6. El mexicano va a ganar; es (a sure thing). _____
7. El agua de la montaña es (pure water). _____
8. Su versión de la historia es (a complete lie). _____
9. El maestro es (a pitiful man). _____
10. (The only thing) que quiero es descansar. _____
11. El es (an old man). _____
12. No me gustan (certain things). _____

B. Descriptive adjectives as subject complements

1. Descriptive adjectives can follow the verbs **ser** or **estar**, *to be*, and function as a subject complement. The adjective always agrees in number and, when possible, in gender with the subject it modifies.

	Subject	Predicate	Subject Complement	
M-sing	El libro	es	nuevo.	*The book is new.*
F-sing	La sopa	está	caliente.	*The soup is hot.*
M-pl	Ellos	están	cansados.	*They are tired.*
F-pl	Ellas	son	hermosas.	*They are beautiful.*

2. An adjective can modify a noun in a previous sentence. It must still agree with the noun it modifies, even though the noun is not present in the same sentence.

Question	Answer
¿De qué color es **el libro**?	**Es rojo**. El libro es rojo.
What color is the book?	*It's red. The book is red.*
¿De qué color es **la casa**?	**Es amarilla**. La casa es amarilla.
What color is the house?	*It's yellow. The house is yellow.*

¿Cómo están **los muchachos**?	Están **enojados**. Los muchachos están enojados.
How are the boys?	*They're mad. The boys are mad.*
¿Cómo están **María y Marta**?	Están **enfermas**. María y Marta están enfermas.
How are María and Marta?	*They're sick. María and Marta are sick.*

3. Sometimes the subject follows the subject complement. This word order emphasizes the adjective over the noun it modifies.

¡Está **caliente** la sopa!	*The soup is **hot**!*
¡Son **nuevos** los libros!	*The books are **new**!*
¡Es **hermosa** mi hija!	*My daughter is **beautiful**!*

EXERCISE 2-5: Answer the following questions by using the correct form of the adjective given in parentheses, and repeating the verb used in the question. Answers are at the end of the chapter.

Example: (rojo) ¿ De qué color son los libros?   *Son rojos.*

1. (aburrido) ¿ Cómo es el libro?

2. (gris) ¿ De qué color es tu traje?

3. (sabroso) ¿ Cómo estuvo la sopa?

4. (cansado) ¿ Cómo están los niños?

5. (bueno) ¿ Cómo son los estudiantes?

6. (mojado) ¿ Cómo llegó tu marido?

7. (rojo) ¿ De qué color son las rosas?

8. (azul) ¿ De qué color son tus ojos?

9. (simpático) ¿ Cómo es el maestro?

10. (hablador) ¿ Cómo son tus primas?

11. (enfermo) ¿ Cómo está tu padre?

12. (malo) ¿ Cómo es el clima del norte?

13. (ocupado) ¿ Cómo está tu madre?

14. (blanco) ¿ De qué color son los paraguas?

15. (largo) ¿ Cómo fue la película?

C. Use of adjectives as nouns

Adjectives can be used as nouns. The noun itself is dropped, but the article (**el, la, los, las**) is retained. Study the following examples.

la casa	*the house*	el libro	*the book*
la casa nueva	*the new house*	el libro rojo	*the red book*
la nueva	*the new one*	el rojo	*the red one*
las mujeres	*the women*	los hombres	*the men*
las mujeres jóvenes	*the young women*	los hombres ricos	*the rich men*
las jóvenes	*the young*	los ricos	*the rich*

Study the following examples of adjectives used as nouns.

Perdí **mi bolsa**.
I lost my purse.

Necesito comprar **una nueva**.
I need to buy a new one.

El parque viejo está lejos.
The old park is far away.

El viejo está lejos.
The old one is far away.

¿Cuál es **el paraguas roto**?
Which is the broken umbrella?

El roto es el blanco y rojo.
*The broken one is the red and
white one.*

Los chicos habladores son mis primos.
The talkative boys are my cousins.

Los habladores son mis primos.
The talkative ones are my cousins.

EXERCISE 2-6: Rewrite the following sentences by expressing each noun phrase given in parentheses with an adjective. Answers are at the end of the chapter.

Example: El (libro azul) es interesante.   *El azul es interesante.*
   1. Mi tía es (la mujer rubia).

   2. ¿Dónde queda (la biblioteca nueva)?

   3. (El restaurante italiano) está aquí.

   4. Voy a comprar (el libro viejo).

   5. (La camisa blanca) está sucia.

   6. Tengo que hablar con (la mujer joven).

   7. Perdí (el anillo favorito).

   8. (El teléfono negro) está roto.

   9. ¿Cuál es (la canción favorita)?

   10. ¿Dónde están (las librerías antiguas)?

D. **Use of more than one adjective**

   1. When two adjectives follow a noun, they are separated by the conjunction **y**, *and.*

   Juana es una mujer **inteligente y trabajadora**.   *Juana is an intelligent and
industrious woman.*

   Vi el mar **verde y hondo**.   *I saw the deep, green sea.*

   2. When more than two adjectives follow a noun, the first adjectives are separated by a comma, and the last two are separated by the conjunction **y**.

   Vi el mar **verde, hondo y majestuoso**.   *I saw the deep, green,
majestic sea.*

   Es un hombre **feo, bajo, pequeño y hablador**.   *He's an ugly, short, little,
talkative man.*

EXERCISE 2-7: Translate the following phrases into Spanish. If you do not know the adjective, look it up in your dictionary. Answers are at the end of the chapter.

   1. the tall, green trees

   2. the small, blond girl

   3. the dear, old friend

4. the old, decrepit house

5. the clear, pure water

6. the long, frustrating conversation

7. the happy, smiling child (*fem*)

8. the hot, salty popcorn

9. the great, famous painting

10. the large, famous university

REMEMBER: Some words such as **grande**, **puro**, and **viejo** change their meaning according to their position before or after the noun they modify. Check your answers.

2-3. Adjectives of Quantity

Adjectives of quantity tell us *how much* or *how many*. Unlike descriptive adjectives, they almost always precede the noun they modify. Study the following list.

poco(a)	*only a little, not much*	Tengo poco tiempo.	*I have only a little time. I don't have much time.*
pocos(as)	*not many, only a few*	Tengo pocos libros.	*I don't have many books. I have only a few books.*
mucho(a)	*a lot of, much*	Tengo mucha energía.	*I have a lot of energy.*
muchos(as)	*lots of, many*	Tengo muchos libros.	*I have lots of books.*
todo el	*all, all the*	Duermo todo el día.	*I sleep all day.*
toda la	*all, all the*	Trabajo toda la noche.	*I work all night.*
todos los	*every, all*	Trabajo todos los días. Todos los muchachos cantan.	*I work every day. All the boys sing.*
todas las	*every, all*	Duermo todas las noches. Todas las muchachas bailan.	*I sleep every night. All the girls dance.*
otro(a)	*another, other*	Quiero otra cerveza.	*I want another beer.*
otros(as)	*other*	Vendrán otros días.	*Other days will come.*
algún(a)	*some*	Algún día sabremos.	*We will know some day.*
algunos(as)	*some*	Tengo algunos libros.	*I have some books.*
ningún(a)	*not . . . any*	No tengo ninguna idea.	*I don't have any idea.*
ningunos(as)	*not . . . any*	No tengo ningunos discos.	*I don't have any records.*
cada	*each, every*	Cada cosa tiene su lugar.	*Each thing has its place.*
		Cada hombre es distinto.	*Each man is different.*

ambos(as)	*both*	Ambas mujeres piensan ir.	*Both women plan to go.*
demasiado(a)	*too much*	Hay demasiado pan.	*There is too much bread.*
demasiados(as)	*too many*	Hay demasiadas personas.	*There are too many people.*

> **NOTE:** **Cada** has only one form. **Ambos** has only a plural form.

EXERCISE 2-8: Fill in the blank with the correct form of the adjective given in parentheses. Answers are at the end of the chapter.

1. (mucho) Tengo _____ mesas en casa.
2. (poco) Yo como _____ carne.
3. (algún) Necesito _____ solución al problema.
4. (otro) No quiero beber _____ copa.
5. (cada) Yo me levanto a las seis _____ día.
6. (todo) Tengo que hablar con _____ los estudiantes.
7. (todo) Roberto duerme _____ la mañana.
8. (todo) Mi hermana vive conmigo _____ el año.
9. (demasiado) Hay _____ sal en la sopa.
10. (ningún) No tengo _____ respuesta.

2-4. Possessive Adjectives

A. Form of possessive adjectives

In Spanish, the possessive adjective changes form in order to agree with *the object possessed*, not the possessor. **Mi, tu,** and **su** agree in number only. **Nuestro** and **vuestro** agree in number *and* in gender with the noun they modify. Study the following chart carefully.

Singular		Plural	
mi libro	*my book*	mis libros	*my books*
mi pluma	*my pen*	mis plumas	*my pens*
tu sombrero	*your hat*	tus sombreros	*your hats*
tu mesa	*your table*	tus mesas	*your tables*
su carro	*his, her, their, your car*	sus carros	*his, her, their your cars*
su casa	*his, her, their, your house*	sus casas	*his, her, their, your houses*
nuestro libro	*our book*	nuestros libros	*our books*
nuestra casa	*our house*	nuestras casas	*our houses*
vuestro libro	*your book*	vuestros libros	*your books*
vuestra pluma	*your pen*	vuestras plumas	*your pens*

EXERCISE 2-9: Fill in the blank with the correct form of the possessive adjective given in parentheses. Answers are at the end of the chapter.

1. (his) Juan compró _____ abrigo ayer.
2. (our) María y yo tenemos _____ paraguas.
3. (my/her) Tengo _____ bicicleta y Alicia tiene _____ carro.
4. (our) Alfredo y yo hablamos con _____ padres todos los días.
5. (his) Rafael dice que _____ tía viene mañana.
6. (her) María dice que _____ primos vienen hoy.
7. (our) Tú y yo tenemos que hablar con _____ hijas.
8. (their) Los niños abren _____ regalos mañana.

9. (my) Yo abrí _____ regalo ayer.

10. (my) No sé donde está _____ cartera.

11. (your) Tendrás que llevar _____ traje de baño.

12. (their) Jaime y Andrés compraron _____ boletos ayer.

B. Clarification of *su* and *sus*

The meaning of **su** and **sus** can be either his, her, their or your. If the meaning is not clear from the context of the sentence, a prepositional phrase, **de** + *proper noun or subject pronoun*, is used to clarify the meaning. If the prepositional phrase is used, **su** is generally replaced by the definite article.

Juan busca **su lápiz**.	*Juan is looking for his pencil.*
Juan busca **el lápiz de ella**.	*Juan is looking for her pencil.*

Study the following examples.

Singular		Plural	
el libro de Juan	*Juan's book*	los libros de Juan	*Juan's books*
el libro de él	*his book*	los libros de él	*his books*
el libro de María	*María's book*	los libros de María	*María's books*
el libro de ella	*her book*	los libros de ella	*her books*
la casa de él	*his house*	las casas de él	*his houses*
la casa de ella	*her house*	las casas de ella	*her houses*
la casa de usted	*your house*	las casas de ustedes	*your houses*
la casa de ellos	*their house*	las casas de ellos	*their houses*

NOTE: When the plural form includes both masculine and feminine direct objects, **ellos** is used: **la casa de María y de Juan; la casa de ellos**. The preposition **de** is repeated before each proper name and object pronoun in a series.

EXERCISE 2-10:   Translate the following phrases into Spanish using the prepositional phrase **de** + _____. Answers are at the end of the chapter.

1. Juan's overcoat

2. María's overcoat

3. the children's toys

4. the women's meeting

5. their (*masc*) record player

6. Mr. and Mrs. López's house

7. his horse

8. the town's mayor

9. the university's library

10. his plan

11. their (*fem*) party

12. Elena and Tomás' letter

13. Miguel and Raúl's cars

14. the summer's heat

15. the student's (*fem*) notebooks

16. the student's (*fem*) notebook

2-5. Demonstrative Adjectives

A. Form of demonstrative adjectives

Study the following forms of the demonstrative adjectives.

	Singular		Plural	
Masc	este	*this*	estos	*these*
Fem	esta	*this*	estas	*these*
Masc	ese	*that*	esos	*those*
Fem	esa	*that*	esas	*those*
Masc	aquel	*that*	aquellos	*those*
Fem	aquella	*that*	aquellas	*those*

EXERCISE 2-11: Rewrite the following sentences by changing the noun phrases given in parentheses from the plural to the singular. Answers are at the end of the chapter.

1. Voy a comprar (aquellos sombreros grandes).

2. Mi madre me regaló (estas cucharas viejas).

3. No necesitamos (aquellas camas viejas).

4. Encontré (esos cuadros mexicanos).

5. Voy a tirar (estos trastes feos).

6. Perdí (aquellas joyas estupendas).

7. Queremos hablar con (aquellos muchachos franceses).

8. Raúl va a leer (estos libros grandes).

9. Tenemos que estudiar (estas fórmulas difíciles).

10. Quiero visitar (aquellos museos famosos).

B. Use of demonstrative adjectives

1. **Este(a)** and **estos(as)** are used to refer to objects or persons close to the speaker.
2. **Ese(a)** and **esos(as)** are used to refer to objects or persons at a physical or temporal distance from the speaker.
3. **Aquel(la)** and **aquellos(as)** are used to refer to objects or persons removed from the speaker by a substantial amount of space or time.

EXERCISE 2-12: Fill in the blank with the correct form of the demonstrative adjective given in parentheses. Answers are at the end of the chapter.

1. (ese) _____ sábanas son nuevas.
2. (este) _____ zapatos son pequeños.

3. (aquel) No me gustó _____ película.
4. (aquel) _____ tiempos eran difíciles.
5. (ese) _____ paraguas no está roto.
6. (este) Voy a terminar _____ cartas mañana.
7. (aquel) Perdí _____ par de zapatos el verano pasado.
8. (este) Me gusta _____ clase de papel.
9. (ese) No quiero hablar con _____ personas.
10. (ese) _____ hombres son mis tíos.

2-6. Comparison of Adjectives

A. Comparative and superlative forms

In English, the comparative and the superlative are formed by adding the endings *-er* and *-est* to the adjective. In Spanish, the comparative is formed by placing **más**, *more*, or **menos**, *less*, before the adjective. The superlative is formed by using the definite article **el, la, los,** or **las,** or the possessive adjective before the noun, followed by **más** + adjective: **el . . . más hermoso, la . . . más hermosa.** Study the following chart.

		Comparative	Superlative
M-sing	un hombre alto *a tall man*	un hombre más alto *a taller man*	el hombre más alto *the tallest man*
F-sing	una mujer flaca *a thin woman*	una mujer más flaca *a thinner woman*	la mujer más flaca *the thinnest woman*
M-pl	los libros caros *the costly books*	unos libros más caros *some more costly books*	los libros más caros *the costliest books*
F-pl	las tazas nuevas *the new cups*	unas tazas más nuevas *some newer cups*	las tazas más nuevas *the newest cups*
	ALSO mis tazas nuevas *my new cups*		mis tazas más nuevas *my newest cups*

REMEMBER: There is no difference between the comparative and the superlative forms *except* for the use of the definite article or the possessive adjective before the modified noun in the superlative form.

EXERCISE 2-13: Rewrite each sentence twice. First change the adjective to the comparative form, then to the superlative form. Answers are at the end of the chapter.

Example: Necesito un coche nuevo.   *Necesito un coche más nuevo.*
                                    Necesito el coche más nuevo.

1. Quiero comprar un sombrero bonito.

2. José tiene una casa vieja.

3. *Don Quixote* es una novela larga.

4. Tengo un traje caro.

5. Prefiero los discos modernos.

6. Necesito una ensalada grande.

7. Quiero unos vestidos nuevos.

B. Irregular forms of comparatives and superlatives

There are four adjectives that have special forms to express the comparative and superlative.

	Comparative	Superlative
bueno	mejor	el, la mejor
good	*better*	los, las mejores
		the best
malo	peor	el, la peor
bad	*worse*	los, las peores
		the worst
grande	mayor	el, la mayor
big, great	*greater, older*	los, las mayores
		the greatest, the oldest
pequeño	menor	el, la menor
small	*lesser, younger*	los, las menores
		the least, the youngest

Pay special attention to the position of each adjective in relation to the noun it modifies in the following sentences.

1. *Comparisons according to quality.*

Jane Eyre es un **buen** libro. ⎫ *Jane Eyre* es un libro **bueno.** ⎭	*Jane Eyre is a good book.*
Don Quixote es un libro **mejor.**	*Don Quixote is a better book.*
War and Peace es **el mejor** libro.	*War and Peace is the best book.*
Esta es una **mala** película. ⎫ Esta es una película **mala.** ⎭	*This is a bad movie.*
Aquella fue una película **peor.**	*That was a worse movie.*
La de anoche fue **la peor** película.	*Last night's was the worst movie.*

> **NOTE:** **Bueno** and **malo** may appear before or after the noun without changing the meaning of the adjective. **Mejor** and **peor** generally precede the noun in the superlative form.

2. *Comparisons according to age.* **Mayor** and **menor** are used to express age when referring to people.

Carlos es mi hermano **menor.**	*Carlos is my younger brother.*
Carlos es el hermano **menor.**	*Carlos is the youngest brother.*
Alicia es una hija **mayor.**	*Alicia is an older daughter.*
Alicia es la hija **mayor.**	*Alicia is the oldest daughter.*

> **NOTE:** The words **joven** and **viejo** are used to describe age in a noncomparative form.
>
> | | |
> |---|---|
> | Carlos es **joven.** | *Carlos is young.* |
> | Alicia es **vieja.** | *Alicia is old.* |

3. *Comparisons according to size.* **Grande** and **pequeño** are used to express size.

La mesa es **grande.**	*The table is big.*
Esta mesa es **más grande** que aquella.	*This table is bigger than that one.*
Mi mesa es **la más grande.**	*My table is the biggest.*
Mi coche es **pequeño.**	*My car is small.*
Tu coche es **más pequeño.**	*Your car is smaller.*
El coche de Jaime es **el maś pequeño.**	*Jaime's car is the smallest.*

EXERCISE 2-14: Translate the English phrases given in parentheses into Spanish. Answers are at the end of the chapter.

1. Raúl es (my oldest brother). _____
2. Esta es (the best novel) del mundo. _____
3. Mi radio es (bad), pero tu radio es (worse). _____
4. Quiero crear (a better world). _____
5. ¿Quién es (the youngest daughter)? _____
6. Tengo (the worst car) de los Estados Unidos. _____
7. No puedo imaginarme (a better plan). _____
8. Rosaura tiene (the best plan). _____
9. (The best novels) son las novelas rusas. _____
10. Tengo que hablar con (the youngest children). _____

C. Use of the comparative and superlative forms

1. The phrases **más ... que** (**más ... de**), *more ... than*, and **menos ... que** (**menos ...de**), *less ... than*, are used to compare one adjective to another. Study the following examples.

Juan es alto.	*Juan is tall.*
Juan es **más** alto **que** María.	*Juan is taller than María.*
Juan es **el** estudiante **más** alto **de** la clase.	*Juan is the tallest student in the class.*

2. **Más de** (more than) and **menos de** (less than) are used with numbers in an affirmative statement. If the statement is negative, however, **más que** is used.

Affirmative: Tengo **más de** diez dólares.	*I have more than ten dollars.*
Negative: No tengo **más que** diez dólares.	*I have no more than ten dollars.*
	OR
	I have only ten dollars.

3. The subject pronouns (**yo**, **tú**, etc.) are used in the comparative form.

Alicia es **menos** alta **que** tú.	*Alicia is shorter (less tall) than you.*
Yo estoy **más** preocupada **que** él.	*I am more worried than he.*

4. In the superlative, the adjective can be used as a noun by dropping the noun and retaining the remaining form.

¿Cuál es **la ciudad más bella**?	**La más bella** es París.
What is the most beautiful city?	*The most beautiful one is Paris.*
¿Quién es **el hijo mayor**?	**El mayor** es Samuel.
Who is the oldest son?	*The oldest is Samuel.*

EXERCISE 2-15: Rewrite the two sentences by changing them into one comparative statement. Answers are at the end of the chapter.

Example: París es bello. Pero Roma es más bella.   *Roma es más bella que París.*

1. Roberto es alto. Pero Juan es más alto.

2. Yo estoy cansada. Pero tú estás más cansado.

3. Mi libro es interesante. Pero tu libro es más interesante.

4. El español es difícil. Pero el japonés es más difícil.

5. Mi idea es mala. Pero tu idea es peor.

6. Esta película es larga. Pero aquella película es más larga.

7. Aquella casa es cara. Pero esta casa es más cara.

8. Mi corbata es roja. Pero tu corbata es más roja.

9. Mis discos son buenos. Pero tus discos son mejores.

10. La sopa está caliente. Pero el guisado está más caliente.

D. Adjectives with *-ísimo*

The absolute superlative may also be formed by adding the ending **-ísimo** to the adjective, meaning *very* or *extremely*.

1. If the adjective ends in a vowel, drop the final vowel and add **-ísimo**.

   ro**jo**   ro**jísimo**

2. If the adjective ends in a consonant, add **-ísimo** directly to the adjective.

   azul   azul**ísimo**

3. Sometimes the adjective must change its spelling in order to accommodate the **-ísimo** ending: **-co** changes to **-qu**, **-go** changes to **-gu**, and **-z** changes to **-c**.

   rico   ri**quísimo**
   largo   lar**guísimo**
   feliz   feli**císimo**

   > **REMEMBER:** There is always an accent over **-ísimo**. The ending must agree in number and gender with the noun it modifies: **-ísimo, -ísima, -ísimos, -ísimas**.

EXERCISE 2-16: Answer the following questions using the absolute superlative and the superlative. Study the examples carefully. Answers are at the end of the chapter.

Example: ¿Es París una bella ciudad?   *Sí, es bellísima. Sí, es la ciudad más bella del mundo.*
¿Es Raúl un muchacho inteligente?   *Sí, es inteligentísimo. Sí, es el muchacho más inteligente del mundo.*

1. ¿Es Manhattan una isla pequeña?

2. ¿Es María una mujer feliz?

3. ¿Es *Moby Dick* una novela larga?

4. ¿Es el presidente un hombre rico?

5. ¿Es la Torre Latina un edificio alto?

6. ¿Es el Paseo de la Reforma una avenida ancha?

7. ¿Es la trucha un pescado barato?

8. ¿Es la comida mexicana una comida buena?

9. ¿Es Mario un cantante malo?

10. ¿Son los libros españoles unos libros caros?

2-7. Comparison of Equalities

A. Use of *tan . . . como* with adjectives or adverbs

In English, *as . . . as* is used to compare two characteristics that are equal. In Spanish, **tan . . . como** is used to express two equal qualities. Study the following examples carefully. Note that **tan . . . como** does not change, but the adjective must agree with the noun it modifies.

Ricardo es **tan** rico **como** María.	*Ricardo is as rich as María.*
Alda es **tan** alta **como** José.	*Alda is as tall as José.*
Las muchachas están **tan** cansadas **como** los muchachos.	*The girls are as tired as the boys.*

EXERCISE 2-17: Rewrite the two sentences to form one statement of equality. Study the example carefully. Answers are at the end of the chapter.

Example: Ricardo es atrevido. Pero María es atrevida también.
María es tan atrevida como Ricardo.

1. La rosa es hermosa. Pero el geranio es hermoso también.

2. El vino es bueno. Per el agua es buena también.

3. El español es difícil. Pero el inglés es difícil también.

4. Las casas son caras. Pero los apartamentos son caros también.

5. Las montañas son peligrosas. Pero el mar es peligroso también.

6. La princesa está triste. Pero el príncipe está triste también.

B. Use of *tanto (-a, -os, -as) . . . como* with nouns

1. In English, *as much . . . as* or *as many . . . as* is used to compare two equal quantities to each other. In Spanish, **tanto (-a, -os, -as) . . . como** is used to compare one noun of equal quantity to another. Since **tanto** modifies the noun it precedes, it functions as an adjective and must change its form according to the number and gender of the noun it modifies. Study the following examples.

Compré **tantos** libros **como** mi hermano.	*I bought as many books as my brother.*
Yo comí **tanta** ensalada **como** tú.	*I ate as much salad as you.*
Los niños duermen **tantas** horas **como** las niñas.	*The little boys sleep as many hours as the little girls.*

2. If the noun being modified is referred to in a previous sentence, it is frequently omitted.

¿Cuánta **ensalada** comiste?	Comí **tanta como** tú.
How much salad did you eat?	*I ate as much as you.*
¿Cuántos **libros** compraste?	Compré **tantos como** mi hermano.
How many books did you buy?	*I bought as many as my brother.*

EXERCISE 2-18: Rewrite the two sentences to form one statement of equality. Study the example carefully before beginning. Answers are at the end of the chapter.

Example: Yo comí mucho pan. Tú comiste mucho pan también.
Tú comiste tanto pan como yo.

1. Mi tía compró muchos sombreros. Mi tío compró muchos sombreros también.

2. Los niños comieron mucho pastel. Los padres comieron mucho pastel también.

3. Mi amiga escribe muchas cartas. Yo escribo muchas cartas también.

4. Yo fui a muchos museos. El fue a muchos museos también.

5. Las muchachas hicieron muchas preguntas. Los muchachos hicieron muchas preguntas también.

6. Yo encontré tres errores. Tú encontraste tres errores también.

7. Yo busqué el libro en cuatro librerías. Tú buscaste el libro en cuatro librerías también.

8. Mi prima bebió dos vasos de leche. Alberto bebió dos vasos de leche también.

2-8. Forms of Adverbs

Adverbs can be formed from most adjectives by adding **-mente** to the *feminine singular* form of the adjective. The **-mente** ending corresponds to the English *-ly* ending.

alegr**e**	*happy*	alegr**emente**	*happily*
trist**e**	*sad*	trist**emente**	*sadly*
enojad**a**	*angry*	enojad**amente**	*angrily*
fácil	*easy*	fácil**mente**	*easily*
cariñbos**a**	*loving*	cariño**samente**	*lovingly*

> **NOTE:** Although the feminine singular form of many adjectives ends in **-a**, many do not: **alegre**, **fácil**, etc. Thus, the adverbial form does not always end in **-a + mente**. If the adjective has a written accent, the accent is retained in the adverb form: **rápido**, **rápidamente**.

A. Adverbs with the prepositional phrase *con* + noun

Adverbs are often formed by using the prepositional phrase **con** + the singular form of the noun. Compare the following lists of adverbs. Note that the meaning is the same in both forms.

con ciudado	ciudadosamente	*carefully*
con gusto	gustosamente	*gladly*
con cariño	cariñosamente	*lovingly*
con dificultad	dificultosamente	*with difficulty*
con ansiedad	ansiosamente	*anxiously*
con lentitud	lentamente	*slowly*
con rapidez	rápidamente	*rapidly*
con paciencia	pacientemente	*patiently*

B. Adverbs not derived from adjectives

Following is a list of some of the more common adverbs that are not derived from adjectives.

mucho	*a lot*	poco	*a little*
muchísimo	*a great deal*	poquísimo	*very little*
mal	*badly*	bastante	*quite, rather*
peor	*worse*	nada	*not at all*
muy	*very*	despacio	*slowly*

tan	*so*	aprisa	*quickly, hurriedly*
algo	*somewhat*	siempre	*always*
demasiado	*too*	nunca	*never*

EXERCISE 2-19: Fill in the blank with the correct form of the adverb by adding **-mente** to the feminine form of the adjective given in parentheses. Answers are at the end of the chapter.

1. (dificultoso) Hablamos alemán_____.
2. (ciudadoso) Los estudiantes escriben_____.
3. (triste) Me contó_____ la historia del accidente.
4. (ansioso) Estabamos esperando el tren_____.
5. (gustoso) Mi madre limpia la cocina_____.
6. (rápido) Me gusta manejar_____.
7. (intenso) El niño miró_____ por la ventana.
8. (cariñoso) Te saludo_____.
9. (paciente) Se sentaba y tejía_____.
10. (lento) Me gusta hacer las cosas_____.

2-9. Use of Adverbs

A. Adverbs that modify verbs

Adverbs that answer the question **¿cómo?**, *how?*, usually follow the verb. A few adverbs such as **rápidamente**, **lentamente**, and **duramente**, may also appear in a masculine singular adjective form: **rápido**, **lento**, **duro**. Study the following examples.

1. *Use of one adverb.*

Ella corre **rápidamente**.	*She runs rapidly.*
Ella corre **rápido**.	
Ella trabaja **despacio**.	*She works slowly.*
Ella trabaja **lentamente**.	

2. *Use of two adverbs.* When two adverbs with the **-mente** ending are used, only the second adverb takes the **-mente** ending.

Andrés trabaja **lenta y ciudadosamente**.	*Andrés works slowly and carefully.*
Tenemos que pensar **ciudadosa y inteligentemente**.	*We must think carefully and intelligently.*
Ellos dibujan **rápidamente y bien**.	*They draw quickly and well.*
Tú corres **despacio y mal**.	*You run slowly and badly.*

> **NOTE:** **Bien** and **mal** are usually placed after the first adverb. Since they do not take the **-mente** ending, the first adverb does.

EXERCISE 2-20: Fill in the blanks by translating the adverbs given in parentheses into Spanish. Use the **-mente** ending whenever possible. Answers are at the end of the chapter.

1. (quickly) Ellos trabajan_____.
2. (happily) Los niños juegan_____.
3. (carefully and quickly) Tengo que trabajar_____.
4. (carefully and well) Hay que hablar_____.
5. (frequently) Mi marido canta_____.
6. (slowly and carefully) Los muchachos hablan_____.
7. (calmly) Quiero ver el programa_____.
8. (sadly) Me contó_____ la historia.
9. (elegantly) Mi hermana se viste_____.
10. (angrily) Me mostró_____ la ventana rota.

B. Adverbs that modify adjectives and other adverbs

Adverbs such as **muy**, **poco**, **demasiado**, and the like are used to express degrees of intensity. Other adverbs that express degree are **relativamente**, **extraordinariamente**, **enormemente**, **extremadamente**, **verdaderamente**, and **realmente**.

1. *Modification of adverbs by other adverbs.*

Affirmative

Canta **muy, muy** bien.	*He (she) sings very, very well.*
Baila **enormemente** bien.	*He (she) dances tremendously well.*
Canta **bastante** mal.	*He (she) sings rather (quite) badly.*
Los niños comen **demasiado** rápido.	*The children eat too quickly.*

Negative

María no habla **nada** bien.	*María does not speak at all well.*
José no habla **muy** bien.	*José does not speak very well.*

2. *Modification of adjectives by adverbs.*

Affirmative

Jaime está **algo** triste.	*Jaime is somewhat sad.*
Antonio es **bastante** alto.	*Antonio is quite tall.*
Elena as **demasiado** hermosa.	*Elena is too beautiful.*
Mis primas son **enormemente** ricas.	*My cousins are enormously rich.*

Negative

Aquel perro es **poco** valiente.	*That dog is not very brave.*
Andrés no es **nada** gordo.	*Andrés is not fat at all.*

> **REMEMBER:** Words such as **poco**, **demasiado**, and **bastante** can be used as both adjectives and adverbs. Adverbs modify verbs, adjectives, and other adverbs. *Adverbs never change their form.* Adjectives modify nouns and pronouns and must agree with the words they modify in number and, if possible, in gender. Compare the following examples.

Adverbs do not change form.

Trabajo **demasiado** rápido.	*I work too rapidly.*
Elena es **demasiado** hermosa.	*Elena is too beautiful.*

Adjectives change form.

Tengo **demasiados** libros.	*I have too many books.*
Me diste **demasiada** sopa.	*You gave me too much soup.*

EXERCISE 2-21: Find the word that is being modified in each of the following sentences. Ask yourself what part of speech it is. Then fill in the blank with the correct form of the word given in parentheses to complete the sentence. Remember, only adjectives change their form. Adverbs stay the same. Answers are at the end of the chapter.

1. (poco) Tengo _____ libros en casa.
2. (bastante) Los niños duermen _____.
3. (bastante) Los niños juegan _____ horas.
4. (demasiado) Hay _____ sillas en el comedor.
5. (demasiado) Los niños hablan _____.
6. (demasiado) Ella es _____ alta.
7. (demasiado) Tengo _____ discos.
8. (muy) Jaime es _____ inteligente.
9. (mucho) Mi casa tiene _____ ventanas.
10. (mucho) Te quiero _____.
11. (mucho) Me gusta tener _____ trabajo.
12. (nada) La maestra no es _____ alegre.

SUMMARY

1. To form the plural of adjectives, (1) if the adjective ends in a vowel, add **-s**, (2) if the adjective ends in a consonant, add **-es**, and (3) if the adjective ends in **-z**, change the **-z** to **-c** and add **-es**.

2. There are three kinds of adjectives that change their form to indicate gender: (1) adjectives ending in **-o**, (2) adjectives ending in **-or**, **-án**, **-ón**, or **-ín**, and (3) adjectives of nationality.

3. All adjectives ending in **-e** have only singular and plural forms. Adjectives ending in a consonant have only singular and plural forms (except those listed in #2 above).

4. Some adjectives drop the final **-o** in the masculine singular form when placed *before* the noun they modify.

5. The meaning of some adjectives changes depending on whether the adjective is placed before or after the noun.

6. A descriptive adjective can take the place of the noun it is modifying by dropping the noun itself and retaining the article.

7. Adjectives of quantity generally precede the noun they modify.

8. Possessive adjectives must agree with the object possessed, not with the person who possesses the object.

9. The meanings of the possessive adjectives **su** and **sus** are not always clear; thus, a prepositional phrase (**de** + proper name or subject pronoun) can be used to clarify the meaning.

10. The demonstrative adjectives **este** (-a, -os, -as), **ese** (-a, -os, -as), and **aquel** (-la, -los, -las) must agree in number and gender with the noun they modify.

11. The comparative is formed by placing **más** or **menos** before the adjective. The superlative is formed by placing an article or a possessive adjective + **más** or **menos** before the adjective.

12. There are four adjectives that have irregular forms to express the comparative and superlative: **mejor**, **peor**, **mayor**, and **menor**.

13. The phrases **más . . . que** and **menos . . . que** are used to compare one adjective to another. **Más . . . de** and **menos . . . de** are used to express the superlative. In affirmative statements about numbers, **más de** and **menos de** are used. **Más que** is used in negative statements about numbers.

14. The absolute superlative is formed by adding the ending **-ísimo** (-a, -os, -as) to the adjective.

15. The phrase **tan . . . como** (*as . . . as*) is used to compare adjectives and adverbs. The word **tan** never changes its form.

16. The phrase **tanto** (-a, -os, -as) **. . . como** (*as much . . . as* or *as many . . . as*) is used to compare nouns. **Tanto** changes its form to agree in number and gender with the noun it modifies.

17. Adverbs are formed by adding **-mente** to the feminine singular form of the adjective. The prepositional phrase **con** + noun also functions like an adverb. All adverbs have a single form that does not change.

18. A few adverbs may appear in a masculine singular adjective form.

19. When two adverbs with the **-mente** ending are used, only the second adverb takes the **-mente** ending.

RAISE YOUR GRADES

☑ **Agreement of adjectives** [Section 2-1]

Change the following sentences from singular to plural. Remember to change all the adjectives to agree with the plural noun. Answers are at the end of the chapter.

Example: La montaña es alta. *Las montañas son altas.*

El postre está delicioso. *Los postres están deliciosos.*

1. Ese árbol es alto y verde.

2. Tu caballo es demasiado nervioso.

3. La niña cansada no está muy contenta.

4. La ensalada es buena, pero demasiado grande.

5. Aquel vaso rojo es de Antonio.

6. Esta carta larga es de Elena.

7. El cuadro de Goya es famoso.

8. El queso francés es sumamente rico.

9. Aquella película vieja es más divertida que esta moderna.

10. Mi perro está más enojado que tu gato.

☑ **Recognition of adjectives** [Sections 2-2 through 2-5]

Read each sentence carefully and underline all adjectives. Choose what kind of adjective each one is from the list at the right. Write in the corresponding letter(s) in the space provided to the left of each sentence. Answers are at the end of the chapter.

Example: _c, a_ *Mis* plumas son *rojas*.

_____ 1. Yo conozco muchas canciones francesas.	a. descriptive adjective
_____ 2. Dejé mis nuevos guantes azules en casa.	b. adjective of quantity
_____ 3. Tengo una buena casa grande y confortable.	c. possessive adjective
_____ 4. Todos mis hermanos son altos.	d. demonstrative adjective
_____ 5. Pocas mujeres llegan tan temprano.	
_____ 6. Aquellas novelas rusas son demasiado largas.	
_____ 7. Estamos cansados porque trabajamos toda la noche.	
_____ 8. Sus ideas son bastante interesantes.	
_____ 9. Estos sombreros no me gustan nada.	
_____ 10. Tenemos demasiados libros en casa ahora.	

☑ **Comparative form of adjectives** [Section 2-6]

Review the form of comparative adjectives. Pay attention to irregular comparatives like **mejor** and **peor**. Then fill in the blank with the correct form of the adjective given in parentheses. Answers are at the end of the chapter.

1. (taller) Mi madre es alta, pero mi padre es_____ .
2. (bigger) La Universidad de México es_____ que la de Madrid.
3. (better) La sopa de hoy es_____ que la sopa de ayer.
4. (older) La Torre Eiffel es_____ que el Edificio Chrysler.
5. (more expensive) Las casas son_____ hoy día.
6. (worse) Esta novela es mala, pero aquella novela es_____ .
7. (less famous) Aquel cuadro de Goya es_____ que sus otros cuadros.
8. (younger) Juan es_____ que Carlos.
9. (smaller) La mesa nueva es_____ .
10. (less interesting) Los cómicos de hoy son_____ que los cómicos de los años cincuenta.

☑ **Use of *más que* and *más de*** [Section 2-6]

Review the use of **más que** and **más de** when referring to statements about numbers. Fill in the blanks with the correct phrase. Answers are at the end of the chapter.

1. No gano_____ cinco dólares la hora.
2. Mi hermano tiene_____ cinco coches.
3. No recibo_____ tres cartas por semana.

4. Recibo＿＿＿＿＿＿＿ diez cartas por mes.
5. Tengo＿＿＿＿＿＿＿ suficiente.
6. Siempre compro＿＿＿＿＿＿＿ tú.
7. Necesitamos＿＿＿＿＿＿＿ diez horas para terminar el trabajo.
8. No tenemos＿＿＿＿＿＿＿ cinco minutos.
9. No encontré＿＿＿＿＿＿＿ una servilleta.
10. Necesito＿＿＿＿＿＿＿ una taza de café diariamente.

✓ **Use of *tan . . . como* and *tanto . . . como*** [Section 2-7]

Read each of the following sentences carefully. Ask yourself what is being compared—an adjective, an adverb, or a noun. After you have identified the word being modified, write in either **tan** or **tanto** (-a, -os, -as) . . . **como** in the spaces provided. Remember that **tanto** modifies nouns only and must agree with them in number and gender. **Tan** modifies adverbs and adjectives and does not change its form. Answers are at the end of the chapter.

Examples: El duerme ＿＿*tan*＿＿ profundamente ＿＿*como*＿＿ un niño.
La niña comió ＿＿*tantas*＿＿ galletas ＿＿*como*＿＿ su hermano.

1. María sabe＿＿＿＿＿＿ canciones＿＿＿＿＿＿ su hermana.
2. Los niños pidieron＿＿＿＿＿＿ dulces＿＿＿＿＿＿ las niñas.
3. Las mujeres corren＿＿＿＿＿＿ rápido＿＿＿＿＿＿ los hombres.
4. Compré＿＿＿＿＿＿ carne＿＿＿＿＿＿ ella.
5. La comida mexicana es＿＿＿＿＿＿ buena＿＿＿＿＿＿ la francesa.
6. Estamos＿＿＿＿＿＿ cansados＿＿＿＿＿＿ ustedes.
7. No tengo＿＿＿＿＿＿ discos＿＿＿＿＿＿ mi hermano.
8. Tuve que esperar＿＿＿＿＿＿ horas＿＿＿＿＿＿ tú.
9. Fernando tiene＿＿＿＿＿＿ valor＿＿＿＿＿＿ un matador de toros.
10. Yo no juego al béisbol＿＿＿＿＿＿ bien＿＿＿＿＿＿ Jackie Robinson.

CHAPTER ANSWERS

EXERCISE 2-1

1. mexicanos *My cousins are Mexican.*
2. japonesas *The Japanese girls are coming*
3. hermosas *The roses are beautiful now.*
4. portuguesa *I like Portuguese literature.*
5. alto *I want to see the tall building.*
6. chillones *The crying children woke me up.*
7. calculadores *Cats are very calculating.*
8. habladoras *My cousins are very talkative.*
9. encantadora *Your aunt is charming.*
10. amarillo *I bought a yellow dress yesterday.*
11. estrecha *It's a very narrow street.*
12. burlones *The students are very mocking.*
13. española *We like Spanish food.*
14. sucia *My shirt is dirty.*
15. suizo *Swiss chocolate is the best.*
16. folklórico *I am interested in folk art.*
17. catalana *We are studying Catalan poetry.*
18. pura *We prefer pure water.*
19. negra *I saw a black eagle.*
20. fresco *The air is cool.*

EXERCISE 2-2

1. los deportes difíciles, *the difficult sports*
2. las iglesias españolas, *the Spanish churches*
3. las lecciones fáciles, *the easy lessons*
4. las aguas sucias, *the dirty waters*
5. las historias verdaderas, *the true stories*
6. los hombres ricos, *the rich men*
7. las muchachas mexicanas, *the Mexican girls*
8. las mujeres altas, *the tall women*
9. las hachas agudas, *the sharp axes*
10. los muchachos trabajadores, *the hard working boys*
11. los españoles tristes, *the sad Spaniards*
12. los maestros criticones, *the critical teachers*
13. los niños holgazanes, *the lazy children*
14. los castillos ingleses, *the English castles*
15. los zapatos blancos, *the white shoes*
16. las habitaciones viejas, *the old rooms*
17. las águilas negras, *the black eagles*
18. las conversaciones frustrantes, *the frustrating conversations*
19. las escaleras grandes, *the big staircases*
20. los crímenes violentos, *the violent crimes*
21. las nubes gordas, *the fat clouds*
22. los manteles blancos, *the white tablecloths*
23. los días grises, *the gray days*
24. las manos blancas, *the white hands*
25. las hojas verdes, *the green leaves*

EXERCISE 2-3

1. ninguna *There isn't any window open.*
2. tercer *I want the third painting.*
3. primeras *I need to read the first pages.*
4. gran *He is a great athlete.*
5. mala *He (She) is a bad person.*
6. algunas *There are some napkins on the table.*
7. buena *It's a good idea.*
8. buen *He's a good doctor.*
9. buenas *They are good teachers.*
10. grandes *I am going to study the great works of art.*

EXERCISE 2-4

1. una personalidad única *Roberto has a unique personality.*
2. medio vaso *I do not want more than half a glass.*
3. El hombre medio *The average man is not very tall.*
4. un gran hombre *Einstein was a great man.*
5. una mujer pobre *Roberta does not have money; she is a poor woman.*
6. una cosa cierta *The Mexican is going to win; it's a sure thing.*
7. agua pura *The mountain water is pure water.*
8. una pura mentira *Her version of the story is a complete lie.*
9. un pobre hombre *The teacher is a pitiful man.*
10. la única cosa *The only thing I want is to rest.*
11. un hombre viejo *He is an old man.*
12. ciertas cosas *I do not like certain things.*

EXERCISE 2-5

1. Es aburrido. *What's the book like? It's boring.*
2. Es gris. *What color is your suit? It's gray.*
3. Estuvo sabrosa. *How was the soup? It was tasty.*
4. Están cansados. *How are the children? They're tired.*
5. Son buenos. *What are the students like? They're good.*
6. Llegó mojado. *How did your husband arrive? He arrived wet.*
7. Son rojas. *What color are the roses? They're red.*
8. Son azules. *What color are your eyes? They're blue.*
9. Es simpático. *What's the teacher like? He's nice.*
10. Son habladoras. *What are your cousins like? They're talkative.*
11. Está enfermo. *How is your father? He's sick.*
12. Es malo. *What's the northern climate like? It's bad.*

13. Está ocupada. *How is your mother? She's busy.*
14. Son blancos. *What color are the umbrellas? They're white.*
15. Fue larga. *How was the movie? It was long.*

EXERCISE 2-6

1. la rubia *My aunt is the blond.*
2. la nueva *Where's the new one?*
3. El italiano *The Italian one is here.*
4. el viejo *I'm going to buy the old one.*
5. La blanca *The white one is dirty.*
6. la joven *I have to talk to the young one.*
7. el favorito *I lost my favorite one.*
8. El negro *The black one is broken.*
9. la favorita *Which one is the favorite?*
10. las antiguas *Where are the old ones?*

EXERCISE 2-7

1. los árboles altos y verdes
2. la muchacha pequeña y rubia
3. el viejo amigo querido
4. la casa vieja y decrépita
5. el agua clara y pura
6. la conversación larga y frustrante
7. la niña feliz y risueña
8. las palomitas saladas y calientes
9. el gran cuadro famoso
10. la universidad famosa y grande

EXERCISE 2-8

1. muchas *I have many tables at home.*
2. poca *I don't eat much meat.* OR *I eat only a little meat.*
3. alguna *I need some solution to the problem.*
4. otra *I don't want to drink another drink.*
5. cada *I get up at six o'clock every day.*
6. todos *I have to speak to all the students.*
7. toda *Roberto sleeps all morning (the whole morning).*
8. todo *My sister lives with me all year (the whole year).*
9. demasiada *There's too much salt in the soup.*
10. ninguna *I don't have any answer.*

EXERCISE 2-9

1. su *Juan bought his overcoat yesterday.*
2. nuestros *María and I have our umbrellas.*
3. mi, su *I have my bicycle and Alicia has her car.*
4. nuestros *Alfredo and I talk with our parents every day.*
5. su *Rafael says that his aunt is coming tomorrow.*
6. sus *María says that her cousins are coming tomorrow.*
7. nuestras *You and I have to talk to our daughters.*

8. sus *The children open their presents tomorrow.*
9. mi *I opened my present yesterday.*
10. mi *I don't know where my wallet is.*
11. tu *You'll have to take your bathing suit.*
12. sus *Jaime and Andrés bought their tickets yesterday.*

EXERCISE 2-10

1. el abrigo de Juan
2. el abrigo de María
3. los juguetes de los niños
4. la reunión de las mujeres
5. el tocadiscos de ellos
6. la casa de los señores López
7. el caballo de él
8. el alcalde del pueblo
9. la biblioteca de la universidad
10. el plan de él
11. la fiesta de ellas
12. la carta de Elena y de Tomás
13. los carros de Miguel y de Raúl
14. el calor del verano
15. los cuadernos de la estudiante
16. el cuaderno de la estudiante

EXERCISE 2-11

1. aquel sombrero grande *I'm going to buy that big hat.*
2. esta cuchara vieja *My mother gave me this old spoon.*
3. aquella cama vieja *We don't need that old bed.*
4. ese cuadro mexicano *I found that Mexican painting.*
5. este traste feo *I am going to throw out this ugly dish.*
6. aquella joya estupenda *I lost that fabulous jewel.*
7. aquel muchacho francés *We want to talk to that French boy.*
8. este libro grande *Raúl is going to read this big book.*
9. esta fórmula difícil *We have to study this difficult formula.*
10. aquel museo famoso *I want to visit that famous museum.*

EXERCISE 2-12

1. Esas *Those sheets are new.*
2. Estos *These shoes are small.*
3. aquella *I didn't like that movie.*
4. Aquellos *Those times were difficult.* OR *Those were hard times.*
5. Ese *That umbrella isn't broken.*
6. estas *I'm going to finish these letters tomorrow.*
7. aquel *I lost that pair of shoes last summer.*
8. esta *I like this kind of paper.*
9. esas *I don't want to talk to those people.*
10. Esos *Those men are my uncles.*

EXERCISE 2-13

1. un sombrero más bonito, el sombrero más bonito *I want to buy a prettier hat. I want to buy the prettiest hat.*
2. una casa más vieja, la casa más vieja *José has an older house. José has the oldest house.*
3. una novela más larga, la novela más larga *Don Quixote is a longer novel. Don Quixote is the longest novel.*
4. un traje más caro, el traje más caro *I have a more expensive suit. I have the most expensive suit.*
5. unos discos más modernos, los discos más modernos *I prefer more modern records. I prefer the most modern records.*
6. una ensalada más grande, la ensalada más grande *I need a bigger salad. I need the biggest salad.*
7. unos vestidos más nuevos, los vestidos más nuevos *I want some newer dresses. I want the newest dresses.*

EXERCISE 2-14

1. mi hermano mayor *Raúl is my oldest brother.*
2. la mejor novela *This is the best novel in the world.*
3. malo, peor *My radio is bad, but your radio is worse.*
4. un mundo mejor *I want to create a better world.*
5. la hija menor *Who is the youngest daughter?*
6. el peor coche *I have the worst car in the United States.*
7. un plan mejor *I can't imagine a better plan.*
8. el mejor plan *Rosaura has the best plan.*
9. Las mejores novelas *The best novels are the Russian novels.*
10. los hijos menores *I have to talk to the youngest children.*

EXERCISE 2-15

1. Juan es más alto que Roberto. *Juan is taller than Roberto.*
2. Tú estás más cansado que yo. *You are more tired than I.*
3. Tu libro es más interesante que mi libro. *Your book is more interesting than my book.*
4. El japonés es más difícil que el español. *Japanese is more difficult than Spanish.*
5. Tu idea es peor que mi idea. *Your idea is worse than my idea.*
6. Aquella película es más larga que esta película. *That movie is longer than this movie.*
7. Esta casa es más cara que aquella casa. *This house is more expensive than that house.*

8. Tu corbata es más roja que mi corbata.
   Your tie is redder than my tie.
9. Tus discos son mejores que mis discos.
   Your records are better than my records.
10. El guisado está más caliente que la sopa.
    The stew is hotter than the soup.

EXERCISE 2-16

1. Sí, es pequeñísima. Sí, es la isla más pequeña del mundo. *Yes, it's very small. Yes, it's the smallest island in the world.*
2. Sí, es felicísima. Sí, es la mujer más feliz del mundo. *Yes, she's very happy. Yes, she's the happiest woman in the world.*
3. Sí, es larguísima. Sí, es la novela más larga del mundo. *Yes, it's very long. Yes, it's the longest novel in the world.*
4. Sí, es riquísimo. Sí, es el hombre más rico del mundo. *Yes, he's very rich. Yes, he's the richest man in the world.*
5. Sí, es altísimo. Sí, es el edificio más alto del mundo. *Yes, it's very tall. Yes, it's the tallest building in the world.*
6. Sí, es anchísima. Sí, es la avenida más ancha del mundo. *Yes, it's very wide. Yes, it's the widest avenue in the world.*
7. Sí, es baratísimo. Sí, es el pescado más barato del mundo. *Yes, it's very cheap. Yes, it's the cheapest fish in the world.*
8. Sí, es buenísima. Sí, es la mejor comida del mundo. *Yes, it's very good. Yes, it's the best food in the world.*
9. Sí, es malísimo. Sí, es el peor cantante del mundo. *Yes, he's extremely bad. Yes, he's the worst singer in the world.*
10. Sí, son carísimos. Sí, son los libros más caros del mundo. *Yes, they're very expensive. Yes, they're the most expensive books in the world.*

EXERCISE 2-17

1. El geranio es tan hermoso como la rosa. *The geranium is as lovely as the rose.*
2. El agua es tan buena como el vino. *Water is as good as wine.*
3. El inglés es tan difícil como el español. *English is as difficult as Spanish.*
4. Los apartamentos son tan caros como las casas. *Apartments are as expensive as houses.*
5. El mar es tan peligroso como las montañas. *The sea is as dangerous as the mountains.*
6. El príncipe está tan triste como la princesa. *The prince is as sad as the princess.*

EXERCISE 2-18

1. Mi tío compró tantos sombreros como mi tía. *My uncle bought as many hats as my aunt.*
2. Los padres comieron tanto pastel como los niños. *The parents ate as much cake as the children.*

3. Yo escribo tantas cartas como mi amiga. *I write as many letters as my friend.*
4. El fue a tantos museos como yo. *He went to as many museums as I.*
5. Los muchachos hicieron tantas preguntas como las muchachas. *The boys asked as many questions as the girls.*
6. Tú encontraste tantos errores como yo. *You found as many errors as I.*
7. Tú buscaste el libro en tantas librerías como yo. *You looked for the book in as many bookstores as I.*
8. Alberto bebió tantos vasos de leche como mi prima. *Alberto drank as many glasses of milk as my cousin.*

EXERCISE 2-19

1. dificultosamente *We speak German with difficulty.*
2. cuidadosamente *The students write carefully.*
3. tristemente *He told me the story of the accident sadly.*
4. ansiosamente *We were waiting for the train anxiously.*
5. gustosamente *My mother cleans the kitchen with pleasure.*
6. rápidamente *I like to drive fast.*
7. intensamente *The child stared intensely through the window.*
8. cariñosamente *I greet you lovingly. OR Best wishes.*
9. pacientemente *She sat and weaved patiently.*
10. lentamente *I like to do things slowly.*

EXERCISE 2-20

1. rápidamente *They work quickly.*
2. alegremente *The children play happily.*
3. cuidadosa y rápidamente *I have to work carefully and quickly.*
4. cuidadosamente y bien *It is necessary to speak carefully and well.*
5. frecuentemente *My husband sings frequently.*
6. lenta y cuidadosamente *The boys speak slowly and carefully.*
7. tranquilamente *I want to see the program calmly.*
8. tristemente *He told me the story sadly.*
9. elegantemente *My sister dresses elegantly.*
10. enojadamente *He showed me the broken window angrily.*

EXERCISE 2-21

1. pocos *I have few books at home.*
2. bastante *The children sleep quite a lot.*
3. bastantes *The children play quite a few hours.*
4. demasiadas *There are too many chairs in the dining room.*

5. demasiado *The children talk too much.*
6. demasiado *She is too tall.*
7. demasiados *I have too many records.*
8. muy *Jaime is very intelligent.*
9. muchas *My house has many (a lot of) windows.*
10. mucho *I love you very much.*
11. mucho *I like to have a lot of work.*
12. nada *The teacher isn't at all cheerful.*

RAISE YOUR GRADES

Agreement of adjectives

1. Esos árboles son altos y verdes. *Those trees are tall and green.*
2. Tus caballos son demasiado nerviosos. *Your horses are too nervous.*
3. Las niñas cansadas no están muy contentas. *The tired little girls are not very happy.*
4. Las ensaladas son buenas, pero demasiado grandes. *The salads are good, but too big.*
5. Aquellos vasos rojos son de Antonio. *Those red glasses are Antonio's.*
6. Estas cartas largas son de Elena. *These long letters are Elena's.*
7. Los cuadros de Goya son famosos. *Goya's paintings are famous.*
8. Los quesos franceses son sumamente ricos. *French cheeses are extremely rich.*
9. Aquellas películas viejas son más divertidas que estas modernas. *Those old movies are more fun than these modern ones.*
10. Mis perros están más enojados que tus gatos. *My dogs are angrier than your cats.*

Recognition of adjectives

1. b, muchas; a, francesas *I know many French songs.*
2. c, mis; a, nuevos; a, azules *I left my new, blue gloves at home.*
3. a, buena; a, grande; a, confortable *I have a good, big, comfortable house.*
4. b, Todos; c, mis; a, altos *All my brothers are tall.*
5. b, pocas *Few women arrive so early.*
6. d, aquellas; a, rusas; a, largas *Those Russian novels are too long.*
7. a, cansados; b, toda *We are tired because we worked all night.*
8. c, Sus; a, interesantes *Their (His, Her) ideas are quite interesting.*
9. d, Estos *I don't like these hats at all.*
10. b, demasiados *We have too many books in the house now.*

Comparative form of adjectives

1. más alto *My mother is tall, but my father is taller.*
2. más grande *The University of Mexico is bigger than that of Madrid.*
3. mejor *Today's soup is better than yesterday's soup.*
4. más vieja *The Eiffel Tower is older than the Chrysler Building.*
5. más caras *Houses are more expensive these days.*
6. peor *This novel is bad, but that novel is worse.*
7. menos famoso *That painting by Goya is less famous than his other paintings.*
8. menor *Juan is younger than Carlos.*
9. más pequeña *The new table is smaller.*
10. menos interesantes *Today's comics are less interesting than the comics of the fifties.*

Use of *más que* and *más de*

1. más que *I make only five dollars an hour.*
2. más de *My brother has more than five cars.*
3. más que *I get just three letters a week.*
4. más de *I get more than ten letters a month.*
5. más que *I have more than enough.*
6. más que *I always buy more than you.*
7. más de *We need more than ten hours to finish the job.*
8. más que *We have just five minutes.*
9. más que *I found only one napkin.*
10. más de *I need more than one cup of coffee a day.*

Use of *tan . . . como* and *tanto . . . como*

1. tantas (modifies noun canciones), como *María knows as many songs as her sister.*
2. tantos (modifies noun dulces), como *The little boys asked for as many candies as the little girls.*
3. tan (modifies adverb rápido), como *The women run as fast as the men.*
4. tanta (modifies noun carne), como *I bought as much meat as she did.*
5. tan (modifies adjective buena), como *Mexican food is as good as French food.*
6. tan (modifies adjective cansados), como *We are as tired as you are.*
7. tantos (modifies noun discos), como *I don't have as many records as my brother.*
8. tantas (modifies noun horas), como *I had to wait as many hours as you did.*
9. tanto (modifies noun valor), como *Fernando has as much bravery (is as brave) as a bullfighter.*
10. tan (modifies adverb bien), como *I don't play baseball as well as Jackie Robinson.*

3 PRESENT TENSE

THIS CHAPTER IS ABOUT

- ☑ **Regular Verbs**
- ☑ **Stem-Changing Verbs**
- ☑ **Orthographic (Spelling) Changes**
- ☑ **Irregular Verbs**
- ☑ **Reflexive Verbs**
- ☑ **Present Progressive Tense**
- ☑ **Use of the Infinitive**
- ☑ **Affirmative and Negative Syntax**
- ☑ **Interrogatives**

3-1. Regular Verbs

A. **The most important difference between Spanish and English verbs is the use of the verb endings in Spanish to signal the doer of the action.**

Unlike English, Spanish seldom uses the subject pronouns (**yo, tú, él, ella,** etc.) except for emphasis or clarification. Instead, the verb ending indicates the doer of the action. For example, **hablo** means *I speak* or *I am speaking.* **Hablamos** means *we speak* or *we are speaking.*

B. **Spanish has four verb forms that are used to address other people directly:** *tú, vosotros, usted,* **and** *ustedes.*

These subject pronouns all mean *you* in English. In general, the familiar second person singular, **tú,** is used with friends, peers, children, and usually with relatives. The familiar second person plural, **vosotros,** is used in everyday speech in Spain. In Latin America, the third person plural, **ustedes,** is used instead of **vosotros** in both formal and informal address.

C. **The use of the informal** *tú* **versus the formal** *usted* **differs greatly according to the culture and the generation of the user.**

Tú is more widely used in Spain, especially among young people. On the other hand, many children in Latin America still use the **usted** form when speaking to their parents. On both continents, **usted** is always used when speaking to anyone providing a service or anyone with whom the speaker is not acquainted. However, it is not exceptional to hear **usted** used by older people who have known each other for years.

Patterns of usage differ more extensively among different generations than between different cultures. In both Spain and Latin America, the post-World War II generations tend to use the **tú** form more extensively. If you are in doubt about which form is correct for your situation, it is always better to use **usted** and to allow the person to whom you are speaking to say, "**por favor, háblame de tú,**" *"please, speak to me using tú."*

D. **There are three conjugations or groups of verbs in Spanish.**

Spanish verbs are classified into these three groups according to their infinitive endings (-ar, -er, and -ir). All verbs with an infinitive ending in **-ar**, such as **hablar**, *to speak*, and **caminar**, *to walk*, belong to the first conjugation. Verbs with an infinitive ending in **-er** such as **correr**, *to run*, and **comer**, *to eat*, belong to the second conjugation. Verbs with an infinitive ending in **-ir**, such as **vivir**, *to live*, and **escribir**, *to write*, belong to the third conjugation.

All present tense verb endings are added to the infinitive stem. The infinitive stem is formed by removing the infinitive ending. For example, **caminar**, *to walk*, = **camin + ar**; **trabajar**, *to work*, = **trabaj + ar**; **vaciar**, *to empty*, = **vaci + ar**. As you can see, the infinitive stem can end in either a vowel or a consonant.

1. *The -ar conjugation.* The **-ar** endings are **-o, -as, -a, -amos, -áis, -an**. Study the first conjugation verb given below.

hablar = habl + ar, *to speak*

(yo)	habl**o**	*I speak, am speaking*
(tú)	habl**as**	*you speak, are speaking*
(él, ella)	habl**a**	*he, she, it speaks, is speaking*
(usted)		*you speak, are speaking*
(nosotros, -as)	habl**amos**	*we speak, are speaking*
(vosotros, -as)	habl**áis**	*you speak (pl), are speaking*
(ellos, ellas)	habl**an**	*they speak, are speaking*
(ustedes)		*you speak (pl), are speaking*

EXERCISE 3-1: Write in the verb ending that corresponds to the subject pronoun given in parentheses. Answers are at the end of the chapter.

1. (nosotros) Cant_____ y bail_____ todos los sábados.
2. (usted) Trabaj_____ muy rápido.
3. (ellos) Cada mañana, and_____ cinco millas.
4. (nosotros) Estudi_____ juntos los fines de semana.
5. (él) Guard_____ sus discos cuidadosamente.
6. (vosotros) Gan_____ más dinero que ellos.
7. (tú) Desayun_____ a las seis, y cen_____ a las diez.
8. (ellos) Siempre habl_____ mucho y escuch_____ muy poco.
9. (ellas) Compr_____ un coche nuevo una vez al año.
10. (ella) Nad_____ y también esquí_____.
11. (yo) Ayud_____ a mis hermanos con frecuencia.
12. (ustedes) Lav_____ los platos inmediamente después de la comida.
13. (él) Siempre dej_____ su coche en el mismo lugar.
14. (yo) Necesit_____ una casa más grande.
15. (usted) Siempre pag_____ la comida.

2. *The -er and -ir conjugation.* Verb endings for **-er** and **-ir** verbs are the same except for the first person plural, **nosotros**, and the second person plural, **vosotros**. The **-er** endings are **-o, -es, -e, -emos, -éis, -en**. The **-ir** endings are **-o, -es, -e, -imos, -ís, -en**. Study the second and third conjugation verbs given below.

comer = com + er, *to eat*

(yo)	com**o**	*I eat, am eating*
(tú)	com**es**	*you eat, are eating*
(él, ella)	com**e**	*he, she, it eats, is eating*
(usted)		*you eat, are eating*
(nosotros, -as)	com**emos**	*we eat, are eating*
(vosotros, -as)	com**éis**	*you ear (pl), are eating*
(ellos, ellas)	com**en**	*they eat, are eating*
(ustedes)		*you eat (pl), are eating*

vivir = viv + ir, *to live*

(yo)	viv**o**	*I live, am living*
(tú)	viv**es**	*you live, are living*
(él, ella)⎫ (usted) ⎬	viv**e**	*he, she, it lives, is living* *you live, are living*
(nosotros, -as)	vivi**mos**	*we live, are living*
(vosotros, -as)	viv**ís**	*you live (pl), are living*
(ellos, ellas)⎫ (ustedes) ⎬	viv**en**	*they live, are living* *you live (pl), are living*

EXERCISE 3-2: Write in the correct form of the verb given in parentheses. First, look at the infinitive ending and ask yourself if the verb belongs to the **-er** or the **-ir** conjugation. Remember that the **nosotros** and **vosotros** forms of **-er** verbs are different from those of **-ir** verbs. Answers are at the end of the chapter.

1. (asisitir) Mi marido _____ a la Escuela de Bellas Artes.
2. (comer) Los bailarines _____ mucha ensalada.
3. (beber) Toda su familia _____ agua con la comida.
4. (recibir) Yo _____ una carta de él cada semana.
5. (aprender) Los estudiantes _____ rápido con aquella maestra.
6. (vivir) Ellos _____ en San Diego durante el verano.
7. (correr) Yo _____ todos los días en el parque.
8. (abrir) El Sr. González _____ el restorán tarde los domingos.
9. (deber) Mi primo _____ mil dólares mensualmente.
10. (sufrir) Vosotros _____ mucho de la contaminación del aire.
11. (subir) Todas las noches, nosotros _____ estas escaleras.
12. (comprender) Vosotros _____ muy bien la lección.
13. (vender) Aquellas muchachas _____ palomitas en la feria.
14. (recibir) Los novelistas latinoamericanos _____ muchos premios.
15. (discutir) El hijo mayor _____ más que sus hermanas menores.
16. (responder) Los niños _____ rápido a las preguntas.
17. (prometer) El presidente _____ muchas cosas al pueblo.
18. (creer) La religión cristiana _____ en una vida eterna.
19. (abrir) Nosotros siempre _____ la tienda a las nueve.
20. (meter) Mi madre nunca _____ a los niños en la cama temprano.

3-2. Stem-Changing Verbs

Stem-changing verbs are regular verbs that change the stem vowel in the first, second, and third person singular and the third person plural forms of the present tense. Stem changes never occur in the first and second person plural forms, **nosotros** and **vosotros**. There are three classes of stem-changing verbs.

A. **Class I stem-changing verbs**

Class I stem-changing verbs belong to the **-ar** and **-er** conjugations. There are two kinds of Class I stem-changing verbs.

> **NOTE:** In addition to stem changes in the present tense forms, Class I stem changes also occur in the polite command forms (see Chapter 7, Section 7-8).

1. **e—ie**. The first kind of Class I stem-changing verbs change the stem vowel from **e** to **ie**. It is important to remember that the **e—ie** change takes place in the verb stem. The stem of the verb is formed by removing the infinitive ending. The verb endings themselves do not change. Study the following examples of stem changes in an **-ar** and **-er** verb.

cerrar = cerr + ar, *to close*

(yo)	c**ie**rro	*I close, am closing*
(tú)	c**ie**rras	*you close, are closing*

(él, ella) \	cierra	*he, she, it closes, is closing*
(usted) /		*you close, are closing*
(nosotros, -as)	cerramos	*we close, are closing*
(vosotros, -as)	cerráis	*you close (pl), are closing*
(ellos, ellas) \	cierran	*they close, are closing*
(ustedes) /		*you close (pl), are closing*

entender = entend + er, *to understand*

(yo)	entiendo	*I understand, am understanding*
(tú)	entiendes	*you understand, are understanding*
(él, ella) \	entiende	*he, she, it understands, is understanding*
(usted) /		*you understand, are understanding*
(nosotros, -as)	entendemos	*we understand, are understanding*
(vosotros, -as)	entendéis	*you understand (pl), are understanding*
(ellos, ellas) \	entienden	*they understand, are understanding*
(ustedes) /		*you understand (pl), are understanding*

The following is a list of common verbs with a Class I **e—ie** stem change.

-ar verbs		-er verbs	
calentar	*to heat*	defender	*to defend*
comenzar	*to begin*	encender	*to light*
despertar	*to awaken*	perder	*to lose*
empezar	*to begin*	querer	*to want, to love*
gobernar	*to govern*		
negar	*to deny*		
nevar	*to snow*		
pensar	*to think*		
quebrar	*to break*		
sentarse	*to sit down*		

EXERCISE 3-3: Write in the correct form of the verb given in parentheses. Remember that stem changes do not occur in the first person plural and second person plural forms, **nosotros** and **vosotros**. Answers are at the end of the chapter.

1. (empezar) Todos los días yo _____ mis estudios al mediodía.
2. (perder) Mi tía siempre _____ sus guantes y sus gafas.
3. (querer) Tu tío _____ más café.
4. (entender) Vosotros _____ los problemas de la vida cotidiana.
5. (nevar) En el norte, _____ muchísimo.
6. (pensar) La maestra _____ que el horario es demasiado complicado.
7. (encender) Nosotros no _____ la luz durante el día.
8. (gobernar) El presidente _____ con el apoyo del pueblo.
9. (querer) Los estudiantes _____ a su maestro.
10. (comenzar) La película _____ a las ocho.

2. o—ue. The second kind of Class I stem-changing verbs change the stem vowel from **o** to **ue**. Study the following examples of **o—ue** changes in an **-ar** and an **-er** verb.

recordar = record + ar, *to remember*

(yo)	recuerdo	*I remember, am remembering*
(tú)	recuerdas	*you remember, are remembering*
(él, ella) \	recuerda	*he, she, it remembers, is remembering*
(usted) /		*you remember, are remembering*
(nosotros, -as)	recordamos	*we remember, are remembering*
(vosotros, -as)	recordáis	*you remember (pl), are remembering*
(ellos, ellas) \	recuerdan	*they remember, are remembering*
(ustedes) /		*you remember (pl), are remembering*

poder = **pod** + **er**, *to be able*

(yo)	**pue**do	*I am able, can*
(tú)	**pue**des	*you are able, can*
(él, ella)		*he, she, it is able, can*
(usted)	**pue**de	*you are able, can*
(nosotros, -as)	podemos	*we are able, can*
(vosotros, -as)	podéis	*you are able (pl), can*
(ellos, ellas)		*they are able, can*
(ustedes)	**pue**den	*you are able (pl), can*

The following is a list of common verbs with a Class I **o—ue** stem change.

-ar verbs		-er verbs	
almorzar	*to eat lunch*	devolver	*to return or give back*
colgar	*to hang up*	envolver	*to cover*
contar	*to count, to tell*	llover	*to rain*
demonstrar	*to demonstrate*	morder	*to bite*
encontrar	*to find or meet*	mover	*to move*
mostrar	*to show*	volver	*to return*
probar	*to taste, to try*		
sonar	*to ring*		
soñar	*to dream*		
volar	*to fly*		

> **NOTE:** The verb **oler**, *to smell*, changes the **o** to **ue** and adds **h**: **hue**lo, **hue**les, **hue**le, olemos, oléis, **hue**len. The verb **jugar**, *to play*, changes the **u** to **ue**: **jue**go, **jue**gas, **jue**ga, jugamos, jugáis, **jue**gan.

EXERCISE 3-4: Write in the correct form of the verb given in parentheses. Answers are at the end of the chapter.

1. (almorzar) Mis hijos _____ en casa a las doce.
2. (colgar) Tomás siempre _____ el teléfono antes que yo.
3. (mostrar) El perro _____ una indiferencia absoluta.
4. (recordar) Ellos _____ todos los detalles de su pasado.
5. (contar) Yo _____ seis tazas y sólo cinco platitos.
6. (envolver) La dependienta siempre _____ el pan en papel blanco.
7. (sonar) La campana no _____ porque está rota.
8. (soñar) Los estudiantes _____ demasiado en clase.
9. (llover) En el desierto, no _____ nunca.
10. (morder) El perro _____ al policía, pero no al vecino.
11. (colgar) Los niños _____ sus chaquetas antes de entrar en el salón.
12. (volar) El superhombre _____ por encima de los rascacielos.
13. (devolver) La madre _____ los libros a la biblioteca.
14. (probar) Yo _____ la sopa para ver si tiene demasiada sal.

B. Class II and Class III stem-changing verbs

Both Class II and Class III stem-changing verbs belong to the **-ir** conjugation. There are two kinds of Class II stem-changing verbs and one kind of Class III stem-changing verbs.

> **NOTE:** Class II stem-changing verbs change the **e** to **i** and **o** to **u** in the present participle forms and in the third person singular and plural preterite forms. Also, Class III stem-changing verbs change the **e** to **i** in the present participle forms and in the third person singular and plural preterite forms. (See Section 3-6 in this chapter and Chapter 5, Section 5-2.)

1. *Class II stem change from* **e**—**ie**. The first kind of Class II stem-changing verbs change the stem vowel from **e** to **ie**. Study the following example.

mentir = **ment** + **ir**, *to lie*

(yo)	miento	*I lie, am lying*
(tú)	mientes	*you lie, are lying*
(él, ella) (usted)	miente	*he, she, it lies, is lying* / *you lie, are lying*
(nosotros, -as)	mentimos	*we lie, are lying*
(vosotros, -as)	mentís	*you lie (pl), are lying*
(ellos, ellas) (ustedes)	mienten	*they lie, are lying* / *you lie (pl), are lying*

2. *Class II stem change from* **o**—**ue**. The second kind of Class II stem-changing verbs change the stem vowel from **o** to **ue**. Study the following example.

morir = **mor** + **ir**, *to die*

(yo)	muero	*I die, am dying*
(tú)	mueres	*you die, are dying*
(él, ella) (usted)	muere	*he, she, it dies, is dying* / *you die, are dying*
(nosotros, -as)	morimos	*we die, are dying*
(vosotros, -as)	morís	*you die (pl), are dying*
(ellos, ellas) (ustedes)	mueren	*they die, are dying* / *you die (pl), are dying*

3. *Class III stem change from* **e**—**i**. Class III stem-changing verbs change the stem vowel from **e** to **i**. Study the following example.

pedir = **ped** + **ir**, *to ask for or request*

(yo)	pido	*I ask for, am asking for*
(tú)	pides	*you ask for, are asking for*
(él, ella) (usted)	pide	*he, she, it asks for, is asking for* / *you ask for, are asking for*
(nosotros, -as)	pedimos	*we ask for, are asking for*
(vosotros, -as)	pedís	*you ask for (pl), are asking for*
(ellos, ellas) (ustedes)	piden	*they ask for, are asking for* / *you ask for (pl), are asking for*

Study the following list of Class II and Class III stem-changing verbs.

Class II		Class III	
e—ie		**e—i**	
consentir	*to consent*	despedir	*to fire, to send off*
herir	*to wound, hurt*	freír	*to fry*
preferir	*to prefer*	medir	*to measure*
sentir	*to feel sorry, regret*	perseguir	*to pursue, persecute*
sugerir	*to suggest*	reír	*to laugh*
		repetir	*to repeat*
o—ue		seguir	*to follow*
dormir	*to sleep*	sonreír	*to smile*

> **NOTE:** The verbs **freír**, *to fry*, **reír**, *to laugh*, and **sonreír**, *to smile*, have a written accent over the **i** in all present tense forms: **río, ríes, ríe, reímos, reís, ríen.**

EXERCISE 3-5: Write in the correct form of the verb given in parentheses. The stem change is given with the verb. Answers are at the end of the chapter.

1. (pedir, i) Yo generalmente _____ permiso primero.
2. (sonreír, i) Mi hermano _____ muchísimo.

3. (mentir, ie) Los políticos _____ demasiado.
4. (dormir, ue) Nosotros _____ mucho los fines de semana.
5. (repetir, i) La maestra _____ el mismo ejercicio con frecuencia.
6. (morir, ue) La esperanza _____ despacio.
7. (consentir, ie) Yo no _____ las demandas de mi suegra.
8. (herir, ie) Mi marido _____ las rodillas con frecuencia.
9. (servir, i) Su tía siempre _____ café con leche.
10. (medir, i) Mi primo no _____ más que cinco pies.
11. (sugerir, ie) El abogado _____ otra táctica de defensa.
12. (freír, i) Todas las mañanas, yo _____ un par de huevos.
13. (reír, i) Las muchachas _____ poco durante el trabajo.

3-3. Orthographic (Spelling) Changes

In Spanish, changes in the spelling system occur according to the pronunciation of the word. There are four kinds of spelling changes in present tense verbs.

A. **Verbs that end in -cer change the c to zc before o and a.**

In the present tense, this change occurs only in the first person singular. The **c** is pronounced like a **k** after the **z**. Study the following examples.

aparecer	*to appear*	apare**zc**o, apareces, aparece, aparecemos, aparecéis, aparecen
conducir	*to drive*	condu**zc**o, conduces, conduce, conducimos, conducís, conducen
introducir	*to introduce*	introdu**zc**o, introduces, introduce, introducimos, introducís, introducen
merecer	*to deserve*	mere**zc**o, mereces, merece, merecemos, merecéis, merecen
ofrecer	*to offer*	ofre**zc**o, ofreces, ofreces, ofrecemos, ofrecéis, ofrecen
reconocer	*to recognize*	recono**zc**o, reconoces, reconoce, reconocemos, reconocéis, reconocen
reducir	*to reduce*	redu**zc**o, reduces, reduce, reducimos, reducís, reducen

B. **Verbs that end in -ger and -gir change the g to j before o and a in order to avoid the hard g of -go and -ga.**

In the present tense, this change occurs only in the first person singular. Study the following examples.

coger	*to pick up*	co**j**o, coges, coge, cogemos, cogéis, cogen
corregir(i)	*to correct*	corri**j**o, corriges, corrige, corregimos, corregís, corrigen
escoger	*to choose*	esco**j**o, escoges, escoge, escogemos, escogéis, escogen
exigir	*to demand*	exi**j**o, exiges, exige, exigimos, exigís, exigen
dirigir	*to direct*	diri**j**o, diriges, dirige, dirigimos, dirigís, dirigen

C. **Verbs that end in -guir change the gu to g before o and a.**

In the present tense, this change occurs only in the first person singular. Study the following examples.

conseguir(i)	*to get*	consi**g**o, consigues, consigue, conseguimos, conseguís, consiguen
distinguir	*to distinguish*	distin**g**o, distingues, distingue, distinguimos, distinguís, distinguen
perseguir(i)	*to pursue*	persi**g**o, persigues, persigue, perseguimos, perseguís, persiguen
seguir(i)	*to follow*	si**g**o, sigues, sigue, seguimos, seguís, siguen

D. **Verbs that end in *-uir* add *y* before *o, e,* and *a*.**

In the present tense, this change occurs in the first, second, and third person singular and plural forms. Study the following examples.

construir	*to build*	construyo, construyes, construye, construimos, construís, construyen
destruir	*to destroy*	destruyo, destruyes, destruye, destruimos, destruís, destruyen
huir	*to flee*	huyo, huyes, huye, huimos, huís, huyen
instruir	*to instruct*	instruyo, instruyes, instruye, instruimos, instruís, instruyen

EXERCISE 3-6: Rewrite the following sentences by changing the verb from first person plural to first person singular. Answers are at the end of the chapter.

Example: Seguimos el mismo camino.   *Sigo el mismo camino.*

1. Siempre conseguimos lo que queremos.
2. No conocemos al presidente todavía.
3. Siempre escogemos el pedazo más grande del pastel.
4. Exigimos mucho de los estudiantes.
5. Construimos de día y destruimos de noche.
6. Aparecemos diariamente a las cinco.
7. Producimos tomates, cebollas, ajos y perejil.
8. Pertenecemos a varias organizaciones del barrio.
9. Corregimos las cartas de los jóvenes.
10. Reconocemos la veracidad de los cuentos de hadas.
11. Ofrecemos una cena con vino, pan, postre y café.
12. Conseguimos los mismos resultados todos los días.
13. Agradecemos infinitamente la bondad del maestro.
14. Traducimos del francés al inglés, pero no al revés.

3-4. Irregular Verbs

Irregular verbs in the present tense are not difficult to learn because most irregularities occur in the first person singular. A few verbs, such as **ser**, *to be*, and **ir**, *to go*, are very irregular, but they are the exception. Some commonly used irregular verbs are given below in the present tense.

A. **Irregular verbs with first person singular change**

1. *First person adds **g** before the **-o** ending.*

hacer	*to do*	ha**g**o, haces, hace, hacemos, hacéis, hacen
poner	*to put*	pon**g**o, pones, pone, ponemos, ponéis, ponen
salir	*to leave*	sal**g**o, sales, sale, salimos, salís, salen
valer	*to be worth*	val**g**o, vales, vale, valemos, valéis, valen

2. *First person adds* **ig** *before the* **-o** *ending.*

| caer | *to fall* | ca**ig**o, caes, cae, caemos, caéis, caen |
| traer | *to bring* | tra**ig**o, traes, trae, traemos, traéis, traen |

3. *First person adds* **g** *before* **-o** *ending.* These verbs also have either a stem change or an orthographic change.

decir (i)	*to say, tell*	di**g**o, dices, dice, decimos, decís, dicen
oír (y)	*to hear*	oi**g**o, oyes, oye, oímos, oís, oyen
tener (ie)	*to have*	ten**g**o, tienes, tiene, tenemos, tenéis, tienen
venir (ie)	*to come*	ven**g**o, vienes, viene, venimos, venís vienen

4. *Verbs with other first person singular irregularities.*

caber	*to fit*	**quep**o, cabes, cabe, cabemos, cabéis, caben
dar	*to give*	**doy**, das, da, damos, dáis, dan
saber	*to know*	**sé**, sabes, sabe, sabemos, sabéis, saben
ver	*to see*	**veo**, ves, ve, vemos, véis, ven

NOTE: The written accent over the **e** of **sé** distinguishes it from the reflexive pronoun, **se**.

EXERCISE 3-7: Study the irregular verbs listed above. Repeat them aloud and listen to the first person irregularity. Note that the remaining forms follow the pattern of regular or stem-changing verbs. Now rewrite the following sentences by changing the verbs to the first person singular. Answers are at the end of the chapter.

Example: Ellos saben mucho. *Sé mucho.*

1. Tenemos mucha leche en la nevera.
2. Venimos al parque todos los días.
3. Ven un partido de béisbol todos los domingos.
4. Hacen todo lo posible para ganar.
5. Ustedes ponen mucha atención en el proyecto.
6. Salimos a las cuatro en punto.
7. Siempre traemos flores para el día de las madres.
8. Saben lo que hacen.
9. Siempre dan la ropa vieja a la iglesia.
10. Tú no cabes en aquella silla.
11. No oyen lo que dicen.
12. Dices muchas cosas pero no haces nada.
13. Oímos la radio todo el día.
14. Ves cosas raras en el desierto.
15. Saben mucho de historia latinoamericana.

B. *Ser, estar,* and *ir*

Ser and **ir** are irregular in all forms of the present tense. **Estar** is irregular in the first, second, and third person singular and third person plural forms. Study the written accents of **estar** carefully. The uses and meanings of **ser** and **estar** are discussed in Chapter 4.

ser, *to be*	estar, *to be*		ir, *to go*	
soy	**estoy**	*I am*	**voy**	*I go, am going*
eres	**estás**	*you are*	**vas**	*you go, are going*
es	**está**	*he, she, it is*	**va**	*he, she, it goes, is going*
		you are		*you go, are going*
somos	estamos	*we are*	**vamos**	*we go, are going*
sois	**estáis**	*you are (pl)*	**vais**	*you go (pl), are going*
son	**están**	*they are (pl)*	**van**	*they go (pl), are going*
		you are (pl)		*you go (pl), are going*

EXERCISE 3-8: Write in the correct form of the verb given in parentheses. Answers are at the end of the chapter.

1. (ir) Ellos _____ al parque los domingos.
2. (ir) Yo _____ al centro por la mañana.
3. (ser) Nosotros _____ franceses.
4. (ser) Los edificios _____ muy altos.
5. (ir) Nosotros _____ pronto.
6. (estar) Yo _____ solo y triste.
7. (estar) María y Carlos _____ en la cocina.
8. (ir) Jaime y Andrés _____ a la playa todos los días.
9. (ser) Tú _____ el primero y yo _____ el tercero.
10. (ser) Ellos _____ muy amigos.

3-5. Reflexive Verbs

Reflexive verbs differ from other verbs in that the doer of the action and the receiver of the action are the same person. In English, this concept is often expressed by using *myself, yourself,* etc. In Spanish, a reflexive verb is always conjugated with a reflexive pronoun: **me lavo,** *I wash myself;* **te lavas,** *you wash yourself,* and so on. Reflexive verbs are listed in the dictionary after the nonreflexive form. For example, **llamar,** *v.t. to call;* **llamar,** *v.r. to be named.* In grammar books, reflexive verbs are often listed with the reflexive pronoun **se** attached to the infinitive: **llamarse,** *to be named.*

A. **Forms of reflexive verbs**

Reflexive verbs always appear with the appropriate reflexive pronoun. It is important to understand that the reflexive pronoun functions as an object pronoun and does not take the place of the subject pronoun: **(yo) me lavo, (tú) te lavas,** and so on. The reflexive pronouns are given below.

me	*myself*	**nos**	*ourselves*
te	*yourself*	**os**	*yourselves*
se	*herself, himself, itself*	**se**	*themselves, yourselves*
	yourself		

Note that the reflexive pronoun **se** is the same for the third person singular and plural. Now study the following example of a reflexive verb.

levantarse, *to get up*

(yo)	me levanto	*I get up, am getting up*
(tú)	te levantas	*you get up, are getting up*
(él, ella) (usted)	se levanta	*he, she gets up, is getting up* / *you get up, are getting up*

(nosotros, -as)	nos levantamos	*we get up, are getting up*
(vosotros, -as)	os levantáis	*you get up (pl), are getting up*
(ellos, ellas) (ustedes)	se levantan	*they get up, are getting up* *you get up (pl), are getting up*

Study the following list of common reflexive verbs. Stem changes are given in parentheses.

acordarse(ue)	*to remember*	equivocarse	*to be mistaken*
acostarse(ue)	*to go to bed, to lie down*	irse	*to go away*
arrepentirse(ie)	*to regret*	llamarse	*to be named*
atreverse	*to dare to*	marcharse	*to go away*
bañarse	*to take a bath*	peinarse	*to comb one's hair*
callarse	*to be quiet*	ponerse	*to put on, to dress*
despedirse(i)	*to take leave, to say goodbye*	quedarse	*to remain*
despertarse	*to wake up*	quejarse	*to complain*
divertirse(ie)	*to enjoy*	sentarse(ie)	*to sit down*
enfadarse	*to get mad, to get angry*	sentirse(ie)	*to feel*
enojarse	*to get mad, to get annoyed*	vestirse(i)	*to dress*

EXERCISE 3-9: Write in the correct form of the reflexive verb given in parentheses. Stem changes are also noted in parentheses. Remember, the reflexive pronoun immediately precedes the verb. Answers are at the end of the chapter.

1. (marcharse) Carlos nunca _____ enojado de la fiesta
2. (sentarse, ie) Mi madre _____ gran parte del día.
3. (ponerse) Todos los días, Jaime _____ el traje azul marino.
4. (divertirse, ie) Robert y George _____ muchísimo.
5. (bañarse) Nosotros _____ por la mañana.
6. (acostarse, ue) Alicia _____ muy temprano.
7. (equivocarse) Yo nunca _____.
8. (levantarse) Vosotros _____ demasiado temprano.
9. (peinarse) Aquel muchacho _____ de una manera muy rara.
10. (acordarse, ue) Yo siempre _____ de todo.
11. (enojarse) El mecánico _____ fácilmente.
12. (llamarse) Tú _____ Mary Jane, ¿verdad?
13. (despedirse, i) Ustedes siempre _____ demasiado pronto.
14. (sentirse, ie) Mi prima _____ muy bien.
15. (despertarse, ie) El pequeño _____ muchas veces durante la noche.

B. Use of reflexive verbs

1. A reflexive verb is used to indicate that the action reflects back upon the doer of the action. Any transitive verb—that is, any action verb that can take a direct object—can usually be used as a reflexive verb. Study the following examples.

Nonreflexive	Reflexive
Lavo las manos de mi hermano.	Me lavo las manos.
I wash my brother's hands.	*I wash my hands.*
La madre acuesta a los niños.	La madre se acuesta.
The mother puts the children to bed.	*The mother goes to bed.*
Pones el vaso en la mesa.	Te pones la corbata roja.
You are putting the glass on the table.	*You are putting on the red tie.*

2. A reflexive verb sometimes differs in meaning from the nonreflexive form. Study the following examples.

	Nonreflexive		Reflexive
comer	*to eat*	comerse	*to eat up*
despedir(i) a	*to fire*	despedirse(i) de	*to take leave*
ir	*to go*	irse	*to go away*
llamar	*to call*	llamarse	*to be named, to be called*
llevar	*to carry*	llevarse	*to take away*
marchar	*to go*	marcharse	*to go away*
poner	*to put*	ponerse	*to wear*
parecer	*to seem*	parecerse	*to look alike*
quedar	*to be left*	quedarse	*to remain, to stay*
sentir(ie)	*to regret*	sentirse(ie)	*to feel*
sonar(ue)	*to ring*	sonarse(ue)	*to blow one's nose*

3. Verbs such as **morir**, **reír**, and **sonreír** often add the reflexive pronoun to emphasize the level of involvement of the subject with the action of the verb. However, the difference between **muero** and **me muero**, for example, cannot be translated into English.

4. The reflexive can be used to mean "to oneself." Study the following examples.

Yo me hablo.	*I talk to myself.*
Ellos se mienten.	*They lie to themselves.*

5. The reflexive can be used to mean "each other." Study the following examples.

Nosotros nos hablamos.	*We talk to each other.*
Vosotros os engañáis.	*You deceive each other.*
Ellos se mienten.	*They lie to each other.*

> **NOTE:** In order to avoid confusion between "to oneself" and "to each other," you can add "**uno(s) a otro(s)**" for the latter meaning.
>
> Ellos se mienten **unos a otros**.   *They lie to each other.*

EXERCISE 3-10: Choose the correct verb form from those given in parentheses that fits the meaning of the sentence. Answers are at the end of the chapter.

1. (Pongo, Me pongo) _____ las rosas en un florero más grande.
2. (pongo, me pongo) Siempre _____ los calcetines primero.
3. (parecen, se parecen) Los gemelos _____ mucho.
4. (parece, se parece) Eduardo _____ cansado.
5. (parezco, me parezco) Yo _____ a mi madre.
6. (llama, se llama) Alda _____ a su novio.
7. (marcha, se marcha) Todo _____ bien.
8. (marchan, se marchan) Los músicos _____ en seguida.
9. (levantas, te levantas) Los domingos _____ a las diez.
10. (Levanto, Me levanto) _____ cinco kilos fácilmente.
11. (acuesto, me acuesto) Siempre _____ a los niños temprano.
12. (acostamos, nos acostamos) Mi marido y yo _____ tarde.
13. (quedan, se quedan) De los cinco postres, sólo _____ dos.
14. (queda, se queda) Este fin de semana, Juan _____ en casa.
15. (bañas, te bañas) Tú siempre _____ con agua fría, ¿verdad?
16. (baño, me baño) No _____ al perro con mucha frecuencia.

3-6. Present Progressive Tense

In English, the present progressive tense consists of the appropriate form of the verb "to be" plus the present participle (the -*ing* form), such as I *am eating* and *Are* you *eating?* In Spanish, the present progressive tense also consists of the appropriate form of **estar** (never **ser**) plus the present participle.

A. Forms of the present participle

1. First conjugation -ar verbs add **-ando** to the infinitive stem to form the present participle.

> trabajar = trabaj + **ando**, **trabajando**, *working*
> jugar = jug + **ando**, **jugando**, *playing*
> pasear = pase + **ando**, **paseando**, *walking around*
> estudiar = estudi + **ando**, **estudiando**, *studying*

2. Second and third conjugation -er and -ir verbs add **-iendo** to the infinitive stem to form the present participle.

> comer = com + **iendo**, **comiendo**, *eating*
> escribir = escrib + **iendo**, **escribiendo**, *writing*
> hacer = hac + **iendo**, **haciendo**, *doing*
> salir = sal + **iendo**, **saliendo**, *leaving*

3. Class II and Class III stem-changing verbs change the **e** of the infinitive stem to **i** before adding the **-iendo** ending.

> conseguir = consigu + iendo, **consiguiendo**, *getting*
> pedir = pid + iendo, **pidiendo**, *asking for*
> repetir = repit + iendo, **repitiendo**, *repeating*
> seguir = sigu + iendo, **siguiendo**, *following*
> sentir = sint + iendo, **sintiendo**, *feeling*
> servir = sirv + iendo, **sirviendo**, *serving*
> venir = vin + iendo, **viniendo**, *coming*
> vestir = vist + iendo, **vistiendo**, *dressing*

> **NOTE:** The present participle of **ser** is **siendo**.

4. Class II stem-changing verbs change the **o** of the infinitive stem to **u** before adding the **-iendo** ending.

> dormir = durm + iendo, **durmiendo**, *sleeping*
> morir = mur + iendo, **muriendo**, *dying*
> poder = pud + iendo, **pudiendo**, *being able*

5. When **i** appears between two vowels, the **i** changes to **y**. Thus, verbs with an infinitive stem that ends in a vowel, such as **leer**, *to read*, and **oír**, *to hear*, change the **-iendo** ending to **-yendo**. Study the following examples.

-er verbs			-ir verbs		
atraer	atra**yendo**	*attracting*	constituir	constitu**yendo**	*constituting*
caer	ca**yendo**	*falling*	construir	constru**yendo**	*building*
creer	cre**yendo**	*believing*	destruir	destru**yendo**	*destroying*
leer	le**yendo**	*reading*	huir	hu**yendo**	*fleeing*
poseer	pose**yendo**	*possessing*	ir	**yendo**	*going*
traer	tra**yendo**	*bringing*	influir	influ**yendo**	*influencing*
			oír	o**yendo**	*listening*

EXERCISE 3-11: First, form the present participle from its infinitive, watching for stem-changing verbs and spelling changes. Then write in the English translation. Answers are at end of the chapter.

1. estudiar	_____ _____		6. hablar	_____ _____
2. romper	_____ _____		7. seguir	_____ _____
3. llover	_____ _____		8. dormir	_____ _____
4. creer	_____ _____		9. almorzar	_____ _____
5. sentir	_____ _____		10. estacionar	_____ _____

11. venir	_____ _____	18. jugar	_____ _____
12. morir	_____ _____	19. huir	_____ _____
13. pedir	_____ _____	20. ser	_____ _____
14. poder	_____ _____	21. estar	_____ _____
15. aprender	_____ _____	22. ir	_____ _____
16. limpiar	_____ _____	23. traer	_____ _____
17. mentir	_____ _____	24. dudar	_____ _____

B. Use of the present progressive tense

The present tense can be used in Spanish to convey the idea of continuous action; however, the present progressive tense is used *only* when the action of the verb is actually taking place. Study the following examples.

| **Estamos hablando** demasiado. | *We are talking too much (right now).* |
| **Estás mintiendo**. | *You are telling a lie (right now).* |

Unlike English, Spanish never uses the present progressive tense to refer to a future event. Note this difference in the examples below.

| **Estoy estudiando** ahora. | *I am studying now.* |
| **Estudio** con Jaime esta noche. | *I am studying with Jaime tonight.* |

EXERCISE 3-12: Rewrite the following sentences by changing the verb from the present to the present progressive tense. Watch out for stem-changing verbs. Answers are at the end of the chapter.

Example: Busco mi carpeta nueva. *Estoy buscando mi carpeta nueva.*

1. Rafael lava la ropa sucia.

2. Los niños miran le tele en su dormitorio.

3. La maestra explica una lección de gramática.

4. Los caballos corren por la playa.

5. Tú pides demasiado dinero.

6. Las muchachas duermen porque están aburridas.

7. El policía persigue al ladrón.

8. Nieva mucho esta mañana.

9. El obispo almuerza con el general.

10. Roberto y Luisa nadan en el mar.

11. Discutimos un tema muy importante.

12. Lees una novela muy aburrida.

13. Vosotros coméis una cena estupenda.

14. Muero de cansancio y aburrimiento.

15. Elena rompe sus viejas cartas de amor.

C. **Present progressive tense with reflexive verbs**

When forming the present progressive tense using reflexive verbs, the reflexive pronoun can be placed either directly preceding the conjugated form of **estar**, or it can be attached to the present participle. If the reflexive pronoun is attached to the present participle, a written accent is required over the **a** of **-ándose** or the **e** of **-iéndose.** Study the following examples.

quejarse, *to complain*

(yo)	**me** estoy quejando OR estoy quejándo**me**	*I am complaining*
(tú)	**te** estás quejando OR estas quejándo**te**	*you are complaining*
(él, ella)⎱ (usted) ⎰	**se** está quejando OR está quejándo**se**	*he, she, it is complaining* *you are complaining*
(nosotros, -as)	**nos** estamos quejando OR estamos quejándo**nos**	*we are complaining*
(vosotros, -as)	**os** estáis quejando OR estáis quejándo**os**	*you are complaining (pl)*
(ellos, ellas)⎱ (ustedes) ⎰	**se** están quejándo OR están quejándo**se**	*they are complaining* *you are complaining (pl)*

> **NOTE:** Both structures are used interchangeably and there is no translatable difference.

EXERCISE 3-13: Rewrite the following sentences by changing the form of the reflexive verb to agree with the subject given in parentheses. Use the syntax of the original sentence. Remember that when the reflexive pronoun is attached to the present participle, a written accent must be placed over **-ándose** and **-iéndose.** Answers are at the end of the chapter.

Examples: Me estoy lavando la cara. (tú) *Te estás lavando la cara.*
           Estamos divirtiéndonos mucho. (él) *Está divirtiéndose mucho.*

1. Roberto se está mintiendo. (ellos)

2. Nosotros nos estamos quejando demasiado. (Los estudiantes)

3. Andrew se está riendo. (yo)

4. Tú te estás acostando temprano. (vosotros)

5. Yo me estoy levantando ahora mismo. (Mis abuelos)

6. María se está vistiendo ahora. (Nosotros)

7. Ella se está peinando en el dormitorio. (nosotros)

8. Rafael se está despertando poco a poco. (yo)

9. Nosotros estamos despidiéndonos de la maestra. (Los estudiantes)

10. Yo estoy acordándome de la pelicula. (tú)

11. Rosaura está muriéndose de risa. (tú)

12. Tú estás sentándote en mi asiento. (El profesor)

13. Yo estoy preguntándome qué pasó. (José)

14. Nosotros estamos levantándonos despacio. (yo)

15. Yo estoy enojándome aquí. (Leopoldo)

16. Tú estás enfadándote demasiado. (yo)

17. José está quejándose de la comida. (Mi suegra)

18. Yo estoy poniéndome el abrigo de pieles. (Carlota)

19. Los estudiantes están gritándose unos a otros. (nosotros)

20. Nosotros estamos engañándonos unos a otros. (ellos)

3-7. Use of the Infinitive

A. The infinitive as object of the verb

1. *Nonreflexive verbs.* The infinitive is used directly after verbs such as **querer**, *to want*; **esperar**, *to expect* or *to hope*; **necesitar**, *to need*; **poder**, *to be able*; and **deber**, *ought to* or *should*. Study the following examples.

Quiero comprar varios vestidos.	*I want to buy several dresses.*
Podemos hacer una ensaladilla rusa.	*We can make a potato salad.*
Espero llegar temprano.	*I hope to arrive early.*

2. *Reflexive verbs.* The reflexive pronoun can be placed either directly before the conjugated verb or attached to the infinitive. Study the following examples.

Quiero lavar**me** la cara.
Me quiero lavar la cara. } *I want to wash my face.*

Podemos llevar**nos** las sobras.
Nos podemos llevar las sobras. } *We can take the leftovers.*

José debe levantar**se** más temprano.
José **se** debe levantar más temprano. } *José should get up earlier.*

REMEMBER: The use of the subject pronoun is optional.

EXERCISE 3-14: Study each sentence below and ask yourself if the verb is reflexive or nonreflexive. If the verb is reflexive, the reflexive pronoun attached to the infinitive must agree with the subject. Complete each sentence by translating the verb given in parentheses into Spanish. Answers are at the end of the chapter.

Example: (to go to bed) Debes ___acostarte___ pronto.

1. (to get up) Lourdes necesita _____ temprano.
2. (to buy) Espero _____ una carpeta más grande.
3. (to feel) Debes _____ mejor pronto.
4. (to say goodbye) Necesitamos _____ de la Sra. Blanco.
5. (to read) Espero _____ toda la Enciclopedia Británica.
6. (to write) Puedes _____ una carta más larga.
7. (to remember) Los estudiantes esperan _____ de la lección de ayer.
8. (to sit down) Necesito _____ un rato.
9. (to put on) Andrew quiere _____ una camisa roja.
10. (to look alike) Las hermanas Jones deben _____ mucho.
11. (to seem) Eloisa quiere _____ una persona seria.
12. (to bring) Ustedes pueden _____ el pan y la mantequilla.
13. (to call) Necesitamos _____ a la tía Barbara.
14. (to wash) Los muchachos deben _____ su propia ropa.

B. *Hay que* and *tener que* + infinitive

There are two grammatical structures that require **que** before the infinitive.

1. *Tener versus tener que*. **Tener** means *to have* (*to possess*). **Tener que** means *to have to* (do something) and is always followed by an infinitive. Study the following examples. Note that the word **que** always immediately precedes the infinitive object.

Tengo dos coches nuevos.	*I have two new cars.*
Tengo que lavar los coches.	*I have to wash the cars.*
Tengo dos coches **que lavar**.	*I have two cars to wash.*
Tengo muchas cosas **que hacer**.	*I have many things to do.*
Tengo que hacer muchas cosas.	*I have to do many things.*
Tú **tienes que acostarte** temprano.	
Tú **te tienes que acostar** temprano.	*You have to go to bed early.*

2. *Hay versus hay que*. **Hay** is a non-conjugatable form of the verb **haber**, *to have*. **Hay** means *there is* or *there are*. **Hay que** means *it is necessary to* or *one must*. This impersonal structure cannot be conjugated. Study the following examples. Note that **que** is never separated from the infinitive.

Hay un problema.	*There's a problem.*
Hay muchos problemas.	*There are many problems.*
Hay un problema **que resolver**.	*There's a problem to resolve.*
Hay muchos problemas **que resolver**.	*There are many problems to resolve.*
Hay que resolver el problema.	*It is necessary to resolve the problem.*
Hay que resolver los problemas.	*It is necessary to resolve the problems.*

EXERCISE 3-15: Study the following sentences. First, try to find the subject. If there is a subject, you must use the conjugated form of the verb **tener** or **tener que** that agrees with the subject. If there is no subject, you must use either **hay** or **hay que**. Remember, **que** always immediately precedes the infinitive. Answers are at the end of the chapter.

Examples: Mis hermanas *tienen que* ir al mercado. (Subj.—*My sisters have to go to the market.*)
Hay que lavar los platos. (No subj.—*It is necessary to wash the dishes.*)
Mi padre *tiene* una casa grande. (Subj.—*My father has a big house.*)
Hay una casa grande. (No subj.—*There is a big house*).

1. Yo _____ muchos vasos viejos para la fiesta.
2. Rosa no puede salir porque ella _____ mucho _____ hacer.
3. _____ una película nueva en el centro.
4. _____ ir muy temprano para comprar las entradas.
5. _____ comer la carne antes del postre.
6. Tú _____ estudiar más, si quieres aprender.
7. Los futbolistas _____ sueño, y _____ acostarse.
8. Nosotros _____ un problema grave y _____ salir.
9. Los estudiantes _____ varias lecciones _____ estudiar.
10. El jefe del instituto _____ entrar a las ocho.
11. _____ ver las flores del desierto en la primavera.
12. Nosotros _____ viajar este verano.
13. Los candidatos _____ muchas reglas _____ aprender.
14. _____ leer *Don Quixote*, por lo menos una vez.
15. Yo _____ leer *Don Quixote*, pero yo _____ leer *Moby Dick* primero.

C. **Infinitive after a preposition**

In English, the *-ing* form is usually used after a preposition. In Spanish, however, a preposition can only be followed by an infinitive. Study the following examples and their English equivalents.

antes de leer   *before reading*
después de empezar   *after beginning*
en vez de salir   *instead of leaving*
sin estudiar   *without studying*
al (a + el) entrar   *upon entering*

> **NOTE:** The use of prepositions with certain verbs is discussed further in Chapter 9.

EXERCISE 3-16: Complete the following sentences by writing in either the infinitive form or the present participle form of the verbs given in parentheses. Answers are at the end of the chapter.

1. (estudiar) Mi amigo quiere _____ el álgebra, pero en este momento estamos _____ gramática.
2. (pintar) En vez de _____ solamente la sala, queremos _____ toda la casa.
3. (mirar) Estoy _____ esta telenovela porque tengo que _____ las noticias después de _____ este programa.
4. (acostarse) Necesitas _____ ahora, en vez de _____ tan tarde.
5. (cantar) Tenemos que _____ una canción mexicana sin _____ la canción que ellos están _____ .
6. (hablar) Los estudiantes están _____ de una cosa importante, pero la maestra quiere _____ de otra cosa.
7. (olvidarse) Queremos _____ de los detalles pequeños, sin _____ de las cosas importantes.
8. (escuchar) Estás _____ a un músico de primera categoría, pero debes _____ a otros músicos también, en vez de _____ solamente a uno.
9. (abrir) Al _____ el regalo de tu padre, debemos _____ todos los regalos, también.
10. (arreglar) Tienes tus propios asuntos que _____ , después de _____ el horario de los niños.

D. The infinitive as subject

In Spanish, the infinitive (sometimes accompanied by the definite article **el**) may be used as the subject of the sentence. Study the following examples.

Hablar es fácil, **hacer** es difícil.   *Talking is easy, doing is difficult.*
El viajar es agradable y educativo.   *Traveling is pleasant and instructive.*

E. The infinitive following verbs of perception and causation

1. *Verbs of perception.* Perception verbs such as **oír**, *to listen,* and **ver**, *to see,* may take both a noun object and an infinitive object. Study the following examples. Notice the use of the personal **a** before the person objects.

   Veo a María.   *I see María.*
   Veo salir a María.   *I see María leaving.*
   Oigo a los niños.   *I hear the children.*
   Oigo llorar a los niños.   *I hear the children crying.*

2. *Verbs of causation.* Causation verbs such as **mandar**, *to order,* **hacer**, *to make,* **dejar**, *to let,* **permitir**, *to permit,* and so forth, may take both an infinitive and a noun object. Study the following examples.

   El jefe **deja salir** temprano **a los**   *The boss lets the employees leave*
       empleados.   *early.*

El entrenador **hace correr a los jugadores**.	*The coach makes the players run.*
La reina no **permite estar de pie a sus súbditos**.	*The queen doesn't allow her subjects to stand.*
La maestra siempre **manda callarse a los estudiantes**.	*The teacher always tells the students to be quiet.*

EXERCISE 3-17: Translate the following sentences into Spanish. Don't forget to use the personal **a** when necessary. Answers are at the end of the chapter.

1. I see Raúl running.

2. The teacher makes the students work.

3. My boss lets Mary leave early.

4. She hears a bird singing.

5. We hear Linda and Robert talking.

6. The neighbor always orders the children to leave.

7. The nurse lets the children play.

8. My cousin always allows her sister to speak first.

F. The infinitive after verbs of motion and beginning

1. The infinitive is preceded by the preposition **a**, *to*, after verbs of motion and beginning, such as **ir**, *to go*, and **empezar**, *to begin*. Study the following examples.

Voy a ir al centro mañana.	*I'm going downtown tomorrow.*
José **sale a comprar** el periódico temprano.	*José goes out to buy the newspaper early.*
Sólo **vengo a despedirme**.	*I'm only coming to say goodbye.*
Empezamos a entender la lección.	*We are beginning to understand the lesson.*
Voy a tener que ir.	*I'm going to have to go.*
Arturo **comienza a cantar** a las seis.	*Arturo begins (will begin) to sing at six o'clock.*
Voy a acostarme temprano.⎱ Me **voy a acostar** temprano.⎰	*I'm going to go to bed early.*

2. In Spanish, the **ir a** + *infinitive* construction is used much more frequently than the future tense. Spanish also uses the present tense with a time expression to indicate an action or event occurring in the future. Study the following examples of present tense used with a future meaning.

Present Tense	ir a + Infinitive
Vuelvo en seguida. *I'll be right back.*	**Voy a volver** en seguida. *I'm going to come back right away.*
Leo tus poemas más tarde. *I'll read your poems later.*	**Voy a leer** tus poemas más tarde. *I'm going to read your poems later.*
Después, **vamos** a la playa. *Later, we'll go to the beach.*	**Vamos a ir** a la playa después. *We're going to go to the beach later.*
Llamo a Stuart mañana. *I'll call Stuart tomorrow.*	**Voy a llamar** a Stuart mañana. *I'm going to call Stuart tomorrow.*

EXERCISE 3-18: Rewrite the following sentences, changing the verb from the present tense to the **ir a** + *infinitive* structure. Watch for reflexive verbs. Remember that the reflexive pronoun must agree with the person and number of the subject. Answers are at the end of the chapter.

Examples: Salgo en cinco minutos. *Voy a salir en cinco minutos.*
Me levanto en un ratito. *Voy a levantarme en un ratito.* (OR *Me voy a levantar.*)

1. Mañana vemos a mi tía.

2. Salgo mañana para Los Angeles.

3. John viene dentro de poco.

4. Angel vuelve mañana.

5. Después pedimos más.

6. Pronto descansamos.

7. Subo en seguida.

8. Me siento aquí con usted.

9. Te sientes mejor pronto.

10. Los muchachos llegan en dos semanas.

11. Alice trabaja mañana.

12. Hago la comida en seguida.

13. Me quedo aquí otro ratito.

14. Mañana la novia se viste de blanco.

15. Compro la carne mañana.

3-8. Affirmative and Negative Syntax

A. Affirmative and negative words

Study the following list of the most frequently used affirmative and negative words.

algo	*something*	nada	*nothing, anything*
alguien	*somebody*	nadie	*nobody*
alguno(-a, -os, -as)	*some, something*	ninguno(-a, -os, -as)	*no, none*
siempre	*always*	nunca	*never*
		jamás	*never, ever*
también	*also*	tampoco	*neither, not either*
o . . . o	*either . . . or*	ni . . . ni	*neither . . . nor*
siquiera	*at least*	ni siquiera	*not even*
ya	*already, now*	ya no	*no longer*

B. Affirmative syntax

One of the most important differences between English and Spanish is the flexibility of the location of the Spanish subject. Compare the following examples of Spanish and English word order. Note the position of the subject in relation to the verb.

Algo tiene que **pasar.**
Tiene que **pasar algo.** } *Something has to happen.*

José **va a ir** con **Elena.**
Va a ir José con **Elena.** } *José is going to go with Elena.*
Va a ir con **Elena** José.

Carlos **está escribiendo un trabajo.**
Está escribiendo Carlos **un trabajo.** } *Carlos is writing a paper.*

> **NOTE:** When the object is much longer than the subject, the subject is generally placed directly after the verb, followed by the object.

C. Negative syntax

1. The negative **no** is always placed directly before the verb, except when the sentence contains a reflexive or object pronoun. Compare the following examples of affirmative and negative syntax.

Affirmative	Negative
Yo hablo.	Yo **no hablo.**
I speak.	*I don't speak.*
Quiero levantarme.	**No quiero levantarme.**
I want to get up.	*I don't want to get up.*
Estoy lavándome la cara.	**No estoy lavándome** la cara.
Me estoy lavando la cara.	**No me estoy lavando** la cara.
I'm washing my face.	*I'm not washing my face.*

2. In addition to the negative **no**, any negative may be placed before the verb in order to form the negative.

Nadie quiere ir.   *Nobody wants to go.*
Nunca hablamos con ella.   *We never talk to her.*
Tampoco baila Antonio.   *Antonio doesn't dance either.*

3. If a negative word is placed after the verb, **no** must be placed before the verb. Unlike English, the double negative is required in Spanish.

Nadie debe gritar.
No debe gritar **nadie.** } *Nobody ought to shout.*

Ni él **ni** ella **quiere** bailar.
No quiere bailar **ni** él **ni** ella. } *Neither he nor she wants to dance.*

No pasa nada aquí.   *Nothing's happening here.*

EXERCISE 3-19: Rewrite the following sentences in the negative, using the same syntax as the original sentence. Answers are at the end of the chapter.

Examples: Algo queremos hacer.   *Nada queremos hacer.*
           Queremos hacer algo.   *No queremos hacer nada.*

1. Alguien está hablando por teléfono.

2. Tenemos que llegar temprano.

3. Mario siempre se viste de negro.

4. Ustedes deben organizar algo.

5. O Carmen o Michael puede traer la sopa.

6. Los fines de semana, me acuesto tarde.

7. Yo me pongo la chaqueta negra con frecuencia.

8. Siempre van al cine los domingos.

9. Daniel se lava el pelo todos los días.

10. Yo quiero ir a París también.

11. Voy a estudiar.

12. Mi primo quiere leer algún libro.

13. Los estudiantes quieren decir algo.

14. Necesitamos algunas mesas más.

15. Quiero algo.

16. Algo está pasando.

17. Los obreros se levantan a las siete también.

18. Va a ir Carlos con María.

19. También vamos a ir nosotros.

20. Siempre comen primero los niños.

D. Special affirmative and negative phrases

1. *Siquiera versus **ni siquiera***. Study the following examples, paying close attention to the word order.

Affirmative

Pepa **siquiera** bebe un vaso de leche.	*Pepa at least drinks a glass of milk.*
Tengo que dormir **siquiera** veinte minutos.	*I have to sleep at least twenty minutes.*

Negative

John **ni siquiera** bebe leche. ⎫
John **no** bebe **ni siquiera** leche. ⎭   *John doesn't even drink milk.*

> **REMEMBER:** If **ni siquiera** follows the verb, **no** must be placed before the verb.

2. *Ya versus **ya no***. Study the following examples, paying attention to word order.

Affirmative

Ya voy a trabajar. ⎫
Voy a trabajar **ya**. ⎭   *I'm going to work now.*
Yo **ya** me levanto temprano. ⎫
Yo me levanto temprano **ya**. ⎭   *I get up early now (nowadays).*

> **NOTE:** **Ya** means *already* when used with the past tense: **ya fui**, *I already went*. (See Chapter 6 for a discussion of past tense.)

Negative

Ya no trabajo.	*I no longer work.*
No trabajo **ya**.	*I don't work any more.*
Ya no me levanto temprano.	*I no longer get up early.*
No me levanto temprano **ya**.	*I don't get up early any more.*

EXERCISE 3-20: Write in the Spanish translation of the phrase given in parentheses. Answers are at the end of the chapter.

1. (no longer) Yo _____ bebo café.
2. (anymore) Yo _____ bebo leche _____ .
3. (not even) Tom _____ camina al supermercado.
4. (at least) Bárbara quiere probar _____ la ensaladilla rusa.
5. (no longer) Los niños _____ quieren jugar al béisbol.
6. (now) Me voy a ir _____ .
7. (now) Los jóvenes _____ comen más carne que antes.
8. (at least) Vamos a ver _____ la *Mona Lisa*.
9. (not even) Elisa _____ sabe tocar la flauta.
10. (anymore) Luis _____ lee novelas francesas _____ .

3-9. Interrogatives

A. Interrogative words

All interrogatives (question words) have a written accent over the stressed vowel and are preceded by an inverted question mark: **¿qué?**, *what?* Study the following list of interrogatives.

¿qué?	*what?*	¿quién(es)?	*who?*
¿cuál?	*which (one)?*	¿cuándo?	*when?*
¿cuáles?	*which (ones)?*	¿dónde?	*where?*
¿cuánto(-a)?	*how much?*	¿por qué?	*why?*
¿cuántos(-as)?	*how many?*	¿cómo?	*how?*

EXERCISE 3-21: Complete the following questions by writing in the interrogative word that corresponds to the words given in parentheses in each statement. Don't forget to include the inverted question mark and the accent. Answers are at the end of the chapter.

Example: José está comiendo
(sopa). ___*¿Qué*___ está comiendo José?

1. Soy (la nueva maestra). _____ es usted?
2. Vamos a ir (mañana). _____ van a ir ustedes?
3. Quiero (café con leche). _____ quiere usted?
4. Mi carpeta está
(en casa de Nuria). _____ está tu carpeta?
5. Quiero (dos) cucharas
de azúcar. _____ cucharas quieres?
6. Steven gana
(mucho) dinero. _____ dinero gana Steven?
7. Eduardo prefiere
vino (tinto). _____ vino prefiere Eduardo?
8. Preferimos bocadillos
(de calamares). _____ bocadillos prefieren ustedes?
9. Hoy día, las mejores
novelas son
(latinoamericanas). _____ son las mejores novelas hoy día?
10. Mi película predilecta
es (*El ladrón
de bicicletas*). _____ es tu película predilecta?
11. Vamos a ir (en avión). _____ vais a ir?
12. Todos los estudiantes
están, menos (Paco). _____ no está?
13. Philip canta (ópera). _____ canta Philip?
14. Voy a terminar
(en dos minutos). _____ vas a terminar?

15. Tengo que
    (lavarme el pelo). _____ tienes que hacer?
16. Alex sabe tocar
    (flamenco). _____ sabe tocar Alex?
17. Vamos a ver (un partido
    de béisbol). _____ van a ver ustedes?
18. Vamos a viajar por los
    Pirineos (en el verano). _____ vais a los Pirineos?
19. Van a ir (mi hermana y
    su familia). _____ van a ir?
20. (Yo) voy con ellos
    al mercado. _____ va a ir con ellos?

B. Interrogative syntax

1. *Position of subject.* In Spanish, the subject follows the verb in order to form a question. The position of the subject after the verb is flexible, however. It may be placed either directly after the verb or at the end of the question. If the subject is contained within the verb ending, the question is signaled by the inverted question mark, and orally, by a change in intonation. Study the following examples carefully. Note the position of the subject.

Statement	Question	Yes/No Answer
Maria llega temprano.	¿**Llega María** temprano? ¿**Llega** temprano **María**?	Sí, llega temprano. No, no llega temprano.
Bob puede ir en coche.	¿**Puede** ir **Bob** en coche? ¿**Puede** ir en coche **Bob**?	Sí, puede. No, no puede.
Los estudiantes están cantando el himno nacional.	¿**Están** cantando **los estudiantes** el himno nacional? ¿**Están** cantando el himno nacional **los estudiantes**?	Sí. No.
Juan tiene que comprar el periódico.	¿**Tiene que** comprar Juan **el periódico**? ¿**Tiene que** comprar **el periódico** Juan?	Sí. No.
Las muchachas se levantan a las seis.	¿**Se levantan las muchachas** a las seis? ¿**Se levantan** a las seis **las muchachas**?	Sí. No.
La capital de España es Madrid.	¿**Es Madrid** la capital de España? ¿**Es** la capital de España **Madrid**?	Sí. No.

2. *The use of* ***tú*** *versus* ***usted.*** **Usted** is generally included in direct address, and **tú** is usually omitted. Study the following examples and note the position of **usted** in the question. It is common usage for **usted** to appear between the conjugated form of the verb and the infinitive or present participle.

tú	usted
¿**Quieres** un vaso de agua?	¿**Quiere usted** un vaso de agua?
¿Te **quieres** sentar aquí?	¿Se **quiere usted** sentar aquí?
¿**Quieres** sentarte aquí?	¿**Quiere usted** sentarse aquí?
¿**Estás** divirtiéndote?	¿**Está usted** divirtiéndose?
¿Te **estás** divirtiendo?	¿Se **está usted** divirtiendo?
¿**Tienes** que estudiar más?	¿**Tiene usted** que estudiar más?

3. *Rhetorical questions.* Both affirmative and negative statements may be turned into questions by adding a tag question such as ¿verdad?, ¿verdad que sí?, and so on. Study the following examples. Note that the inverted question mark is placed before the tag question, not before the entire sentence.

Quieres dormir, ¿verdad?	*You want to sleep, right?*
Quieres dormir, ¿verdad que sí?	*You want to sleep, don't you?*
No conoces a Daniel, ¿verdad?	*You don't know Daniel, right?*
No conoces a Daniel, ¿verdad que no?	*You don't know Daniel, do you?*
Comes muchos plátanos, ¿no?	*You eat a lot of bananas, right?*

EXERCISE 3-22:   Rewrite the following statements as questions, using the subject or subject pronoun given in parentheses. Remember, **usted** is included in the question, but **tú** is omitted. Answers are at the end of the chapter.

Examples: Tengo que estudiar. (tú)   *¿Tienes que estudiar?*
Tengo que irme. (usted)   *¿Tiene usted que irse?*
Bob es el primo de ella. (Bob)   *¿Es Bob el primo de ella?*

1. Necesito estudiar más. (tú)

2. Quiero ir al cine. (usted)

3. John llega primero. (John)

4. Alice es la capitana de su equipo. (Alice)

5. Mi padre es mexicano. (tu padre)

6. Tengo seis hijos. (usted)

7. Puedo venir mañana. (tú)

8. Me acuesto a las 11:00. (usted)

9. Los estudiantes están cansados. (los estudiantes)

10. Voy a ver una película. (tú)

11. María va al cine con Jorge. (ella)

12. París es la capital de Francia. (París)

13. El mejor lanzador es Fernando Valenzuela. (él)

14. Tengo que hacer una pregunta. (tú)

15. Tengo que despedirme de Vanessa. (usted)

16. Arturo sabe cocinar bien. (él)

17. El Sr. y la Sra. Moreno vienen pronto. (ellos)

18. Nosotros tenemos que hacer muchas cosas. (ustedes)

19. Estoy lavándome los dientes. (tú)

20. Jaime está tocando el piano. (Jaime)

C. Question words with prepositions

In English, prepositions are commonly separated from the question word in everyday speech. In Spanish, the preposition always precedes the interrogative and is never separated from it: **¿Con quien hablas?** *With whom are you speaking* (*Who are you speaking to*)? Study the following list of interrogatives used with prepositions.

¿a quién? **¿a** quiénes?	*to whom?*	**¿por** qué?	*why?*
¿con quién? **con** quiénes?	*with whom?*	**¿para** qué?	*what for?*
¿de quién? **¿de** quiénes?	*whose?*	**¿de** qué?	*about what? of what?*
		¿a dónde?	*to where?*
		¿de dónde?	*from where?*

EXERCISE 3-23: Complete the following sentences by translating the interrogative given in parentheses. Answers are at the end of the chapter.

1. (whose) _____ es aquel sombrero feo?
2. (where) _____ van Lucy y Ricardo?
3. (with whom, pl.) _____ van ustedes al cine?
4. (why) _____ estás estudiando tanto?
5. (to whom) _____ vas a dar tu tocadiscos viejo?
6. (about what) _____ estáis hablando vosotros?
7. (where) _____ van tus padres?
8. (from where) _____ es tu abuelo?
9. (whose, pl.) _____ son estos vasos y aquellos platos?
10. (with whom) _____ hablan ustedes el español?

D. *Cuál(-es)* versus *qué*

Cuál and **cuáles** are used with the verb **ser** except when the question asks a definition, in which case, **qué** is used. Study the following examples.

¿Cuáles son los cinco continentes?	*What are the five continents?*
¿Cuál es la industria más importante de México?	*What is Mexico's most important industry?*
¿Qué es la poesía?	*What is poetry?*

EXERCISE 3-24: Complete the following questions by writing in either **qué**, **cuál**, or **cuáles**. Don't forget the inverted question mark. Answers are at the end of the chapter.

1. _____ es el arte moderno?
2. _____ es el mejor libro español?
3. _____ es un refrán?
4. _____ son los grandes ríos del mundo?
5. _____ es una jirafa?
6. _____ de esos tres animales es una jirafa?
7. _____ quieres?
8. _____ de los dos vestidos quieres?
9. _____ tienes que estudiar?
10. _____ tema vas a elegir?

SUMMARY

1. Spanish has three verb conjugations: **-ar**, **-er**, and **-ir** verbs. Regular verbs add the following present tense endings to the infinitive stem.

-ar	-o, -as, -a, -amos, -áis, -as
-er	-o, -es, -e, -emos, -éis, -en
-ir	-o, -es, -e, -imos, -ís, -en

2. Stem-changing verbs change a vowel in the infinitive stem before adding the present tense verb endings. This change occurs in the first, second, and third person singular and third person plural forms, never in the **nosotros** and **vosotros** forms. There are three kinds of stem changes: **o-ue, e-ei,** and **e-i.**

3. Orthographic (spelling) changes occur for phonetic reasons. For example, the hard **g** is spelled **ga, gue, gui, go,** and **gu.** Most orthographic changes in the present tense occur in the first person singular form: **conocer, conoczco; coger, cojo; seguir, sigo.** When **i** appears between two vowels, the **i** changes to **y** in all forms: **huir, huyo, huyes,** etc.

4. Most irregular changes in present tense verbs occur in the first person singular form. Some verbs add **g** before the first person **-o** ending: **tener, tengo.** Verbs like **ser, estar,** and **ir** are irregular in all forms and must be memorized.

5. Reflexive verbs are conjugated with the reflexive pronouns: **me, te, se, nos, os, se.** Reflexive pronouns are placed either directly before the conjugated verb form, or they are attached to the infinitive or present participle: **él no se está sentando,** *he isn't sitting down;* **yo no tengo que irme,** *I don't have to go;* **él no está sentándose,** *he isn't sitting down.*

6. There are five main uses of reflexive verbs: (1) The object of the verb is the doer of the action: **él se lava,** *he washes himself.* (2) The addition of the reflexive pronoun changes the meaning of the verb: **llevar,** *to carry;* **llevarse,** *to take away.* (3) The addition of the reflexive pronoun emphasizes the involvement of the subject in the verb action, but does not change the essential meaning of the verb: **río,** *I laugh;* **me río,** *I laugh.* (4) The reflexive pronoun functions as an indirect object meaning "to oneself": **él se miente,** *he lies to himself;* **ellos se mienten,** *they lie to themselves.* (5) The plural reflexive pronouns can mean "to each other." The phrase **uno a otro** or **unos a otros** can be added for clarification: **Ellos se mienten uno a otro,** *They lie to each other.*

7. The present progressive tense is formed by conjugating the verb **estar** + the present participle: **estoy cantando,** *I'm singing;* **estás escribiendo,** *you're writing.*

8. To form the present participle, add **-ando** to the infinitive stem of **-ar** verbs, and **-iendo** to the infinitive stem of **-er** and **-ir** verbs. Verbs ending in **-ir** that change the **e-ie** or the **e-i** also change the **e-i** before adding **-iendo: mentir, miento, mintiendo; pedir, pido, pidiendo. Morir** and **dormir** change the **o-u** in the present participle: **muriendo, durmiendo.** When the reflexive pronoun is attached to the present participle, there is a written accent over **-ándose** and **-iéndose.**

9. The present progressive tense is only used to refer to actions taking place at the moment of speaking: **Estoy hablando por teléfono,** *I'm talking on the telephone* (right now).

10. When the infinitive follows **querer, necesitar, esperar, deber, poder,** and the like, it is not preceded by a preposition: **debo estudiar,** *I should study.* When the infinitive is a reflexive verb, the reflexive pronoun either precedes the conjugated verb or is attached to the infinitive: **debo acostarme, me debo acostar,** *I should go to bed.*

11. The infinitive always follows **tener que** and **hay que.** When the infinitive is separated from the conjugated verb by a noun object, **que** immediately precedes the infinitive: **Tengo que hacer mi tarea,** *I have to do my homework;* **Tengo tarea que hacer,** *I have homework to do.* **Hay** and **hay que** do not change their form.

12. Only an infinitive may follow a preposition. It is usually translated as a present participle: **al abrir la puerta,** *upon opening the door;* **antes de empezar a gritar,** *before beginning to yell.*

13. The infinitive (sometimes accompanied by the definite article **el**) may be used as the subject of the sentence.

14. The infinitive can be used with a noun object following **ver, oír,** and other verbs of perception: **Oígo cantar la alondra;** *I hear the lark singing.*

15. The infinitive can be used with a noun object following verbs of causation such as **mandar,** and **hacer: Mando cerrar esta tienda;** *I am ordering this store to be closed.*

16. Infinitives are preceded by **a** when following verbs of motion or beginning: **Empiezo a entender;** *I'm beginning to understand;* **Voy a ir a comprar algo;** *I'm going to go to buy something.*

17. Spanish syntax (the order of words) is different from English syntax. In English, the subject always precedes the verb: *I'm going with you too*; *This car isn't running very well*. In Spanish, the subject is often placed either directly after the verb or at the end of the sentence: **Voy yo contigo también**; **No funciona muy bien este coche**.

18. To form a negative statement, **no** or any other negative such as **nada, nadie**, and the like, is placed before the verb: **Yo no como mucho**; *I don't eat a lot*; **Nadie come**, *Nobody is eating*. If a negative other than **no** follows the verb, **no** must always precede the verb: **Usted no está comiendo nada**; *You aren't eating anything*. The double negative is correct Spanish grammar: **Nadie come nada**, *Nobody is eating anything*.

19. The subject follows the verb to form a question. The question is framed by an inverted question mark at the beginning of the question, and a normal question mark at the end.

20. The subject pronoun **tú** is usually omitted in direct address questions. The subject pronoun **usted** is generally placed after the conjugated verb form: **¿Quieres ir? ¿Quiere usted ir?** *Do you want to go?*

21. When the interrogative requires a preposition, the preposition always precedes the interrogative and is never separated from it: **¿A dónde vas?** *Where are you going (to)?*

22. **Cuál** or **cuáles** is used before the verb **ser** except when the question asks a definition, in which case, **qué** is used: **¿Cuál** (*which one*) **es la ciudad más grande del mundo?** *What is the biggest city in the world?* But, **¿Qué es una ciudad?** *What is (the definition of) a city?*

RAISE YOUR GRADES

☑ **Present tense verb endings** [Section 3-1]

Review the chart of present tense verb endings in Section 3-1. Note the differences and similarities between the three conjugations. Then write in the correct verb endings in the following sentences. Answers are at the end of the chapter.

1. Los Dodgers casi siempre gan_____ .
2. ¿Aprend_____ los estudiantes mucho en clase?
3. Nosotros sufr_____ mucho durante el invierno.
4. Mi tía cocin_____ arroz con pollo con frecuencia.
5. Vosotros pag_____ la cena y nosotros pag_____ las entradas.
6. Mis padres recib_____ una llamada diaria de mi hermano.
7. Nosotros no comprend_____ la sicología freudiana.
8. Vosotros discut_____ mucho sin resolver nada.
9. Mi hermana siempre ayud_____ a todos nosotros.
10. Nosotros viv_____ en el paraíso del Pacífico.
11. Roberto y Magda cre_____ que va a llover.
12. Yo escrib_____ docenas de cartas a mis amigos.
13. Tú no tom_____ café, ¿verdad?
14. Nosotros no entend_____ nada de motores.
15. ¿Compr_____ usted la comida en el supermercado?
16. Todos los días, ellos sub_____ a ver a su abuela.
17. Tú respond_____ a todas las preguntas, ¿no?
18. Los atletas corr_____ cinco millas todos los días.
19. ¿Beb_____ ellos leche, jugo o agua mineral?
20. ¿Alcanz_____ la gasolina hasta la próxima gasolinera?

☑ **Stem-changing verbs** [Section 3-2]

There are three possible infinitive stem changes: **o—ue, e—ie**, and **e—i**. Write in the infinitive form of the verb given in parentheses below. Add **se** to the infinitive form of reflexive verbs. Answers are at the end of the chapter.

Examples: (Quiero) agua.   *querer*

(Me siento) mal.   *sentirse*

1. No (entienden) las reglas del béisbol.   _____
2. Los niños están (pidiendo) más refrescos.   _____
3. Silencio, por favor, la niña está (durmiendo).   _____
4. Ya no (me acuesto) tarde.   _____
5. Ustedes (piensan) demasiado en las glorias del pasado. _____
6. (Defiendes) bien tu punto de vista.   _____
7. (Pierdo) la paciencia cuando tengo que esperar.   _____
8. Sus amigos (vuelven) mañana.   _____
9. Aquel hombre (se llama) López   _____
10. ¿A qué hora (almuerzas)?   _____
11. (Huele) a leche quemada.   _____
12. Con este calor, las flores (se mueren) pronto.   _____
13. Los pequeños (se sientan) en el suelo.   _____
14. Ellos están (despidiéndose) de la Sra. Morelos.   _____
15. Raúl (se sonrie) poco.   _____
16. En Seattle, (llueve) mucho.   _____
17. (Pruebo) la sopa primero.   _____
18. Ella (cuenta) una historia larga y triste.   _____
19. (Prefieren) ir en coche.   _____
20. (Sigo) el consejo de mi maestro.   _____

☑ Irregular verbs [Section 3-4]

Rewrite the following sentences by changing the verb from the first person plural to the first person singular. Watch out for reflexive verbs and change the reflexive pronoun, too, when it is necessary to do so. Answers are at the end of the chapter.

1. Vamos a irnos ahora mismo.

2. Estamos despidiéndonos de la Sra. Jones.

3. Sabemos algo de la historia latinoamericana.

4. Merecemos unas vacaciones largas.

5. Exigimos una comida sin sal.

6. Nos parecemos mucho al abuelo materno.

7. Salimos a ver una película a las siete.

8. Seguimos las instrucciones del profesor.

9. Huimos de las preocupaciones cotidianas.

10. Corremos mucho y nunca nos caemos.

☑ Reflexive verbs [Section 3-5]

Write in the reflexive pronoun that agrees with the subject wherever a reflexive verb is used. Answers are at the end of the chapter.

1. Tenemos que acordar _____ de las servilletas
2. Las muchachas _____ están despertando ahora mismo.
3. Yo _____ peino solamente una vez al día.
4. No hay que enfadar _____, Sra. García.
5. Los estudiantes discuten todo y nunca _____ callan.
6. No _____ arrepiento de nada.
7. Vamos a divertir _____ mucho.

8. No _____ atreves a probar la salsa, ¿verdad?
9. Tus amigos _____ quejan de todo, pero no quieren marchar _____ .
10. Durante el día, nunca puedo sentar _____ .

☑ Use of the infinitive [Section 3-7]

The infinitive is preceded by the preposition **a** when used after verbs of motion. The infinitive is used after **tener que** and **hay que**. The infinitive is always used after prepositions. Complete the following sentences by translating the English phrases given in parentheses into Spanish. Answers are at the end of the chapter.

1. Empiezo (to understand) la lección.   _____
2. Daniel (has to go to bed) todas las noches a las nueve.   _____
3. (We can rest) después de la fiesta.   _____
4. Patricia (is going to leave) de su oficina en cinco minutos.   _____
5. Nosotros (have to cut) el césped este fin de semana.   _____
6. (After running), empezamos a (to feel) cansados.   _____
7. (Before going), necesitamos (to say goodbye).   _____
8. (Instead of walking), podemos ir en coche.   _____
9. (I don't want to complain) de la mala comida.   _____
10. (He can't sleep) durante una tempestad.   _____
11. Cuando empieza la música, los jóvenes (begin to dance).   _____
12. Nosotros (can't eat) pasta todos los días porque engorda mucho. _____
13. (It is not necessary to exercise) más que media hora   _____
14. Vosotros (must want) más café, ¿verdad?   _____
15. Mi padre siempre grita (upon answering the telephone).   _____

☑ Negative syntax [Section 3-8]

Review the list of common negatives and study the examples of negative syntax. Then rewrite the following sentences in the negative. Answers are at the end of the chapter.

1. Quiero discutir algo con usted.

2. Tenemos que salir temprano.

3. Me voy a casar mañana.

4. Él se llama Roberto Luis.

5. Alguien está cantando en la calle.

6. Siempre como más que usted.

7. Ellos van a conducir también.

8. O Mario o Raúl va a cantar.

9. Quiero postre.

10. Hay mucho que hacer.

☑ Interrogatives [Section 3-9]

Review the list of question words in Section 3-9. Next, study the use of **qué** versus **cuál** and the use of question words with prepositions. Then complete the following questions by choosing the correct interrogative from those given in parentheses. Answers are at the end of the chapter.

1. (Dónde, A dónde) _____ está el hilo negro?
2. (Quién, De quién) _____ es esta pluma nueva?
3. (Con quiénes, De quiénes) _____ vamos a ir?
4. (Qué, De qué) _____ estáis hablando?

5. (Dónde, De dónde) _____ viene usted?

6. (Quién, Con quién) _____ es el presidente de México?

7. (Qué, Cuál) _____ es un villancico?

8. (Qué, Cuál) _____ es la capital del estado de Nueva York?

9. (Dónde, A dónde) _____ van a jugar los niños?

10. (Quiénes, De quiénes) _____ son estas cintas de jazz?

☑ **The use of *tú* versus *usted* in questions** [Section 3-9]

Rewrite the following questions by changing the form of direct address from **tú** to **usted**. Remember, **usted** follows the conjugated form of the verb. Answers are at the end of the chapter.

Example: ¿Qué estás haciendo? *¿Qué está usted haciendo?*

1. ¿A dónde vas?

2. ¿Quiéres sentarte aquí?

3. ¿Cómo te llamas?

4. ¿A qué hora te quieres marchar?

5. ¿Necesitas descansar más tiempo?

6. ¿Te estás poniendo el vestido nuevo?

7. ¿Cuándo te vas a casar?

8. ¿De qué te estás quejando?

9. ¿Te acuerdas del apellido del dentista?

10. ¿Estás bañándote con agua fría?

CHAPTER ANSWERS

EXERCISE 3-1

1. cantamos, bailamos *We sing and dance every Saturday.*
2. trabaja *You work very fast.*
3. andan *Every morning they walk five miles.*
4. estudiamos *We study together on weekends.*
5. guarda *He puts away his records carefully.*
6. ganáis *You make more money than them.*
7. desayunas, cenas *You have breakfast at six and you have dinner at ten.*
8. hablan, escuchan *They always talk a lot and listen very little.*
9. compran *They buy a new car once a year.*
10. nada, esquía *She swims and also skis.*
11. ayudo *I often help my brothers.*
12. lavan *You wash the dishes immediately after the meal.*
13. deja *He always leaves his car in the same place.*
14. necesito *I need a bigger house.*
15. paga *You always pay for the meal.*

EXERCISE 3-2

1. asiste *My husband attends the School of Fine Arts.*
2. comen *Dancers eat a lot of salad.*
3. bebe *His whole family drinks water with the meal.*
4. recibo *I receive a letter from him every week.*
5. aprenden *The students learn quickly from that teacher.*
6. viven *They live in San Diego during the summer.*
7. corro *I run every day in the park.*
8. abre *Mr. González opens the restaurant late on Sundays.*
9. debe *My cousin owes a thousand dollars a month.*
10. sufrís *You suffer a lot from air pollution.*
11. subimos *Every night we walk up these stairs.*
12. comprendéis *You understand the lesson very well.*

13. venden   *Those girls sell popcorn at the fair.*
14. reciben   *Latin American novelists receive lots of prizes.*
15. discute   *The oldest son argues more than his younger sisters.*
16. responden   *The children answer the questions quickly.*
17. promete   *The president promises the people many things.*
18. cree   *The Christian religion believes in eternal life.*
19. abrimos   *We always open the store at nine.*
20. mete   *My mother never puts the children to bed early.*

EXERCISE 3-3

1. empiezo   *I begin my studies every day at noon.*
2. pierde   *My aunt always loses her gloves and her eyeglasses.*
3. quiere   *Your uncle wants more coffee.*
4. entendéis   *You understand the problems of daily life.*
5. nieva   *In the north, it snows a great deal.*
6. piensa   *The teacher thinks that the schedule is too complicated.*
7. encendemos   *We do not turn the lights on during the day.*
8. gobierna   *The president governs with the support of the people.*
9. quieren   *The students love their teacher.*
10. comienza   *The movie begins at eight.*

EXERCISE 3-4

1. almuerzan   *My children eat lunch at home at noon.*
2. cuelga   *Tomás always hangs up the telephone before I do.*
3. muestra   *The dog shows absolute indifference.*
4. recuerdan   *They remember all the details of their past.*
5. cuento   *I count six cups and only five saucers.*
6. envuelve   *The shop assistant always wraps the bread in white paper.*
7. suena   *The bell does not ring because it is broken.*
8. sueñan   *The students dream too much in class.*
9. llueve   *In the desert, it never rains.*
10. muerde   *The dog bites the policeman, but not the neighbor.*
11. cuelgan   *The children hang up their jackets before entering the living room.*
12. vuela   *Superman flies higher than the skyscrapers.*
13. devuelve   *The mother returns the books to the library.*
14. pruebo   *I taste the soup to see if it has too much salt.*

EXERCISE 3-5

1. pido   *I generally ask permission first.*
2. sonríe   *My brother smiles a lot.*
3. mienten   *Politicians lie too much.*
4. dormimos   *We sleep a lot on weekends.*
5. repite   *The teacher repeats the same exercise frequently.*
6. muere   *Hope dies slowly.*
7. consiento   *I do not consent to my mother-in-law's demands.*
8. hiere   *My husband hurts his knees frequently.*
9. sirve   *His aunt always serves coffee with milk.*
10. mide   *My cousin is just five feet tall.*
11. sugiere   *The lawyer suggests another defense tactic.*
12. frío   *Every morning I fry a couple of eggs.*
13. ríen   *The girls do not laugh much during work.*

EXERCISE 3-6

1. consigo, quiero   *I always get what I want.*
2. conozco   *I haven't met the president yet.*
3. escojo   *I always choose the biggest piece of cake.*
4. Exijo   *I demand a great deal from the students.*
5. Construyo, destruyo   *I build by day and destroy by night.*
6. Aparezco   *I appear daily at five.*
7. Produzco   *I produce tomatoes, onions, garlic, and parsley.*
8. Pertenezco   *I belong to several neighborhood organizations.*
9. Corrijo   *I correct the youngsters' letters.*
10. Reconozco   *I recognize the truthfulness of fairy tales.*
11. Ofrezco   *I offer a dinner with wine, bread, dessert, and coffee.*
12. Consigo   *I get the same results every day.*
13. Agradezco   *I am immensely grateful for the teacher's goodness.*
14. Traduzco   *I translate from French to English but not the other way around.*

EXERCISE 3-7

1. Tengo   *I have plenty of milk in the refrigerator.*
2. Vengo   *I come to the park every day.*
3. Veo   *I see a baseball game every Sunday.*
4. Hago   *I do everything possible to win.*
5. Pongo   *I give a lot of attention to the project.*
6. Salgo   *I leave at four on the dot.*
7. traigo   *I always bring flowers for mother's day.*
8. Sé, hago   *I know what Im doing.*
9. doy   *I always give old clothes to the church.*
10. quepo   *I don't fit in that chair.*
11. Oigo, digo   *I don't hear what I say.*

12. Digo, hago *I say a lot but I don't do anything.*
13. Oigo *I listen to the radio all day.*
14. Veo *I see strange things in the desert.*
15. Sé *I know a lot about Latin American history.*

EXERCISE 3-8

1. van *They go to the park on Sundays.*
2. voy *I go downtown in the morning.*
3. somos *We are French.*
4. son *The buildings are very high.*
5. vamos *We're going soon.*
6. estoy *I'm alone and sad.*
7. están *María and Carlos are in the kitchen.*
8. van *Jaime and Andrés go to the beach every day.*
9. eres, soy *You're the first and I'm the third.*
10. son *They are very good friends.*

EXERCISE 3-9

1. se marcha *Carlos never leaves the party angry.*
2. se sienta *My mother sits down the better part of the day.*
3. se pone *Every day, Jaime puts on his navy blue suit.*
4. se divierten *Robert and George have a lot of fun.*
5. nos bañamos *We take a bath in the morning.*
6. se acuesta *Alicia goes to bed very early.*
7. me equivoco *I'm never wrong.*
8. os levantáis *You get up too early.*
9. se peina *That boy combs his hair strangely.*
10. me acuerdo *I always remember everything.*
11. se enoja *The mechanic gets annoyed easily.*
12. te llamas *Your name is Mary Jane, right?*
13. se despiden *You always say goodbye too soon.*
14. se siente *My cousin feels very well.*
15. se despierta *The little boy wakes up often during the night.*

EXERCISE 3-10

1. Pongo *I put the roses in a bigger vase.*
2. me pongo *I always put on my socks first.*
3. se parecen *The twins look a lot alike.*
4. parece *Eduardo seems tired.*
5. me parezco *I look like my mother.*
6. llama *Alda calls her boyfriend.*
7. marcha *Everything is going well.*
8. se marchan *The musicians are going away right now.*
9. te levantas *On Sundays you get up at ten.*
10. Levanto *I lift five kilos easily.*
11. acuesto *I always put the children to bed early.*
12. nos acostamos *My husband and I go to bed late.*

13. quedan *Of the five desserts, only two remain.*
14. se queda *This weekend, Juan is staying at home.*
15. te bañas *You always bathe in cold water, don't you?*
16. baño *I don't bathe the dog very often.*

EXERCISE 3-11

1. estudiando *studying*
2. rompiendo *breaking*
3. lloviendo *raining*
4. creyendo *believing*
5. sintiendo *feeling*
6. hablando *speaking*
7. siguiendo *following*
8. durmiendo *sleeping*
9. almorzando *having lunch*
10. estacionando *parking*
11. viniendo *coming*
12. muriendo *dying*
13. pidiendo *asking for*
14. pudiendo *being able*
15. aprendiendo *learning*
16. limpiando *cleaning*
17. mintiendo *lying*
18. jugando *playing*
19. huyendo *fleeing*
20. siendo *being*
21. estando *being*
22. yendo *going*
23. trayendo *bringing*
24. dudando *doubting*

EXERCISE 3-12

1. está lavando *Rafael is washing the dirty clothes.*
2. están mirando *The children are watching television in their bedroom.*
3. está explicando *The teacher is giving a grammar lesson.*
4. están corriendo *The horses are running down the beach.*
5. estás pidiendo *You are asking for too much money.*
6. están durmiendo *The girls are sleeping because they are bored.*
7. está persiguiendo *The policeman is chasing the thief.*
8. Está nevando *It's snowing a lot this morning.*
9. está almorzando *The bishop is having lunch with the general.*
10. están nadando *Roberto and Luisa are swimming in the sea.*
11. estamos discutiendo *We are discussing an important topic.*
12. estás leyendo *You are reading a very boring novel.*
13. estáis comiendo *You are eating a wonderful dinner.*

14. Estoy muriendo *I'm dying of tiredness and boredom.*
15. está rompiendo *Elena is tearing up her old love letters.*

EXERCISE 3-13

1. Ellos se están mintiendo. *They are lying to themselves.*
2. Los estudiantes se están quejando demasiado. *The students are complaining too much.*
3. Yo me estoy riendo. *I'm laughing.*
4. Vosotros os estáis acostando temprano. *You're going to bed early.*
5. Mis abuelos se están levantando ahora mismo. *My grandparents are getting up right now.*
6. Nosotros nos estamos vistiendo ahora. *We're getting dressed now.*
7. Nosotros nos estamos peinando en el dormitorio. *We are combing our hair in the bedroom.*
8. Yo me estoy despertando poco a poco. *I'm waking up little by little.*
9. Los estudiantes están despidiéndose de la maestra. *The students are saying goodbye to the teacher.*
10. Tú estás acordándote de la película. *You're remembering the movie.*
11. Tú estás muriéndote de risa. *You're dying of laughter.*
12. El profesor está sentándose en mi asiento. *The professor is sitting in my seat.*
13. José está preguntándose qué pasó. *José is asking himself what happened.*
14. Yo estoy levantándome despacio. *I'm getting up slowly.*
15. Leopoldo está enojándose aquí. *Leopoldo is getting mad here.*
16. Yo estoy enfadándome demasiado. *I'm getting too angry.*
17. Mi suegra está quejándose de la comida. *My mother-in-law is complaining about the meal.*
18. Carlota está poniéndose el abrigo de pieles. *Carlota is putting on her fur coat.*
19. Nosotros estamos gritándonos unos a otros. *We're yelling at each other.*
20. Ellos están engañándose unos a otros. *They're deceiving each other.*

EXERCISE 3-14

1. levantarse *Lourdes has to get up early.*
2. comprar *I hope to buy a bigger folder.*
3. sentirte *You ought to feel better soon.*
4. despedirnos *We have to say goodbye to Mrs. Blanco.*
5. leer *I hope to read the whole Encyclopedia Brittanica.*
6. escribir *You can write a longer letter.*

7. acordarse *The students hope to remember yesterday's lesson.*
8. sentarme *I need to sit down for a while.*
9. ponerse *Andrew wants to put on a red shirt.*
10. parecerse *The Jones sisters must look a lot alike.*
11. parecer *Eloisa wants to seem a serious person.*
12. traer *You can bring the bread and the butter.*
13. llamar *We need to call Aunt Barbara.*
14. lavar *The boys must wash their own clothes.*

EXERCISE 3-15

1. tengo *I have a lot of old glasses for the party.*
2. tiene . . . que *Rosa can't go out because she has a lot to do.*
3. Hay *There's a new movie downtown.*
4. Hay que *It is necessary to go very early to buy the tickets.*
5. Hay que *It is necessary to eat the meat before the dessert.*
6. tienes que *You have to study more if you want to learn.*
7. tienen, tienen que *The football players are sleepy and they have to go to bed.*
8. tenemos, tenemos que *We have a serious problem and we have to leave.*
9. tienen . . . que *The students have several lessons to study.*
10. tiene que *The head of the institute has to get to work at eight.*
11. Hay que *It is necessary to see the desert flowers in the spring.*
12. tenemos que *We have to travel this summer.*
13. tienen . . . que *The candidates have a lot of rules to learn.*
14. Hay que *It is necessary to read* Don Quixote *at least once.*
15. Tengo que, tengo que *I have to read* Don Quixote, *but I have to read* Moby Dick *first.*

EXERCISE 3-16

1. estudiar, estudiando *My friend wants to study algebra, but right now we're studying grammar.*
2. pintar, pintar *Instead of painting just the living room, we want to paint the whole house.*
3. mirando, mirar, mirar *I'm watching this soap opera because I have to watch the news after I watch this program.*
4. acostarte, acostarte *You have to go to bed now, instead of going to bed so late.*
5. cantar, cantar, cantando *We have to sing a Mexican song without singing the song that they're singing.*

6. hablando, hablar *The students are talking about something important, but the teacher wants to talk about something else.*

7. olvidarnos, olvidarnos *We want to forget about the small details without forgetting about the important things.*

8. escuchando, escuchar, escuchar *You're listening to a first-class musician, but you should listen to other musicians too, instead of just one.*

9. abrir, abrir *On opening your father's gift, we should open all the other gifts too.*

10. arreglar, arreglar *You have your own affairs to arrange, after arranging the children's schedule.*

EXERCISE 3-17

1. Veo correr a Raúl.
2. El maestro hace trabajar a los estudiantes.
3. Mi jefe deja salir temprano a Mary.
4. Ella oye cantar un pájaro.
5. Oímos hablar a Linda y a Roberto.
6. El vecino siempre manda salir a los niños.
7. La enfermera deja jugar a los niños.
8. Mi prima siempre deja hablar primero a su hermana.

EXERCISE 3-18

1. vamos a ver *Tomorrow we're going to see my aunt.*
2. Voy a salir *I'm going to leave tomorrow for Los Angeles.*
3. va a venir *John is going to come soon.*
4. va a volver *Angel is going to return tomorrow.*
5. vamos a pedir *We're going to ask for more later.*
6. vamos a descansar *We're going to rest soon.*
7. Voy a subir *I'm going to come right up.*
8. Me voy a sentar *I'm going to sit down here with you.*
9. Te vas a sentir *You're going to feel better soon.*
10. van a llegar *The boys are going to arrive in two weeks.*
11. va a trabajar *Alice is going to work tomorrow.*
12. Voy a hacer *I'm going to make the meal immediately.*
13. Me voy a quedar *I'm going to stay here a little while longer.*
14. se va a vestir *Tomorrow the bride is going to dress in white.*
15. Voy a comprar *I'm going to buy the meat tomorrow.*

EXERCISE 3-19

1. Nadie está hablando por teléfono. *Nobody is speaking on the telephone.*
2. No tenemos que llegar temprano. *We don't have to arrive early.*

3. Mario nunca se viste de negro. *Mario never dresses in black.*
4. Ustedes no deben organizar nada. *You shouldn't organize anything.*
5. Ni Carmen ni Michael puede traer la sopa. *Neither Carmen nor Miguel can bring the soup.*
6. Los fines de semana, no me acuesto tarde. *On weekends, I don't go to bed late.*
7. Yo no me pongo la chaqueta negra con frecuencia. *I don't often put on my black jacket.*
8. Nunca van al cine los domingos. *They never go to the movies on Sunday.*
9. Daniel no se lava el pelo todos los días. *Daniel doesn't wash his hair every day.*
10. Yo no quiero ir a París tampoco. *I don't want to go to Paris either.*
11. No voy a estudiar. *I'm not going to study.*
12. Mi primo no quiere leer ningún libro. *My cousin doesn't want to read any book.*
13. Los estudiantes no quieren decir nada. *The students don't want to say anything.*
14. No necesitamos ningunas mesas más. *We don't need any more tables.*
15. No quiero nada. *I don't want anything.*
16. Nada está pasando. *Nothing is happening.*
17. Los obreros no se levantan a las siete tampoco. *The workers don't get up at seven either.*
18. No va a ir Carlos con María. *Carlos isn't going to go with María.*
19. Tampoco vamos a ir nosotros. *We aren't going to go either.*
20. Nunca comen primero los niños. *The children never eat first.*

EXERCISE 3-20

1. ya no *I no longer drink coffee.*
2. no . . . ya *I don't drink milk any more.*
3. ni siquiera *Tom doesn't even walk to the supermarket.*
4. siquiera *Barbara at least wants to try the potato salad.*
5. ya no *The children no longer want to play baseball.*
6. ya *I am going to go now.*
7. ya *Young people now eat more meat than before.*
8. siquiera *We are going to see at least the Mona Lisa.*
9. ni siquiera *Elisa doesn't even know how to play the flute.*
10. no . . . ya *Luis doesn't read French novels anymore.*

EXERCISE 3-21

1. ¿Quién *Who are you?*
2. ¿Cuándo *When are you going to go?*
3. ¿Qué *What do you want?*
4. ¿Dónde *Where is your folder?*

5. ¿Cuántas *How many spoonfuls do you want?*
6. ¿Cuánto *How much money does Steven make?*
7. ¿Cuál *Which wine does Eduardo prefer?*
8. ¿Cuáles *Which sandwiches do you prefer?*
9. ¿Cuáles *Which are the best novels these days?*
10. ¿Cuál *What is your favorite movie?*
11. ¿Cómo *How are you going to go?*
12. ¿Quién *Who isn't here?*
13. ¿Qué *What does Philip sing?*
14. ¿Cuándo *When are you going to finish?*
15. ¿Qué *What do you have to do?*
16. ¿Qué *What does Alex know how to play?*
17. ¿Qué *What are you going to see?*
18. ¿Cuándo *When are you going to the Pyrenees?*
19. ¿Quiénes *Who is going to go?*
20. ¿Quién *Who is going to go with them?*

EXERCISE 3-22

1. ¿Necesitas estudiar más? *Do you need to study more?*
2. ¿Quiere usted ir al cine? *Do you want to go to the movies?*
3. ¿Llega John primero? *Does John arrive first?*
4. ¿Es Alice la capitana de su equipo? *Is Alice the captain of her team?*
5. ¿Es mexicano tu padre? *Is your father Mexican?*
6. ¿Tiene usted seis hijos? *Do you have six children?*
7. ¿Puedes venir mañana? *Can you come tomorrow?*
8. ¿Se acuesta usted a las 11:00? *Do you go to bed at 11:00?*
9. ¿Están cansados los estudiantes? *Are the students tired?*
10. ¿Vas a ver una película? *Are you going to see a movie?*
11. ¿Va al cine ella con Jorge? *Is she going to the movies with Jorge?*
12. ¿Es París la capital de Francia? *Is Paris the capital of France?*
13. ¿Es él el mejor lanzador? *Is he the best pitcher?*
14. ¿Tienes que hacer una pregunta? *Do you have to ask a question?*
15. ¿Tiene usted que despedirse de Vanessa? *Do you have to say goodbye to Vanessa?*
16. ¿Sabe él cocinar bien? *Does he know how to cook well?*
17. ¿Vienen ellos pronto? *Are they coming soon?*
18. ¿Tienen ustedes que hacer muchas cosas? *Do you have to do many things?*
19. Estás lavándote los dientes? *Are you brushing your teeth?*
20. ¿Está tocando Jaime el piano? OR ¿Esta tocando el piano Jaime? *Is Jaime playing the piano?*

EXERCISE 3-23

1. ¿De quién *Whose is that ugly hat?*
2. ¿A dónde *Where are Lucy and Ricardo going?*
3. ¿Con quiénes *With whom are you going to the movies?*
4. ¿Por qué *Why are you studying so much?*
5. ¿A quién *To whom are you going to give your old record player?*
6. ¿De qué *What are you talking about?*
7. ¿A dónde *Where are your parents going?*
8. ¿De dónde *Where is your grandfather from?*
9. ¿De quiénes *Whose are these glasses and those plates?*
10. ¿Con quién *With whom do you speak Spanish?*

EXERCISE 3-24

1. ¿Qué *What is modern art?*
2. ¿Cuál *Which is the best Spanish book?*
3. ¿Qué *What is a proverb?*
4. ¿Cuáles *What (which ones) are the great rivers of the world?*
5. ¿Qué *What is a giraffe?*
6. ¿Cuál *Which of those three animals is a giraffe?*
7. ¿Qué *What do you want?*
8. ¿Cuál *Which of the two dresses do you want?*
9. ¿Qué *What do you have to study?*
10. ¿Cuál *Which topic are you going to choose?*

RAISE YOUR GRADES

Present tense verb endings

1. ganan *The Dodgers almost always win.*
2. Aprenden *Do the students learn a lot in class?*
3. sufrimos *We suffer a lot during the winter.*
4. cocina *My aunt cooks rice with chicken frequently.*
5. pagáis, pagamos *You pay for the supper and we'll pay for the tickets.*
6. reciben *My parents receive a daily phone call from my brother.*
7. comprendemos *We don't understand Freudian psychology.*
8. discutís *You discuss a lot without resolving anything.*
9. ayuda *My sister always helps all of us.*
10. vivimos *We live in the paradise of the Pacific.*
11. creen *Roberto and Magda think (believe) it is going to rain.*
12. escribo *I write dozens of letters to my friends.*
13. tomas *You don't drink coffee, right?*

14. entendemos *We don't understand any-thing about motors.*
15. Compra *Do you buy the food in the super-market?*
16. suben *Every day they go up to see their grandmother.*
17. respondes *You answer all the questions, right?*
18. corren *The athletes run five miles every day.*
19. Beben *Do they drink milk, juice, or min-eral water?*
20. Alcanza *Will the gasoline last (be suffi-cient) until the next gas station?*

Stem-changing verbs

1. entender *They don't understand the rules of baseball.*
2. pedir *The children are asking for more soft drinks.*
3. dormir *Silence, please, the little girl is sleeping.*
4. acostarse *I no longer go to bed late.*
5. pensar *You think too much about the glo-ries of the past.*
6. defender *You defend your point of view well.*
7. perder *I lose patience when I have to wait.*
8. volver *Their friends are returning tomorrow.*
9. llamarse *That man is named Mr. López.*
10. almorzar *What time do you eat lunch?*
11. oler *It smells like burnt milk.*
12. morirse *In this heat, the flowers die soon.*
13. sentarse *The little ones sit on the floor.*
14. despedirse *They are saying goodbye to Mrs. Morelos.*
15. sonreírse *Raúl smiles very little.*
16. llover *In Seattle, it rains a lot.*
17. probar *I'll taste the soup first.*
18. contar *She tells a long, sad story.*
19. preferir *They prefer to go by car.*
20. seguir *I follow the advice of my teacher.*

Irregular verbs

1. Voy a irme *I'm going to leave right now.*
2. Estoy despidiéndome *I'm saying goodbye to Mrs. Jones.*
3. Sé algo *I know something about Latin American history.*
4. Merezco *I deserve a long vacation.*
5. Exijo *I demand a saltless dinner.*
6. Me parezco *I look a lot like my maternal grandfather.*
7. Salgo *I'm leaving to see a movie at seven.*
8. Sigo *I follow the professor's instructions.*
9. Huyo *I flee from daily worries.*
10. Corro, me caigo *I run a lot and I never fall.*

Reflexive verbs

1. nos *We have to remember the napkins.*
2. se *The girls are waking up right now.*
3. me *I comb my hair only once a day.*

4. se *It is not necessary to get mad, Mrs. García.*
5. se *The students argue about everything and they never shut up.*
6. me *I'm not sorry about anything.* OR *I don't regret anything.*
7. nos *We are really going to enjoy ourselves.*
8. te *You don't dare to taste the salsa, right?*
9. se, se *Your friends complain about every-thing, but they don't want to leave.*
10. me *During the day, I can never sit down.*

Use of the infinitive

1. a entender *I'm beginning to understand the lesson.*
2. tiene que acostarse OR tiene que irse a la cama *Daniel has to go to bed every night at nine.*
3. Podemos descansar *We can rest after the party.*
4. va a salir *Patricia is going to leave her office in five minutes.*
5. tenemos que cortar *We have to cut the grass this weekend.*
6. Después de correr, sentirnos *After run-ning, we begin to feel tired.*
7. Antes de irnos, despedirnos *Before going, we need to say goodbye.*
8. En vez de caminar *Instead of walking, we can go by car.*
9. No quiero quejarme OR No me quiero quejar *I don't want to complain about the bad food.*
10. No puede dormir *He can't sleep during a storm.*
11. empiezan a bailar *When the music begins, the young people begin to dance.*
12. no podemos comer *We can't eat pasta every day because it puts a lot of weight on.*
13. No hay que hacer ejercicio *It is not neces-sary to exercise more than a half hour.*
14. debéis querer *You must want more coffee, right?*
15. al contestar el teléfono *My father always yells upon answering the telephone.*

Negative syntax

1. No quiero discutir nada con usted. *I don't want to argue about anything with you.*
2. No tenemos que salir temprano. *We don't have to leave early.*
3. No me voy a casar mañana. *I'm not go-ing to get married tomorrow.*
4. Él no se llama Roberto Luis. *His name isn't Roberto Luis.*
5. Nadie está cantando en la calle. *Nobody is singing in the street.*
6. Nunca como más que usted. *I never eat more than you.*
7. Ellos no van a conducir tampoco. *They aren't going to drive either.*
8. Ni Mario ni Raúl va a cantar. *Neither Mario nor Raúl is going to sing.*

9. No quiero postre.   *I don't want dessert.*
10. No hay nada que hacer. OR No hay mucho que hacer.   *There is nothing to do.* OR *There isn't a lot to do.*

Interrogatives
1. ¿Dónde   *Where is the black thread?*
2. ¿De quién   *Whose new pen is this?*
3. ¿Con quiénes   *With whom are we going to go?*
4. ¿De qué   *What are you talking about?*
5. ¿De dónde   *Where are you coming from?*
6. ¿Quién   *Who is the president of Mexico?*
7. ¿Qué   *What is a Christmas Carol?*
8. ¿Cuál   *What (which city) is the capital of New York state?*
9. ¿A dónde   *Where are the children going to play?*
10. ¿De quiénes   *Whose jazz tapes are these?*

The use of tú versus *usted* in questions
1. ¿A dónde va usted?   *Where are you going?*
2. ¿Quiere usted sentarse aquí?   *Do you want to sit here?*
3. ¿Cómo se llama usted?   *What is your name?*
4. ·¿A qué hora se quiere usted marchar?   *What time do you want to leave?*
5. ¿Necesita usted descansar más tiempo?   *Do you need to rest longer?*
6. ¿Se está usted poniendo el vestido nuevo?   *Are you putting on your new dress?*
7. ¿Cuándo se va usted a casar?   *When are you going to get married?*
8. ¿De qúe se está usted quejando?   *What are you complaining about?*
9. ¿Se acuerda usted del apellido del dentista?   *Do you remember the dentist's last name?*
10. ¿Está usted bañándose con agua fría?   *Are you taking a bath in cold water?*

 # SER AND ESTAR

THIS CHAPTER IS ABOUT

☑ **Use of** *ser*
☑ **Use of** *estar*
☑ **Adjectives with** *ser* **and** *estar*
☑ *ser* **and** *estar* **with Past Participles**
☑ *estar* **with Present Participles**

Review the present tense forms of **ser** and **estar** given in Chapter 3, Section 3-4B. These two verbs are both translated as *to be*. To Spanish speakers, however, they have widely different meanings. You cannot use **estar** in situations where you must use **ser**, nor can you use **ser** in situations where you must use **estar**. It is important that you learn when to use each verb.

4-1. Use of *ser*

Ser is used to refer to the essential characteristics of a person or thing (color, size, material, occupation, nationality, identity). **Ser** is also used to indicate time, dates, and ownership.

> **REMEMBER:** In Spanish, the subject pronoun *it* is contained in the verb and does not exist separately.
>
> **Es** un perro.   *It's a dog.*
> **Es** una buena película.   *It's a good movie.*

A. *Ser* tells who or what someone or something is.

Soy mujer.	*I am a woman.*
Es un elefante.	*It's an elephant.*
Rogelio no **es** mi hermano.	*Rogelio isn't my brother.*
¿Quién **es** usted?	*Who are you?*
Sois españoles, ¿verdad?	*You're Spanish, right?*

> **REMEMBER:** The subject pronoun (**yo, tú, usted, él, ella**, etc.) is often *not* used in Spanish. When translating from Spanish to English, always check the verb ending, then supply the corresponding English pronoun if necessary.

B. *Ser* is used to refer to the unchanging qualities of a person or thing.

Mario **es** alto y gordo.	*Mario is tall and fat.*
Las casas **son** modernas y limpias.	*The houses are modern and clean.*
Ellas no **son** bajas, son altas.	*They are not short; they're tall.*
María **es** maravillosa.	*María is wonderful.*

> **REMEMBER:** Adjectives following **ser** must always agree with the subject in number and gender.

C. *Ser* **is used with the preposition** *de* (*of* or *from*) **to indicate origin, material, or possession.**

Origin

Ellos **son** de Nueva York.	*They're from New York.*

ALSO NOTE

Yo **soy** argentino.	*I'm Argentine.*

Material

La guitarra **es** de madera.	*The guitar is made of wood.*
Es una rosa de papel.	*It's a paper rose.*

Possession

Aquella pluma **es** de Pedro.	*That pen is Pedro's.*
Este carro **es** de mi madre.	*This car is my mother's.*

D. *Ser* **is used when referring to the time, the day, or the date.**

> **NOTE:** The singular **es** is used when referring to one o'clock plus or minus the number of minutes up to thirty. The plural **son** is used for the rest of the hours. To refer to time in the past tense, the imperfect forms of **ser** (**era**, **eran**) are used.

Es la una.	*It is one o'clock.*
Es la una y cinco.	*It is five minutes after one.*
Son las dos.	*It is two o'clock.*
Eran las seis de la mañana.	*It was six o'clock in the morning.*
¿Qué hora **es**?	*What time is it?*
Hoy **es** martes.	*Today is Tuesday.*
Los domingos **son** para descansar.	*Sundays are for resting.*
La navidad **es** el 25 de diciembre.	*Christmas is December 25.*
Mi cumpleaños **es** el 14 de abril.	*My birthday is April 14.*

E. *Ser* **is used to mean** *to take place.*

La reunion **es** en casa de mi tía.	*The meeting is (taking place) at my aunt's house.*

> **CAUTION:** Don't confuse this use of **ser** with the use of **estar** to show *location* (see Section 4-2).
>
> Roma **está** en Italia.   *Rome is in Italy.*

EXERCISE 4-1: Translate the following sentences into Spanish. Answers are at the end of the chapter.

1. You (*usted*) are a good person.

2. Who am I?

3. Leandro isn't from San Diego.

4. The students are Japanese.

5. To be or not to be; that is the question.

6. Miguel is a student.

7. You (*tú*) and I are friends, but we're not brothers.

8. The music is Cuban, but the orchestra is from Mexico.

9. The big car is Juan's.

10. The concert is (taking place) at Elena's house.

4-2. Use of *estar*

Estar is used to indicate location and position. **Estar** also expresses changing conditions such as health and mood, unexpected changes in the condition of a person, place, or thing, and conditions that cause emotion.

> **REMEMBER:** Always use the accented **á** in **estás**, **está**, **estáis**, and **están**.

A. *Estar* is used to indicate location and position.

No quiero **estar** aquí.	*I don't want to be here.*
Tu abrigo **está** en aquella silla.	*Your overcoat is on that chair.*
¿Dónde **está** mi sombrero?	*Where's my hat?*
París **está** en Francia.	*Paris is in France.*

> **REMEMBER:** It is sometimes necessary to provide the word *here* in order to translate the meaning of **estar**.

Dile que no estoy.	*Tell him I'm not here.*
Mis padres no **están**.	*My parents aren't here.*

B. *Estar* is used to indicate changing conditions.

Los niños **están** enfermos.	*The children are sick.*
Estoy preocupado.	*I'm worried.*
La sopa **está** fria.	*The soup is cold.*
Estamos cansados.	*We are tired.*
La princesa **está** triste.	*The princess is sad.*
El cuarto **está** sucio.	*The room is dirty.*

C. *Estar* is used to express sudden changes or conditions that cause emotion.

Estás muy guapo esta noche.	*You're looking very handsome this evening.*
Estamos muy valientes.	*We're very brave (right now).*
El día **está** precioso.	*It's a lovely day (today).*

EXERCISE 4-2: Circle the correct form of **ser** or **estar** in each sentence below. Answers are at the end of the chapter.

1. Mi vestido (es, está) de lana.
2. Mis hijos no (son, están).
3. (Es, Está) una muchacha bonita.
4. No (es, está) ni gordo ni flaco.
5. ¿Dónde (son, están) las revistas nuevas?
6. ¿Qué hora (es, está)?
7. Tú y yo (somos, estamos) muy buenos amigos.
8. ¿De dónde (eres, estás) tú?
9. La fiesta va a (ser, estar) en casa de Julia.
10. Hoy (es, está) mi cumpleaños.
11. Después de trabajar, los obreros (son, están) cansados.
12. Cómo (son, están) ustedes?
13. Tú (eres, estás) muy guapa esta noche.
14. Hoy (soy, estoy) muy contenta.

4-3. Adjectives with *ser* and *estar*

Some adjectives have different meanings depending on whether they are used with **ser** or **estar**. Study the following list of special meanings.

aburrido

ser aburrido	*to be boring*	Es un hombre aburrido.	*He's a boring man.*
estar aburrido	*to be bored*	Estoy cansada y aburrida.	*I'm tired and bored.*

alto

ser alto	*to be tall*	La montaña es alta.	*The mountain is tall.*
estar alto	*to be placed high*	No puedo abrir la ventana. Está demasiado alta.	*I can't open the window. It's too high.*

bajo

ser bajo	*to be short*	Es gordo y bajo.	*He's fat and short.*
estar bajo	*to be placed low*	El libro está bajo la mesa.	*The book is under the table.*

bueno

ser bueno	*to be good (person or thing)*	Es una buena película.	*It's a good movie.*
estar bueno	*to taste good*	La sopa está muy buena.	*The soup tastes very good.*

callado

ser callado	*to be a quiet person*	Mi hermana es muy callada. Nunca habla.	*My sister is the quiet type. She never talks.*
estar callado	*to keep quiet*	Los niños están callados por el momento.	*The children are keeping quiet for the time being.*

enfermo

ser enfermo	*to be an invalid*	Mi tío es un enfermo.	*My uncle is an invalid.*
estar enfermo	*to be sick*	Ella tiene catarro. Está enferma.	*She has a cold. She's sick.*

listo

ser listo	*to be clever*	Eres un chico listo.	*You're a smart boy.*
estar listo	*to be ready*	Espera, no estoy listo.	*Wait, I'm not ready.*

malo

ser malo	*to be bad (person or thing)*	Es un hombre malo.	*He is a bad man.*
estar malo	*to be sick*	Mi madre está mala.	*My mother is sick.*

rico

ser rico	*to be rich*	Es una mujer rica.	*She is a rich woman.*
estar rico	*to taste good*	Es un pastel rico.	*It is a delicious cake.*

seguro

ser seguro	*to be safe; to be reliable*	Es una casa segura.	*It is a safe house.*
estar seguro	*to be certain*	No estoy seguro.	*I am not sure.*

verde

ser verde	*to be green (in color)*	El vestido es verde.	*The dress is green.*
estar verde	*to be unripe*	La fruta está verde.	*The fruit is unripe.*

REMEMBER: Always use **estar** to indicate the condition of being dead.

Las flores **están** muertas.   *The flowers are dead.*
Mi abuelo **está** muerto.   *My grandfather is dead.*

EXERCISE 4-3: Complete the following sentences with the correct present tense form of **ser** or **estar**. Answers are at the end of the chapter.

1. ¿Dónde _____ los niños?
2. Miguel _____ de Canadá.
3. No podemos ir. Mi hijo _____ malo. (*he's sick*)
4. Mi hermano _____ ingeniero, y ahora _____ en México.
5. La fiesta _____ (*takes place*) en casa de Carlos porque sus padres no _____ .
6. La casa _____ de Juan y _____ verde y blanca.
7. La casa _____ sucia, pero las ventanas _____ limpias.
8. Todas mis hermanas _____ listas. (*they're smart*)
9. *Don Quijote* _____ una novela larga, pero no _____ aburrida.
10. _____ las tres de la tarde.
11. La lección _____ difícil, y los estudiantes _____ cansados y aburridos.
12. ¿Cómo _____ ustedes?
13. ¿De qué _____ tu bolsa, de plástico o de piel?
14. Tú y yo no _____ listos (*ready*).
15. Hoy _____ jueves.
16. Yo no _____ muerto todavía.
17. Barcelona _____ en España.
18. Carlos _____ en España, pero _____ mexicano.
19. No quiero la manzana porque _____ verde (*unripe*).
20. Usted cocina bien, la sopa _____ rica.

4-4. *ser* and *estar* with Past Participles

A. *ser* + past participle = passive voice

Combining a present or preterite form of **ser** with the past participle of another verb is one way to express the passive voice (see Chapter 6 for a discussion of the past participle). Note that you use this construction only when an *action* is being described and when there is a *doer* of that action; in other words, the action is not happening by itself. The doer need not actually be mentioned in the sentence. However, if the doer is present, the doer is introduced by the preposition **por**.

El banco **es abierto** todos los días **por** el gerente.   *The bank is opened every day by the manager.*
El martes, el banco **fue abierto por** las cajeras.   *On Tuesday, the bank was opened by the cashiers.*

B. *estar* + past participle = a condition resulting from an action

Combining a present or imperfect form of **estar** with the past participle of another verb is a way of expressing a condition resulting from an action. Note that you use this construction when you are describing the *result* of an action rather than the action itself and when there is *no doer* of the action either mentioned or implied.

Fui al banco, pero **estaba cerrado.**   *I went to the bank, but it was closed.*

El banco **está abierto** hasta las 6:00.   *The bank is open until 6:00.*

C. **Comparison of the uses of *ser* and *estar* with past participles**

The best way to distinguish when to use **ser** or **estar** with a past participle is to remember that **ser** is used to indicate an *action*, while **estar** is used to describe the *result* of an action. Study the examples below.

action

La tarta de manzana **fue acabada** por mi hermano.

The apple pie was finished (eaten up) by my brother.

result

La tarta de manzana **está acabada**.

The apple pie is finished. (There is no more left.)

action

El coche **fue lavado** ayer.

The car was washed yesterday.

result

El coche **está lavado**.

The car is washed.

> **REMEMBER:** When a past participle follows **ser** or **estar**, it functions like an adjective and must agree with its noun antecedent in number and gender.

EXERCISE 4-4: Each of the following sentences contains a form of **ser** or **estar** with the past participle of another verb. Change each sentence from singular to plural, as shown in the examples. You will need to review the preterite forms of **ser** and the imperfect forms of **estar**, as well as the list of irregular past participles in Chapter 6 of this book. Answers are at the end of the chapter.

Examples: La casa fue quemada por los soldados. *Las casas fueron quemadas por los soldados.*

La ventana está cerrada. *Las ventanas están cerradas.*

1. El vaso fue roto por los niños.

2. El poema fue leído en la reunión.

3. La carta está escrita.

4. Todos los días, la tienda es abierta a las 9:00 en punto.

5. La nueva silla estaba rota.

6. El país fue conquistado por los españoles.

7. El pájaro está muerto.

8. El juguete fue escondido por la madre.

9. La ventana estaba cerrada por la mañana.

10. El carro fue robado por una banda de ladrones.

11. El árbol fue destruido por el viento.

4-5. *estar* with Present Participles

Estar is combined with the present participles of other verbs to form the progressive tenses. (See Chapter 3 for a review of the present progressive tenses. Other progressive tenses are discussed in later chapters.)

El niño **está haciendo** su tarea.

The child is doing his homework.

Estoy mirando la tele.

I'm watching television.

REMEMBER: **Estar** must change to agree with the subject, but the present participle (**-ando, -iendo**) never changes its form.

Estoy mirando la tele.   *I'm watching television.*
Estamos mirando la tele.   *We are watching television.*

EXERCISE 4-5: Circle the correct form of **ser** or **estar** in each sentence below. Answers are at the end of the chapter.

1. (*Soy/Estoy*) haciendo un vestido nuevo.
2. En su casa, las ventanas (*son/están*) abiertas siempre.
3. Ahora, los muchachos (*son/están*) cantando canciones populares.
4. Creo que las maletas (*son/están*) perdidas.
5. La cosa (*es/está*) hecha.

SUMMARY

1. **Ser** and **estar** are both translated as *to be*, but they are not interchangeable—each has its own special uses.
2. **Ser** is used to refer to essential characteristics, such as identity and nationality, and unchanging qualities, such as color, size, and the like.
3. **Ser** is used with the preposition **de** (*of* or *from*) to indicate origin, material, or possession.
4. **Ser** is used when referring to the time, the day, or the date.
5. **Ser** is used to mean *to take place*.
6. **Estar** is used to indicate location and position.
7. **Estar** is used to indicate a temporary or changing condition in health, mood, temperature, and the like.
8. **Estar** is used to express sudden changes or conditions that cause emotion.
9. Some adjectives have different meanings depending on whether they are used with **ser** or **estar**.
10. Combining **ser** with the past participle of another verb is one way to express the passive voice. You can use this construction only when an *action* is being described and when that action has a *doer*, either mentioned or implied.
11. Combining **estar** with the past participle of another verb is a way of expressing a condition resulting from an action.
12. **Estar** is combined with the present participles of other verbs to form the progressive tenses.

RAISE YOUR GRADES

For each sentence in the column on the left, decide why **ser** or **estar** has been used. Then find that reason in the column on the right and write its letter next to the number of each sentence in the space provided. You may use the same letter more than once. Answers are at the end of the chapter.

_____ 1. Soy de la Argentina.
_____ 2. Los niños están aburridos.
_____ 3. La pluma es de mi tía.
_____ 4. Mi padre está malo.
_____ 5. La carta fue escrita ayer.
_____ 6. Los españoles están cantando.
_____ 7. La fiesta es en casa de Alicia.
_____ 8. Es un gran hombre.
_____ 9. La carne está fria otra vez.
_____ 10. Las sillas están rotas.
_____ 11. El cuarto del niño está sucio.

ser
a. identity
b. nationality
c. origin
d. profession
e. material
f. "to take place"
g. essential characteristic
h. time
i. action (passive voice)
j. possession

_____12. El abrigo es de lana.

_____13. Es una casa grande y hermosa.

_____14. Estamos en la sala.

_____15. Mi hermano es vendedor.

_____16. Las ventanas están demasiado altas.

_____17. Es un hombre alto.

_____18. Somos japoneses.

_____19. ¿Cómo estas?

_____20. Hoy es martes.

estar

k. location or position

l. health

m. mood

n. temporary or changing condition

o. progressive tense

p. result of action

CHAPTER ANSWERS

EXERCISE 4-1

1. Usted es una buena persona.
2. ¿Quién soy yo?
3. Leandro no es de San Diego.
4. Los estudiantes son japoneses.
5. Ser o no ser; ésa es la cuestión.
6. Miguel es un estudiante.
7. Tú y yo somos amigos, pero no somos hermanos.
8. La música es cubana, pero la orquesta es de México.
9. El carro grande es de Juan.
10. El concierto es en casa de Elena.

EXERCISE 4-2

1. es *My dress is made of wool.*
2. están *My children aren't here.*
3. Es *She is a pretty girl.*
4. es *He is neither fat nor thin.*
5. están *Where are the new magazines?*
6. es *What time is it?*
7. somos *You and I are very good friends.*
8. eres *Where are you from?*
9. ser *The party is going to take place at Julia's house.*
10. es *Today is my birthday.*
11. están *After working, the workers are tired.*
12. están *How are you?*
13. estás *You are looking very pretty tonight.*
14. estoy *I am very happy today.*

EXERCISE 4-3

1. están *Where are the children?*
2. es *Miguel is from Canada.*
3. está *We can't go. My son is sick.*
4. es, está *My brother is an engineer, and he is in Mexico now.*
5. es, están *The party is at Carlos's house because his parents are not home.*
6. es, es *The house is Juan's, and it is green and white.*
7. está, están *The house is dirty, but the windows are clean.*
8. son *All of my sisters are smart.*

9. es, es *Don Quixote is a long novel, but it is not boring.*
10. Son *It's three o'clock in the afternoon.*
11. es, están *The lesson is difficult, and the students are tired and bored.*
12. están *How are you?*
13. es *What is your purse made of, plastic or leather?*
14. estamos *You and I are not ready.*
15. es *Today is Thursday.*
16. estoy *I am not dead yet.*
17. está *Barcelona is in Spain.*
18. está, es *Carlos is in Spain, but he is Mexican.*
19. está *I do not want the apple because it is unripe.*
20. está *You cook well; the soup is tasty.*

EXERCISE 4-4

1. Los vasos fueron rotos por los niños. *The glasses were broken by the children.*
2. Los poemas fueron leídos en la reunión. *The poems were read at the meeting.*
3. Las cartas están escritas. *The letters are written.*
4. Todos los días, las tiendas son abiertas a las 9:00 en punto. *Every day, the stores are opened at 9:00 sharp.*
5. Las nuevas sillas estaban rotas. *The new chairs were broken.*
6. Los paises fueron conquistados por los españoles. *The countries were conquered by the Spaniards.*
7. Los pájaros están muertos. *The birds are dead.*
8. Los juguetes fueron escondidos por la madre. *The toys were hidden by the mother.*
9. Las ventanas estaban cerradas por la mañana. *The windows were closed in the morning.*
10. Los carros fueron robados por una banda de ladrones. *The cars were stolen by a gang of thieves.*
11. Los árboles fueron destruidos por el viento. *The trees were destroyed by the wind.*

EXERCISE 4-5

1. Estoy   *I am making a new dress.*
2. están   *In his house, the windows are always open.*
3. están   *Now the boys are singing popular songs.*
4. están   *I think the suitcases are lost.*
5. está   *The thing is done.*

RAISE YOUR GRADES

1. c   *I am from Argentina.*
2. m   *The children are bored.*
3. j   *The pen is my aunt's.*
4. l   *My father is sick.*
5. i   *The letter was written yesterday.*

6. o   *The Spaniards are singing.*
7. f   *The party is at Alicia's house.*
8. g   *He is a great man.*
9. n   *The meat is cold again.*
10. p   *The chairs are broken.*
11. n   *The child's room is dirty.*
12. e   *The overcoat is made of wool.*
13. g   *It is a big, beautiful house.*
14. k   *We are in the living room.*
15. d   *My brother is a salesman.*
16. k   *The windows are too high.*
17. g   *He is a tall man.*
18. b   *We are Japanese.*
19. l   *How are you?*
20. h   *Today is Tuesday.*

5 THE PRETERITE AND THE IMPERFECT

THIS CHAPTER IS ABOUT

☑ **Preterite of Regular Verbs**
☑ **Preterite of Irregular Verbs**
☑ **Use of the Preterite**
☑ **Forms of the Imperfect Indicative**
☑ **Use of the Imperfect**
☑ **Comparison of the Preterite and the Imperfect**
☑ **Use of *ser, estar*, and *haber* in the Preterite and Imperfect**
☑ **Comparison of the Past Progressive and the Imperfect**

There are two past tenses in Spanish, the preterite and the imperfect indicative.

5-1. Preterite of Regular Verbs

A. *-ar* verbs

The preterite of regular **-ar** verbs is formed by dropping the infinitive ending and adding the endings **-é, -aste, -ó, -amos, -asteis, -aron** to the infinitive stem. Note the written accent over the first and third person singular endings: **-é, -ó**. This written accent prevents confusion with present tense endings. The first person plural ending, **-amos**, is the same for both the present and the preterite. Study the following example.

hablar = habl + ar

(yo)	habl**é**	*I talked, did talk*
(tú)	habl**aste**	*you talked, did talk*
(él, ella) (usted)	habl**ó**	*he, she talked, did talk* / *you talked, did talk*
(nosotros, -as)	habl**amos**	*we talked, did talk*
(vosotros, -as)	habl**asteis**	*you talked (pl), did talk*
(ellos, ellas) (ustedes)	habl**aron**	*they talked, did talk* / *you talked (pl), did talk*

EXERCISE 5-1: Write in the correct preterite form of the verb given in parentheses. Watch out for reflexive verbs and use the reflexive pronoun that agrees with the subject. Answers are at the end of the chapter.

1. (acostarse) Jaime y Carlos _____ tarde.
2. (cerrar) Yo _____ todas las ventanas.
3. (llorar) El muchacho _____ muchísimo.
4. (enseñar) Ayer, la maestra _____ las reglas de la pronunciación del español.
5. (enojarse) Nosotros _____ con él el verano pasado.
6. (callarse) Los estudiantes _____ de repente.
7. (espantar) El perro _____ al gato.

8. (caminar) Tú _____ más rápido que yo.

9. (lavar) Ayer, vosotros _____ la ropa en el río.

10. (charlar) Mi madre _____ mucho con los vecinos.

11. (bañarse) Nosotros _____ en la piscina.

12. (esperar) El otro día, nosotras _____ veinte minutos.

13. (terminar) El albañil _____ el cuarto de baño el jueves.

14. (desayunar) Pedro _____ huevos con chorizo.

15. (cenar) Tú _____ muy tarde la otra noche.

B. *-er* and *-ir* verbs

The preterite of regular **-er** and **-ir** verbs is formed by dropping the infinitive ending and adding the endings -**í**, -**iste**, -**ió**, -**imos**, -**isteis**, -**ieron** to the infinitive stem. Note the written accent over the first and third person singular endings: -**í**, -**ió**. The first person plural ending, -**imos**, is the same for the present and the preterite of **-ir** verbs but not **-er** verbs. Study the following examples.

correr = corr + er

(yo)	corrí	*I ran, did run*
(tú)	corriste	*you ran, did run*
(él, ella) (usted)	corrió	*he, she, it ran, did run* *you ran, did run*
(nosotros, -as)	corrimos	*we ran, did run*
(vosotros, -as)	corristeis	*you ran (pl), did run*
(ellos, ellas) (ustedes)	corrieron	*they ran, did run* *you ran (pl), did run*

vivir = viv + ir

(yo)	viví	*I lived, did live*
(tú)	viviste	*you lived, did live*
(él, ellas) (usted)	vivió	*he, she, it lived, did live* *you lived, did live*
(nosotros, -as)	vivimos	*we lived, did live*
(vosotros, -as)	vivisteis	*you lived (pl), did live*
(ellos, ellas) (ustedes)	vivieron	*they lived, did live* *you lived (pl), did live*

> **NOTE:** The preterite first and third person singular forms of the verb **ver**, *to see*, do not have a written accent because they are words of a single syllable: **vi** and **vio**.

EXERCISE 5-2: Write in the correct preterite form of the verbs given in parentheses. Be careful not to confuse the first and third person singular endings -**í** and -**ió**. Answers are at the end of the chapter.

1. (romper) Yo _____ el florero más bonito que tengo.

2. (abrir) Ayer, los mecánicos no _____ el taller.

3. (ver) Nosotros _____ a mi prima la semana pasada.

4. (escoger) Mary Jane _____ dos novelas policíacas y una biografía.

5. (recibir) Mis abuelos _____ mi carta anteayer.

6. (distinguir) Tú _____ entre el arte clásico y el arte moderno.

7. (interrumpir) El político _____ bruscamente al periodista.

8. (salir) Ayer, yo _____ tarde del trabajo.

9. (llover) El otro día, _____ durante dos horas.

10. (escribir) El verano pasado, mi amiga _____ una novela.

11. (volver) Vosotros _____ muy cansados del viaje.

12. (vender) La semana pasada, Robert _____ su coche viejo.

13. (perder) Andrew _____ su reloj en el parque.
14. (nacer) Los hermanos _____ el quince de septiembre.
15. (entender) Vosotros no _____ bien la lección.

5-2. Preterite of Irregular Verbs

The irregular preterite endings are **-e, -iste, -o, -imos, -isteis, -ieron**. Note that the irregular preterite endings have no written accents. Irregular preterite endings cannot be confused with present tense endings because they are not attached to the infinitive stem. It is necessary to memorize the irregular preterite stems.

A. Irregular preterite stems

The following common verbs have irregular stems in the preterite. To help in memorization, they have been grouped by some common stem irregularities.

1. *uv* in the preterite stem.

andar	*to walk*	and**uv**e, and**uv**iste, and**uv**o, and**uv**imos, and**uv**isteis, and**uv**ieron
estar	*to be*	est**uv**e, est**uv**iste, est**uv**o, est**uv**imos, est**uv**isteis, est**uv**ieron
tener	*to have*	t**uv**e, t**uv**iste, t**uv**o, t**uv**imos, t**uv**isteis, t**uv**ieron

> **NOTE:** Verbs ending in **-tener**, such as **obtener**, **retener**, and **contener**, are conjugated like **tener**.

2. *u* in the preterite stem.

caber	*to fit*	cupe, cupiste, cupo, cupimos, cupisteis, cupieron
poder	*to be able*	pude, pudiste, pudo, pudimos, pudisteis, pudieron
poner	*to put*	puse, pusiste, puso, pusimos, pusisteis, pusieron
saber	*to know*	supe, supiste, supo, supimos, supisteis, supieron

3. *i* in the preterite stem.

hacer	*to do, to make*	hice, hiciste, hizo, hicimos, hicisteis, hicieron
querer	*to want*	quise, quisiste, quiso, quisimos, quisisteis, quisieron
venir	*to come*	vine, viniste, vino, vinimos, vinisteis, vinieron

> **NOTE:** In the third person singular of **hacer**, **c** changes to **z**: **hizo**.

4. *j* in the preterite stem. Note that the third person plural ending for these verbs is **-eron**, rather than **-ieron**.

decir	*to say, to tell*	dije, dijiste, dijo, dijimos, dijisteis, dijeron
reducir	*to lessen, to reduce*	reduje, redujiste, redujo, redujimos, redujisteis, redujeron
traer	*to bring*	traje, trajiste, trajo, trajimos, trajisteis, trajeron.

> **NOTE:** Verbs ending in **-cir**, such as **conducir**, **traducir**, and **producir**, are conjugated like **reducir**.

EXERCISE 5-3: Rewrite the following sentences by changing the preterite verb from the singular to the plural form. Answers are at the end of the chapter.

1. Traje sal, pimienta, moztaza y mayonesa.

2. Ella quiso ir pero no pudo.

3. Tú pusiste la fruta en la nevera, ¿verdad?

4. Traduje *La guerra y la paz* del ruso el español.

5. Él no vino a la playa con Samuel.

6. Hice una paella muy rica.

7. El perro no cupo en el apartamento de Patricia.

8. Dijiste muchas cosas pero no hiciste nada.

9. Pude hacer lo que quise.

10. Estuviste en París mucho tiempo.

B. *Dar*, *ser*, and *ir*

The verbs **dar**, *to give*, **ser**, *to be*, and **ir**, *to go*, are completely irregular in the preterite and must be memorized. Note that **dar** takes the endings of **-er** and **-ir** verbs in the preterite. Also note that **ser** and **ir** are the same in the preterite.

dar	*to give*	**di, diste, dio, dimos, disteis, dieron**
ser	*to be*	**fui, fuiste, fue, fuimos, fuisteis, fueron**
ir	*to go*	**fui, fuiste, fue, fuimos, fuisteis, fueron**

EXERCISE 5-4: Rewrite the following sentences by changing the verb from the present tense to the preterite. Answers are at the end of the chapter.

1. Siempre damos la ropa vieja a los amigos.

2. Voy al mercado por la mañana.

3. Usted es un maestro muy bueno.

4. Doy a cada muchacho una foto de la boda.

5. Ellos son músicos de mucho talento.

6. Quiero ir a la playa temprano.

7. No cabemos todos en un solo coche.

8. Mis primos tienen que estudiar día y noche.

9. José compone todos mis electrodomésticos.

10. Los estudiantes quieren hablar con el rector de la universidad.

11. Todo el mundo dice que Picasso es un gran pintor.

12. Me pongo la corbata roja en vez de la corbata azul.

13. No traemos nada de comer.

14. Vengo a despedirme de usted.

15. Ellos ponen primero el mantel y después los cubiertos.

16. Digo todo lo que tengo que decir.

17. Estamos todo el verano en San Francisco.

18. Mi primo anda dos millas a la escuela.

19. La maestra no hace errores.

20. Ellos quieren creer en la inmortalidad.

C. **Stem-changing verbs**

Class II and Class III verbs ending in **-ir** change the preterite stem in the third person singular and plural.

1. *Stem changes from o to u.*

| morir | *to die* | morí, moriste, murió, morimos, moristeis, murieron |
| dormir | *to sleep* | dormí, dormiste, durmió, dormimos, dormisteis, durmieron |

> **NOTE:** **Morir** and **dormir** are the only important verbs in this category.

2. *Stem changes from e to i.*

mentir	*to lie*	mentí, mentiste, mintió, mentimos, mentisteis, mintieron
divertirse	*to enjoy oneself, to have fun*	me divertí, te divertiste, se divirtió, nos divertimos, os divertisteis, se divirtieron
sentirse	*to feel*	me sentí, te sentiste, se sintió, nos sentimos, os sentisteis, se sintieron
pedir	*to ask for, to request*	pedí, pediste, pidió, pedimos, pedisteis, pidieron
reír	*to laugh*	reí, reíste, rió, reímos, reísteis, rieron
seguir	*to follow*	seguí, seguiste, siguió, seguimos, seguisteis, siguieron

EXERCISE 5-5: Rewrite the following sentences by substituting the same preterite form of the verb given in parentheses for the italicized preterite form of the verb within the sentence. Answers are at the end of the chapter.

1. (divertirse) Anoche, Leticia y Helen *se sonrieron* mucho en la fiesta.

2. (ponerse) Ana *vistió* un abrigo de pieles y una bufanda de seda.

3. (herirse) El niño *se hizo daño* al subir la escalera.

4. (pedir) Las muchachas *ofrecieron* agua de limón con hielo.

5. (perseguir) El espía *siguió* al sospechoso cautelosamente.

6. (repetir) El vecino *contó* un chiste muy viejo pero muy chistoso.

7. (servir) Anoche, *dimos* a todos los invitados champán y perdices.

8. (mentir) *Hablaste* mucho acerca de ese asunto.

9. (sentirse) Anoche, todos *durmieron* bien.

10. (preferir) Mi madre *quiso* llegar antes que yo al restorán.

D. **Orthographic changes of verbs ending in *-car*, *-gar*, and *-zar***

All **-ar** verbs ending in **-car**, **-gar**, and **-zar** change the spelling of the first person singular preterite.

1. *-car verbs change the* **c** *to* **qu** *before -e.*

acercarse	*to approach*	me acer**qu**é
buscar	*to look for*	bus**qu**é
colocar	*to put in place*	colo**qu**é
explicar	*to explain*	expli**qu**é
masticar	*to chew*	masti**qu**é
practicar	*to practice*	practi**qu**é
sacar	*to take out*	sa**qu**é
significar	*to mean, to signify*	signifi**qu**é
tocar	*to touch, to play an instrument*	to**qu**é

2. *-gar verbs change the* **g** *to* **gu** *before -e.*

castigar	*to punish*	casti**gu**é
entregar	*to hand over*	entre**gu**é
jugar(ue)	*to play*	ju**gu**é
juzgar	*to judge*	juz**gu**é
llegar	*to arrive*	lle**gu**é
negar(ie)	*to negate, deny*	ne**gu**é
pagar	*to pay*	pa**gu**é
rogar(ue)	*to beg for, beseech*	ro**gu**é

3. *-zar verbs change the* **z** *to* **c** *before -e.*

abrazar	*to hug, to embrace*	abra**c**é
alcanzar	*to reach*	alcan**c**é
alzar	*to raise*	al**c**é
comenzar(ie)	*to begin*	comen**c**é
empezar(ie)	*to begin, to start*	empe**c**é
gozar	*to enjoy*	go**c**é
realizar	*to realize a profit, to fulfill*	reali**c**é
tropezar	*to trip, to stumble upon*	trope**c**é

EXERCISE 5-6: Rewrite the following sentences by omitting the subject and changing the verb form to the preterite first person singular. Answers are at the end of the chapter.

Example: Ayer, mi novio pagó el cine y la cena.   *Ayer, pagué el cine y la cena.*

1. Mi hermano nunca realizó el sueño de ser jugador de béisbol.

2. Los muchachos se acercaron lentamente a la piscina.

3. El verano pasado, empezamos a creer en la realidad de los duendes.

4. Ayer, buscaste un periódico y encontraste muchos.

5. La maestra explicó un problema difícil de matemáticas.

6. Mi padre no gozó del viaje.

7. Linda tropezó al subir la escalera.

8. Negamos la realidad de los seres extraterrestres.

9. Llegaron a tiempo.

10. El jefe alzó el salario de todos los empleados.

11. Los estudiantes comenzaron a reír.

12. El pianista tocó una sonata de Mozart.

13. Los obreros colocaron los ladrillos encima de la muralla.

14. Sacamos varias latas de atún de la bolsa de papel.

15. Los niños no alcanzaron el punto más alto del cerro.

E. **Orthographic changes from *i* to *y***

Verbs ending in **-uir**, such as **sustituir** and **huir**, change the **i** to **y** in the third person singular and plural in the preterite. **Caer, creer, leer,** and **oír** also change the **i** to **y** in the third person singular and plural. These four verbs have a written accent over the **i** in all forms.

> **NOTE:** Other common verbs ending in **-uir** are **construir, destruir,** and **incluir**.

caer	*to fall*	caí, caíste, cayó, caímos, caísteis, cayeron
creer	*to believe*	creí, creíste, creyó, creímos, creísteis, creyeron
huir	*to flee*	huí, huíste, huyó, huímos, huísteis, huyeron
leer	*to read*	leí, leíste, leyó, leímos, leísteis, leyeron
oír	*to hear*	oí, oíste, oyó, oímos, oísteis, oyeron

EXERCISE 5-7: Rewrite the following sentences by changing the verb from the present to the preterite tense. Begin each sentence with **ayer**. Answers are at the end of the chapter.

Example: Todas las tardes, Emilio oye las noticias en la radio.
Ayer, Emilio oyó las noticias en la radio.

1. Todas las mañanas, mi padre lee el periódico.

2. Dices cosas raras pero no mientes.

3. Todos los días, el niño huye de su hermano mayor.

4. Siempre sustituyes la fruta y el postre por la carne y el arroz.

5. Siempre crees lo que lees sin cuestionarlo.

6. Siempre caes porque subes demasiado rápido.

7. Me siento triste porque no incluyen a Fernando en la invitación.

8. Nos sentamos después de desayunar y leemos novelas.

9. Todos los días, los niños se ríen cuando oyen la radio.

10. Siempre destruyen un edificio para construir otro nuevo.

5-3. Use of the Preterite

A. The preterite is used to express an action or series of actions completed in the past.

Fui al centro temprano.	*I went downtown early.*
Después de levantarse, el muchacho **salió** al patio, **vio** dos ardillas, les **dio** algo de comer y **entró** otra vez en la casa.	*After getting up, the boy went out to the patio, saw two squirrels, gave them something to eat, and went back into the house again.*
Ayer **llovió**.	*It rained yesterday.*

B. The preterite is used to indicate the beginning or the end of an action that took place in the past.

El hombre **empezó** a hablar.	*The man began to speak.*
De repente, **dejó** de nevar.	*Suddenly, it stopped snowing.*

C. The preterite is used to state a fact about an event or series of events that took place in a completed time period.

Mi suegra sólo **estuvo** aquí quince minutos.	*My mother-in-law was only here fifteen minutes.*
El siglo XVIII **fue** un siglo de muchas revoluciones.	*The eighteenth century was a century of many revolutions.*

EXERCISE 5-8: Translate the following sentences into Spanish. Answers are at the end of the chapter.

1. It rained yesterday.

2. The boys went to the beach.

3. She went downtown, ate lunch, and bought a pair of shoes.

4. I couldn't open the door.

5. Before going to the store, I cleaned the kitchen.

6. We couldn't sleep last night.

7. I arrived late; the class began at eight.

8. I never felt worse.

9. The children went to the movies.

10. I believed everything that he said.

11. He translated *Don Quixote* from Spanish to English.

12. Elizabeth gave her father a new tie.

13. You (*tú*) didn't see José last night?

14. They began to eat the salad but they didn't drink anything.

15. We asked permission before entering.

16. He never told a lie.

17. I studied French all day.

18. I already paid the bill.

19. The Spaniards arrived before the English and the French.

20. You (*tú*) began to read at the age of three.

21. What did she say?

22. Who went with Mary to the store?

23. Why did you (*tú*) open the door?

24. What time did you (*usted*) return?

25. When did you (*tú*) go to bed last night?

5-4. Forms of the Imperfect Indicative

Imperfect verb forms are easy to learn because there are only three verbs that are irregular.

A. *-ar* verbs

The imperfect indicative of **-ar** verbs is formed by dropping the infinitive ending and adding **-aba, -abas, -aba, -ábamos, -abais, -aban** to the infinitive stem. Note the written accent over **-ábamos**. Study the following example.

hablar = habl + ar

(yo)	habl**aba**	*I was speaking, used to speak*
(tú)	habl**abas**	*you were speaking, used to speak*
(él, ella) (usted)	habl**aba**	*he, she, it was speaking, used to speak* / *you were speaking, used to speak*
(nosotros, -as)	habl**ábamos**	*we were speaking, used to speak*
(vosotros, -as)	habl**abais**	*you were speaking (pl), used to speak*
(ellos, ellas) (ustedes)	habl**aban**	*they were speaking, used to speak* / *you were speaking (pl), used to speak*

B. Regular *-er* and *-ir* verbs

The imperfect indicative of regular **-er** and **-ir** verbs is formed by dropping the infinitive ending and adding **-ía, -ías, -ía, -íamos, -íais, -ían** to the infinitive stem. Note the written accent over the **í** in all forms. Study the following examples.

comer = com + er

(yo)	com**ía**	*I was eating, used to eat*
(tú)	com**ías**	*you were eating, used to eat*
(él, ella) (ustedes)	com**ía**	*he, she, it was eating, used to eat* / *you were eating, used to eat*
(nosotros, -as)	com**íamos**	*we were eating, used to eat*
(vosotros, -as)	com**íais**	*you were eating (pl), used to eat*
(ellos, ellas) (ustedes)	com**ían**	*they were eating, used to eat* / *you were eating (pl), used to eat*

vivir = viv + ir

(yo)	viv**ía**	*I was living, used to live*
(tú)	viv**ías**	*you were living, used to live*
(él, ella) (usted)	viv**ía**	*he, she, it was living, used to live* / *you were living, used to live*
(nosotros, -as)	viv**íamos**	*we were living, used to live*
(vosotros, -as)	viv**íais**	*you were living (pl), used to live*
(ellos, ellas) (ustedes)	viv**ían**	*they were living, used to live* / *you were living (pl), used to live*

C. *Ir*, *ser*, **and** *ver*

The verbs **ir**, **ser**, and **ver** are irregular in the imperfect indicative and must be memorized. Study the following conjugations.

ir	*to go*	**iba, ibas, iba, íbamos, ibais, iban**
ser	*to be*	**era, eras, era, éramos, erais, eran**
ver	*to see*	**veía, veías, veía, veíamos, veíais, veían**

EXERCISE 5-9: Fill in the correct imperfect indicative form of the verb or verbs given in parentheses. Remember that **ir**, **ser**, and **ver** are irregular. Answers are at the end of the chapter.

1. (hablar, trabajar) Yo siempre _____ y _____ al mismo tiempo.
2. (ser, comer) Cuando José _____ pequeño, no _____ mucho.
3. (vivir, caminar) Cuando nosotros _____ en California, no _____ nunca.
4. (acostarse) Antes, los niños _____ más temprano.
5. (venir, sentirse) Mientras yo _____ por el camino, _____ mal.
6. (lavar) Antes de comprar una máquina de lavar, mi madre _____ la ropa a mano.
7. (bañarse) De niños, nosotros _____ todos los sábados.
8. (ser, ir) Cuando mis primas _____ pequeñas, _____ al cine todos los domingos.
9. (ver, ayudar) Cuando yo _____ a mi madre cansada, _____ con el trabajo de la casa.
10. (callarse, saber) Los estudiantes _____ cuando no _____ las respuestas.
11. (romper) Todos los días, el camarero _____ dos o tres copas.
12. (preferir) A veces, nosotros _____ comer fruta en vez de pasteles.
13. (brillar, reírse) Cuando el sol _____ , los niños _____ todo el día.
14. (brotar) Todas las primaveras, _____ flores en mi pueblo.
15. (llover) En el Caribe, _____ todas las tardes a las cinco.
16. (coser, mirar) Mi abuela _____ y _____ la tele a la vez.
17. (escribir, hacer) Yo siempre _____ por la mañana y _____ ejercicio por la tarde.
18. (querer, caber) Nosotros _____ meter el pavo en el horno, pero no _____ .
19. (poner) Después de desayunar, Ana siempre _____ la mesa para la cena.
20. (hacer) ¿Qué _____ tú esta mañana?
21. (estar) ¿Quiénes _____ en casa ayer?
22. (tocar) ¿Cuántas horas _____ usted el piano cuando era joven?
23. (andar) ¿Por qué _____ usted con tanta prisa?
24. (decir) ¿Qué _____ tú?
25. (cantar) ¿Por qué _____ ustedes tan fuerte?

5-5. Use of the Imperfect

A. **The imperfect is used to indicate an action or series of actions that are in progress in the past.**

Mientras José **cantaba**, Elena **bailaba**.

While Jose sang (was singing), Elena danced (was dancing).

Iba a ir a la playa, pero **llovía** demasiado.

I was going to go to the beach, but it was raining too hard.

B. **The imperfect is used to indicate a repeated, customary action.**

In English, this concept is often expressed by "used to."

Antes **fumaba** mucho, pero casi no fumo ya.   *Before, I used to smoke a lot, but I hardly smoke at all now.*

Mis padres **iban** a la biblioteca todos los domingos.   *My parents went (used to go) to the library every Sunday.*

C. **The imperfect is used to describe a state of mind, a physical state, or the physical environment in the past.**

Era una noche oscura y borrascosa.   *It was a dark and stormy night.*
Quería ir al cine pero me **sentía** demasiado deprimido.   *I wanted to go to the movies, but I felt too depressed.*
Luisa se **vestía** de negro y **llevaba** una bolsa blanca.   *Luisa wore (was wearing) black and carried (was carrying) a white purse.*

D. **The imperfect is used to express the time of day in the past.**

Era la una de la mañana.   *It was one o'clock in the morning.*

EXERCISE 5-10: Translate the following sentences into Spanish. Answers are at the end of the chapter.

1. I used to walk to school every day.

2. When Michael was a baby, he cried a lot.

3. It was a very beautiful day.

4. Catherine used to play the piano a lot.

5. I always cooked and my brother washed the dishes.

6. The students used to ask a lot of questions.

7. We didn't usually get up late.

8. The teacher (*f*) usually taught spelling first.

9. My boss used to get angry frequently.

10. He was only five years old, but he knew Greek, Latin, and Italian.

11. He almost never paid the bill.

12. Belinda always hugged and kissed everyone.

13. I used to like summer more than spring.

14. What were you (*tú*) doing?

15. Where was he going?

16. Did you (*tú*) used to write many letters?

17. Were José and Marcela at the party?

18. What was Michael looking at?

19. With whom was Lourdes dancing?

20. It was raining all day yesterday.

5-6. Comparison of the Preterite and the Imperfect

A. **The main difference between the preterite and the imperfect is between a completed action (preterite) and an incomplete or continuous action or state of being (imperfect).**

The preterite is used to indicate specific actions completed at a particular moment in time. The imperfect is used to describe the background in which the completed action occurs. This background may be the description of the physical environment, an emotional or physical state of a person, or an action that is in progress at the same time that the completed action takes place. Study the following examples carefully.

	Background		Completed Action
Action in progress	Teresa escribía a máquina *Teresa was typing*	cuando *when*	Pepe llamó por telefono. *Pepe called on the telephone.*
Description of physical environment	Llovía y nevaba *It was raining and snowing*	pero *but*	los exploradores llegaron a la cumbre. *the explorers reached the mountain top.*
Action in progress	Mario cruzaba el salón *Mario was crossing the room*	cuando *when*	tropezó con la mecedora. *he tripped on the rocking chair.*
Description of physical environment and mental state	Era un día gris y me sentía triste y solo *It was a gray day and I was feeling sad and alone*	cuando *when*	vinieron mis amigos con flores y música. *my friends came with flowers and music.*

EXERCISE 5-11: Read each of the following sentences for comprehension. Then complete the sentence by selecting the correct verb form from those given in parentheses. Finally, translate the sentence into English. Answers are at the end of the chapter.

1. Cuando Jesús (entraba, entró), los niños (estudiaban, estudiaron) silenciosamente.

2. El día que mi primo (nacía, nació), yo (llegaba, llegué) primero al hospital.

3. (Eran, Fueron) las cinco de la tarde cuando (empezaba, empezó) a llover.

4. Todos (estaban, estuvieron) muy sorprendidos cuando de repente (hablaba, habló) Fernando.

5. Cuándo (veías, viste) a Gloria, ¿qué abrigo (llevaba, llevó)?

6. Yo (tenía, tuve) ocho años cuando (íbamos, fuimos) a vivir a Oregon.

7. Mientras Jaime (leía, leyó), su hermano (tocaba, tocó) la guitarra.

8. Un día, mientras usted (estaba, estuvo) fuera, (venía, vino) un hombre a casa pero no me (decía, dijo) su nombre.

9. El otro día, mientras los niños (cenaban, cenaron), la tierra (empezaba, empezó) a temblar y (salíamos, salimos) corriendo de la casa.

10. Cuando tu hermana (se casaba, se casó), tú (tenías, tuviste) sarampión y por eso no (ibas, fuiste) a la boda.

B. Some verbs change their meaning, depending on whether the preterite or the imperfect tense is used.

The preterite always emphasizes the completed action, but the imperfect leaves the result of the action in doubt. Study the following examples carefully.

Conocer, *to know, to meet, to be acquainted with*

Completed action	Conocí a Pepe el 17 de octubre.
	I met Pepe on October 17.
Continuous state	Antes, conocíamos Londres muy bien.
	We used to know London very well.

Saber, *to know, to find out*

Completed action	Los investigadores nunca supieron toda la verdad.
	The researchers never found out the whole truth.
Continuous mental state	Yo sabía mucha poesía de memoria.
	I used to know a lot of poetry by heart.

Querer, *to want*

Definite result	Ella no quiso hablar.
	She refused to speak.
Indefinite result	Ella no quería escribir más.
	She didn't want to write anymore.

Tener que, *to have to*

Definite result	El tuvo que ir a comprar pan.
	He had to go buy bread. (He did go.)
Indefinite result	El tenía que estudiar.
	He was supposed to (had to) study. (We don't know if he did.)

Ir a, *to go to, going to*

Definite result	El fue a buscar a Joe
	He went to look for Joe.
Indefinite result	El iba a buscar a Joe.
	He was going to look for Joe. (We don't know if he did.)

Poder, *to be able*

Definite result	Yo pude levantar el escritorio.
	I was able to lift the desk.
Indefinite result	Yo podía llevar a Emma en mi coche.
	I could take Emma in my car.

Vestirse, *to get dressed*

Definite result	Aquella mañana, ella se vistió temprano.
	That morning, she got dressed early.
Description of condition	Siempre se vestía de blanco.
	She was always dressed in white.

EXERCISE 5-12: Rewrite the following sentences by translating the English phrase given in parentheses into Spanish. Answers are at the end of the chapter.

1. Qué (were you doing) cuando los estudiantes (began to laugh)?

2. El año pasado, Isabel (met) a Carolina.

3. (I wasn't able to) terminar el almuerzo.

4. Los niños (found out) que los dulces (were not) en la cocina.

5. Cuando José (was) joven, nunca (knew) lo que (he was doing).

6. ¿Qué (were you going to buy) para la fiesta de Carlos?

7. ¿(Did Mary go) a la playa con Miguel?

8. ¿Por qué (didn't you want) escoger un sombrero más grande?

9. (They left) temprano porque (they weren't able) oír al orador.

10. (I was going to buy) un caballo pero (I bought) un perro grande.

11. El día que (I saw) a Michelle, (she was wearing) zapatos de tenis.

12. (We found out) que Bárbara y Luis (were) hermanos.

13. Timothy siempre (knew) los nombres de todos los ríos del mundo.

14. Los muchachos (wanted to get up) pero (they refused) verstirse.

15. (We met) a tu hermana cuando (we were traveling) en Francia.

5-7. Use of *ser*, *estar*, and *haber* in the Preterite and Imperfect

A. Use of *ser* and *estar* in the preterite

The preterite forms of **ser** and **estar** are used to state a fact about a person, thing, or condition or event that is perceived by the speaker as being completed within a specific time period in the past. Study the following examples.

ser

Yo **fui** discípulo de Freud también.
I was a student of Freud too. (I am no longer his student.)

La mañana de mi cumpleaños **fue** una mañana estupenda.
The morning of my birthday was a wonderful morning. (It is over.)

estar

Miguel **estuvo** enfermo tres días.
Miguel was sick for three days. (He is no longer sick.)

Los muebles **estuvieron** mojados durante mucho tiempo.
The furniture was wet for a long time. (Now it is dry.)

> **NOTE:** See Chapter 4 for a comparison of the uses of **ser** versus **estar**.

B. Use of *ser* and *estar* in the imperfect

The imperfect forms of **ser** and **estar** are used to describe a condition or event that is perceived by the speaker as taking place in the past and having no definite ending. Study the following examples.

ser

Yo **era** discípulo de Freud cuando vivía en Austria.
I was a student of Freud while I was living in Austria.

La mañana de mi cumpleaños **era** una mañana estupenda. Vinieron muchos amigos y trajeron regalos.
The morning of my birthday was wonderful. Many friends came and brought presents.

> **NOTE:** The description of the morning provides a background for the action.

estar

Aquel día, Miguel **estaba** enfermo.
That day, Miguel was sick. (He was sick the whole day, and we do not know if he got better.)

Los muebles **estaban** mojados y yo no sabía qué hacer.
The furniture was wet and I didn't know what to do. (The condition continued unchanged.)

C. Use of *haber* in the preterite and imperfect

The preterite form of **haber**, **hubo**, is seldom used. The imperfect form, **había**, is frequently used and translates as *there was*, *there were*, or *there used to be*. Study the following examples.

Cuando éramos jovenes, **había** menos tráfico.   *When we were young, there was less traffic.*

Fui a la tienda, pero no **había** huevos.   *I went to the store, but there weren't any eggs.*

EXERCISE 5-13: Read the following paragraph in its entirety. Then complete each sentence by choosing the correct preterite or imperfect form of the verb given in parentheses. Then translate the paragraph into English. Answers are at the end of the chapter.

(*1*) Mi abuelo siempre me (contaba, contó) historias de su niñez en México. (*2*) Cuando (era, fue) joven, su familia (vivía, vivió) en un pueblito que (se llamaba, se llamó) Río Blanco. (*3*) Un día, mi abuelo y su hermano mayor (se levantaban, se levantaron) temprano y (se iban, se fueron) al río. (*4*) El hermano de mi abuelo (era, fue) alto, fuerte y de carácter bondadoso. (*5*) Nunca (se enojaba, se enojó) con nadie. (*6*) Aquel día, el sol (brillaba, brilló) y no (había, hubo) ni una nube en el cielo. (*7*) Los hermanos (se sentaban, se sentaron) junto al río. (*8*) De repente, mi abuelo (resbalaba, resbaló) y (se caía, se cayó) al agua. (*9*) (Empezaba, Empezó) a gritar "¡Socorro! ¡Socorro! ¡No sé nadar!" (*10*) Pero su hermano no (hacía, hizo) nada. "Hermano, ayúdame," (gritaba, gritó) mi abuelo. (*11*) "Ayúdate a ti mismo," (contestaba, contestó) su hermano, con la misma sonrisa de siempre. (*12*) Y entonces, tranquilamente (entraba, entró) al agua y (se acercaba, se acercó) a mi abuelo. (*13*) Entonces, mi abuelo (dejaba, dejó) de gritar y (veía, vio) que en el río solamente (había, hubo) medio metro de agua.

5-8. Comparison of the Past Progressive and the Imperfect

A. The past progressive is formed by conjugating the imperfect of *estar* with a present participle.

Estaba nevando.   *It was snowing.*
Los niños **estaban durmiendo**.   *The children were sleeping.*

> **NOTE:** See Chapter 3, Section 3-6, for a review of the present participle.

B. **The past progressive is used only to express an action that is actually occurring at a specific moment in the past.**

Although the imperfect can also be used to express an action that is actually occurring at a specific moment in the past, the past progressive is used when the speaker wishes to emphasize the immediacy of the action taking place in the past.

1. *Action is occurring.*

Imperfect	Ellos **miraban** la televisión cuando llegaron sus padres.
	They were watching television when their parents arrived.
OR	
Past progressive	Ellos **estaban mirando** la televisión cuando llegaron sus padres.
	They were watching television when their parents arrived.

2. *Habitual action.*

Imperfect	Ellos **miraban** la televisión con frecuencia.
	They used to watch television frequently.

EXERCISE 5-14: Rewrite the following sentences by changing the verb given in parentheses from the imperfect to the past progressive. Answers are at the end of the chapter.

1. (Llovía) mucho aquella mañana.

2. ¿Qué (miraban)?

3. ¿(Cantabas)?

4. No entramos porque Juan y Pedro (dormían).

5. El agua (subía) rápidamente.

6. ¿Por qué (reías) tanto?

7. José (se bañaba) despacio.

8. En aquel momento, (me levantaba).

9. Yo no (decía) nada.

10. ¿Con quién (peleaba) Emma?

REMEMBER: The reflexive pronoun either precedes the conjugated form of **estar** or is attached to the present participle: **me** estaba levantando, estaba levantándo**me**.

SUMMARY

1. The preterite endings of regular **-ar** verbs are **-é, -aste, -ó, -amos, -asteis, -aron**.
2. The preterite endings of regular **-er** and **-ir** verbs are **-í, -iste, -ió, -imos, -isteis, -ieron**.
3. Preterite endings of regular verbs are added to the infinitive stem, which is formed by dropping the infinitive ending.
4. The preterite endings of irregular verbs are **-e, -iste, -o, -imos, -isteis, -ieron**.
5. The preterite endings of irregular verbs are added to irregular preterite stems which must be memorized.
6. The verbs **dar, ser,** and **ir** are completely irregular in the preterite and must be memorized.

7. Stem-changing -ir verbs change the preterite stem in the third person singular and plural. For example, **dormir** changes the **o** to **u**: **durmió, durmieron**. **Mentir** changes the **e** to **i**: **mintió, mintieron**.

8. Orthographic changes occur in all -ar verbs ending in -car, -gar, and -zar before the first person singular preterite ending -é. Verbs ending in -car change the **c** to **qu**. Verbs ending in -gar change the **g** to **gu**. Verbs ending in -zar change the **z** to **c**.

9. In the preterite, **caer, creer, leer, oír**, and verbs ending in -uir, such as **construir**, change the **i** to **y** in the third person singular and plural.

10. The preterite is used to express (1) a completed action or series of actions, (2) the beginning or ending of an action that took place in the past, and (3) a statement of fact about an action occurring in the past and completed within a specific time frame.

11. The imperfect endings for -ar verbs are -aba, -abas, -aba, -ábamos, -abais, -aban.

12. The imperfect endings for regular -er and -ir verbs are -ía, -ías, -ía, -íamos, -íais, -ían.

13. Only three verbs, **ir, ser**, and **ver**, are irregular in the imperfect and must be memorized.

14. The imperfect is used to express (1) an action or series of actions in progress in the past, (2) a repeated, customary action, and (3) an emotional or physical condition existing in the past.

15. The imperfect tense is used to express the time of day in the past.

16. The main difference between the preterite and the imperfect is between a completed action in the past (preterite) and an incomplete or continuous action or state of being in the past (imperfect).

17. The use of the preterite versus the imperfect depends upon the meaning the user wants to convey. Certain verbs, such as **saber, conocer, poder**, etc., change their meaning according to the tense used.

18. The preterite forms of **ser** and **estar** are used to state a fact that is perceived by the speaker to be completed within a specific time period in the past.

19. The imperfect forms of **ser** and **estar** are used to describe a condition or event that is perceived by the speaker as taking place in the past and having no definite ending.

20. The preterite form of **haber, hubo**, is seldom used. The imperfect form, **había**, is frequently used, and translates as *there was, there were*, or *there used to be*.

21. The past progressive is formed by conjugating the imperfect tense of **estar** + the present participle.

22. Either the imperfect or the past progressive may be used to indicate an action that is in progress at a specific moment in the past. However, the past progressive is often used when the speaker wishes to emphasize the immediacy of the action taking place in the past.

RAISE YOUR GRADES

☑ **Forms of the preterite** [Sections 5-1 and 5-2]

Complete the following sentences by writing in the correct preterite form of the verb or verbs given in parentheses. Watch for irregular verbs, stem-changing verbs, and verbs with orthographic changes. Answers are at the end of the chapter.

1. (buscar, encontrar) Yo _____ mi cartera, pero no _____ nada.
2. (estar, salir) José y Rosa solamente _____ cinco minutos y después _____ juntos.
3. (ir, tener que) Nosotros _____ porque _____ despedirnos de los señores Smith.
4. (despertarse) Hoy, el niño _____ muy tarde.
5. (sentirse) Mis hijos _____ tristes después de escuchar la noticia.
6. (hacer, decir) Los estudiantes _____ todo el trabajo y no _____ nada a la maestra.
7. (traer) Carlos _____ unos discos nuevos de jazz.
8. (pedir) Los muchachos _____ ayuda a la enfermera.
9. (morirse) Mis plantas _____ de repente.
10. (trabajar, ganar) Ellos _____ todo el día, pero no _____ mucho.

11. (divertirse) Leonor no _____ mucho en el concierto.
12. (acercarse) Los leones _____ lentamente al río.
13. (empezar, poder) Yo _____ a correr, pero no _____ alcanzar el autobús.
14. (realizar) Yo nunca _____ mi sueño de ser violinista.
15. (leer) Michelle _____ una novela de Balzac anoche.
16. (llegar) Yo _____ primero y Linda _____ a las diez.
17. (ser) Nosotros nunca _____ aficionados a las carreras de caballos.
18. (tener) En la reunión, ustedes _____ la oportunidad de hacer muchas preguntas.
19. (dormir) Aquella noche, las mujeres _____ mal.
20. (vestirse, irse) Carlos _____ rápidamente y _____ de la casa.

☑ Forms of the imperfect [Section 5-4]

Complete the following sentences by changing the verb or verbs given in parentheses from the preterite to the imperfect. Answers are at the end of the chapter.

1. (Tuvimos que) acostarnos temprano. Todas las noches, _____ temprano.
2. Una vez (nadé) en el río Mississippi. Cuando era joven, _____ en el río Mississippi todos los veranos.
3. Anoche, (cayeron) todas las hojas. Las hojas _____ lentamente.
4. Los niños (se rieron) cuando (vieron) a los payasos. Los niños siempre _____ cuando _____ a los payasos.
5. Ese día, los abogados (se durmieron) delante del juez. Los abogados siempre _____ delante del juez.
6. El señor Black (abrió) su tienda temprano. El señor Black generalmente _____ su tienda temprano.
7. De repente, los hombres (se callaron) y (escucharon) atentamente a las mujeres. Normalmente, los hombres no _____ y tampoco _____ atentamente a las mujeres.
8. Los novios (dieron) cien dólares a los músicos. En los buenos tiempos, los novios _____ dinero a los musicos.
9. Mi padre (construyó) una casa nueva. Antes, mucha gente _____ su propia casa.
10. Yo no (me levanté) tarde esta mañana. Cuando era joven, _____ tarde los fines de semana.
11. Cuando Alejandro (destruyó) el castillo de arena, Marcela (hizo) otro más grande. Siempre que Alejandro _____ el castillo de arena, Marcela _____ otro más grande.
12. Yo (toqué) el piano en la boda de mi hermana. De niña, yo _____ el piano tres horas todos los días.
13. Ellos no (dijeron) nada. Ella nunca _____ nada en las reuniones de los miercoles.
14. Yo (fui) jugador de béisbol durante un año. Cuando _____ joven, _____ un buen jugador de béisbol.
15. Juan (estuvo) en México el año pasado. Juan _____ en México cuando oyó la noticia.
16. Nadie (vino) a la fiesta. Nadie _____ nunca a nuestras fiestas.
17. Mi tía (puso) el florero en medio de la mesa. Mi tía siempre _____ el florero en medio de la mesa.
18. Ayer (fuimos) a ver la nueva película de Buñuel. Siempre _____ a ver la nueva película de Buñuel.
19. Los estudiantes (se callaron) de repente. Cuando hablaba la maestra, los estudiantes _____ .
20. Pedro (fue) al circo y (se divirtió) mucho. Cuando Pedro _____ al circo, siempre _____ mucho.

☑ The preterite versus the imperfect [Section 5-6]

Study the following list of uses of the preterite and the imperfect. Then read each sentence carefully and select the preterite or imperfect form of the verb or verbs given in parentheses that best fits the context of the sentence. Choose the reason or reasons for your selection from the list of uses and write in the corresponding letter or letters in the space provided to the left of each sentence. Answers are at the end of the chapter.

Preterite	Imperfect
a. Completed action	*d.* Action in progress
b. Beginning or end of an action	*e.* Habitual action
c. Statement of a completed action or event in a specific time frame	*f.* Description of physical or mental state
	g. **Estar** + present participle
	h. Clock time

_____ 1. Cuando Laura (abrió, abría) la puerta, Beth (estuvo, estaba) cantando.

_____ 2. Mientras Pepe (corrió, corría) por la calle, (empezó, empezaba) a llover.

_____ 3. Yo (logré, lograba) levantar la silla porque no (pesó, pesaba) mucho.

_____ 4. Cuando mis hijos (fueron, iban) a España, (aprendieron, aprendían) a hablar bien el español.

_____ 5. El abogado (habló, hablaba) mientras (escuchó, escuchaban) el acusado y el juez.

_____ 6. (Fueron, Eran) las cinco de la tarde cuando el policía (se cayó, se caía) del caballo.

_____ 7. Cuando José (jugó, jugaba) al béisbol, siempre (llevó, llevaba) una camiseta roja.

_____ 8. (Llovió, Llovía) mucho y por eso Teresa (dejó, dejaba) de caminar y (volvió, volvía) a casa.

_____ 9. Ayer, (estuvimos, estábamos) muy cansados y (nos acostamos, nos acostábamos) a las nueve.

_____ 10. Cuando el niño (oyó, oía) los pájaros por primera vez, (empezó, empezaba) a reír.

_____ 11. Mientras los albañiles (estuvieron, estaban) construyendo el techo, (dejó, dejaba) de llover.

_____ 12. (Nevó, Nevaba) aquella noche y por eso (fuimos, íbamos) en coche.

_____ 13. Cuando Angel (fue, era) pequeño, (anduvo, andaba) horas y horas por el rancho de su padre.

_____ 14. Mozart (fue, era) el compositor más famoso del siglo XVIII.

_____ 15. Yo (tuve, tenía) mucho frío y por eso (me puse, me ponía) la chaqueta.

☑ **Verbs with special meanings** [Section 5-6]

Some verbs change their meaning depending on whether they are used in the preterite or the imperfect. The preterite indicates a completed action, and therefore implies a definite result. The imperfect indicates an action or intended action with no known result. Complete each of the following sentences by translating the italicized English phrase into Spanish, using the verb given in parentheses. Answers are at the end of the chapter.

1. (no querer) Los obreros *refused to* trabajar después de las seis. _____

2. (conocer) Irma y Mario *met* a Fernando el verano pasado. _____

3. (saber) Yo nunca *knew* hacer bien el arroz. _____

4. (poder) Ustedes *were able to* levantar el sillón porque pesaba poco. _____

5. (tener que) Los muchachos *were supposed to* cortar la yerba. _____

6. (saber) *We found out* la verdad ayer. _____

7. (tener que) Yo *had to* estudiar mucho para aprobar el examen. _____

8. (conocer) Antes, nosotros *used to be familiar with* Londres pero ya no. _____

9. (ir) El profesor *went* a pedir permiso al decano. _____

10. (ir) Yo *was going* a acostarme temprano anoche. _____

CHAPTER ANSWERS

EXERCISE 5-1

1. se acostaron   *Jaime and Carlos went to bed late.*

2. cerré   *I closed all the windows.*

3. lloró   *The boy cried a great deal.*

4. enseñó   *Yesterday, the teacher taught Spanish pronunciation rules.*

5. nos enojamos   *We got angry with him last summer.*

6. se callaron *The students fell silent suddenly.*
7. espantó *The dog scared the cat.*
8. caminaste *You walked more quickly than I did.*
9. lavasteis *Yesterday, you washed the clothes in the river.*
10. charló *My mother chatted a lot with the neighbors.*
11. nos bañamos *We swam in the pool.*
12. esperamos *The other day, we waited twenty minutes.*
13. terminó *The construction worker finished the bathroom on Thursday.*
14. desayunó *Pedro had eggs and sausage.*
15. cenaste *You had dinner very late the other night.*

EXERCISE 5-2

1. rompí *I broke the prettiest flower vase that I have.*
2. abrieron *Yesterday, the mechanics did not open the workshop.*
3. vimos *We saw my cousin last week.*
4. escogió *Mary Jane chose two mystery novels and a biography.*
5. recibieron *My grandparents received my letter the day before yesterday.*
6. distinguiste *You distinguished between classical art and modern art.*
7. interrumpió *The politician brusquely interrupted the journalist.*
8. salí *Yesterday, I left work late.*
9. llovió *The other day, it rained for two hours.*
10. escribió *Last summer, my friend wrote a novel.*
11. volvisteis *You returned very tired from the trip.*
12. vendió *Last week, Robert sold his old car.*
13. perdió *Andrew lost his watch in the park.*
14. nacieron *The brothers were born on the fifteenth of September.*
15. entendisteis *You didn't understand the lesson well.*

EXERCISE 5-3

1. Trajimos *We brought salt, pepper, mustard, and mayonnaise.*
2. Ellas quisieron, pudieron *They wanted to go but they couldn't.*
3. Vosotros pusisteis *You put the fruit in the refrigerator, right?*
4. Tradujimos *We translated* War and Peace *from Russian to Spanish.*
5. Ellos no vinieron *They didn't come to the beach with Samuel.*
6. Hicimos *We made a delicious paella.*
7. cupieron *The dogs didn't fit in Patricia's apartment.*
8. Dijisteis, hicisteis *You said many things but you didn't do anything.*

9. Pudimos, quisimos *We were able to do what we wanted.*
10. Estuvisteis *You were in Paris for a long time.*

EXERCISE 5-4

1. dimos *We alway gave the old clothes to friends.*
2. Fui *I went to the market in the morning.*
3. fue *You were a very good teacher.*
4. Di *I gave each boy a photo of the wedding.*
5. fueron *They were very talented musicians.*
6. Quise *I wanted to go to the beach early.*
7. cupimos *We didn't all fit in a single car.*
8. tuvieron *My cousins had to study day and night.*
9. compuso *José fixed all my appliances.*
10. quisieron *The students wanted to talk with the rector of the university.*
11. dijo, fue *Everyone said that Picasso was a great painter.*
12. Me puse *I put on my red tie instead of my blue tie.*
13. trajimos *We didn't bring anything to eat.*
14. Vine *I came to say goodbye to you.*
15. pusieron *First they put on the table cloth and then the silverware.*
16. Dije, tuve *I said everything I had to say.*
17. Estuvimos *We spent the whole summer in San Francisco.*
18. anduvo *My cousin walked two miles to school.*
19. hizo *The teacher didn't make any mistakes.*
20. quisieron *They wanted to believe in immortality.*

EXERCISE 5-5

1. se divirtieron *Last night, Leticia and Helen had a lot of fun at the party.*
2. se puso *Ana put on a fur coat and a silk scarf.*
3. se hirió *The child cut himself going up the stairs.*
4. pidieron *The girls asked for lemonade with ice.*
5. persiguió *The spy chased the suspect cautiously.*
6. repitió *The neighbor repeated a very old but funny joke.*
7. servimos *Last night, we served all the guests champagne and partridge.*
8. Mentiste *You lied a great deal about that matter.*
9. se sintieron *Last night, everyone felt well.*
10. prefirió *My mother preferred to arrive before me at the restaurant.*

EXERCISE 5-6

1. realicé *I never fulfilled my dream of being a baseball player.*
2. Me acerqué *I slowly approached the swimming pool.*

3. empecé   *Last summer, I began to believe in the reality of ghosts.*
4. busqué, encontré   *Yesterday, I looked for a newspaper and I found a lot of them.*
5. expliqué   *I explained a difficult mathematics problem.*
6. gocé   *I didn't enjoy the trip.*
7. Tropecé   *I tripped while going up the stairs.*
8. Negué   *I denied the reality of extraterrestrial beings.*
9. Llegué   *I arrived on time.*
10. Alcé   *I raised the salary of all the employees.*
11. Comencé   *I began to laugh.*
12. Toqué   *I played a Mozart sonata.*
13. Coloqué   *I placed the bricks on top of the wall.*
14. Saqué   *I took several cans of tuna from the paper bag.*
15. No alcancé   *I didn't reach the highest point of the hill.*

EXERCISE 5-7

1. leyó   *Yesterday, my father read the newspaper.*
2. dijiste, mentiste   *Yesterday, you said strange things but you didn't lie.*
3. huyó   *Yesterday, the child fled from his older brother.*
4. substituiste   *Yesterday, you substituted fruit and dessert for meat and rice.*
5. creíste, leíste   *Yesterday, you believed what you read without questioning it.*
6. caíste, subiste   *Yesterday, you fell because you went up too fast.*
7. me sentí, incluyeron   *Yesterday, I felt sad because they didn't include Fernando in the invitation.*
8. nos sentamos, leímos   *Yesterday, we sat down after breakfast and read novels.*
9. se rieron, oyeron   *Yesterday, the children laughed when they listened to the radio.*
10. destruyeron   *Yesterday, they destroyed a building in order to build a new one.*

EXERCISE 5-8

1. Llovió ayer.
2. Los muchachos fueron a la playa.
3. Ella fue al centro, almorzó y compró un par de zapatos.
4. No pude abrir la puerta.
5. Antes de ir a la tienda, limpié la cocina.
6. No pudimos dormir anoche.
7. Llegué tarde; la clase empezó a las ocho.
8. Nunca me sentí peor.
9. Los niños fueron al cine.
10. Creí todo lo que dijo.
11. Tradujo *Don Quixote* del español al inglés.
12. Elizabeth dio una corbata nueva a su padre.
13. ¿No viste a José anoche?
14. Empezaron a comer la ensalada pero no bebieron nada.
15. Pedimos permiso antes de entrar.
16. Nunca mintió.
17. Estudié francés todo el día.
18. Ya pagué la cuenta.
19. Los españoles llegaron antes que los ingleses y los franceses.
20. Empezaste a leer a los tres años de edad.
21. ¿Qué dijo ella?
22. ¿Quién fue con Mary a la tienda?
23. ¿Por qué abriste la puerta?
24. ¿A qué hora volvió usted?
25. ¿Cuándo te acostaste anoche?

EXERCISE 5-9

1. hablaba, trabajaba   *I always talked and worked at the same time.*
2. era, comía   *When José was little, he didn't eat very much.*
3. vivíamos, caminábamos   *When we lived in California, we never walked.*
4. se acostaban   *In the past, children used to go to bed earlier.*
5. venía, me sentía   *While I was coming down the road, I felt ill.*
6. lavaba   *Before buying a washing machine, my mother used to wash the clothes by hand.*
7. nos bañábamos   *When we were children, we used to take a bath every Saturday.*
8. eran, iban   *When my cousins were little, they used to go to the movies every Sunday.*
9. veía, ayudaba   *When I saw my mother (was) tired, I helped with the housework.*
10. se callaban, sabían   *The students kept quiet when they didn't know the answer.*
11. rompía   *Every day, the waiter broke two or three glasses.*
12. preferíamos   *At times, we preferred to eat fruit rather than pie.*
13. brillaba, se reían   *When the sun shone, the children laughed all day.*
14. brotaban   *Every spring, flowers bloomed in my home town.*
15. llovía   *In the Caribbean, it rained every afternoon at five.*
16. cosía, miraba   *My grandmother sewed and watched television at the same time.*
17. escribía, hacía   *I always wrote in the morning and did exercise in the afternoon.*
18. queríamos, cabía   *We wanted to put the turkey in the oven, but it didn't fit.*
19. ponía   *After having breakfast, Ana always set the table for dinner.*
20. hacías   *What were you doing this morning?*
21. estaban   *Who was at home yesterday?*
22. tocaba   *How many hours did you play the piano when you were young?*
23. andaba   *Why were you walking so fast?*
24. decías   *What were you saying?*
25. cantaban   *Why were you singing so loud?*

EXERCISE 5-10

1. Yo andaba a la escuela todos los días.
2. Cuando Michael era niño, lloraba mucho.

3. Hacía (Era) un día muy hermoso.
4. Catherine tocaba el piano mucho.
5. Yo siempre cocinaba y mi hermano lavaba los platos.
6. Los estudiantes hacían muchas preguntas.
7. Generalmente, no nos levantábamos tarde.
8. Generalmente, la maestra enseñaba ortografía primero.
9. Mi jefe se enfadaba con frecuencia.
10. Solamente tenía cinco años, pero sabía griego, latín e italiano.
11. Casi nunca pagaba la cuenta.
12. Belinda siempre abrazaba y besaba a todo el mundo.
13. Me gustaba el verano más que la primavera.
14. ¿Qué hacías?
15. ¿Adónde iba?
16. ¿Escribías muchas cartas?
17. ¿Estaban José y Marcela en la fiesta?
18. ¿Qué miraba Michael?
19. ¿Con quién bailaba Lourdes?
20. Ayer, llovía todo el día.

EXERCISE 5-11

1. entró, estudiaban *When Jesús came in, the children were studying quietly.*
2. nació, llegué *The day my cousin was born, I arrived at the hospital first.*
3. Eran, empezó *It was five in the afternoon when it began to rain.*
4. estaban, habló *Everyone was very surprised when suddenly Fernando spoke.*
5. viste, llevaba *When you saw Gloria, what coat was she wearing?*
6. tenía, fuimos *I was eight years old when we went to live in Oregon.*
7. leía, tocaba *While Jaime read, his brother played the guitar.*
8. estaba, vino, dijo *One day while you were out, a man came to the house but he didn't tell me his name.*
9. cenaban, empezó, salimos *The other day, while the children were eating, the earth began to tremble and we ran out of the house.*
10. se casó, tenías, fuiste *When your sister got married, you had measles and so you didn't go to the wedding.*

EXERCISE 5-12

1. hacías, empezaron a reír *What were you doing when the students began to laugh?*
2. conoció *Last year, Isabel met Caroline.*
3. No pude *I wasn't able to finish lunch.*
4. supieron, no estaban *The children found out that the candy wasn't in the kitchen.*
5. era, sabía, hacía *When José was young, he never knew what he was doing.*
6. ibas a comprar *What were you going to buy for Carlos's party?*
7. Fue Mary *Did Mary go to the beach with Miguel?*

8. querías *Why didn't you want to choose a bigger hat?*
9. Salieron, no pudieron *They left early because they weren't able to hear the speaker.*
10. Iba a comprar, compré *I was going to buy a horse but I bought a big dog.*
11. vi, vestía *The day I saw Michelle, she was wearing tennis shoes.*
12. Supimos, eran *We found out that Barbara and Luis were brother and sister.*
13. sabía *Timothy always knew the names of all the rivers of the world.*
14. querían levantarse, no quisieron *The boys wanted to get up but they refused to get dressed.*
15. Conocimos, viajabamos *We met your sister when we were traveling in France.*

EXERCISE 5-13

1. contaba *My grandfather always told me stories about his childhood in Mexico.*
2. era, vivía, se llamaba *When he was young, his family lived in a little town called Río Blanco.*
3. se levantaron, se fueron *One day, my grandfather and his older brother got up early and went down to the river.*
4. era *My grandfather's brother was tall, strong, and good-natured.*
5. se enojaba *He never got mad (used to get mad) at anyone.*
6. brillaba, había *That day, the sun was shining and there wasn't a cloud in the sky.*
7. se sentaron *The brothers sat down beside the river.*
8. resbaló, se cayó *Suddenly, my grandfather slipped and fell into the water.*
9. Empezó *He began to yell, "Help! Help! I don't know how to swim."*
10. hizo, gritó *But his brother didn't do anything. "Brother, help me," yelled my grandfather.*
11. contestó *"Help yourself," answered his brother, with his same habitual smile.*
12. entró, se acercó *And then, he calmly entered the water and approached my grandfather.*
13. dejó, vio, había *Then, my grandfather stopped yelling and saw that there was only two feet of water in the river.*

EXERCISE 5-14

1. Estaba lloviendo *It was raining a lot that morning.*
2. estaban mirando *What were they looking at?*
3. ¿Estabas cantando? *Were you singing?*
4. estaban durmiendo *We didn't go in because Juan and Pedro were sleeping.*
5. estaba subiendo *The water was rising fast.*

6. estabas riendo *Why were you laughing so much?*
7. estaba bañándose *José was bathing slowly.*
8. estaba levantándome *At that moment, I was getting up.*
9. estaba diciendo *I wasn't saying anything.*
10. estaba peleando *Who was Emma fighting with?*

RAISE YOUR GRADES

Forms of the preterite

1. busqué, encontré *I looked for my briefcase but I didn't find anything.*
2. estuvieron, salieron *José and Rosa were here for only five minutes and then they left together.*
3. fuimos, tuvimos que *We went because we had to say goodbye to Mr. and Mrs. Smith.*
4. se despertó *Today, the child woke up very late.*
5. se sintieron *My children felt sad after hearing the news.*
6. hicieron, dijeron *The students did all the work and didn't say anything to the teacher.*
7. trajo *Carlos brought some new jazz records.*
8. pidieron *The boys asked the nurse for help.*
9. se murieron *My plants died suddenly.*
10. trabajaron, ganaron *They worked all day, but they didn't earn much.*
11. se divirtió *Leonor didn't have much fun at the concert.*
12. se acercaron *The lions slowly approached the river.*
13. empecé, pude *I began to run, but I couldn't catch up to the bus.*
14. realicé *I never fulfilled my dream of being a violinist.*
15. leyó *Michelle read a novel by Balzac last night.*
16. llegué, llegó *I arrived first and Linda arrived at ten.*
17. Fuimos *We were never fans of horse racing.*
18. tuvieron *In the meeting, you had the opportunity to ask many questions.*
19. durmieron *That night, the women slept badly.*
20. Se vistió, se fue *Carlos got dressed quickly and went out of the house.*

Forms of the imperfect

1. teníamos que *We had to go to bed early every night.*
2. nadaba *When I was young, I swam (used to swim) in the Mississippi every summer.*
3. caían *The leaves fell slowly.*
4. se reían, veían *The children always laughed (used to laugh) when they saw the clowns.*
5. se dormían *The lawyers always slept (used to sleep) in front of the judge.*
6. abría *Mr. Black generally opened his store early.*
7. se callaban, escuchaban *Normally, the men didn't keep quiet or listen attentively to the women.*
8. daban *In the good old days, the bride and groom used to give money to the musicians.*
9. construía *Before, many people built their own house.*
10. me levantaba *When I was young, I got up late on weekends.*
11. destruía, hacía *Whenever Alejandro destroyed the sand castle, Marcela made a bigger one.*
12. tocaba *When I was a little girl, I played (used to play) the piano three hours every day.*
13. decía *She never said (used to say) anything in the Wednesday meetings.*
14. era, era *When I was young, I was a good baseball player.*
15. estaba *Juan was in Mexico when he heard the news.*
16. venía *Nobody ever came (used to come) to our parties.*
17. ponía *My aunt always put the flower vase in the middle of the table.*
18. íbamos *We always went (used to go) to see Buñuel's new movies.*
19. se callaban *When the teacher talked, the students kept quiet.*
20. iba, se divertía *When Pedro went to the circus, he always had a lot of fun.*

The preterite versus the imperfect

1. a, g; abrió, estaba *When Laura opened the door, Beth was singing.*
2. d, b; corría, empezó *While Pepe ran through the street, it began to rain.*
3. a, f; logré, pesaba *I managed to lift the chair because it didn't weigh very much.*
4. a, a; fueron, aprendieron *When my children went to Spain, they learned to speak Spanish very well.*
5. d, d; hablaba, escuchaban *The lawyer spoke while the defendant and the judge listened.*
6. h, a; eran, se cayó *It was five o'clock in the afternoon when the policeman fell off the horse.*
7. d, e; jugaba, llevaba *When José played baseball, he always used to wear a red t-shirt.*
8. f, b, a; Llovía, dejó, volvió *It was raining very hard and therefore Teresa stopped walking and returned home.*
9. f, a; estábamos, nos acostamos *Yesterday, we were very tired and went to bed at nine.*
10. a, b; oyó, empezó *When the child heard the birds for the first time, he began to laugh.*

11. g, b; estaban, dejó *When the construction workers were building the roof, it stopped raining.*
12. f, a; nevaba, fuimos *It was snowing that night and therefore we went by car.*
13. f, e; era, andaba *When Angel was a small child, he used to walk for hours and hours around his father's ranch.*
14. c; fue *Mozart was the most famous composer of the eighteenth century.*
15. f, a; tenía, me puse *I was very cold and therefore I put on a jacket.*

Verbs with special meanings.
1. no quisieron *The workers refused to work after six.*
2. conocieron *Irma and Mario met Fernando last summer.*
3. sabía *I never knew how to make rice well.*
4. pudieron *You were able to lift the armchair because it weighed very little.*
5. tenían que *The boys were supposed to cut the grass.*
6. Supimos *We found out the truth yesterday.*
7. tuve que *I had to study a lot in order to pass the exam.*
8. conocíamos *In the past (before), we used to be familiar with London, but not now (no longer).*
9. fue *The professor went to ask permission from the dean.*
10. Iba *I was going to go to bed early last night.*

6 FUTURE, CONDITIONAL, AND COMPOUND TENSES

6-1. Forms of the Future Tense

A. Regular verbs

The future tense of regular **-ar**, **-er**, and **-ir** verbs is formed by adding the endings **-é, -ás, -á, -emos, -éis, -án** to the infinitive. Note the written accent over all future endings except the first person plural form, **-emos**. The future tense endings cannot be confused with the preterite endings because they are added to the infinitive. Study the following examples.

trabajar, *to work*

yo	trabajar**é**	*I will work*
tú	trabajar**ás**	*you will work*
él, ella } usted	trabajar**á**	*he, she, it will work* *you will work*
nosotros(-as)	trabajar**emos**	*we will work*
vosotros(-as)	trabajar**éis**	*you will work (pl)*
ellos, ellas } ustedes	trabajar**án**	*they will work* *you will work (pl)*

leer, *to read*

yo	leer**é**	*I will read*
tú	leer**ás**	*you will read*
él, ella } usted	leer**á**	*he, she, it will read* *you will read*
nosotros(-as)	leer**emos**	*we will read*
vosotros(-as)	leer**éis**	*you will read (pl)*
ellos, ellas } ustedes	leer**án**	*they will read* *you will read (pl)*

abrir, *to open*

yo	abrir**é**	*I will open*
tú	abrir**ás**	*you will open*

117

él, ella⎫	abrir**á**	*he, she, it will open*
usted ⎭		*you will open*
nosotros(-as)	abrir**emos**	*we will open*
vosotros(-as)	abrir**éis**	*you will open (pl)*
ellos, ellas⎫	abrir**án**	*they will open*
ustedes ⎭		*you will open (pl)*

EXERCISE 6-1: Complete the following sentences by writing in the correct future form of the verb given in parentheses. Remember that reflexive verbs require a reflexive pronoun that must agree with the subject. Answers are at the end of the chapter.

1. (hablar) ¿ _____ usted mañana en el mitin?
2. (vivir) Nosotros _____ muchos años.
3. (dormir) Pronto las niñas _____ .
4. (levantarse) Tengo mucho que hacer; por eso _____ temprano.
5. (sentirse) Si te vas, los estudiantes _____ mal.
6. (bailar) ¿Cuántas horas _____ usted en la fiesta?
7. (comprar) Si recibes el dinero, ¿qué _____ ?
8. (comer) Nosotros _____ mucho.
9. (limpiar) Mi marido _____ la cocina y yo _____ el cuarto de baño.
10. (estudiar) Los muchachos _____ esta noche pero tú no _____ hasta mañana por la tarde.
11. (romper) Vosotros no _____ ni los vasos ni las tazas.
12. (mirar) La maestra _____ despacio la tarea de todos los estudiantes.
13. (ver) José nunca _____ a su novia otra vez.
14. (escribir) ¿ _____ tú mañana a tus padres?
15. (viajar) El verano próximo, vosotros _____ por toda Europa.
16. (comprender) Roberto y Miguel no _____ nunca las quejas de sus amigos.
17. (volver) Mis abuelos _____ mañana.
18. (casarse) ¿Cuándo _____ Leonor y Pedro?
19. (dar) Yo _____ quinientos dólares por aquel coche viejo.
20. (ir) Tú no _____ nunca a Suecia.

B. Irregular verbs

There are twelve verbs that change their stems before adding the future endings.

1. Five verbs drop the **e** of the **-er** infinitive ending.

caber	*to fit*	**cabr**é, **cabr**ás, **cabr**á, **cabr**emos, **cabr**éis, **cabr**án
haber	*to have*	**habr**é, **habr**ás, **habr**á, **habr**emos, **habr**éis, **habr**án
poder	*to be able*	**podr**é, **podr**ás, **podr**á, **podr**emos, **podr**éis, **podr**án
querer	*to want, to love*	**querr**é, **querr**ás, **querr**á, **querr**emos, **querr**éis, **querr**án
saber	*to know*	**sabr**é, **sabr**ás, **sabr**á, **sabr**emos, **sabr**éis, **sabr**án

2. Five verbs replace the vowel of the **-er** and **-ir** infinitive endings with **d**.

poner	*to put, to place*	**pondr**é, **pondr**ás, **pondr**á, **pondr**emos, **pondr**éis, **pondr**án
salir	*to leave*	**saldr**é, **saldr**ás, **saldr**á, **saldr**emos, **saldr**éis, **saldr**án
tener	*to have*	**tendr**é, **tendr**ás, **tendr**á, **tendr**emos, **tendr**éis, **tendr**án
valer	*to be worth*	**valdr**é, **valdr**ás, **valdr**á, **valdr**emos, **valdr**éis, **valdr**án
venir	*to come*	**vendr**é, **vendr**ás, **vendr**á, **vendr**emos, **vendr**éis, **vendr**án

3. The future stem of **decir** is **dir-**, and the future stem of **hacer** is **har-**. Study these verbs carefully. Note that even though the stem is irregular, the future endings are the same.

decir   *to say, to tell*   **dir**é, **dir**ás, **dir**á, **dir**emos, **dir**éis, **dir**án
hacer   *to do, to make*   **har**é, **har**ás, **har**á, **har**emos, **har**éis, **har**án

EXERCISE 6-2: Answer the following questions with a verb in the future tense, using the answer cue given in parentheses. Answers are at the end of the chapter.

Example: ¿Podrás llegar temprano? (sí)   *Sí, podré llegar temprano.*

1. ¿A qué hora vendrás mañana? (a las cinco)

2. ¿Qué dirás mañana en la reunión? (muchas cosas importantes)

3. ¿Vendrán Cecilia y Jane a la cena? (no)

4. No querrás cantar en la fiesta? (no)

5. ¿Cuándo podrás dejar el trabajo? (en la primavera)

6. ¿Tendrás que levantarte temprano mañana? (sí)

7. ¿Podrá usted acostarse pronto? (no)

8. ¿Saldrán ustedes a las ocho? (sí)

9. ¿Qué querrán comer los niños? (hamburguesas y helado)

10. ¿Cuánto valdrá la casa en cinco años? (mucho más)

11. ¿Cuántos errores harás en el examen? (pocos)

12. ¿Qué dirá el jefe? (nada)

13. ¿Cabremos todos en el coche? (no)

14. ¿Sabrás lo que tendrás que hacer? (sí)

15. ¿Saldréis vosotros antes que Julia? (sí)

6-2. Use of the Future Tense

A. **The future tense is used to express two different meanings.**

   1. *Future time.* In Spanish, as in English, the future tense is used to indicate an action, event, or condition that will take place in the future.

      Iré temprano a tu casa mañana.   *I'll go to your house early tomorrow.*

   2. *Present probability.* The future tense is used to express the possibility of an action or event that might be occurring in the present.

      ¿Qué hora **será**?   { *What time might it be?*
                            { *What time do you suppose it is?*

      Serán las once.   { *It must be eleven o'clock.*
                         { *It's probably eleven o'clock.*

¿Qué **tendrá** ese muchacho?

$$\left\{\begin{array}{l}\textit{What could be the matter with that boy?}\\\textit{What do you suppose is the matter with}\\\quad\textit{that boy?}\end{array}\right.$$

Tendrá un dolor de cabeza.

$$\left\{\begin{array}{l}\textit{He must have a headache.}\\\textit{He probably has a headache.}\end{array}\right.$$

B. **The future of** *haber*
   1. The future form of **haber**, **habrá**, means *there will be.*

      Habrá mucha gente en el cine.   *There will be a lot of people at the movies.*

   2. **Habrá que** + the infinitive means *it will be necessary.*

      Habrá que cortar el césped primero.   *It will be necessary to cut the grass first.*

C. **The future progressive tense**

   The future progressive tense is formed by conjugating **estar**, *to be*, in the future tense + the present participle. Like the future tense, it also has two meanings.

   1. *Specific future time period.* The future progressive is used to indicate an event or action that will take place at a specific moment or during a specific time period in the future.

      Mañana **estaré estudiando**.   *Tomorrow I'll be studying.*

   2. *Present probability.* The future progressive is used to suggest probability or conjecture concerning an event taking place in the present.

      ¿Qué **estarán pensando** de nosotros?   *What do you suppose they're thinking about us?*

EXERCISE 6-3:   Complete the following sentences by changing the verb from the preterite to the future tense. Pay attention to the placement of reflexive pronouns if the verb is reflexive. Answers are at the end of the chapter.

Example: Ayer fui a la biblioteca. Mañana, *iré a la biblioteca* otra vez.

   1. El invierno pasado, tuve que comprar un coche nuevo. Este verano, _____ también.
   2. Pagamos la cuenta la semana pasada. La semana próxima, _____ otra vez.
   3. Ayer vinieron mis primos y mis tíos. Mañana, _____ otra vez.
   4. El año pasado, Angel trajo su guitarra a la fiesta. Este año, _____ otra vez.
   5. Ayer, nadie dijo nada en la reunión. Pasado mañana, _____ tampoco.
   6. El sábado pasado me levanté muy temprano. El sábado próximo, _____ también.
   7. Los estudiantes dieron un regalo a la maestra el año pasado. En navidades, _____ también.
   8. Ayer hice un pastel de manzana. Este fin de semana, _____ también.
   9. La última vez, Jorge e Isabel salieron muy temprano. Esta vez, _____ también.
   10. ¿Cuánto valió aquella casa en 1980? ¿Cuánto _____ en 1990?
   11. José Luis tuvo fiebre ayer. José Luis no _____ mañana.
   12. Yo nunca conocí a una estrella de cine. Yo nunca _____ .
   13. ¿Cuánto dió Pepe por aquel coche? ¿Cuánto _____ ?

14. ¿Con quiénes fueron los muchachos? ¿Con quiénes _____ ?
15. ¿Qué tuviste que estudiar para el examen? ¿Qué _____ ?

6-3. Forms of the Conditional

A. Regular verbs

The conditional of regular **-ar**, **-er**, and **-ir** verbs is formed by adding the endings **-ía**, **-ías**, **-ía**, **-íamos**, **-íais**, **-ían** to the infinitive. Note the written accent over the **í** in all forms. The conditional cannot be confused with the imperfect because the endings are added to the infinitive. Study the following examples.

trabajar, *to work*

yo	trabajaría	*I would work*
tú	trabajarías	*you would work*
él, ella usted	trabajaría	*he, she, it would work* *you would work*
nosotros(-as)	trabajaríamos	*we would work*
vosotros(-as)	trabajaríais	*you would work (pl)*
ellos, ellas ustedes	trabajarían	*they would work* *you would work (pl)*

leer, *to read*

yo	leería	*I would read*
tú	leerías	*you would read*
él, ella usted	leería	*he, she, it would read* *you would read*
nosotros(-as)	leeríamos	*we would read*
vosotros(-as)	leeríais	*you would read (pl)*
ellos, ellas ustedes	leerían	*they would read* *you would read (pl)*

abrir, *to open*

yo	abriría	*I would open*
tú	abrirías	*you would open*
él, ella usted	abriría	*he, she, it would open* *you would open*
nosotros(-as)	abriríamos	*we would open*
vosotros(-as)	abriríais	*you would open (pl)*
ellos, ellas ustedes	abrirían	*they would open* *you would open (pl)*

B. Irregular verbs

The same verbs that are irregular in the future tense are also irregular in the conditional. Study the following conjugations carefully. Note that both the future and the conditional endings are added to the *same* irregular stems.

caber	*to fit*	**cabría, cabrías, cabría, cabríamos, cabríais, cabrían**
decir	*to say, to tell*	**diría, dirías, diría, diríamos, diríais, dirían**
haber	*to have*	**habría, habrías, habría, habríamos, habríais, habrían**
hacer	*to do, to make*	**haría, harías, haría, haríamos, haríais, harían**
poder	*to be able*	**podría, podrías, podría, podríamos, podríais, podrían**
poner	*to put, to place*	**pondría, pondrías, pondría, pondríamos, pondríais, pondrían**
querer	*to want, to love*	**querría, querrías, querría, querríamos, querríais, querrían**
saber	*to know*	**sabría, sabrías, sabría, sabríamos, sabríais, sabrían**
salir	*to leave*	**saldría, saldrías, saldría, saldríamos, saldríais, saldrían**

tener	*to have*	**tendría, tendrías, tendría, tendríamos, tendríais, tendrían**
valer	*to be worth*	**valdría, valdrías, valdría, valdríamos, valdríais, valdrían**
venir	*to come*	**vendría, vendrías, vendría, vendríamos, vendríais, vendrían**

EXERCISE 6-4: Rewrite the following statements as questions, changing the verb from the present tense to the conditional. Remember that questions are formed by reversing the order of the subject and verb. Subject pronouns are usually omitted, except for the use of **usted**. For a review of interrogative syntax, see Chapter 3, Section 3-8. Answers are at the end of the chapter.

Example: José va todos los días al museo.　*¿Iría José todos los días al museo?*

1. Miguel bebe café con leche.

2. Tú hablas con todo el mundo.

3. Tenemos que descansar antes de ir.

4. Este terreno vale mucho dinero.

5. Usted puede venir a las seis.

6. María se siente triste.

7. Los estudiantes leen libros de historia.

8. Los abuelos van a la playa.

9. Alicia se enoja con David.

10. Usted viene más tarde.

11. Vosotros coméis pescado.

12. Ellos escriben una carta todos los días.

13. Los estudiantes esperan al maestro.

14. Tú haces lo mismo que yo.

15. Usted pone el mantel blanco.

6-4. Use of the Conditional

A. **The conditional is used to indicate the possibility of an action that is related to specific circumstances.**

Possible Action	Related Circumstances
Me **gustaría** ir	contigo al cine.
I would like to go	*with you to the movies.*
Yo **bebería** leche	pero no hay.
I would drink milk	*but there isn't any.*
Ella **llamaría** al médico	en caso de emergencia.
She would call the doctor	*in case of an emergency.*

B. **The conditional is used to express the probability that an action occurred in the past.**

> Después de viajar tantas horas, **estarían** cansados.
> *After traveling so many hours, they were probably tired (OR they must have been tired).*

C. **The use of the future versus the conditional.**

1. The future tense is used in a dependent clause following a present tense main clause.

Main Clause—Present	Dependent Clause—Future
El jefe **dice**	que todos **tendrán** que salir.
The boss says	*that everyone will have to leave.*
María **promete**	que ellos **llegarán** a la hora.
María promises	*that they will arrive on time.*

2. The conditional is used in a dependent clause following a past tense main clause.

Main Clause—Preterite	Dependent Clause—Conditional
El jefe **dijo**	que todos **tendrían** que salir.
The boss said	*that everyone would have to leave.*
María **prometió**	que ellos **llegarían** a la hora.
María promised	*that they would arrive on time.*

D. **The conditional of *haber***

1. The conditional form of **haber**, **habría**, means *there would be.*

> El director dijo que **habría** cincuenta   *The director said that there would*
> personas en la reunión.   *be fifty people at the meeting.*

2. **Habría que** + the infinitive means *it would be necessary to.*

> **Habría que hablar** con el señor Blanco.   *It would be necessary to talk to*
> *Mr. Blanco.*

E. **The conditional progressive**

The conditional progressive is formed by conjugating **estar** in the conditional + the present participle.

> Andrew dijo que **estaría trabajando**   *Andrew said that he would be working*
> tarde.   *late.*

EXERCISE 6-5: Rewrite the following sentences by changing the verb of the main clause from the present to the preterite, and the verb of the dependent clause from the future to the conditional. Before beginning the exercise, study the example carefully. Answers are at the end of the chapter.

> Example: La maestra dice que terminará pronto.   *La maestra dijo que terminaría pronto.*

1. Los niños prometen que comerán mucho.

2. Mi padre dice que estará en casa temprano.

3. La maestra insiste en que habrá que leer *Hamlet*.

4. Los obreros declaran que ya no trabajarán.

5. El señor Moreno decide lo que habrá que comprar.

6. Creo que tendremos que darnos prisa.

7. La señora Black dice que se irá a dormir a las once.

8. Usted piensa que nadie vendrá a la fiesta, ¿verdad?

9. José cree que lloverá mucho.

10. Todos dicen que querrán postre.

6-5. Forms of the Past Participle

In English, the past participle usually ends in *-ed*, as in *walked* or *cooked*. However, there are also many irregular past participles, such as *written*, *read*, or *done*. Spanish also has both regular and irregular past participles.

A. Regular past participles

The past participle of all **-ar** verbs is formed by dropping the infinitive ending and adding **-ado** to the infinitive stem. The past participle of regular **-er** and **-ir** verbs is formed by dropping the infinitive ending and adding **-ido** to the infinitive stem. Study the following examples.

amar	*to love*	am**ado**	*loved*
comer	*to eat*	com**ido**	*eaten*
vivir	*to live*	viv**ido**	*lived*

B. Irregular past participles

1. *Past participles ending in* **-to**.

abrir	*to open*	abier**to**	*opened*
cubrir	*to cover*	cubier**to**	*covered*
descubrir	*to discover*	descubier**to**	*discovered*
freír	*to fry*	fri**to**	*fried*
morir	*to die*	muer**to**	*dead*
poner	*to put*	pues**to**	*put*
resolver	*to resolve*	resuel**to**	*resolved*
romper	*to break*	ro**to**	*broken*
ver	*to see*	vis**to**	*seen*
volver	*to return*	vuel**to**	*returned*

> **NOTE:** The **-to** ending is always added to a changed stem. Be careful to study the entire word.

2. *Past participles ending in* **-cho**.

decir	*to say, to tell*	di**cho**	*said, told*
hacer	*to do, to make*	he**cho**	*done, made*
satisfacer	*to satisfy*	satisfe**cho**	*satisfied*

> **NOTE:** Some verbs such as **caer, creer. leer, oír,** and **traer** require an accent over the í of **-ído**: caído: caído, creído, leído, oído, traído. The past participle of **ir** is **ido.**

EXERCISE 6-6: Write in the past participle and the English translation for the following verbs. Answers are at the end of the chapter.

Example: estudiar *estudiado, studied*

1. decir_____
2. cortar_____
3. poner_____
4. acostar_____

5. creer_____
6. cantar_____
7. comer_____
8. establecer_____

9. ser _____
10. dar _____
11. dormir _____
12. despertar _____
13. tener _____
14. poder _____
15. hacer _____
16. escribir _____
17. romper _____

18. crear _____
19. averiguar _____
20. leer _____
21. ver _____
22. herir _____
23. llover _____
24. estar _____
25. volver _____

6-6. Forms of the Compound Tenses in the Indicative

In English, the compound tenses are formed with the auxiliary verb *to have* + the past participle: *I have read, he had slept,* etc. In Spanish, the compound tenses are also formed by conjugating the auxiliary verb **haber**, *to have* + the past participle. In Spanish, the conjugated form of **haber** is used only to form the compound tenses. There are five compound tenses in the indicative. The compound tenses in the subjunctive are discussed in Chapter 7.

A. The present perfect tense

The present perfect tense is formed by conjugating **haber** in the present tense + the past participle. Study the following chart, paying careful attention to the English translations.

yo	**he**	amado / comido / vivido	*I*	*have*	*loved / eaten / lived*
tú	**has**	amado / comido / vivido	*you*	*have*	*loved / eaten / lived*
él, ella / usted	**ha**	amado / comido / vivido	*he, she, it / you*	*has / have*	*loved / eaten / lived*
nosotros(-as)	**hemos**	amado / comido / vivido	*we*	*have*	*loved / eaten / lived*
vosotros(-as)	**habéis**	amado / comido / vivido	*you (pl)*	*have*	*loved / eaten / lived*
ellos, ellas / ustedes	**han**	amado / comido / vivido	*they / you (pl)*	*have*	*loved / eaten / lived*

EXERCISE 6-7: Translate the English verb forms given in parentheses into Spanish. First, locate the subject of the sentence. Remember that the verb **haber** must be conjugated to agree with the subject, and that the past participle does not change. Answers are at the end of the chapter.

1. Yo (have gone) a la playa. _____
2. Marianela (has eaten) tres langostas. _____
3. Mi padre (has said) lo mismo muchas veces. _____
4. Nosotros (have sung) aquella canción en todas las reuniones. _____
5. Ustedes (have seen) cosas raras en su vida. _____
6. José nunca (has made) tantos errores. _____
7. Los estudiantes todavía no (have finished) *Don Quixote.* _____
8. Vosotros (have heard) la noticia, ¿verdad? _____
9. Tú (have been able) contestar todas las preguntas. _____

10. Yo (have been) estudiante durante toda la vida. _____

11. El señor Black (has opened) el restaurán temprano. _____

12. Ustedes (have broken) mi silla favorita. _____

13. Vosotros (have arrived) demasiado tarde. _____

14. Los muchachos (have promised) limpiar bien la cocina. _____

15. Tú (have worked) con ella antes, ¿verdad? _____

B. The pluperfect tense

The pluperfect tense, el **pluscuamperfecto**, is formed by conjugating **haber** in the imperfect tense + the past participle. Study the following chart, paying careful attention to the English translations.

yo	**había**	trabajado aprendido recibido	*I*	*had*	*worked* *learned* *received*	
tú	**habías**	trabajado aprendido recibido	*you*	*had*	*worked* *learned* *received*	
él, ella} usted	**había**	trabajado aprendido recibido	*he, she, it}* *you*	*had*	*worked* *learned* *received*	
nosotros(-as)	**habíamos**	trabajado aprendido recibido	*we*	*had*	*worked* *learned* *received*	
vosotros(-as)	**habíais**	trabajado aprendido recibido	*you (pl)*	*had*	*worked* *learned* *received*	
ellos, ellas} ustedes	**habían**	trabajado aprendido recibido	*they* *you (pl)}*	*had*	*worked* *learned* *received*	

> **NOTE:** The preterite perfect (**hube comido, hubiste hablado**, etc.) is never used in spoken Spanish or in ordinary written communication, such as letters or reports. It is used strictly in literary works.

Luego que **hube terminado** de hablar, el público irrumpió en aplausos.	*As soon as I had finished speaking, the public broke into applause.*

EXERCISE 6-8: Write in the correct pluperfect form of the verb given in parentheses. First, find the subject of the sentence and make sure that the conjugated form of **haber** agrees with it. Answers are at the end of the chapter.

Example: (trabajar) Mario *había trabajado* mucho.

1. (hacer) Yo _____ el trabajo.
2. (leer) Los estudiantes _____ la mitad del libro de texto.
3. (publicar) El poeta _____ sus poemas a una edad temprana.
4. (saber) Nosotros _____ la verdad.
5. (salir) Ustedes ya _____ cuando llegaron los músicos.
6. (pagar) Yo siempre _____ mis deudas rápidamente.
7. (jugar) Los niños _____ durante muchas horas.
8. (escribir) Vosotros _____ bastantes cartas el año pasado
9. (poder) Ustedes no _____ asistir al partido de béisbol.
10. (ver) Nosotros _____ París en el año 1968.

C. The future perfect tense

The future perfect tense is formed by conjugating **haber** in the future tense + the past participle. Study the following chart, paying careful attention to the English translations.

yo	**habré**	acabado / leído / salido	*I*	*will have*	*finished / read / left*
tú	**habrás**	acabado / leído / salido	*you*	*will have*	*finished / read / left*
él, ella / usted	**habrá**	acabado / leído / salido	*he, she it / you*	*will have*	*finished / read / left*
nosotros(-as)	**habremos**	acabado / leído / salido	*we*	*will have*	*finished / read / left*
vosotros(-as)	**habréis**	acabado / leído / salido	*you (pl)*	*will have*	*finished / read / left*
ellos, ellas / ustedes	**habrán**	acabado / leído / salido	*they / you (pl)*	*will have*	*finished / read / left*

> **REMEMBER:** In the future tense, there is a written accent over all final vowels except for the first person plural, **habremos**.

EXERCISE 6-9: Locate the subject of the sentence. Then translate the English verb forms given in parentheses into Spanish. Answers are at the end of the chapter.

Example: Para entonces, ellos (will have left). <u>*habrán salido*</u>.
1. Yo (will have slept) doce horas. _____
2. Para mañana, nosotros (will have seen) todo lo que podemos ver. ____
3. Creo que Andrew (will have eaten) todo el helado. _____
4. Ustedes (will have done) las cosas más urgentes. _____
5. Para la primavera, los estudiantes (will have finished) el proyecto. __
6. Para mañana, ellos (will have made) muchas llamadas telefónicas. __
7. Vosotras (will have gone) tres veces a España. _____
8. Ellos (will have heard) la noticia ya. _____
9. La señora Rojas (will have closed) la tienda. _____
10. Tú (will have broken) todas las reglas del juego. _____

D. The conditional perfect tense

The conditional perfect tense is formed by conjugating **haber** in the conditional + the past participle. Study the following chart, paying careful attention to the English translations.

yo	**habría**	dejado / tenido / sufrido	*I*	*would have*	*left / had / suffered*
tú	**habrías**	dejado / tenido / sufrido	*you*	*would have*	*left / had / suffered*
él, ella / usted	**habría**	dejado / tenido / sufrido	*he, she, it / you*	*would have*	*left / had / suffered*

nosotros(-as)	**habríamos**	dejado tenido sufrido	*we*		*would have*	left had suffered
vosotros(-as)	**habríais**	dejado tenido sufrido	*you (pl)*		*would have*	left had suffered
ellos, ellas ustedes	**habrían**	dejado tenido sufrido	*they you (pl)*		*would have*	left had suffered

EXERCISE 6-10: Locate the subject of the sentence. Then write in the correct conditional perfect form of the verb given in parentheses. Answers are at the end of the chapter.

Example: (estar) Yo *habría estado* en casa a tiempo pero no era posible.
1. (decir) En este caso, yo no _____ nada.
2. (dejar) En esa ocasión, nosotros _____ una propina más grande.
3. (preferir) Los estudiantes _____ leer una novela más corta que *La guerra y la paz.*
4. (tener) El verano pasado, tú _____ más tiempo.
5. (trabajar) Las muchachas _____ más que los muchachos.
6. (hacer) Vosotros _____ el mismo error.
7. (salir) En caso de lluvia, todos _____ temprano.

6-7. Use of the Compound Tenses

The use of the compound tenses in Spanish should present few problems to you because they are used in the same circumstances as in English. The main differences are syntactical changes in questions and negative statements.

A. Questions using the compound tenses

In English, the subject of the question is placed between the auxiliary verb and the past participle: *Have you eaten yet?* In Spanish, the conjugated form of the auxiliary verb **haber** is never separated from the past participle under any circumstances. Study the following examples. Pay close attention to the placement of the Spanish equivalent of adverbs such as *ever* and *yet.*

¿**Has probado** anguilas alguna vez?	*Have you ever tried eels?*
¿**Han salido** ya los niños?	*Have the children left already?*
¿**Has visitado** Madrid ya?	*Have you visited Madrid already?*
¿**Había fumado** Antonio durante muchos años?	*Had Antonio smoked for many years?*

B. Negative statements using the compound tenses

Negative statements using the compound tenses are formed in the same way as all negative statements. The negative is placed before the conjugated form of **haber.** Study the following examples.

Tú **no has comido** nada todavía.	*You haven't eaten anything yet.*
¿**No habían visto** ya tus padres el museo?	*Hadn't your parents already seen the museum?*
Yo **no he podido** trabajar mucho todavía.	*I haven't been able to work much yet.*

C. Reflexive verbs in the compound tenses

The reflexive pronoun is almost always placed directly before the conjugated form of the auxiliary verb **haber.** In a negative sentence, the negative is placed directly before the reflexive pronoun. If the complete verb form contains either an infinitive or a present participle, the reflexive pronoun can be attached to the end of the infinitive or present participle. In these instances, the negative comes before the auxiliary verb **haber**. Study the following examples.

Affirmative

{ Mario **se había levantado** temprano aquella mañana.
Mario had gotten up early that morning.

Negative

{ Mario **no se había levantado** temprano aquella mañana.
Mario had not gotten up early that morning.

Infinitive

{ Me **he tenido que levantar** temprano toda la semana.
OR
He tenido que levantarme temprano toda la semana.
I've had to get up early all week.

Present Participle

{ **Nos hemos estado preocupando** mucho de Elena.
OR
Hemos estado preocupándonos mucho de Elena.
We've been worrying a lot about Elena.

D. *Poder* and *deber* + the compound tenses

Poder and **deber** are conjugated in the imperfect with **haber** + the past participle to express the idea of "what might have been." Study the following examples and their English equivalents carefully.

Yo **podía haber dormido** veinticuatro horas seguidas.

I could have slept twenty-four hours straight.

No **debíamos haber salido** tan pronto.

We shouldn't have left so soon.

Me **podía haber levantado** a las seis.
OR
Podía haberme levantado a las seis.

{ *I could have gotten up at six.*

EXERCISE 6-11: Translate the following English sentences into Spanish using the correct form of the auxiliary verb **haber** + the past participle of the verb given in parentheses. Answers are at the end of the chapter.

Example: (terminar) Have you (*usted*) finished your soup? *¿Ha terminado usted la sopa?*

1. (estar) Have you (*tú*) been sick long?

2. (probar) Have you (*ustedes*) tried the salad?

3. (ver) I have never seen Paris.

4. (salir) I should have left earlier.

5. (comer) I could have eaten more rice.

6. (leer) She hasn't read *Don Quixote* yet.

7. (casarse) He has never gotten married.

8. (decir) You (*usted*) have always told the truth.

9. (levantarse) The children had gotten up too early.

10. (lavarse) We have already washed our hands.

11. (ponerse) I should have worn a hat.

12. (enfadarse) He has never gotten mad easily.

13. (quejarse) Have you (*tú*) ever complained?

14. (escuchar) Haven't you (*vosotros*) ever listened to Miguel?

15. (ir) Have you (*usted*) ever gone to Australia?

6-8. The Passive Voice

The passive voice is used when an action occurs and the doer of the action is omitted; for example, *The letter was written*. There are two passive constructions in Spanish.

A. The passive construction with *se*

1. *The impersonal subject* **se**. Study the following comparison of active and passive constructions. Note that in the passive construction, the verb must agree in number with the subject being acted upon. The impersonal subject **se** remains the same in both the singular and the plural.

Active—The doer of the action is present.
Juan rompió la jarra.   *Juan broke the pitcher.*
Juan y Carlos rompieron la jarra.   *Juan and Carlos broke the pitcher.*

Passive—The doer of the action is absent.
Se rompió la jarra.   *The pitcher was broken.*
Se rompieron las jarras.   *The pitchers were broken.*

EXERCISE 6-12: Change the following statements from the active to the passive voice. First, eliminate the doer of the action and substitute **se**. Then change the verb, if necessary, to agree in number with the subject being acted upon.

Examples: Los niños bebieron la leche.   *Se bebió la leche.*
               Yo hablo italiano y francés.   *Se hablan italiano y francés.*

1. Jorge comió el pastel.

2. Los estudiantes leyeron la novela.

3. Caruso cantó las operas de Verdi.

4. Carlos no hizo ningún error.

5. Hablo inglés.

6. No hablo italiano.

7. El jefe abrió el restaurán a las cinco.

8. Recibimos los recados.

9. Luisa cuenta historias muy extrañas.

10. No dije nada.

11. Alguien perdió un guante.

12. Manuel no compró mi libro.

13. Los muchachos limpiaron la cocina.

14. La lluvia manchó los muebles.

15. No ganaste el partido.

2. *Other impersonal expressions using* ***se***. **Se** + the third person singular of a verb also means *one, people, they, it is,* and so on. Study the following examples and their possible translations.

Se dice que ganarán los Dodgers.
They say
People say } *that the Dodgers will win.*
It is said

No **se sale** de aquí sin pagar un dineral.
You don't leave here
People don't leave here } *without paying a*
One doesn't leave here } *lot of money.*

> **REMEMBER:** This construction uses only the third person singular form of the verb.

EXERCISE 6-13: Translate the following Spanish sentences into English. Supply the two best possible translations. Answers are at the end of the chapter.

1. Se dice que irá mucha gente a la fiesta.

2. Aquí se habla solamente español.

3. No se aprende sin estudiar.

4. Se prohibe fumar aquí.

5. Se cree que alguien mató a Mozart.

B. The passive construction with *ser* + the past participle

The conjugated form of **ser** + the past participle is used when the doer of the action is present in the sentence. This construction of the passive voice is nearly identical to the English construction. Since the past participle is considered an adjective in this construction, it must agree in number and gender with the subject. Study the following examples.

La carta **fue escrita** por el maestro.
The letter was written by the teacher.

Las casas **son pintadas** por el dueño una vez al año.
The houses are painted by the owner once a year.

El horario **fue decidido** por la Sra. Sánchez.
The schedule was decided by Mrs. Sánchez.

Los crímenes **serán investigados** por la policía.
The crimes will be investigated by the police.

> **NOTE:** Verbs that express feeling, such as **querer**, *to want or to love*, **amar**, *to love*, and **admirar**, *to admire*, require the preposition **de** rather than **por: Juanita es admirada de todos.** *Juanita is admired by everyone.*

EXERCISE 6-14: Use the expression given in parentheses to change the following sentences from the passive construction with **se** to the passive construction with **ser** + the past participle. Answers are at the end of the chapter.

Examples: Se abrieron todas las ventanas. (por mi hermano)
Todas las ventanas fueron abiertas por mi hermano.
Se corta el césped con frecuencia. (por el vecino)
El césped es cortado con frecuencia por el vecino.

1. Se construyó el puente el año pasado. (por el ingeniero)

2. Se discutirá el asunto mañana. (por el jefe)

3. Se leyó una obra de Shakespeare el semestre pasado. (por los estudiantes)

4. Se escucha todo. (por los niños)

5. Se jugó un buen partido. (por todos)

6. Se cambiaron las llaves de la casa. (por Jorge)

7. Anoche, se dijeron muchas tonterías. (por tus hermanos)

8. Se compraron los muebles en aquella tienda. (por el Sr. White)

9. Se comieron los pasteles. (por Jaime)

10. Se anunciarán los premios la semana que viene. (por la maestra)

SUMMARY

1. The future tense endings are **-é, -ás, -á, -emos, -éis, -án**. Both regular and irregular verbs use the same endings in the future tense.

2. The future tense of regular **-ar**, **-er**, and **-ir** verbs is formed by adding the future endings to the infinitive. There are twelve verbs with irregular future stems that must be memorized.

3. The future tense is used to express both future time and probability in the present. For example, **María estará enferma** can mean *María will be sick (later)* or *María must be sick (now)*. The meaning depends on the context of the sentence.

4. The future form of **haber**, **habrá**, means *there will be*. **Habrá que** + infinitive means *it will be necessary to*.

5. The future progressive tense is formed by conjugating **estar** in the future tense + the present participle. It is used to indicate an event or action that will take place at a specific future time or to express probability or conjecture in the present.

6. The conditional endings are **-ía, -ías, -ía, -íamos, -íais, -ían**. These endings are added to the infinitive of regular verbs. The same twelve verbs that are irregular in the future tense are irregular in the conditional.

7. The meaning of the conditional is expressed in English by the auxiliary verb, *would*: **Tendríamos que salir temprano**; *We would have to leave early*. The conditional can also express probability that an action occurred in the past. For example, **María estaría enferma** can mean *María would be sick* or *María must have been sick*.

8. When the main clause of a sentence is followed by a dependent clause, a present tense main clause is followed by a future tense dependent clause. A past tense main clause is followed by a conditional tense dependent clause.

9. The conditional form of **haber**, **habría**, means *there would be*. **Habría que** + infinitive means *it would be necessary to*.

10. The conditional progressive tense is formed by conjugating **estar** in the conditional + the present participle. **Carmen dijo que hoy estaría estudiando en casa.** *Carmen said that she would be studying at home today.*

11. The past participle ending of regular **-ar** verbs is **-ado**: **amado**, *loved*. The past participle ending of regular **-er** and **-ir** verbs is **-ido**: **comido**, *eaten*; **vivido**, *lived*.

12. There are some irregular past participles ending in **-to** and **-cho** that must be memorized.

13. The compound tenses are formed by conjugating the auxiliary verb **haber**, *to have*, + the past participle. The compound tenses include all tenses in the indicative and the subjunctive. There are five compound tenses in the indicative. Shown below is an

example of **haber escrito**, *to have written*, conjugated in the first person singular indicative of the compound tenses.

Present perfect	**he escrito**	*I have written*
Pluperfect	**había escrito**	*I had written*
Future perfect	**habré escrito**	*I will have written*
Conditional perfect	**habría escrito**	*I would have written*
Preterite perfect	**hube escrito**	*I had written*

Remember that the preterite perfect is a written form only and is very rarely used.

14. The meanings of the compound tenses in Spanish are practically the same as in English: **Nunca he escrito al presidente**; *I have never written to the president.* However, as the example shows, there are some differences in syntax. The most important thing to remember is that the auxiliary verb and the past participle, **he escrito**, form the complete verb and can never be separated by a negative or a pronoun.

15. There are two constructions of the passive voice. The most commonly used construction is **se** + the verb + the subject acted upon: **Se pagó la cuenta**; *The bill was paid.* **Se** is also used in impersonal expressions such as *one, it is, they,* etc. For example, **se dice** can mean *it is said, they say, one says,* or *you say.*

16. When the doer of the action is present, the passive construction used is subject + **ser** + the past participle + **por** ___. In this construction, the past participle is used as an adjective and must agree with the subject in number and gender: **La cuenta fue pagada por Emilio**; *The bill was paid by Emilio.* Verbs that express feeling require the preposition **de** rather than **por**: **Arturo es amado de las niñas**; *Arturo is loved by the girls.*

RAISE YOUR GRADES

☑ **Future and conditional forms** [Sections 6-1 and 6-3]

Write in the correct form of the verb given in parentheses, according to the tense specified. Remember that there are twelve verbs with irregular stems in the future and conditional. Answers are at the end of the chapter.

Example: (quedarse, fut.) Mañana, yo *me quedaré* en casa.

1. (beber, cond.) Los niños _____ leche, pero no hay.
2. (tener, cond.) En ese caso, yo no _____ nada que decir.
3. (escribir, fut.) Nosotros _____ a mamá la semana que viene.
4. (casarse, fut.) Ellos _____, pero quieren esperar hasta mayo.
5. (salir, fut.) Vosotros _____ pronto, ¿verdad?
6. (valer, cond.) Mi casa _____ mucho más dinero, pero no tiene piscina.
7. (conocer, fut.) Mañana, tú _____ a toda la familia.
8. (empezar, cond.) Ellos dijeron que _____ tarde.
9. (decir, fut.) Seguramente, las muchachas no _____ nada.
10. (hacer, cond.) ¿Qué _____ tú en mi caso?
11. (saber, fut.) Mañana, todo el mundo _____ la verdad.
12. (abrir, fut.) ¿Quién _____ la sesión?
13. (sentarse, fut.) Nosotros _____ aquí.
14. (irse, cond.) Yo _____ ahora mismo pero no puedo.
15. (romper, cond.) Los niños _____ los platos.
16. (callarse, fut.) ¿Cuándo _____ aquel hombre?
17. (levantarse, fut.) ¿A qué hora _____ tus padres?
18. (tener, fut.) ¿Qué _____ usted que hacer mañana?
19. (ser, cond.) No _____ mala idea ir al cine esta noche.
20. (querer, fut.) ¿Qué _____ comer vosotros?

☑ **Sequence of tenses with future and conditional** [Section 6-4]

Select the correct verb from those given in parentheses to complete the following sentences. Remember, in dependent clauses, the future tense follows the present and the conditional follows the past tenses. Answers are at the end of the chapter.

1. María y Ana dijeron que (harán, harían) el postre.
2. Mis padres insistieron en que (habrá que, habría que) llegar a casa antes de las once.
3. Los novios piensan que (se casarán, se casarían) en el mes de junio.
4. Mi hermana creía que nadie (vendrá, vendría) a verle.
5. Dices que ellos (tendrán que, tendrían que) pagar las entradas.
6. El jefe afirma que (podremos, podríamos) salir temprano el sábado.
7. Usted dice que las tiendas (estarán, estarían) abiertas hasta las nueve.
8. Mis padres creen que (haremos, haríamos) demasiado ruido.
9. Luisa prometió que (se acostará, se acostaría) a las diez.
10. Raúl dice que (estará, estaría) jugando con sus primos.

☑ **The past participle** [Section 6-5]

Complete the following sentences by writing in the past participle form of the verb given in parentheses. Answers are at the end of the chapter.

1. (querer) He _____ hablar con ella desde hace mucho tiempo.
2. (poder) No hemos _____ conseguir entradas para el concierto.
3. (estar) Ella ha _____ viviendo en México.
4. (romper) Julia ha _____ las ventanas.
5. (ver) Vosotros habéis _____ el Mediterráneo, ¿verdad?
6. (escuchar) Nunca habían _____ una conferencia tan interesante.
7. (abrir) ¿Has _____ mis cartas?
8. (decir) He _____ a todos que a las siete vamos a cenar.
9. (morir) Ha _____ el canario de la tía Marcela.
10. (poner) ¿No han _____ ustedes la mesa todavía?
11. (freír) El cocinero ha _____ dos pollos.
12. (volver) Las golondrinas han _____ a Capistrano.
13. (dormir) Los chicos no han _____ bastante.
14. (resolver) Vosotros todavía no habéis _____ vuestros problemas.
15. (hacer) No hemos _____ ningún error.

☑ **Use of compound tenses** [Section 6-7]

Carefully review the examples of the compound tenses given in Section 6-7, comparing the Spanish to the English translations. Then change the following statements into questions, using the cue word or words given in parentheses. Answers are at the end of the chapter.

Example: He visitado Madrid muchas veces. (cuántas veces—tú)
  ¿Cuántas veces has visitado Madrid?

1. Andrew ha trabajado toda la semana. (cuánto tiempo—él)

2. Nunca habíamos estado en París. (alguna vez—ustedes)

3. Los empleados se han quejado del jefe varias veces. (alguna vez—los empleados)

4. Los muchachos han podido abrir la puerta. (quién)

5. Mis padres no han visto el río Amazonas todavía. (ya—tus padres)

6. No hemos comido todavía. (ya—ustedes)

7. Jaime no se había quejado nunca. (alguna vez—Jaime)

8. Hemos bailado toda la noche. (cuánto tiempo—ustedes)

9. La maestra ha salido ayer. (cuándo—ella)

10. Los niños habían jugado toda la tarde. (cuánto tiempo—ellos)

☑ **The passive voice** [Section 6-8]

Change the following sentences from the passive construction using **ser** + the past participle to the passive construction using **se** + verb + subject acted upon.

Example: Las puertas fueron abiertas temprano.   *Se abrieron las puertas temprano.*

1. Los edificios fueron construidos en la Edad Media.

2. Aquella canción es cantada en todas las fiestas.

3. La comida fue hecha ayer.

4. Las cartas fueron escritas por la tarde.

5. Las ventanas son rotas con frecuencia.

6. Una alondra fue vista en la madrugada.

7. La mesa fue puesta temprano.

8. Las sábanas fueron lavadas y planchadas.

9. Las sillas son pintadas todos los años.

10. Los libros fueron devueltos ayer.

CHAPTER ANSWERS

EXERCISE 6-1

1. Hablará   *Will you speak tomorrow at the meeting?*
2. viviremos   *We'll live for many years.*
3. dormirán   *The girls will sleep soon.*
4. me levantaré   *I have a lot to do; that's why I'll get up early.*
5. se sentirán   *If you go, the students will feel bad.*
6. bailará   *How many hours will you dance at the party?*
7. comprarás   *If you get the money, what will you buy?*
8. comeremos   *We'll eat a lot.*
9. limpiará, limpiaré   *My husband will clean the kitchen and I'll clean the bathroom.*
10. estudiarán, estudiarás   *The boys will study tonight but you won't study until tomorrow afternoon.*
11. romperéis   *You won't break either the glasses or the cups.*
12. mirará   *The teacher will take a slow look at all the students' homework.*
13. verá   *José will never see his girlfriend again.*
14. Escribirás   *Will you write your parents tomorrow?*
15. viajaréis   *Next summer, you'll travel around all of Europe.*
16. comprenderán   *Roberto and Miguel will never understand their friends' complaints.*
17. volverán   *My grandparents will return tomorrow.*
18. se casarán   *When will Leonor and Pedro get married?*
19. daré   *I'll give five hundred dollars for that old car.*
20. irás   *You'll never go to Sweden.*

EXERCISE 6-2

1. Vendré mañana a las cinco.   *I'll come tomorrow at five.*
2. Diré muchas cosas importantes en la reunión.   *I'll say a lot of important things at the meeting.*
3. No, no vendrán Cecilia y Jane a la cena.   *No, Cecilia and Jane won't come to the dinner.*
4. No, no querré cantar en la fiesta.   *No, I won't want to sing at the party.*

5. Podré dejar el trabajo en la primavera. *I'll be able to leave work in the spring.*

6. Sí, tendré que levantarme temprano mañana. *Yes, I'll have to get up early tomorrow.*

7. No, no podré acostarme pronto. *No, I won't be able to go to bed early.*

8. Sí, saldremos a las ocho. *Yes, we'll leave at eight.*

9. Los niños querrán comer hamburguesas y helado. *The children will want to eat hamburgers and ice cream.*

10. La casa valdrá mucho más en cinco años. *The house will be worth much more in five years.*

11. Haré pocos errores en al examen. *I'll make few mistakes on the exam.*

12. El jefe no dirá nada. *The boss won't say anything.*

13. No, no cabremos todos en el coche. *No, we won't all fit in the car.*

14. Sí, sabré lo que tendré que hacer. *Yes, I'll know what I'll have to do.*

15. Sí, saldremos nosotros antes que Julia. *Yes, we'll leave before Julia.*

EXERCISE 6-3

1. tendré que comprar un coche nuevo *This summer, I'll have to buy a new car too.*

2. pagaremos la cuenta *Next week, we'll pay the bill again.*

3. vendrán mis primos y mis tíos *Tomorrow, my cousins and my aunts and uncles will come again.*

4. Ángel traerá su guitarra a la fiesta *This year, Ángel will bring his guitar to the party again.*

5. nadie dirá nada en la reunión *The day after tomorrow, nobody will say anything in the meeting either.*

6. me levantaré muy temprano *Next Saturday, I'll get up very early also.*

7. darán un regalo a la maestra *At Christmas, they'll also give the teacher a gift.*

8. haré un pastel de manzana *This weekend, I'll also make an apple pie.*

9. Jorge e Isabel saldrán temprano *This time, Jorge and Isabel will also leave early.*

10. valdrá aquella casa *How much will that house be worth in 1990?*

11. tendrá fiebra *José Luis will not have a fever tomorrow.*

12. conoceré a una estrella de cine *I'll never meet a movie star.*

13. dará Pepe por aquel coche *How much will Pepe give for that car?*

14. irán los muchachos *With whom will the boys go?*

15. tendrás que estudiar para el examen *What will you have to study for the exam?*

EXERCISE 6-4

1. ¿Bebería Miguel café con leche? *Would Miguel drink coffee with milk?*

2. ¿Hablarías tú con todo el mundo? *Would you talk with everyone?*

3. ¿Tendríamos que descansar antes de ir? *Would we have to rest before going?*

4. ¿Valdría este terreno mucho dinero? *Would this land be worth a lot of money?*

5. ¿Podría usted venir a las seis? *Would you be able to come at six?*

6. ¿Se sentiría María triste? *Would María feel sad?*

7. ¿Leerían los estudiantes libros de historia? *Would the students read history books?*

8. ¿Irían los abuelos a la playa? *Would our grandparents go to the beach?*

9. ¿Se enojaría Alicia con David? *Would Alicia get annoyed with David?*

10. ¿Vendría usted más tarde? *Would you come later?*

11. ¿Comeríais vosotros pescado? *Would you eat fish?*

12. ¿Escribirían ellos una carta todos los días? *Would they write a letter every day?*

13. ¿Esperarían los estudiantes al maestro? *Would the students wait for the teacher?*

14. ¿Harías tú lo mismo que yo? *Would you do the same as I?*

15. ¿Pondría usted el mantel blanco? *Would you set out the white table cloth?*

EXERCISE 6-5

1. prometieron, comerían *The children promised that they would eat a lot.*

2. dijo, estaría *My father said that he would be home early.*

3. insistió, habría que *The teacher insisted that it would be necessary to read Hamlet.*

4. declararon, trabajarían *The workers stated that they wouldn't work anymore.*

5. decidió, habría que *Mr. Moreno decided what it would be necessary to buy.*

6. Creí, tendríamos que *I thought that we would have to hurry.*

7. dijo, iría *Mrs. Black said that she would go to sleep at eleven.*

8. pensó, vendría *You thought that nobody would come to the party, right?*

9. creyó, llovería *José thought that it would rain a lot.*

10. dijeron, querrían *They all said that they would want dessert.*

EXERCISE 6-6

1. dicho *said*

2. cortado *cut*

3. puesto *put*

4. acostado *laid down*

5. creído *believed*
6. cantado *sung*
7. comido *eaten*
8. establecido *established*
9. sido *been*
10. dado *given*
11. dormido *slept*
12. despertado *woken*
13. tenido *had*
14. podido *been able*
15. hecho *done*
16. escrito *written*
17. roto *broken*
18. creado *created*
19. averiguado *found out*
20. leído *read*
21. visto *seen*
22. herido *wounded*
23. llovido *rained*
24. estado *been*
25. vuelto *returned*

EXERCISE 6-7

1. he ido *I have gone to the beach.*
2. ha comido *Marianela has eaten three lobsters.*
3. ha dicho *My father has said the same thing many times.*
4. hemos cantado *We have sung that song at all of the meetings.*
5. han visto *You have seen strange things in your life.*
6. ha hecho *José has never made so many mistakes.*
7. han terminado *The students still haven't finished* Don Quixote.
8. habéis oído *You have heard the news, right?*
9. has podido *You have been able to answer all the questions.*
10. he sido *I have been a student all my life.*
11. ha abierto *Mr. Black has opened the restaurant early.*
12. han roto *You have broken my favorite chair.*
13. habéis llegado *You have arrived too late.*
14. han prometido *The boys have promised to clean the kitchen well.*
15. has trabajado *You have worked with her before, right?*

EXERCISE 6-8

1. había hecho *I had done the work.*
2. habían leído *The students had read half the textbook.*
3. había publicado *The poet had published his poems at an early age.*
4. habíamos sabido *We had known the truth.*
5. habían salido *You had already left when the musicians arrived.*
6. había pagado *I had always paid my debts quickly.*
7. habían jugado *The children had played for many hours.*
8. habíais escrito *You had written quite a few letters last year.*
9. habían podido *You had not been able to attend the baseball game.*
10. habíamos visto *We had seen Paris in 1968.*

EXERCISE 6-9

1. habré dormido *I will have slept twelve hours.*
2. habremos visto *By tomorrow, we will have seen all that we can see.*
3. habrá comido *I think that Andrew will have eaten all the ice cream.*
4. habrán hecho *You will have done the most urgent things.*
5. habrán terminado *By spring, the students will have finished the project.*
6. habrán hecho *By tomorrow, they will have made many telephone calls.*
7. habréis ido *You will have gone to Spain three times.*
8. habrán oído *They will have heard the news already.*
9. habrá cerrado *Mrs. Rojas will have closed the store.*
10. habrás roto *You will have broken all the rules of the game.*

EXERCISE 6-10

1. habría dicho *In this case, I wouldn't have said anything.*
2. habríamos dejado *On that occasion, we would have left a bigger tip.*
3. habrían preferido *The students would have preferred to read a shorter novel than* War and Peace.
4. habrías tenido *Last summer, you would have had more time.*
5. habrían trabajado *The girls would have worked harder than the boys.*
6. habríais hecho *You would have made the same mistake.*
7. habrían salido *In case of rain, they all would have left early.*

EXERCISE 6-11

1. ¿Has estado enfermo mucho tiempo?
2. ¿Han probado ustedes la ensalada?
3. Nunca he visto París.
4. Debía haber salido más temprano.
5. Podía haber comido más arroz.
6. No ha leído *Don Quixote* todavía.
7. Nunca se ha casado.
8. Siempre ha dicho usted la verdad. OR Usted siempre ha dicho la verdad.

9. Los niños se habían levantado demasiado temprano.
10. Ya nos hemos lavado las manos.
11. Debía haberme puesto un sombrero. OR Me debía haber puesto un sombrero.
12. Nunca se ha enfadado fácilmente.
13. ¿Te has quejado alguna vez?
14. ¿Nunca habéis escuchado a Miguel?
15. ¿Ha ido usted alguna vez a Australia?

EXERCISE 6-12

1. Se comió el pastel. *The cake was eaten.*
2. Se leyó la novela. *The novel was read.*
3. Se cantaron las óperas de Verdi. *Verdi's operas were sung.*
4. No se hizo ningún error. *No mistake was made.*
5. Se habla inglés. *English is spoken.*
6. No se habla italiano. *Italian is not spoken.*
7. Se abrió el restaurán a las cinco. *The restaurant was opened at five.*
8. Se recibieron los recados. *The messages were received.*
9. Se cuentan historias muy extrañas. *Strange stories are told.*
10. No se dijo nada. *Nothing was said.*
11. Se perdió un guante. *A glove was lost.*
12. No se compró mi libro. *My book was not bought.*
13. Se limpió la cocina. *The kitchen was cleaned.*
14. Se mancharon los muebles. *The furniture was stained.*
15. No se ganó el partido. *The game wasn't won.*

EXERCISE 6-13

1. *It's said (They say) that a lot of people will go to the party.*
2. *Only Spanish is spoken here. (They only speak Spanish here.)*
3. *You don't (One doesn't) learn without studying.*
4. *It is forbidden (They forbid you) to smoke here.*
5. *It is believed (They believe) that someone killed Mozart.*

EXERCISE 6-14

1. El puente fue construido el año pasado por el ingeniero. *The bridge was built by the engineer.*
2. El asunto será discutido mañana por el jefe. *The matter will be discussed tomorrow by the boss.*
3. Una obra de Shakespeare fue leída por los estudiantes el semestre pasado. *A work of Shakespeare was read by the students last semester.*
4. Todo es escuchado por los niños. *Everything is heard by the children.*
5. Un buen partido fue jugado por todos. *A good game was played by all.*
6. Las llaves de la casa fueron cambiadas por Jorge. *The keys to the house were changed by Jorge.*
7. Anoche, muchas tonterías fueron dichas por tus hermanos. *Last night, many foolish things were said by your brothers.*
8. Los muebles fueron comprados en aquella tienda por el Sr. White. *The furniture was bought in that store by Mr. White.*
9. Los pasteles fueron comidos por Jaime. *The cakes were eaten by Jaime.*
10. Los premios serán anunciados por la maestra la semana que viene. *The prizes will be announced by the teacher next week.*

RAISE YOUR GRADES

Future and conditional forms
1. beberían *The children would drink milk, but there isn't any.*
2. tendría *In that case, I would have nothing to say.*
3. escribiremos *We'll write Mom next week.*
4. se casarán *They will get married, but they want to wait until May.*
5. saldréis *You'll leave soon, won't you?*
6. valdría *My house would be worth much more money, but it doesn't have a swimming pool.*
7. conocerás *Tomorrow, you will meet the whole family.*
8. empezarían *They said that they would begin late.*
9. dirán *Surely, the girls won't say anything.*
10. harías *What would you do in my case?*
11. sabrá *Tomorrow, everyone will know the truth.*
12. abrirá *Who will open the session?*
13. nos sentaremos *We will sit here.*
14. me iría *I would go now but I can't.*
15. romperían *The children would break the dishes.*
16. se callará *When will that man shut up?*
17. se levantarán *What time will your parents get up?*
18. tendrá *What will you have to do tomorrow?*
19. sería *It wouldn't be a bad idea to go to the movies tonight.*
20. querréis *What will you want to eat?*

Sequence of tenses with future and conditional
1. harían *María and Ana said that they would make dessert.*
2. habría que *My parents insisted that it would be necessary to arrive home before eleven.*
3. se casarán *The bride and groom think that they will get married in June.*

4. vendría *My sister believed that nobody would come to see her.*
5. tendrán que *You say that they will have to pay for the tickets.*
6. podremos *The boss affirms that we will be able to leave early on Saturday.*
7. estarán *You say that the stores will be open until nine.*
8. haremos *My parents believe that we will make too much noise.*
9. se acostaría *Luisa promised that she would go to bed at ten.*
10. estará *Raúl says that he will be playing with his cousins.*

The past participle

1. querido *I have wanted to talk with her for a long time.*
2. podido *We haven't been able to get tickets for the concert.*
3. estado *She has been living in Mexico.*
4. roto *Julia has broken the windows.*
5. visto *You've seen the Mediterranean, haven't you?*
6. escuchado *They had never heard such an interesting lecture.*
7. abierto *Have you opened my letters?*
8. dicho *I've told everyone that we're going to have dinner at seven.*
9. muerto *Aunt Marcela's canary has died.*
10. puesto *Haven't you set the table yet?*
11. frito *The cook has fried two chickens.*
12. vuelto *The swallows have returned to Capistrano.*
13. dormido *The kids haven't slept enough.*
14. resuelto *You still haven't resolved your problems.*
15. hecho *We haven't made any mistakes.*

Use of compound tenses

1. ¿Cuánto tiempo ha trabajado él? *How much time has he worked?*
2. ¿Habían estado ustedes alguna vez en París? *Had you ever been to Paris?*
3. ¿Se han quejado los empleados del jefe alguna vez? *Have the employees ever complained about the boss?*
4. ¿Quién ha podido abrir la puerta? *Who has been able to open the door?*
5. ¿Ya han visto tus padres el río Amazonas? *Have your parents already seen the Amazon River?*
6. ¿Ya han comido ustedes? *Have you eaten already?*
7. ¿Se había quejado Jaime alguna vez? *Had Jaime ever complained?*
8. ¿Cuánto tiempo han bailado ustedes? *How long have you danced?*
9. ¿Cuándo ha salido ella? *When has she left?*
10. ¿Cuánto tiempo habían jugado ellos? *How long had they played?*

The passive voice

1. Se construyeron los edificios en la Edad Media. *The buildings were built in the Middle Ages.*
2. Se canta aquella canción en todas las fiestas. *That song is sung at all the parties.*
3. Se hizo la comida ayer. *The food was prepared yesterday.*
4. Se escribieron las cartas por la tarde. *The letters were written in the afternoon.*
5. Se rompen las ventanas con frecuencia. *The windows are often broken.*
6. Se vio una alondra en la madrugada. *A lark was seen at daybreak.*
7. Se puso la mesa temprano. *The table was set early.*
8. Se lavaron y se plancharon las sábanas. *The sheets were washed and ironed.*
9. Se pintan las sillas todos los años. *The chairs are painted every year.*
10. Se devolvieron los libros ayer. *The books were returned yesterday.*

7 SUBJUNCTIVE AND IMPERATIVE

THIS CHAPTER IS ABOUT

☑ Forms of the Present Subjunctive
☑ Use of the Subjunctive
☑ Forms of the Imperfect Subjunctive
☑ Use of the Imperfect Subjunctive
☑ Use of the Subjunctive with Conjunctions
☑ Forms of the Perfect Subjunctive
☑ Use of the Perfect Subjunctive
☑ Forms of the Imperative
☑ Use of the Imperative
☑ Colloquial Uses of the Subjunctive

English speakers rarely use the subjunctive mode. Consequently, no distinction is made in English between the subjunctive and the indicative. Spanish speakers, on the other hand, cannot express themselves without using the subjunctive mode, because it is used in commands and in many dependent clauses. The essential difference between the indicative and the subjunctive is the difference between a fact (indicative) and a possibility, uncertainty, or wish (subjunctive). Study the following examples.

Indicative	Subjunctive
Mario **viene** mañana.	Quizá **venga** Mario mañana.
Mario is coming tomorrow. (fact)	*Perhaps Mario will come tomorrow. (possibility)*
Creo que **es** una novela interesante.	Dudo que **sea** una novela interesante.
I think it is an interesting novel. (fact)	*I doubt that it is an interesting novel. (uncertainty)*
Quiero **almorzar**.	Quiero que tú **almuerces** conmigo.
I want to eat lunch. (fact)	*I want you to eat lunch with me. (possibility or wish)*

7-1. Forms of the Present Subjunctive

A. Regular verbs

The present subjunctive endings of all verbs are attached to the stem of the first person singular form of the present indicative. The present subjunctive endings of regular -ar verbs change the **a** to **e**. The present subjunctive endings of regular -er and -ir verbs change the **e** to **a**. Study the following chart.

hablar	*to speak*	hable, hables, hable, hablemos, habléis, hablen
beber	*to drink*	beba, bebas, beba, bebamos, bebáis, beban
vivir	*to live*	viva, vivas, viva, vivamos, viváis, vivan

B. Stem-changing verbs

1. *Class I stem-changing verbs.* Recall that Class I stem-changing verbs include both **-ar** and **-er** verbs with stem changes of **e-ie** and **o-ue**. These same change patterns are followed in the present subjunctive. Remember, stem changes do not occur in the first and second person plural forms, **nosotros** and **vosotros**. Study the following examples of common Class I stem-changing verbs.

almorzar (ue)	*to have lunch*	almuerce, almuerces, almuerce, almorcemos, almorcéis, almuercen
cerrar (ie)	*to close*	cierre, cierres, cierre, cerremos, cerréis, cierren
contar (ue)	*to count*	cuente, cuentes, cuente, contemos, contéis, cuenten
despertar (ie)	*to awaken*	despierte, despiertes, despierte, despertemos, despertéis, despierten
empezar (ie)	*to begin*	empiece, empieces, empiece, empecemos, empecéis, empiecen
encontrar (ue)	*to find*	encuentre, encuentres, encuentre, encontremos, encontréis, encuentren.
entender (ie)	*to understand*	entienda, entiendas, entienda, entendamos, entendáis, entiendan
mostrar (ue)	*to show*	muestre, muestres, muestre, mostremos, mostréis, muestren
pensar (ie)	*to think*	piense, pienses, piense, pensemos, penséis, piensen
perder (ie)	*to lose*	pierda, pierdas, pierda, perdamos, perdáis, pierdan
probar (ue)	*to prove, to taste*	pruebe, pruebes, pruebe, probemos, probéis, prueben
querer (ie)	*to want, to love*	quiera, quieras, quiera, queramos, queráis, quieran
volver (ue)	*to return*	vuelva, vuelvas, vuelva, volvamos, volváis, vuelvan

2. *Class II stem-changing verbs.* Recall that Class II stem-changing verbs end in **-ir**. They follow a pattern of stem changes from **o-ue** and **e-ie**. This pattern of stem changes is followed in the present subjunctive except that the first and second person plural forms also have stem changes from **e-i** or **o-u**. Study the following list of common Class II stem-changing verbs.

consentir (ie)	*to consent*	consienta, consientas, consienta, consintamos, consintáis, consientan
dormir (ue)	*to sleep*	duerma, duermas, duerma, durmamos, durmáis, duerman
mentir (ie)	*to lie*	mienta, mientas, mienta, mintamos, mintáis, mientan
morir (ue)	*to die*	muera, mueras, muera, muramos, muráis, mueran
sentir (ie)	*to feel*	sienta, sientas, sienta, sintamos, sintáis, sientan

3. *Class III stem-changing verbs.* Recall that Class III stem-changing verbs end in **-ir** and change **e-i**. This stem change occurs in *all* forms of the present subjunctive. Study the following list of common Class III stem-changing verbs.

freír (i)	*to fry*	fría, frías, fría, friamos, friáis, frían
medir (i)	*to measure*	mida, midas, mida, midamos, midáis, midan
pedir (i)	*to ask for*	pida, pidas, pida, pidamos, pidáis, pidan

| reír (i) | *to laugh* | ría, rías, ría, riamos, riáis, rían |
| seguir (i) | *to follow* | siga, sigas, siga, sigamos, sigáis, sigan |

NOTE: See Chapter 3, Section 3-2 for a review of stem-changing verbs in the present indicative.

C. Orthographic (spelling) changes

Some verbs change the final consonant of the stem before adding the present subjunctive endings.

1. Verbs that end in **-zar** change the **z** to **c** before **e**.

almorzar (ue)	*to have lunch*	almuerce, almuerces, almuerce, almorcemos, almorcéis, almuercen
avanzar	*to advance*	avance, avances, avance, avancemos, avancéis, avancen
comenzar (ie)	*to begin*	comience, comiences, comience, comencemos, comencéis, comiencen
empezar (ie)	*to begin*	empiece, empieces, empiece, empecemos, empecéis, empiecen

2. Verbs that end in **-ger** and **-gir** change the **g** to **j** before **a**.

| coger | *to pick up* | coja, cojas, coja, cojamos, cojáis, cojan |
| dirigir | *to direct* | dirija, dirijas, dirija, dirijamos, dirijáis, dirijan |

3. Verbs that end in **-guir** change the **gu** to **g** before **a**.

| distinguir | *to distinguish* | distinga, distingas, distinga, distingamos, distingáis, distingan |
| seguir | *to follow* | siga, sigas, siga, sigamos, sigáis, sigan |

4. Verbs that end in **-car** change the **c** to **qu** before **e**.

buscar	*to look for*	busque, busques, busque, busquemos, busquéis busquen
sacar	*to take out*	saque, saques, saque, saquemos, saquéis, saquen
tocar	*to touch, to play*	toque, toques, toque, toquemos, toquéis, toquen

5. Verbs that end in **-cer** and **-cir** change the **c** to **zc** before **a**.

| conocer | *to know* | conozca, conozcas, conozca, conozcamos, conozcáis, conozcan |
| traducir | *to translate* | traduzca, traduzcas, traduzca, traduzcamos, traduzcáis, traduzcan |

6. Verbs that end in **-uir** add **y** before **a**.

| huir | *to flee* | huya, huyas, huya, huyamos, huyáis, huyan |
| instruir | *to instruct* | instruya, instruyas, instruya, instruyamos, instruyáis, instruyan |

NOTE: See Chapter 3, Section 3-3 for a review of orthographic changes in the present indicative.

D. Irregular first person stems

Recall the verbs with irregular first person singular stems in the present indicative (Chapter 3, Section 3-4). Since the present subjunctive endings are added to the first person singular form of the present indicative, it follows that these same verbs are irregular in the present subjunctive. Study the following list.

caber	*to fit*	**quepa, quepas, quepa, quepamos, quepáis, quepan**
caer	*to fall*	**caiga, caigas, caiga, caigamos, caigáis, caigan**
decir	*to say*	**diga, digas, diga, digamos, digáis, digan**
hacer	*to do, to make*	**haga, hagas, haga, hagamos, hagáis, hagan**
oír	*to hear*	**oiga, oigas, oiga, oigamos, oigáis, oigan**
poner	*to put*	**ponga, pongas, ponga, pongamos, pongáis, pongan**
salir	*to leave*	**salga, salgas, salga, salgamos, salgáis, salgan**
tener	*to have*	**tenga, tengas, tenga, tengamos, tengáis, tengan**

E. Irregular verbs

There are six verbs that are irregular in the present subjunctive that must be memorized.

dar	*to give*	**dé, des, dé, demos, deis, den**
estar	*to be*	**esté, estés, esté, estemos, estéis, estén**
haber	*to have (aux.)*	**haya, hayas, haya, hayamos, hayáis, hayan**
ir	*to go*	**vaya, vayas, vaya, vayamos, vayáis, vayan**
saber	*to know*	**sepa, sepas, sepa, sepamos, sepáis, sepan**
ser	*to be*	**sea, seas, sea, seamos, seáis, sean**

EXERCISE 7-1: Write in the correct present subjunctive forms that correspond to the subject pronouns given below. Use the verb given in parentheses.

1. (enseñar) yo _____, nosotros _____, ellas _____, él _____
2. (ir) nosotros _____, vosotros _____, tú _____, ella _____
3. (buscar) tú _____, ellos _____, vosotros _____, yo _____
4. (dar) yo _____, ellos _____, nosotros _____, tú _____
5. (cerrar) vosotros _____, tú _____, usted _____, nosotros _____
6. (llegar) yo _____, ellas _____, ustedes _____, vosotros _____
7. (vivir) él _____, nosotros _____, yo _____, ella _____
8. (ser) tú _____, él _____, ellas _____, yo _____
9. (empezar) tú _____, ustedes _____, vosotras _____, usted _____
10. (probar) ellos _____, yo _____, ella _____, usted _____
11. (saber) vosotras _____, yo _____, nosotros _____, usted _____
12. (tener) nosotros _____, ella _____, ustedes _____, tú _____
13. (sacar) tú _____, vosotros _____, nosotros _____, él _____
14. (salir) yo _____, ellas _____, nosotros _____, usted _____
15. (estar) tú _____, nosotros _____, ellas _____, él _____

7-2. Use of the Subjunctive

Various types of verbs or expressions that must be followed by the subjunctive are categorized below. *Do not let these categories confuse you.* In general, it is only necessary to remember that the subjunctive must be used in dependent clauses in which there is a change of subject and when the sentence expresses a feeling or possibility rather than a fact.

A. **The subjunctive is used in dependent clauses following verbs of emotion, doubt, uncertainty, or denial, and verbs of desire or command.**

The subjunctive is only required when there is a change of subject. When there is no change of subject, the infinitive is used.

Yo quiero que tú **vayas**.   *I want you to go. (change of subject)*
BUT
Yo quiero ir.   *I want to go. (no change of subject)*

1. *Verbs of emotion.* Some common verbs of emotion are given below.

esperar	*to hope*	estar contento de	*to be pleased*
temer	*to fear*	sentir	*to be sorry, to regret*
algegrarse	*to be glad*		

> **Temo** que los muchachos **digan** que no.   *I'm afraid the boys might say no.*
> **Espero** que Marta **llegue** pronto.   *I hope Marta arrives soon.*

2. *Verbs of doubt, uncertainty, or denial.* Some common verbs of doubt, uncertainty, or denial are given below.

negar	*to deny*	no pensar	*not to think*
dudar	*to doubt*	no creer	*not to believe, not to think*

> **No creo** que **venga** mucha gente.   *I don't think that many people will come.*
> **Dudo** que José **tenga** más de   *I doubt that José is more than 40*
>   cuarenta años.   *years old.*

3. *Verbs of desire or command.* Some common verbs of desire or command are given below.

querer	*to want*	pedir	*to ask for*
preferir	*to prefer*	sugerir	*to suggest*
mandar	*to order*	decir	*to tell (someone to do something)*
necesitar	*to need*		

> **Queremos** que los niños **coman** pescado.   *We want the children to eat fish.*
> Te **pido** que no te **vayas**.   *I'm asking you not to go.*

EXERCISE 7-2: Write in the correct present subjunctive form of the verb given in parentheses. When you finish, read the sentence out loud and translate it into English. Remember that the subjunctive verb form must agree with the subject of the dependent clause. Answers are at the end of the chapter.

1. (comer) No creo que ellos _____ carne.
2. (acostarse) Su madre prefiere que Leonila _____ temprano.
3. (ser) ¿No pensáis vosotras que la ganadora _____ Josefina?
4. (tener) Siento mucho que ustedes no _____ más tiempo.
5. (irse) Dudo que Carlos _____ a vivir a Francia.
6. (callarse) Mando que todos _____ inmediatamente.
7. (buscar) Queremos que ustedes _____ al hermano de Juan.
8. (pagar) Prefiero que ellos no _____ la cuenta.
9. (decir) Yo no creo que Norma _____ nada a sus amigas.
10. (seguir) Pedimos que los estudiantes nos _____ en coche.
11. (casarse) Los padres no quieren que sus hijos _____ .
12. (tocar) La maestra manda que sus alumnos _____ el piano tres horas diarias.
13. (coger) Espero que ustedes no _____ mi catarro.
14. (pedir) Quiero que todos _____ más dinero al jefe.
15. (volver) Quiero que vosotros _____ a casa muy pronto.
16. (querer) No creo que ustedes _____ estar aquí.
17. (poder) Yo no creo que Sara _____ ganar.
18. (estar) Laura niega que su tía _____ en casa.
19. (atacar) Enrique duda que el perro _____ .
20. (encender) Quiero que usted _____ mi cigarro.

B. **The subjunctive is used in dependent clauses following impersonal expressions.**

1. *Common impersonal expressions.* The following is a list of common impersonal expressions that require the use of the subjunctive in a dependent clause if the dependent clause contains a subject.

es dudoso	*it's doubtful*	es posible	*it's possible*
es importante	*it's important*	es preciso	*it's necessary*
es imposible	*it's impossible*	es probable	*it's probable, likely*
es (una) lástima	*it's a pity*	es raro	*it's unusual, strange*
es necesario	*it's necessary*	es urgente	*it's urgent*

NOTE: The presence of the negative, such as **no es importante**, or **no es necesario**, has no effect on the use of the subjunctive with these expressions.

2. *Subject in dependent clause.* The subjunctive is used in dependent clauses following an impersonal expression only when the dependent clause contains a subject. When there is no subject, the infinitive is used after impersonal expressions.

Es importante que los niños **coman** verduras.

It is important that the children eat vegetables. (subject in dependent clause)

BUT

Es importante **comer** bien.

It is important to eat well. (no subject in dependent clause)

3. *Negative expressions of fact.* The subjunctive is not used in a dependent clause after affirmative impersonal expressions of fact. However, these impersonal expressions do require the subjunctive when they are used with the negative. Study the following examples of negative impersonal expressions that require the subjunctive.

Affirmative—Indicative		Negative—Subjunctive	
es verdad	*it's true*	no es verdad	*it's not true*
es cierto	*it's certain*	no es cierto	*it's not certain*
es evidente	*it's evident*	no es evidente	*it's not evident*
es claro	*it's clear*	no es claro	*it's not clear*
es seguro	*it's sure*	no es seguro	*it's not sure*

Es verdad que Julia **está** en casa.

It's true that Julia is home. (affirmative—indicative)

BUT

No es verdad que Julia **esté** en casa.

It's not true that Julia is home. (negative—subjunctive)

EXERCISE 7-3: Complete each sentence by changing the words given in parentheses into a dependent clause. Make sure that the subject and verb of the dependent clause agree. Answers are at the end of the chapter.

Examples: Es urgente (Alda llegar temprano).   *Es urgente que Alda llegue temprano.*

Es dudoso (los niños levantarse tarde).   *Es dudoso que los niños se levanten tarde.*

1. Es una lástima (Mary no trabajar).

2. Es importante (nosotros pensar seriamente).

3. Es necesario (los niños beber leche).

4. Es dudoso (Antonio venir a tiempo).

5. Es raro (los estudiantes callarse en clase).

6. Es posible (los futbolistas no jugar mañana).

7. Es imposible (Manuel casarse con Julieta).

8. Es urgente (el mitin empezar a las cinco).

9. Es preciso (tú buscar a Claudio).

10. Es posible (él tener fiebre).

11. Es necesario (nosotros seguir el mismo camino).

12. Es raro (tu primo pedir dinero)

13. Es importante (todos oír las instrucciones).

14. Es dudoso (ustedes acostarse temprano).

15. Es preciso (vosotros poner la mesa).

C. **The subjunctive is used in dependent clauses when the noun modified by the dependent clause does not refer to a specific person or thing.**

Quiero comprar una silla que **sea** cómoda.	*I want to buy a chair that is comfortable. (the chair may or may not exist)*
BUT	
Eliseo compró una silla que **es** muy cómoda.	*Eliseo bought a chair that is very comfortable. (the chair exists)*
Necesito un ayudante que **sepa** hablar inglés y español.	*I need an assistant who knows how to speak English and Spanish. (such a person may or may not exist)*
BUT	
Necesito al ayudante que **sabe** hablar inglés y español.	*I need the assistant who knows how to speak English and Spanish. (this person exists)*

> **NOTE:** The personal **a** is not used when the antecedent is indefinite.

D. **The subjunctive is always used in dependent clauses that modify words formed by adding -*quiera* to words such as *cuando*, *donde*, *quien*, etc.**

Study the following list and examples.

cualquiera	*whichever*	dondequiera	*wherever*
cuandoquiera	*whenever*	quienquiera	*whoever*
comoquiera	*however*		

Quienquiera que **coma** en ese restaurán se enferma.	*Whoever eats in that restaurant gets sick.*
Dondequiera que tú **estés**, yo te sigo.	*Wherever you may be, I'll follow you.*

E. **The subjunctive is used in dependent clauses that modify a negative antecedent.**

No hay nadie que lo **haga** mejor.	*There is no one who does it better.*
Ella **no come nada** que **tenga** azúcar.	*She doesn't eat anything that contains sugar.*

EXERCISE 7-4: Write in the correct form of the verb given in parentheses. If the antecedent is a specific person or thing, use the present indicative. If the antecendent is indefinite, use the present subjunctive. Answers are at the end of the chapter.

Examples: (conocer) Quiero hablar con **alguien** que *conozca* bien las computadoras. (indefinite—subjunctive)

(conocer) Quiero hablar con la persona que *conoce* bien las computadoras. (definite—indicative)

1. (ir) Voy a ir dondequiera que tú _____ .
2. (conocer) Quiero hablar con la enfermera que _____ a mi tía.

3. (conducir) Necesitamos una persona que _____ bien un coche.
4. (querer) Mi hermano conoce a un matrimonio que _____ vender todos sus libros.
5. (tener) Cuandoquiera que tú _____ tiempo, comeremos juntos.
6. (acostarse) Mi madre es una persona que siempre _____ tarde.
7. (saber) Jorge busca una novia que _____ esquiar.
8. (decir) Cualquier cosa que él _____ será sensata.
9. (levantarse) Necesitamos un ayudante que _____ temprano.
10. (casarse) Tengo que hablar con los novios que _____ el sábado.
11. (volver) Hablaré con el estudiante que _____ primero.
12. (parecerse) Tenemos una amiga que _____ mucho a Bette Davis.
13. (tocar) El jefe necesita un músico que _____ la trompeta y la guitarra.
14. (dar) Quiero hablar con la mujer que _____ clases de piano.
15. (portarse) Daré un premio a todos los niños que _____ bien.

7-3. Forms of the Imperfect Subjunctive

A. Regular verbs

The imperfect subjunctive of regular **-ar**, **-er**, and **-ir** verbs is formed by dropping the **-ron** ending of the third person plural preterite indicative and adding either **-ra**, **-ras**, **-ra**, **-ramos**, **-rais**, **-ran**, or **-se**, **-ses**, **-se**, **-semos**, **-seis**, **-sen**. Both sets of endings have the same meaning, but the **-ra** endings are usually used in conversation, whereas the **-se** endings are used in literature. Study the following charts.

-ra endings

hablar, *to speak*	comer, *to eat*	vivir, *to live*
hablara	comiera	viviera
hablaras	comieras	vivieras
hablara	comiera	viviera
habláramos	comiéramos	viviéramos
hablarais	comierais	vivierais
hablaran	comieran	vivieran

-se endings

hablar, *to speak*	comer, *to eat*	vivir, *to live*
hablase	comiese	viviese
hablases	comieses	vivieses
hablase	comiese	viviese
hablásemos	comiésemos	viviésemos
hablaseis	comieseis	vivieseis
hablasen	comiesen	viviesen

> **NOTE:** There is a written accent over the **a** or **e** of the first person plural stem of all imperfect subjunctives, both regular and irregular.

B. Irregular verbs

All verbs with an irregular stem in the preterite indicative use that stem to form the imperfect subjunctive (see Chapter 5, Section 5-2 for a review of irregular verbs in the preterite).

1. *Irregular preterite stems.* The following verbs add **-iera**, etc., or **iese**, etc., to the irregular preterite stem.

andar	*to walk*	**anduv-**	anduviera	anduviese
caber	*to fit*	**cup-**	cupiera	cupiese
dar	*to give*	**d-**	diera	diese
estar	*to be*	**estuv-**	estuviera	estuviese

haber	to have (aux)	**hub-**	hub**iera**	hub**iese**
hacer	to do	**hic-**	hic**iera**	hic**iese**
poder	to be able	**pud-**	pud**iera**	pud**iese**
poner	to put	**pus-**	pus**iera**	pus**iese**
querer	to want	**quis-**	quis**iera**	quis**iese**
saber	to know	**sup-**	sup**iera**	sup**iese**
tener	to have	**tuv-**	tuv**iera**	tuv**iese**
venir	to come	**vin-**	vin**iera**	vin**iese**

2. *Stem-changing verbs.* Stem-changing verbs ending in **-ir** add **-iera**, etc., or **-iese**, etc., to the irregular third person preterite stem (see Chapter 3, Section 3-2 for a list of **-ir** stem-changing verbs). Three examples are given below.

sentir	to regret, feel	**sint-**	sint**iera**	sint**iese**
morir	to die	**mur-**	mur**iera**	mur**iese**
pedir	to ask for	**pid-**	pid**iera**	pid**iese**

3. *Irregular preterite stems ending in j.* Verbs with irregular third person preterite stems ending in **j** add **-era**, etc., or **-ese**, etc. Study the following examples.

decir	to say	**dij-**	dij**era**	dij**ese**
traducir	to translate	**traduj-**	traduj**era**	traduj**ese**
traer	to bring	**traj-**	traj**era**	traj**ese**

4. *Irregular preterite stems ending in y.* Verbs with irregular third person preterite stems ending in **y** add **-era**, etc., or **-ese**, etc. Study the following examples.

caer	to fall	**cay-**	cay**era**	cay**ese**
creer	to believe	**crey-**	crey**era**	crey**ese**
huir	to flee	**huy-**	huy**era**	huy**ese**
leer	to read	**ley-**	ley**era**	ley**ese**
oír	to hear	**oy-**	oy**era**	oy**ese**

5. *Ir and ser.* **Ir** and **ser** have the same irregular forms in the imperfect subjunctive.

ir	*to go*	**fuera, fueras, fuera, fuéramos, fuerais, fueran**
		fuese, fueses, fuese, fuésemos, fueseis, fuesen
ser	*to be*	**fuera, fueras, fuera, fuéramos, fuerais, fueran**
		fuese, fueses, fuese, fuésemos, fueseis, fuesen

EXERCISE 7-5: Rewrite the following sentences by replacing the italicized verb with the correct imperfect subjunctive form of each verb given in parentheses. Answers are at the end of the chapter.

1. (decir, pedir, leer) El jefe mandó a Emilio que *trajera* algo.

2. (bailar, comer, dormir) Mi madre pidió que los chicos *caminaran* menos.

3. (estudiar, oir, traducir) La maestra quería que los estudiantes *trabajaran* con más atención.

4. (ir, viajar, salir) Yo quería que tú *entraras* conmigo.

5. (saber, llegar, sentarse) Manolo insistió en que vosotros *comierais* primero.

6. (caer, conducir, cantar) No queríamos que Violeta *hablase*.

7. (venir, salir, marcharse) Sentimos mucho que ustedes *llegasen* tan temprano.

8. (sentarse, ir, salir) Eloisa esperaba que la abuela *subiese* en el coche.

9. (cocinar, correr, leer) Yo no pensaba que tú *bailaras* tanto.

10. (llegar, estar, salir) El jefe quería que todos *entraran* temprano.

NOTE: Esperar in the past tenses means *expected* in English (see no. 8 above).

7-4. Use of the Imperfect Subjunctive

Like the present subjunctive, the imperfect subjunctive is used in dependent clauses following verbs of emotion, doubt, or desire, and following certain impersonal expressions, indefinite antecedents, or negative antecedents. The use of the imperfect subjunctive instead of the present subjunctive depends on the tense of the verb in the main clause. The rules for the correct *sequence of tenses* are given below.

The *present* or *future indicative* in the main clause is followed by the *present subjunctive* in the dependent clause.

The *imperfect indicative*, the *preterite*, or the *conditional* in the main clause is followed by the *imperfect subjunctive* in the dependent clause.

Study the following examples carefully.

Main Clause	Dependent Clause
Yo **espero** que *(pres. ind.)* *I hope that*	Reynaldo **venga**. *(pres. subj.)* *Reynaldo comes.*
Ellos **necesitarán** una persona que *(fut. ind.)* *They need a person to*	**cuide** la casa. *(pres. subj.)* *take care of the house.*
Yo **esperé** que *(pret.)* *I expected*	Reynaldo **viniera**. *(imp. subj.)* *Reynaldo to come.*
Yo **esperaba** que *(imp.)* *I was expecting*	Reynaldo **viniera**. *(imp. subj.)* *Reynaldo to come.*
Ellos **necesitarían** una persona que *(cond.)* *They would need someone to*	**cuidara** la casa. *(imp. subj.)* *take care of the house.*

EXERCISE 7-6: Rewrite the following sentences by replacing the verb of the main clause with the verb given in parentheses, then changing the verb in the dependent clause in accordance with the rules for sequence of tenses. Translate the sentence into English. Answers are at the end of the chapter.

Examples: (quería) Quiero que venga Alicia.
Quería que viniera Alicia.
(dirá) El jefe dijo que trabajáramos el sábado.
El jefe dirá que trabajemos el sábado.

1. (pensaba) No pienso que Pepe camine a casa.

2. (esperaríamos) Esperamos que vengan todos.

3. (creí) No creo que el perro ataque a nadie.

4. (quisieron) Mis padres quieren que toquemos el violín.

5. (creía) Yo no creo que te parezcas a tus hermanos.

6. (esperamos) Esperábamos que Carlos pagara la cuenta.

7. (dudan) Dudaron que ustedes ganaran.

8. (quieren) Ustedes querían que fuéramos a otro sitio.

9. (quiero) No quise que sacarais los platos nuevos.

10. (manda) La maestra mandó que empezáramos a las nueve.

11. (esperaría) Espero que llegues temprano.

12. (necesitaría) Necesito un ayudante que sepa escribir bien.

13. (quería) María quiere comprar una casa que tenga piscina.

14. (había) No hay nadie que toque mejor el piano.

15. (creía) No creo que usted conozca al señor López.

16. (era) Es necesario que ustedes se levanten a las seis.

17. (sería) Es preciso que se callen todos.

18. (estaba) No está claro que quepan todas las maletas.

19. (sería) Será imposible que traigas a tanta gente.

20. (era) No es cierto que Julia y David se casen.

7-5. Use of the Subjunctive with Conjunctions

A. **Certain conjunctions are *always* followed by the subjunctive in the dependent clause.**
Study the following list of these conjunctions and the examples.

a no ser que	*unless*	a fin de que	*so that, for the purpose of*
a menos que	*unless*	para que	*so that, in order that*
con tal que	*provided that*	sin que	*without*
en caso de que	*in case*	como si	*as if*
antes de que	*before*		

NOTE: **Como si** always takes the imperfect subjunctive.

Habrá comida para todos, **con tal que** no **venga** el equipo de fútbol. *There will be food for everyone, provided that the football team doesn't come.*
Se levantó temprano **para que** todos **pudieran** despedirse de él. *He got up early so that everyone could say goodbye to him.*
Ahora habla **como si fuera** abogado. *Now he talks as if he were a lawyer.*

REMEMBER: The rules for sequence of tenses apply when deciding whether to use the present or imperfect subjunctive after these conjunctions, except in the case of **como si**.

EXERCISE 7-7: Read the following sentences carefully. Then rewrite the two sentences as one complete sentence, using the conjunction given in parentheses and changing the verb in the dependent clause from the indicative to the subjunctive. After writing the new sentence, read it out loud and translate it into English. Answers are at the end of the chapter.

Example: Alda vendrá a la fiesta. Eliseo llega hoy. (a no ser que)
Alda vendrá a la fiesta a no ser que Eliseo llegue hoy.

1. Hoy nos levantamos temprano. María desayuna con nosotros. (para que)

2. Yo no como helado. Mi marido no engorda. (a fin de que)

3. Pepe no sale nunca. Los amigos le invitan. (a menos que)

4. Mi madre ponía un plato más. Alguien venía a cenar. (en caso de que)

5. Los muchachos salieron de casa. El tocadiscos se rompió. (antes de que)

6. Raimundo comió un pastel entero. Nadie dijo nada. (sin que)

7. Siempre llevamos el paraguas. Hay lluvia. (en caso de que)

8. Leonardo no va a ninguna parte. Marta le acompaña. (sin que)

9. Yo jugaría al ajedrez. Tú querías jugar. (con tal que)

10. Yo no bailaría. Tú podías bailar conmigo. (a menos que)

11. Nadie piensa ir. Hace buen tiempo. (a no ser que)

12. Vamos en mi coche. Caben las maletas. (con tal que)

13. Contaron la historia. Supe la verdad. (para que)

14. Magda baila. Es una bailarina. (como si)

15. Jaime habló. Estaba muy cansado. (como si)

B. **Conjunctions of time require the use of the subjunctive in dependent clauses when the action or condition in the dependent clause has not yet taken place.**

If the action or condition takes place or has taken place at a specific time, the indicative is used. Study the following conjunctions of time and the examples.

antes de que	*before*	luego que	
cuando	*when*	en cuanto	
hasta que	*until*	tan pronto como	*as soon as*
después (de) que	*after*	así que	

Juan siempre llama **cuando estamos** comiendo. *(fact, specific time, indicative)*

Juan always calls when we are eating.

Juan llamó ayer **cuando** Alicia no **estaba**. *(fact, specific time, indicative)*

Juan called yesterday when Alicia wasn't here.

Juan llamará **cuando** Alicia **esté** en casa. *(unspecific future time, subjunctive)*

Juan will call when Alicia is home.

Juan dijo que llamaría **cuando** Alicia **estuviera** en casa. *(unspecific future time, subjunctive)*

Juan said that he would call when Alicia is home.

> **NOTE:** **Antes de que** is the only conjunction of time that invariably takes the subjunctive. The use of **hasta que** requires a negative when the subjunctive is employed. Study the following examples. This use of the negative is colloquial and must be memorized.

No quiso salir **hasta que dejó** de llover. *(specific time, indicative)*

He didn't want to leave until it stopped raining. (it stopped raining and he left)

No quiso salir **hasta que no dejara** de llover. *(unspecific future time, subjunctive)*

He didn't want to leave until it stopped raining. (it is still raining and he is still here)

EXERCISE 7-8: Rewrite the following sentences by changing the verb in the main clause from the past to the future tense, and the verb in the dependent clause from the indicative to the subjunctive. Answers are at the end of the chapter.

Example: Mario salió en cuanto llegaron los músicos.
Mario saldrá en cuanto lleguen los músicos.

1. Los padres lloraron cuando los novios se casaron.

2. Todos se callaron cuando Gilberto cantó el himno nacional.

3. Los amigos volvieron al pueblo así que pasaron cinco años.

4. Los estudiantes no contestaron hasta que llegó la maestra.

5. No nos casamos hasta que vino el abuelo.

6. La familia compró casa después de que María gano la lotería.

7. Todos se levantaron de la mesa luego que se sirvió el café.

8. Había silencio después de que salieron los niños.

9. Adolfo abrió la puerta en cuanto llegaron las visitas.

10. Marilyn empezó a llorar tan pronto como su hijo salió al escenario.

C. **Certain conjunctions can be followed by either the subjunctive or the indicative.**

If the action in the dependent clause already has taken place, the indicative is used. If the action has not yet taken place, the subjunctive is used. Study the following list and the examples carefully.

aunque	*although, even though*	de modo que	*so that*
a pesar de que	*in spite of the fact that*	de manera que	*in such a way that*

NOTE: The conjunction **a pesar de que** is generally used with events that have already taken place.

Main Clause	Conjunction	Dependent Clause
Martín habló mucho	⎰aunque ⎱a pesar de que	nadie le escuchó. *(indic.)*
Martín talked a lot	⎰*even though* ⎱*in spite of the fact that*	*nobody listened to him.*
Martín hablará mucho	aunque	nadie le escuche. *(subj.)*
Martín will talk a lot	*even though*	*nobody listens to him.*
El maestro hizo el examen	⎰de modo que ⎱de manera que	todos aprobaron. *(indic.)*
The teacher made the exam	*in such a way that*	*everyone passed.*
El maestro hizo el examen	⎰de modo que ⎱de manera que	todos aprobaran. *(subj.)*
The teacher made the exam	*in such a way that*	*everyone would pass.*

EXERCISE 7-9: Select the verb form given in parentheses that completes the sentence correctly. Then read the sentence out loud and translate it into English. Answers are at the end of the chapter.

1. Adela pagó la cuenta aunque no (tenía, tuviera, tenga) mucho dinero.
2. Abriremos los regalos cuando tu padre (llegó, llegara, llegue).
3. Metimos los muebles en la casa antes de que (empezó, empezara, empiece) a llover.

4. Hablaban muy bajo de modo que nadie (oiga, oyera, oye) nada.
5. Nadie gritó a pesar de que la situación (era, fuera, fueron) peligrosa.
6. Pondremos un disco de modo que todos nosotros (bailaran, bailen, bailemos).
7. Raúl empezó a sonreír luego que (vio, viera, ve) a su padre.
8. Hicimos una fiesta grande para que todos los niños (participen, participaron, participaran).
9. Andrés salió calladamente sin que nadie le (oiga, oye, oyera).
10. Me iré de vacaciones aunque solamente (tuve, tenía, tenga) una semana.

7-6. Forms of the Perfect Subjunctive

There are two perfect subjunctive tenses in Spanish: present perfect and pluperfect.

A. Present perfect subjunctive

The present perfect subjunctive is formed by conjugating the auxiliary verb **haber**, *to have*, in the present subjunctive + the past participle. Study the following chart.

yo	**haya**	hablado / aprendido / vivido
tú	**hayas**	hablado / aprendido / vivido
él, ella / usted	**haya**	hablado / aprendido / vivido
nosotros(-as)	**hayamos**	hablado / aprendido / vivido
vosotros(-as)	**hayáis**	hablado / aprendido / vivido
ellos, ellas / ustedes	**hayan**	hablado / aprendido / vivido

B. Pluperfect subjunctive

The pluperfect subjunctive is formed by conjugating the auxiliary verb **haber**, *to have*, in the imperfect subjunctive + the past participle. Study the following chart.

yo	**hubiera** / **hubiese**	hablado / aprendido / vivido
tú	**hubieras** / **hubieses**	hablado / aprendido / vivido
él, ella / usted	**hubiera** / **hubiese**	hablado / aprendido / vivido
nosotros(-as)	**hubiéramos** / **hubiésemos**	hablado / aprendido / vivido
vosotros(-as)	**hubierais** / **hubieseis**	hablado / aprendido / vivido
ellos, ellas / ustedes	**hubieran** / **hubiesen**	hablado / aprendido / vivido

7-7. Use of the Perfect Subjunctive

A. Sequence of tenses

1. *The present perfect subjunctive.* The present perfect subjunctive is used in a dependent clause when the verb in the main clause is in the present or future tense and the action in the dependent clause has already taken place.

> **Es** maravilloso que *(pres.)* Ricardo **haya hecho** eso. *(pres. perf. subj.)*
> *It's wonderful that* *Ricardo did (has done) that.*
>
> **Dudarán** que tú *(future)* **hayas terminado** ese libro. *(pres. perf. subj.)*
> *They'll doubt that* *you finished (have finished) the book.*

> NOTE: The English translation of this construction varies according to the context of the sentence.

2. *The pluperfect subjunctive.* The pluperfect subjunctive is used in a dependent clause when the verb in the main clause is in a past tense and the action in the dependent clause has already taken place.

> **Era** maravilloso que *(imp.)* María **hubiera llegado** tan temprano.
>   *(plup. subj.)*
> *It was wonderful that* *María arrived (had arrived) so early.*
>
> Nosotros **queríamos** que *(imp.)* la fiesta **hubiera terminado** más tarde.
>   *(plup. subj.)*
> *We wanted* *the party to have ended later.*
> OR
> *We wished that* *the party would have ended later.*
>
> El maestro **dudó** que *(pret.)* los alumnos **hubieran aprendido** bien la
>   lección. *(plup. subj.)*
> *The teacher doubted that* *the students had learned the lesson well.*

EXERCISE 7-10: Complete the following sentences by filling in the correct perfect subjunctive form of the verb given in parentheses. When the sentence is completed, translate it into English. Answers are at the end of the chapter.

Examples: (levantarse) Dudo que los niños *se hayan levantado* todavía.
(pagar) Él quería que su hijo *hubiera pagado* la cuenta.

1. (salir) No creo que nadie _____ todavía.
2. (estar) Dudé que Miguel _____ en la oficina.
3. (ir) José no quería que nosotros _____ juntos al cine.
4. (publicar) David esperaba que alguien _____ su poesía.
5. (llegar) Espero que no _____ el tren.
6. (leer) Queremos que todos _____ la misma novela para la clase.
7. (terminar) Los maestros esperan que todos los alumnos _____ su tarea a las tres.
8. (decir) El jefe no quería que nosotros _____ nada sobre el nuevo puesto.
9. (poner) Las muchachas dudaban que Ricardo _____ la mesa.
10. (levantarse) Temo que mi hermano no _____ .
11. (casarse) Los padres temían que los jóvenes _____ sin permiso.
12. (hacer) Ustedes no creen que yo _____ el arroz, ¿verdad?
13. (irse) No es posible que todos _____ .
14. (romperse) Dudo que todos los vasos _____ .
15. (escribir) Era necesario que tú _____ una carta.

B. Contrary to fact or *si* clauses

The following is an example of a contrary to fact structure in English: *If I were young, I would run ten miles every day. (But I am not young.)* In Spanish, the **si** clause uses either the imperfect or the pluperfect subjunctive, and the main clause uses the conditional or the conditional perfect. Study the following examples, paying attention to the sequence of tenses.

Si yo **tuviera** tiempo *(contrary to fact clause, subj.)*   **viajaría** a Inglaterra. *(main clause, cond.)*
If I had time   *I would travel to England.*

Si **hubieras llegado** antes *(contrary to fact clause, subj.)*   **habrías** visto a Pepe. *(main clause, cond. perf.)*
If you had arrived sooner   *you would have seen Pepe.*

Si **hubiera habido** menos gente *(contrary to fact clause, subj.)*   la fiesta **habría** sido mas divertida. *(main clause, cond. perf.)*
If there had been fewer people   *the party would have been more fun.*

> **NOTE:** The present subjunctive is never used in **si** clauses. In a **si** clause that states a condition, the present indicative is used: **Si *tengo* tiempo, iré mañana.** *If I have time, I'll go tomorrow.*

EXERCISE 7-11: Translate the following sentences into Spanish using the verbs given in parentheses. Pay close attention to the sequence of tenses. Answers are at the end of the chapter.

1. (ser, estudiar) If I were a student, I would study Spanish.

2. (estar, venir) If I had been sick, I would not have come.

3. (tener, irse) If he had time, he would go to Mexico.

4. (tener, hacer) If he had had time, he would have made the dinner.

5. (conocer, visitar) If we knew the president, we would visit the White House.

6. (saber, decir) If we had known the truth, we would not have said anything.

7. (poder comer, comer) If I could eat something, I would eat some bread and jam.

8. (poder beber, beber) If I could drink something, I would drink milk.

9. (no hablar, callarse) If you (tú) wouldn't talk, we would be quiet too.

10. (callarse, oír) If you had been quiet, you would have heard the speech.

7-8. Forms of the Imperative

In English, there is only one form of direct address: *you.* Consequently, there is only one form of direct command: *stop, go, sit, stand, etc.* Furthermore, there is no grammatical difference between affirmative and negative commands: *stop, don't stop.* In Spanish, there are four forms of direct address: **tú, usted, vosotros(-as),** and **ustedes.** Therefore, there are four forms of direct address in the affirmative, and there are also four forms of direct address in the negative.

A. Formal commands

1. *Regular verbs.* The third person singular and plural forms of the present subjunctive are used with **usted** and **ustedes** in formal or polite commands. Study the following chart. Note that the affirmative and negative forms of formal commands are the same.

Aff. Sing.	Neg. Sing.	Aff. Pl.	Neg. Pl.
hable usted	no **hable** usted	**hablen** ustedes	no **hablen** ustedes
coma usted	no **coma** usted	**coman** ustedes	no **coman** ustedes
abra usted	no **abra** usted	**abran** ustedes	no **abran** ustedes

2. *Irregular verbs.* Any verb that has an irregular present subjunctive form also uses this form in the imperative. The following are some of the more common irregular formal command forms. See Section 7-1D for a complete review of the irregular present subjunctive.

Infinitive	Singular	Plural
decir, *to say*	**diga** usted	**digan** ustedes
hacer, *to do*	**haga** usted	**hagan** ustedes
oír, *to hear*	**oiga** usted	**oigan** ustedes
poner, *to put*	**ponga** usted	**pongan** ustedes
salir, *to leave*	**salga** usted	**salgan** ustedes
venir, *to come*	**venga** usted	**vengan** ustedes

Stem-changing verbs

Infinitive	Singular	Plural
cerrar (ie), *to close*	**cierre** usted	**cierren** ustedes
contar (ue), *to count*	**cuente** usted	**cuenten** ustedes
dormir (ue), *to sleep*	**duerma** usted	**duerman** ustedes
pedir (i), *to ask for*	**pida** usted	**pidan** ustedes
volver (ue), *to return*	**vuelva** usted	**vuelvan** ustedes

Orthographic-changing verbs

Infinitive	Singular	Plural
buscar, *to look for*	**busque** usted	**busquen** ustedes
coger, *to pick up*	**coja** usted	**cojan** ustedes
empezar, *to begin*	**empiece** usted	**empiecen** ustedes
llegar, *to arrive*	**llegue** usted	**lleguen** ustedes
seguir, *to follow*	**siga** usted	**sigan** ustedes

Other irregular verbs

Infinitive	Singular	Plural
dar, *to give*	**dé** usted	**den** ustedes
estar, *to be*	**esté** usted	**estén** ustedes
ir, *to go*	**vaya** usted	**vayan** ustedes
saber, *to know*	**sepa** usted	**sepan** ustedes
ser, *to be*	**sea** usted	**sean** ustedes

NOTE: There are written accents over **dé**, **esté**, and **estén**.

EXERCISE 7-12: Write in the correct formal command form of the verb given in parentheses. Then translate the sentence into English. Answers are at the end of the chapter.

Example: (decir) ___*Diga*___ usted algo. *Say something.*

1. (escribir) No _____ usted todavía.

2. (llorar) No _____ usted tanto.

3. (hacer) No _____ usted nada.

4. (empezar) _____ usted ahora mismo.

5. (venir) _____ usted aquí.

6. (oír) _____ usted, por favor.

7. (hablar) _____ ustedes más fuerte.

8. (cerrer) No _____ usted la puerta.

9. (buscar) No _____ usted nada ahora.

10. (volver) _____ usted mañana.

11. (seguir) No _____ usted mi consejo.

12. (pagar) _____ ustedes la cuenta.

13. (fumar) No _____ usted aquí, por favor.

14. (avanzar) _____ usted dos pasos.

15. (ir) _____ ustedes con él.

16. (ser) No _____ ustedes impertinentes.

17. (dar) No _____ usted nada.

18. (ensenar) _____ ustedes las fotos.

19. (leer) _____ ustedes los libros.

20. (dormir) No _____ ustedes, por favor.

B. Informal or familiar commands

1. *Regular verbs.* The singular affirmative **tú** command is the same as the third person singular form of the present indicative. The plural affirmative **vosotros(-as)** command is formed by replacing the final **r** of the infinitive form with **d**. The spoken stress is always on the final syllable. Both the singular and the plural negative familiar command forms are the same as the present subjunctive forms. Study the following chart.

Aff. Sing.	Neg. Sing	Aff. Pl.	Neg. Pl.
habla	no **hables**	**hablad**	no **habléis**
come	no **comas**	**comed**	no **comáis**
abre	no **abras**	**abrid**	no **abráis**

NOTE: The pronouns **tú** and **vosotros(-as)** are generally not used with the familiar command forms.

2. *Irregular verbs.* There are nine verbs with an irregular form in the affirmative singular only. The remaining three command forms of these verbs are regular. Study the following list.

Infinitive	Aff. Sing.	Neg. Sing.	Aff. Pl.	Neg. Pl.
decir, *to say*	**di**	no digas	decid	no digáis
hacer, *to do*	**haz**	no hagas	haced	no hagáis
ir, *to go*	**ve**	no vayas	id	no vayáis
poner, *to put*	**pon**	no pongas	poned	no pongáis
salir, *to leave*	**sal**	no salgas	salid	no salgáis
ser, *to be*	**se**	no seas	sed	no seáis
tener, *to have*	**ten**	no tengas	tened	no tengáis
valer, *to help*	**val**	no valgas	valed	no valgáis
venir, *to come*	**ven**	no vengas	venid	no vengáis

EXERCISE 7-13: Write in the correct familiar command form of the verb given in parentheses. Then translate the sentence into English. Answers are at the end of the chapter.

1. (tomar) _____ (*tú*) un vaso de vino.

2. (beber) No_____ (*vosotros*) agua.

3. (correr) No_____ (*tú*) tanto.

4. (caminar) _____ (*vosotros*) más despacio.

5. (poner) _____ (*tú*) la mesa.

6. (ahorrar) No_____ tu dinero.

7. (pegar) No_____ a tu hermano.

8. (hacer) _____ lo que te digo.

9. (gritar) No_____ (*vosotros*).

10. (comenzar) _____ (*vosotras*) ahora.

11. (decir) No_____ (*tú*) nada.

12. (bailar) _____ (*vosotros*), por favor.

13. (salir) _____ (*tú*) ahora mismo.

14. (ir) No_____ (*tú*) a clase.

15. (limpiar) _____ (*tú*) la cocina.

16. (pedir) _____ permiso a tu madre.

17. (ser) No_____ (*tú*) tonto.

18. (dormir) _____ (*vosotros*) bien.

19. (cerrar) _____ (*tú*) la puerta.

20. (venir) _____ (*tú*) aca.

7-9. Use of the Imperative

A. Direct command

In formal or polite speech, **usted** and **ustedes** are generally used with the imperative: **Tome *usted* otra galleta, por favor**; *Take another cracker, please.* In informal speech, the subject pronouns **tú** and **vosotros(-as)** are used only for emphasis.

EXERCISE 7-14: Rewrite the following sentences by changing the formal **usted** or **ustedes** command to the informal **tú** or **vosotros(-as)** command. Then translate the sentence into English. Answers are at the end of the chapter.

Example: No abra usted la ventana.   *No abras la ventana. Don't open the window.*

1. Diga usted la verdad.

2. No caiga usted de la escalera.

3. Beba usted otra taza de café.

4. No saquen ustedes los libros todavía.

5. Venga usted conmigo.

6. No piense usted mucho.

7. No despierte usted a la niña.

8. Fría usted un par de huevos.

9. No duerma usted.

10. Vendan ustedes los libros viejos.

11. Dé usted a Manuel algún consejo, por favor.

12. No dé usted dulces a los niños, por favor.

13. No jueguen ustedes cerca de la piscina.

14. No vaya usted con él.

15. No sea usted tan impaciente.

16. Enseñe usted los dibujos a todo el mundo.

17. No mienta usted.

18. Lea usted *La guerra y la paz.*

19. Almuerce usted conmigo, por favor.

20. Devuelva usted mis libros mañana, por favor.

21. Huela usted la sopa.

22. No pierda usted mi paraguas.

23. Responda usted ahora mismo.

24. Suban ustedes la escalera muy despacio, por favor.

25. No grite usted tanto, por favor.

B. Reflexive verbs

Reflexive verbs have the same command forms as other verbs except for the placement of the reflexive pronoun. In affirmative commands in the **tú**, **usted**, and **ustedes** forms, the reflexive pronoun is attached to the verb: **siéntate, siéntese, siéntense**. Note the written accent over the third to the last syllable. In the **vosotros** form, the **d** is dropped and the reflexive pronoun is added: **sentaos**. The only exception is **irse**, which retains the **d**: **idos**. In negative commands, the reflexive pronoun precedes the verb: **no te sientes, no se siente, no os sentéis, no se sienten**. Study the following examples.

casarse, *to get married*
Cásate con Miguel.	*Marry Miguel.*
No te cases con Claudio.	*Don't marry Claudio.*
Casaos en la primavera.	*Get married in spring.*
No os caséis en diciembre.	*Don't get married in December.*

levantarse, *to get up*
Levántate temprano.	*Get up early.*
No te levantes todavía.	*Don't get up yet.*
Levantaos ahora mismo.	*Get up right now.*
No os levantéis de la mesa.	*Don't get up from the table.*

EXERCISE 7-15:   Change the negative commands to the affirmative and the affirmative commands to the negative. After rewriting the command, translate the sentence into English. Answers are at the end of the chapter.

Example: (irse) No se vaya usted.   *Váyase usted. Go away.*

1. (peinarse) Péinate de otro mod .

2. (sentarse) Siéntense ustedes aquí.

3. (ponerse) No te pongas aquel sombrero.

4. (enojarse) !Enójate más!

5. (lavarse) Lavaos la cara.

6. (reirse) Ríete de mí.

7. (equivocarse) Equivocaos mucho.

8. (asustarse) No te asustes.

9. (quedarse) Quédate con nosotros.

10. (quitarse) Quítese usted el abrigo.

11. (irse) No se vaya usted ahora.

12. (acostarse) Acuéstense ustedes pronto.

13. (despedirse) Despídete de tu abuela.

14. (quejarse) No se queje usted de la comida.

15. (enfadarse) No te enfades.

C. Indirect commands

There are two forms of indirect commands in Spanish: **que** + present subjunctive and first person plural present subjunctive.

1. *Que* + *present subjunctive.* Study the following examples of this indirect command structure, paying careful attention to the placement of reflexive pronouns and the English translations.

Nonreflexive

Affirmative

Que entre George primero.
Let George come in first.

Negative

Que no lo **haga** George.
Don't let George do it.

Reflexive

Affirmative

Que se ponga María el vestido azul.
Have María put on her blue dress.

Negative

Que no te pongas enferma.
May you not get sick.

2. *First person plural subjunctive.* Study the following examples of this indirect command structure, paying careful attention to the placement of reflexive pronouns. Note that the final **s** is dropped before adding the first person reflexive pronoun, **nos**, in the affirmative.

Nonreflexive

Affirmative

Escribamos una novela.
Let's write a novel.

Negative

No bailemos.
Let's not dance.

Reflexive

Affirmative

Casémonos.
Let's get married.

Negative

No nos casemos todavía.
Let's not get married yet.

> **NOTE:** **Vamos a** + infinitive can also mean *Let's _____*.
> **Vamos a comer** and **comamos** both mean *Let's eat.* The subjunctive form of **ir**, **vayamos**, is not used as a command. Instead, the present indicative form of **irse**, **Vámonos**, *Let's go*, is used.

EXERCISE 7-16: Translate the following sentences into Spanish using the verb given in parentheses. Answers are at the end of the chapter.

Examples: (sentirse) May you (*tú*) feel better. *Que te sientas mejor.*
(volver) Have Liza return tomorrow *Que vuelva Liza mañana.*
(escribirse) Let's write each other. *Escribámonos.*

1. (ponerse) May you (*tú*) get better soon.

2. (poner) Have Jaime set the table.

3. (sentirse) May they (*ellos*) feel better soon.

4. (sentirse) May you (*ustedes*) feel better soon.

5. (caerse) May you (*usted*) not fall down.

6. (sentarse) Have Andrew sit down first.

7. (lavar) Let Anthony wash the dishes.

8. (vivir) May you (*tú*) live forever.

9. (morirse) May he never die.

10. (tener) May you (*vosotros*) have a lot of luck.

11. (descansar) May you (*ustedes*) rest well.

12. (traer) May it bring luck.

13. (leer) Have Manuel read the letter.

14. (abrir) Have Alice open the door.

15. (entrar) Have the children come in now.

16. (escaparse) Let's run away to Mexico.

17. (salir) Let's not go outside now.

18. (levantarse) Let's not get up.

19. (enojarse) Let's not be mad.

20. (acostarse) Let's go to bed.

7-10. Colloquial Uses of the Subjunctive

A. *Quisiera*

Quisiera means *would like* and is a polite form of the verb **querer**, *to want*: **Yo quisiera decirte algo**. *I would like to tell you something*. It is used in two kinds of basic sentence structures.

1. *Quisiera* + *infinitive (no change of subject)*.

El **quisiera estudiar** ruso.	*He would like to study Russian.*
No **quisiéramos ir** tan lejos.	*We wouldn't like to go so far away.*

2. *Quisiera* + *que* + *subjunctive (change of subject)*.

Yo **quisiera que** él **estudiara** alemán.	*I would like him to study German.*
El **quisiera que** nosotros **nos hubiéramos** ido a otra parte.	*He would like us to have gone somewhere else.*
	OR
	He wishes that we would have gone somewhere else.

NOTE: When **quisiera** is followed by the subjunctive, it can use only the imperfect or pluperfect subjunctive.

EXERCISE 7-17: Rewrite the following sentences using the subject or subject pronouns given in parentheses, and changing from **quisiera** + infinitive to **quisiera** + imperfect subjunctive. Watch out for reflexive verbs. After you rewrite the sentence, translate it into English. Answers are at the end of the chapter.

Example: Quisiera bailar. (él, tú)

Él quisiera que tú bailaras. He would like you to dance.

1. Yo quisiera comer. (él, tú)

2. Quisiéramos comprar una casa. (nosotros, él)

3. Quisiera despedirme. (nosotros, él)

4. Ellos quisieran sentarse. (yo, vosotros)

5. Él quisiera tocar el piano. (ellos, ella)

6. Yo quisiera jugar al ajedrez. (José, nosotros)

7. Quisiera quedarme. (nosotros, tú)

8. Los niños quisieran beber algo. (María, vosotros)

9. Manolo quisiera dejar el trabajo. (tú, yo)

10. Yo quisiera quitarme el abrigo. (yo, todos)

B. *Ojalá*

The word **ojalá** is derived from an Arabic expression meaning *May Allah grant that* _____. It is used today to mean *I wish* or *I hope*, in two basic sentence structures.

1. *Ojalá* **(que)** + *present subjunctive*. When **ojalá** is used with the present subjunctive, it means *I hope*.

Ojalá seamos millonarios.	*I hope that we will be millionaires.*
Ojalá no **hayan** comido toda la ensalada.	*I hope that they haven't eaten all the salad.*

2. *Ojalá* **(que)** + *imperfect or pluperfect subjunctive*. When **ojalá** is used with the imperfect or pluperfect subjunctive, it means *I wish*.

Ojalá fuéramos millonarios.	*I wish that we were millionaires.*
Ojalá no **hubieran** comido toda la ensalada.	*I wish that they hadn't eaten all the salad.*

C. *Quizá* **and** *tal vez*

Quiza and **tal vez**, *perhaps*, are usually used with the present or present perfect subjunctive.

Quizá venga Carlos a la fiesta.	*Perhaps Carlos will come to the party.*
Tal vez Carlos **haya venido** ya.	*Perhaps Carlos has already come.*

EXERCISE 7-18: Translate the following sentences into Spanish, using the verb given in parentheses. Answers are at the end of the chapter.

1. (poder ir) I hope I can go to the beach.

2. (poder ir) I wish I could go to the beach.

3. (ir) I wish we had gone to the beach.

4. (salir) I hope Mario has already left.

5. (estar) Perhaps he is at home.

6. (ir) Maybe Mario will go to Argentina.

7. (poder acostarse) I wish I could go to bed.

8. (poder ir) Perhaps we can go to Uruguay next year.

SUMMARY

1. The present subjunctive endings of **-ar** regular verbs are **-e, -es, -e, -emos, -éis, -en.** The present subjunctive endings of regular **-er** and **-ir** verbs are **-a, -as, -a, -amos, -áis, -an.** The present subjunctive stem is the same as the first person singular present indicative stem: **habl-, escrib-, viv-.**

2. Any verb with a stem change in the first person singular present indicative has the same stem change in the subjunctive: **teng-, pued-, quier-,** and so forth. Some subjunctive stems require spelling changes before the subjunctive endings: **empezar—empiece, empieces,** etc.; **coger—coja, cojas,** etc.

3. The verbs **dar, estar, haber, ir, saber,** and **ser** are irregular in the present subjunctive and must be memorized.

4. The subjunctive is used in dependent clauses with a change of subject (*a*) after verbs of emotion, doubt, uncertainty, or denial, and verbs of desire or command, such as **temer, dudar,** and **querer;** (*b*) after impersonal expressions such as **es necesario** and **es imposible;** (*c*) after indefinite antecedents; (*d*) after words that end with **-quiera,** such as **cualquiera, quienquiera,** and **dondequiera;** and (*e*) after negative antecedents, such as **nada** or **nadie.**

5. The imperfect subjunctive endings of regular verbs are **-ra, -ras, -ra, -ramos, -rais, -ran,** or **-se, -ses, -se, -semos, -seis, -sen.** The **-ra** endings are used more frequently than the **-se** endings in spoken Spanish. Imperfect subjunctive endings are added to the third person plural preterite indicative stem, which is formed by dropping the **-ron** ending: **habla-, escribie-, vivie-.**

6. Verbs with an irregular preterite stem in the indicative use the same stem to form the imperfect subjunctive: **anduv-, sup-,** etc. Verbs with irregular preterite stems add either **-iera** or **-iese** endings, except for verbs with irregular stems ending in **j** or **y,** which add **-era** or **-ese: trajera, influyera. Ir** and **ser** are irregular and must be memorized.

7. When using the subjunctive, the rules for the sequence of tenses are (*a*) present and future indicative in main clauses are followed by the present subjunctive in dependent clauses; and (*b*) imperfect indicative, preterite, and conditional in main clauses are followed by the imperfect subjunctive in dependent clauses.

8. Certain conjunctions are always followed by the subjunctive in dependent clauses: **a no ser que, a menos que, con tal que, en caso de que, antes de que, a fin de que, para que, sin que,** and **como si.**

9. Conjunctions of time, such as **cuando, hasta que,** and so forth, are followed by the subjunctive if the action in the dependent clause is in the future. If the action in the dependent clause has already taken place, the indicative is used. **Antes de que** always takes the subjunctive.

10. Other conjunctions, such as **aunque** and **a pesar de que,** function like conjunctions of time. The use of the subjunctive versus the indicative depends upon whether the action in the dependent clause has or has not taken place.

11. The present perfect and pluperfect subjunctive are formed by conjugating the auxiliary verb **haber** in the present and imperfect subjunctive respectively with a past participle: **haya ido; hubiera (hubiese) ido.**

12. When using the perfect subjunctive, the rules for the sequence of tenses are (*a*) present and future indicative in main clauses are followed by the present perfect subjunctive in dependent clauses; (*b*) imperfect indicative, preterite, and conditional in main clauses are followed by the pluperfect subjunctive.

13. The perfect subjunctives are used to indicate actions that have already taken place, that might have taken place, or that one wishes had taken place.

14. The rules for the sequence of tenses of **si** clauses are (*a*) present indicative in dependent (**si**) clause is followed by the future indicative in the main clause; (*b*) imperfect subjunctive in dependent (**si**) clause is followed by the conditional in the main clause; and (*c*) the pluperfect subjunctive in dependent (**si**) clause is followed by the conditional perfect in the main clause.

15. The third person present subjunctive forms are used for both affirmative and negative formal commands: (**no**) **hable usted**; (**no**) **hablen ustedes**.

16. The third person singular present indicative form is used for the affirmative **tú** command: **habla** (**tú**). The second person singular present subjunctive form is used for the negative **tú** command: **no hables** (**tú**).

17. To form the **vosotros(-as)** affirmative command, drop the final **r** of the infinitive and add **d**: **hablad, comed, escribid**. The second person plural present subjunctive form is used for the negative **vosotros(-as)** command: **no habléis, no comáis, no escribáis**.

18. The formal **usted** and **ustedes** pronouns are almost always used with the command form. The informal **tú** and **vosotros(-as)** pronouns are usually not used. The reflexive pronouns are attached to the verb in affirmative commands. The reflexive pronouns are placed before the verb in negative commands.

19. There are two forms of indirect commands: **que** + present subjunctive; and present subjunctive first person plural.

20. The subjunctive is used after **quisiera**, *would be*, **ojalá**, *I wish* or *I hope*, and **quizá** or **tal vez**, *perhaps*.

RAISE YOUR GRADES

☑ **Verbs requiring the subjunctive** [Section 7-2]

Identify the meaning of the verb in the main clause by choosing one of the three categories listed below and writing in the corresponding letter in the space provided to the left of each sentence. Then complete the sentence by writing in the correct present or imperfect subjunctive form of the verb given in parentheses. Answers are at the end of the chapter.

> *a.* emotion   *b.* doubt, denial   *c.* desire

Example: (ir) ___*c*___ Quiero que tú ___*vayas*___ a la tienda.

1. (traer) _____ Tememos que nadie _____ un sacacorchos.
2. (oír) _____ Raúl espera que todos _____ su concierto en la radio.
3. (ganar) _____ Carlos no cree que nosotros _____ el partido de béisbol.
4. (tener) _____ Pido que tú _____ paciencia.
5. (saber) _____ Dudo que ella _____ traducir bien la poesía.
6. (dar) _____ Me alegro de que los estudiantes _____ tanta comida a los pobres.
7. (estar) _____ Jesús dudaba que nosotros _____ en casa.
8. (acostarse) _____ Queríamos que los niños _____ temprano.
9. (salir) _____ Adolfo necesitó que alguien _____ con él.
10. (vivir) _____ Andrew no creía que Jaime _____ en ese apartamento.
11. (buscar) _____ Prefiero que tú _____ a otra persona.
12. (haber) _____ Espero que pronto _____ paz.
13. (callarse) _____ Yo no quería que nadie _____ nunca.
14. (haber) _____ José no creía que _____ más arroz.
15. (caer) _____ Temo que Eva _____.

☑ **Sequence of tenses** [Sections 7-2, 7-4, and 7-7]

The most important general rule for the sequence of tenses is that past time in the main clause can never be followed by present or future time in the dependent clause. In the following sentences, write in the tense of the italicized verb in the main clause in the space provided to the left of the sentence. Then choose the verb given in parentheses that correctly completes the sentence. Answers are at the end of the chapter.

Example: _____imperfect_____ Mis padres *querían* que (*acabáramos*, acabaremos, acabemos) temprano.

1. _____ *Sería* imposible que muchas flores (crezcan, crecieran, crecieron) en aquel desierto.
2. _____ *Pedíamos* a todos que (traigan, traerían, trajeran) algo de comer.
3. _____ *Quise* que Leonila (era, fuera, sería) invitada en vez de Mario.
4. _____ *Iremos* cuando (tuvimos, teníamos, tengamos) más tiempo.
5. _____ Pepe *duda* que (habrá, hay, haya) un partido de fútbol el domingo.
6. _____ *Siento* mucho que (hubieras estado, has estado, hayas estado) enferma.
7. _____ Los niños *necesitan* que alguien (ayuda, ayudara, ayude) con el transporte.
8. _____ Yo *esperaba* que no (venga, viniera, vino) nadie.
9. _____ El jefe *pedía* a todos que (se sentaban, se sentaron, se sentaran).
10. _____ *Temo* mucho que (han cerrado, hayan cerrado, hubieran cerrado) el banco.
11. _____ *No pensábamos* que (habías llegado, hubieras llegado, hayas llegado).
12. _____ Alda *necesita* una secretaria que (sabía, supiera, sepa) japonés.
13. _____ Yo *quería* que (te sientas, te sentaras, te sentarás) a mi lado.
14. _____ *Espero* que todos (se despidieron, se despiden, se despidan) temprano.
15. _____ Ellos *esperaban* que (ganaba, ganara, gane) Rosa.

☑ **The infinitive *versus* the subjunctive construction** [Sections 7-2, 7-4, and 7-5]

One of the important differences between English and Spanish is the use in Spanish of **que** + the subjunctive in a dependent clause when there is a change of subject. However, a simple infinitive construction is used when there is no change of subject. Change each of the following sentences from an infinitive construction to the **que** + subjunctive construction, using the change of subject given in parentheses. Answers are at the end of the chapter.

Examples: Quiero leer *La guerra y la paz*. (Mario) *Quiero que Mario lea* La guerra y la paz.
Iré antes de comer. (los niños) *Iré antes de que los niños coman.*

1. Espero casarme esta primavera. (Lourdes y Manolo)

2. Yo sentía mucho perder el partido. (las muchachas)

3. Saldremos después de cenar. (mis padres)

4. Lavaré los platos antes de acostarme. (todos)

5. Temo perder el tren. (ustedes)

6. Estudio para aprender más. (mis hijos)

7. Yo esperaba llegar antes del almuerzo. (tú)

8. Yo quería vender la casa. (usted)

9. Necesito volver a casa después del cine. (alguien)

10. Quería tocar el piano. (Jaime)

11. Me gusta cantar y bailar. (los jóvenes)

12. Estoy contento de sentarme aquí tranquilamente. (los muchachos)

13. Yo necesitaba trabajar muchas horas. (mi hermano)

14. Quiero estar en la primera fila. (los estudiantes)

15. Yo tocaba el piano para oír música. (los amigos).

☑ *Si* clauses [Section 7-7]

There are two kinds of **si** clauses. **Si** clauses that state a condition use the present tense and are followed by the main clause in the future tense. **Si** clauses that make a contrary to fact statement use the imperfect or pluperfect subjunctive, and are followed by the conditional or conditional perfect. In the following sentences, change the conditional **si** clause to a **si** clause making a contrary to fact statement. Answers are at the end of the chapter.

Example: Si gano mucho dinero, iré a París.   *Si ganara mucho dinero, iría a París.*

1. Si Raúl practica mucho, ganará el premio.

2. Si los niños no se han acostado, pueden salir.

3. Si todos se callan, oiremos mejor.

4. Si los estudiantes saben la lección, la maestra les dará una hora libre.

5. Si los estudiantes han aprendido bien la lección, estarán contentos.

6. Si soy el rey, perdonaré a todos.

7. Si corremos todas las mañanas, perderemos peso.

8. Si viene Antonia, me pelearé con ella.

9. Si hay más té, tomaré otra taza.

10. Si abro la puerta, entrará mucho viento.

☑ Direct commands [Section 7-8]

There is no easy way to become accustomed to using the many different forms of affirmative and negative direct commands. It is necessary to practice a great deal. In the following sentences, write in the opposite of the command given, and its English translation. When you are finished, practice reading the commands out loud. Answers are at the end of the chapter.

Example: Diga usted la verdad. *No diga usted la verdad. Don't tell the truth.*

1. No te comas el pastel.

2. Siéntate.

3. No te acuestes.

4. Pide un vaso de agua.

5. No des el coche a Luisa.

6. Vaya usted al mercado.

7. No vengáis tarde.

8. Poned la mesa, por favor.

9. Ponte el vestido rojo.

10. Cállate.

11. Acérquense ustedes.

12. No te acuerdes de eso.

13. No se alegren ustedes.

14. Almuerza conmigo.

15. No te despiertes.

16. Pagad la cuenta.

17. Péinate otra vez.

18. Rompa usted los platos.

19. Sigan ustedes mi consejo.

20. Ten paciencia conmigo.

CHAPTER ANSWERS

EXERCISE 7-1

1. enseñe, enseñemos, enseñen, enseñe
2. vayamos, vayáis, vayas, vaya
3. busques, busquen, busquéis, busque
4. dé, den, demos, des
5. cerréis, cierres, cierre, cerremos
6. llegue, lleguen, lleguen, lleguéis
7. viva, vivamos, viva, viva
8. seas, sea, sean, sea
9. empieces, empiecen, empecéis, empiece
10. prueben, pruebe, pruebe, pruebe
11. sepáis, sepa, sepamos, sepa
12. tengamos, tenga, tengan, tengas
13. saques, saquéis, saquemos, saque
14. salga, salgan, salgamos, salga
15. estés, estemos, estén, esté

EXERCISE 7-2

1. coman   *I don't think they eat meat.*
2. se acueste   *Her mother prefers that Leonila go to bed early.*
3. sea   *Don't you think that Josefina is the winner?*
4. tengan   *I'm very sorry you don't have more time.*
5. se vaya   *I doubt that Carlos will go to live in France.*
6. se callen   *I order everyone to shut up immediately.*

7. busquen   *We want you to look for Juan's brother.*
8. paguen   *I prefer them not to pay the bill.*
9. diga   *I don't think that Norma will say anything to her friends.*
10. sigan   *We ask that the students follow us by car.*
11. se casen   *Parents don't want their children to get married.*
12. toquen   *The teacher orders her pupils to play the piano three hours a day.*
13. cojan   *I hope you don't catch my cold.*
14. pidan   *I want everyone to ask the boss for more money.*
15. volváis   *I want you to return home very soon.*
16. quieran   *I don't think you want to be here.*
17. pueda   *I don't think Sara can win.*
18. esté   *Laura denies that her aunt is home.*
19. ataque   *Enrique doubts that the dog will attack.*
20. encienda   *I want you to light my cigarette.*

EXERCISE 7-3

1. Es una lástima que Mary no trabaje.   *It's a shame that Mary doesn't work.*
2. Es importante que nosotros pensemos seriamente.   *It's important for us to think seriously.*

3. Es necesario que los niños beban leche. *It's necessary for the children to drink milk.*
4. Es dudoso que Antonio venga a tiempo. *It's doubtful that Antonio will come in time.*
5. Es raro que los estudiantes se callen en clase. *It's unusual for the students to be quiet in class.*
6. Es posible que los futbolistas no jueguen mañana. *It's possible that the football players won't play tomorrow.*
7. Es imposible que Manuel se case con Julieta. *It's impossible for Manuel to get married to Julieta.*
8. Es urgente que el mitin empiece a las cinco. *It is urgent that the meeting begin at five.*
9. Es preciso que tú busques a Claudio. *It is necessary for you to look for Claudio.*
10. Es posible que él tenga fiebre. *It's possible that he has a fever.*
11. Es necesario que nosotros sigamos el mismo camino. *It's necessary for us to follow the same path.*
12. Es raro que tu primo pida dinero. *It's unusual for your cousin to ask for money.*
13. Es importante que todos oigan las instrucciones. *It's important for everyone to hear the instructions.*
14. Es dudoso que ustedes se acuesten temprano. *It's doubtful that you will go to bed early.*
15. Es preciso que vosotros pongáis la mesa. *It's necessary for you to set the table.*

EXERCISE 7-4

1. vayas *I'll go wherever you go.*
2. conoce *I want to talk to the nurse who knows my aunt.*
3. conduzca *We need a person who drives a car well.*
4. quiere *My brother knows a couple who want to sell all their books.*
5. tengas *Whenever you have time, we'll eat together.*
6. se acuesta *My mother is a person who always goes to bed late.*
7. sepa *Jorge is looking for a girlfriend who knows how to ski.*
8. diga *Whatever he says will be sensible.*
9. se levante *We need a helper who will get up early.*
10. se casan *I have to talk to the bride and groom who are getting married on Saturday.*
11. vuelva *I'll talk with the student who comes back first.*
12. se parece *We have a friend who looks a lot like Bette Davis.*
13. toque *The boss needs a musician who plays the trumpet and the guitar.*
14. da *I want to talk to the woman who gives piano lessons.*
15. se porten *I'll give a prize to all the children who behave well.*

EXERCISE 7-5

1. dijera, pidiera, leyera *The boss ordered Emilio to say, ask for, read, something.*
2. bailaran, comieran, durmieran *My mother asked the boys to dance, eat, sleep, less.*
3. estudiaran, oyeran, tradujeran *The teacher wanted the students to study, hear, translate, more attentively.*
4. fueras, viajaras, salieras *I wanted you to go, travel, leave, with me.*
5. supierais, llegarais, os sentarais *Manolo insisted that you know, arrive, sit down, first.*
6. cayese, condujese, cantase *We didn't want Violeta to fall, drive, sing.*
7. viniesen, saliesen, se marchasen *We were very sorry that you came, left, departed, so early.*
8. se sentase, fuese, saliese *Eloisa expected her grandmother to sit down, go, leave, in the car.*
9. cocinaras, corrieras, leyeras *I didn't think that you cooked, ran, read, so much.*
10. llegaran, estuvieran, salieran *The boss wanted everyone to arrive, be, leave, early.*

EXERCISE 7-6

1. caminara *I didn't think that Pepe would walk home.*
2. vinieran *We would hope that they would all come.*
3. atacara *I didn't think that the dog would attack anyone.*
4. tocáramos *My parents wanted us to play the violin.*
5. te parecieras *I didn't think that you looked like your brothers.*
6. pague *We hope that Carlos will pay the bill.*
7. ganen *They doubt that you'll win.*
8. vayamos *You want us to go somewhere else.*
9. saquéis *I don't want you to take out the new dishes.*
10. empecemos *The teacher orders us to begin at nine.*
11. llegaras *I would hope that you would arrive early.*
12. supiera *I would need a helper who knew how to write well.*
13. tuviera *Maria wanted to buy a house that had a swimming pool.*
14. tocara *There was no one who played the piano better.*
15. conociera *I didn't think that you knew Mr. López.*
16. se levantaran *It was necessary for you to get up at six.*
17. se callaran *It would be necessary for everyone to be quiet.*
18. cupieran *It was not clear whether all the luggage would fit.*

19. trajeras   *It would be impossible for you to bring so many people.*
20. se casaran   *It wasn't true that Julia and David got married.*

EXERCISE 7-7

1. Hoy nos levantamos temprano para que María desayune con nosotros.   *We are getting up early today so that María can have breakfast with us.*
2. Yo no como helado a fin de que mi marido no engorde.   *I don't eat ice cream so that my husband won't gain weight.*
3. Pepe no sale nunca a menos que los amigos le inviten.   *Pepe never goes out unless his friends invite him.*
4. Mi madre ponía un plato más en caso de que alguien viniera a cenar.   *My mother set an extra plate in case anyone came to dinner.*
5. Los muchachos salieron de casa antes de que el tocadiscos se rompiera.   *The boys left the house before the record player broke.*
6. Raimundo comió un pastel entero sin que nadie dijera nada.   *Raimundo ate a whole cake without anyone saying anything.*
7. Siempre llevamos el paraguas en caso de que haya lluvia.   *We always carry an umbrella in case it rains.*
8. Leonardo no va a ninguna parte sin que Marta le acompañe.   *Leonardo doesn't go anywhere without Marta accompanying him.*
9. Yo jugaría al ajedrez con tal que tú quisieras jugar.   *I would play chess provided that you wanted to play.*
10. Yo no bailaría a menos que tú pudieras bailar conmigo.   *I wouldn't dance unless you could dance with me.*
11. Nadie piensa ir a no ser que haga buen tiempo.   *Nobody's thinking of going unless the weather is good.*
12. Vamos en mi coche con tal que quepan las maletas.   *Let's go in my car provided that the luggage fits.*
13. Contaron la historia para que supiera la verdad.   *They told the story so that I would know the truth.*
14. Magda baila como si fuera una bailarina.   *Magda dances as though she were a ballerina.*
15. Jaime habló como si estuviera muy cansado.   *Jaime spoke as though he were very tired.*

EXERCISE 7-8

1. llorarán, se casen   *The parents will cry when the bride and groom are married.*
2. callarán, cante   *Everyone will be quiet when Gilberto sings the national anthem.*
3. volverán, pasen   *The friends will return to the town as soon as five years pass.*

4. no contestarán, hasta que no llegue   *The students will not answer until the teacher arrives.*
5. nos casaremos, hasta que no venga   *We won't get married until grandfather comes.*
6. comprará, gane   *The family will buy a house after María wins the lottery.*
7. se levantarán, se sirva   *Everyone will get up from the table as soon as the coffee is served.*
8. Habrá, salgan   *There will be silence after the children leave.*
9. abrirá, lleguen   *Adolfo will open the door as soon as the guests arrive.*
10. empezará, salga   *Marilyn will begin to cry as soon as her son comes on stage.*

EXERCISE 7-9

1. tenía   *Adela paid the bill although she didn't have much money.*
2. llegue   *We'll open the gifts when your father arrives.*
3. empezara   *We put the furniture inside the house before it started raining.*
4. oyera   *They talked in a very low voice so that no one would hear.*
5. era   *No one yelled in spite of the fact that the situation was dangerous.*
6. bailemos   *We'll put on a record so that all of us can dance.*
7. vio   *Raúl began to smile as soon as he saw his father.*
8. participaran   *We gave a big party so that all the children could participate.*
9. oyera   *Andrés left quietly without anyone hearing him.*
10. tenga   *I'll go on vacation even if I have only a week.*

EXERCISE 7-10

1. haya salido   *I don't think that anyone has left yet.*
2. hubiera estado   *I doubted that Miguel had been in the office.*
3. hubiéramos ido   *José didn't want us to have gone to the movies together.*
4. hubiera publicado   *David expected someone to have published his poetry.*
5. haya llegado   *I hope that the train has not arrived.*
6. hayan leído   *We want everyone to have read the same novel for the class.*
7. hayan terminado   *The teachers hope that all the pupils will have finished their homework at three.*
8. hubiéramos dicho   *The boss didn't want us to have said anything about the new position.*
9. hubiera puesto   *The girls doubted that Ricardo had set the table.*
10. se haya levantado   *I fear that my brother has not gotten up.*

11. se hubieran casado *The parents feared that the young people had gotten married without their permission.*
12. haya hecho *You don't believe that I've made the rice, do you?*
13. se hayan ido *It's not possible that everyone has gone.*
14. se hayan roto *I doubt that all the glasses have been broken.*
15. hubieras escrito *It was necessary for you to have written a letter.*

EXERCISE 7-11

1. Si yo fuera estudiante, estudiaría el español.
2. Si yo hubiera estado enfermo, no habría venido.
3. Si él tuviera tiempo, se iría a México.
4. Si hubiera tenido tiempo, habría hecho la cena.
5. Si conociéramos al presidente, visitaríamos la Casa Blanca.
6. Si hubiéramos sabido la verdad, no habríamos dicho nada.
7. Si pudiera comer algo, comería un poco de pan con mermelada.
8. Si pudiera beber algo, bebería leche.
9. Si tú no hablaras, nosotros nos callaríamos también.
10. Si tú te hubieras callado, habrías oído el discurso.

EXERCISE 7-12

1. escriba *Don't write yet.*
2. llore *Don't cry so much.*
3. haga *Don't do anything.*
4. Empiece *Begin right now.*
5. Venga *Come here.*
6. Oiga *Listen, please.*
7. Hablen *Speak louder.*
8. cierre *Don't close the door.*
9. busque *Don't look for anything now.*
10. Vuelva *Come back tomorrow.*
11. siga *Don't take my advice.*
12. Paguen *Pay the bill.*
13. fume *Don't smoke here, please.*
14. Avance *Take two steps forward.*
15. Vayan *Go with him.*
16. sean *Don't be impertinent.*
17. dé *Don't give (away) anything.*
18. Enseñen *Show the photos.*
19. Lean *Read the books.*
20. duerman *Don't sleep, please.*

EXERCISE 7-13

1. Toma *Have a glass of wine.*
2. bebáis *Don't drink water.*
3. corras *Don't run so much.*
4. Caminad *Walk more slowly.*
5. Pon *Set the table.*
6. ahorres *Don't save your money.*
7. pegues *Don't hit your brother.*
8. Haz *Do what I tell you.*
9. gritéis *Don't yell.*
10. Comenzad *Begin now.*
11. digas *Don't say anything.*
12. Bailad *Dance, please.*
13. Sal *Leave right now.*
14. vayas *Don't go to class.*
15. Limpia *Clean the kitchen.*
16. Pide *Ask your mother for permission.*
17. seas *Don't be a jerk.*
18. Dormid *Sleep well.*
19. Cierra *Close the door.*
20. Ven *Come here.*

EXERCISE 7-14

1. Di *Tell the truth.*
2. caigas *Don't fall down the stairs.*
3. Bebe *Drink another cup of coffee.*
4. saquéis *Don't bring out the books yet.*
5. Ven *Come with me.*
6. pienses *Don't think a lot.*
7. despiertes *Don't wake the little girl up.*
8. Fríe *Fry a couple of eggs.*
9. duermas *Don't sleep.*
10. Vended *Sell the old books.*
11. Da *Give Manuel some advice, please.*
12. des *Don't give the children candy, please.*
13. juguéis *Don't play near the swimming pool.*
14. vayas *Don't go with him.*
15. seas *Don't be so impatient.*
16. Enseña *Show everyone the drawings.*
17. mientas *Don't lie.*
18. Lee *Read* War and Peace.
19. Almuerza *Have lunch with me, please.*
20. Devuelve *Return my books tomorrow, please.*
21. Huele *Smell the soup.*
22. pierdas *Don't lose my umbrella.*
23. Responde *Answer right now.*
24. Subid *Go up the stairway very slowly, please.*
25. grites *Don't yell so much, please.*

EXERCISE 7-15

1. No te peines *Don't comb your hair differently.*
2. Ne se sienten *Don't sit down here.*
3. Ponte *Put that hat on.*
4. No te enojes *Don't get more annoyed.*
5. No os lavéis *Don't wash your face.*
6. No te rías *Don't laugh at me.*
7. No os equivoquéis *Don't make many mistakes.*
8. Asústate *Be frightened.*
9. No te quedes *Don't stay with us.*
10. No se quite *Don't take off your coat.*
11. Váyase *Go now.*
12. No se acuesten *Don't go to bed soon.*

13. No te despidas *Don't say goodbye to your grandmother.*
14. Quéjese *Complain about the food.*
15. Enfádate *Get mad.*

EXERCISE 7-16

1. Que te pongas mejor pronto.
2. Que ponga la mesa Jaime.
3. Que se sientan mejor pronto.
4. Que se sientan ustedes mejor pronto.
5. Que no se caiga usted.
6. Que se siente primero Andrew.
7. Que lave los platos Anthony.
8. Que vivas para siempre.
9. Que nunca se muera.
10. Que tengáis mucha suerte.
11. Que descansen ustedes bien.
12. Que traiga suerte.
13. Que lea la carta Manuel.
14. Que abra la puerta Alicia.
15. Que entren los niños ahora.
16. Escapémonos a México.
17. No salgamos ahora.
18. No nos levantemos.
19. No nos enojemos.
20. Acostémonos.

EXERCISE 7-17

1. Él quisiera que tú comieras. *He would like you to eat.*
2. Nosotros quisiéramos que él comprara una casa. *We would like him to buy a house.*
3. Nosotros quisiéramos que él se despidiera. *We would like him to say goodbye.*
4. Yo quisiera que vosotros os sentarais. *I would like you to sit down.*
5. Ellos quisieran que ella tocara el piano. *They would like her to play the piano.*
6. José quisiera que nosotros jugáramos al ajedrez. *José would like us to play chess.*
7. Nosotros quisiéramos que tú te quedaras. *We would like you to stay.*
8. María quisiera que vosotros bebierais algo. *María would like you to drink something.*
9. Tú quisieras que yo dejara el trabajo. *You would like me to quit my job.*
10. Yo quisiera que todos se quitaran los abrigos. *I would like everyone to take off their coats.*

EXERCISE 7-18

1. Ojalá pueda ir a la playa.
2. Ojalá pudiera ir a la playa.
3. Ojalá hubiéramos ido a la playa.
4. Ojalá haya salido ya Mario.
5. Quizá esté en casa.
6. Tal vez vaya Mario a la Argentina.
7. Ojalá pudiera acostarme.
8. Quizá podamos ir a Uruguay el año próximo.

RAISE YOUR GRADES

Verbs requiring the subjunctive

1. a; traiga *We fear that no one will bring a corkscrew.*
2. a; oigan *Raúl hopes that everyone will hear his concert on the radio.*
3. b; ganemos *Carlos doesn't think that we'll win the baseball game.*
4. c; tengas *I ask you to be patient.*
5. b; sepa *I doubt that she knows how to translate poetry well.*
6. a; den *I'm glad that the students are giving so much food to the poor.*
7. b; estuviéramos *Jesús doubted that we were home.*
8. c; se acostaran *We wanted the children to go to bed early.*
9. c; saliera *Adolfo needed someone to go out with him.*
10. b; viviera *Andrew didn't think that Jaime lived in that apartment.*
11. c; busques *I prefer you to look for someone else.*
12. a; haya *I hope that there's peace soon.*
13. c; se callara *I didn't want anyone to be quiet ever.*
14. b; hubiera *José didn't think that there was any more rice.*
15. a; caiga *I fear that Eva will fall.*

Sequence of tenses

1. conditional; crecieran *It would be impossible for many flowers to grow in that desert.*
2. imperfect; trajeran *We asked everyone to bring something to eat.*
3. preterite; fuera *I wanted Leonila to be invited instead of Mario.*
4. future; tengamos *We'll go when we have more time.*
5. present; haya *Pepe doubts that there is a football game on Sunday.*
6. present; hayas estado *I'm very sorry that you've been sick.*
7. present; ayude *The children need someone to help with transportation.*
8. imperfect; viniera *I expected that nobody would come.*
9. imperfect; se sentaran *The boss asked everyone to sit down.*
10. present; hayan cerrado *I fear very much that they have closed the bank.*
11. imperfect; hubieras llegado *We didn't think you had arrived.*
12. present; sepa *Alda needs a secretary who knows Japanese.*
13. imperfect; te sentaras *I wanted you to sit next to me.*
14. present; se despidan *I hope everyone says goodbye early.*
15. imperfect; ganara *They expected Rosa to win.*

The infinitive *versus* the subjunctive construction

1. Espero que Lourdes y Manolo se casen esta primavera. *I hope that Lourdes and Manolo get married this spring.*
2. Yo sentía mucho que las muchachas perdieran el partido. *I was very sorry that the girls lost the game.*
3. Saldremos después de que mis padres cenen. *We will leave after my parents have dinner.*
4. Lavaré los platos antes de que todos se acuesten. *I'll wash the dishes before everyone goes to bed.*
5. Temo que ustedes pierdan el tren. *I fear that you will miss the train.*
6. Estudio para que mis hijos aprendan más. *I study so that my children learn more.*
7. Yo esperaba que tú llegaras antes del almuerzo. *I expected you to come before lunch.*
8. Yo quería que usted vendiera la casa. *I wanted you to sell the house.*
9. Necesito que alguien vuelva a casa después del cine. *I need someone to return home after the movie.*
10. Quería que Jaime tocara el piano. *I wanted Jaime to play the piano.*
11. Me gusta que los jóvenes canten y bailen. *I like young people to sing and dance.*
12. Estoy contento de que los muchachos se sienten aquí tranquilamente. *I'm pleased that the boys are seated here quietly.*
13. Yo necesitaba que mi hermano trabajara muchas horas. *I needed my brother to work many hours.*
14. Quiero que los estudiantes estén en la primera fila. *I want the students to be in the first row.*
15. Yo tocaba el piano para que los amigos oyeran música. *I played the piano so that my friends would hear music.*

Si clauses

1. practicara, ganaría *If Raúl practiced a lot, he would win the prize.*
2. se hubieran acostado, podrían *If the children hadn't gone to bed, they could go out.*
3. se callaran, oiríamos *If everyone kept quiet, we would hear better.*
4. supieran, daría *If the students knew the lesson, the teacher would give them an hour off.*
5. hubieran aprendido, estarían *If the students had learned the lesson, they would be happy.*
6. fuera, perdonaría *If I were the king, I would pardon everyone.*
7. *corriéramos, perderíamos* *If we ran every morning, we would lose weight.*
8. *viniera, me pelearía* *If Antonia came, I'd fight with her.*
9. hubiera, tomaría *If there were more tea, I'd have another cup.*
10. abriera, entraría *If I opened the door, it would be too windy.*

Direct commands

1. Cómete *Eat up the cake.*
2. No te sientes *Don't sit down.*
3. Acuéstate *Go to bed.*
4. No pidas. *Don't ask for a glass of water.*
5. Da *Give Luisa the car.*
6. No vaya *Don't go to the market.*
7. Venid *Come late.*
8. No pongáis *Please don't set the table.*
9. No te pongas *Don't put on the red dress.*
10. No te calles *Don't be quiet.*
11. No se acerquen *Don't come close.*
12. Acuérdate *Remember that.*
13. Alégrense *Be happy.*
14. No almuerces *Don't have lunch with me.*
15. Despiértate *Wake up.*
16. No paguéis *Don't pay the bill.*
17. No te peines *Don't comb your hair again.*
18. No rompa *Don't break the dishes.*
19. No sigan *Don't take my advice.*
20. No tengas *Don't be patient with me.*

8 PRONOUNS

THIS CHAPTER IS ABOUT

- ☑ **Subject Pronouns**
- ☑ **Prepositional Pronouns**
- ☑ **Object Pronouns**
- ☑ **Use of Object Pronouns**
- ☑ **Position of Object Pronouns**
- ☑ **Double Object Pronouns**
- ☑ **Reflexive Pronouns**
- ☑ **Special Uses of Indirect Object Pronouns**
- ☑ **Possessive and Demonstrative Pronouns**
- ☑ **Relative Pronouns**

8-1. Subject Pronouns

In Spanish, subject pronouns are generally used only for emphasis or clarification. However, there are other important differences between Spanish and English in the use of subject pronouns. Study the chart of subject pronouns given below.

	Singular		Plural
yo	*I*	**nosotros(-as)**	*we*
tú	*you (fam.)*	**vosotros(-as)**	*you (fam.)*
él	*he, it*	**ellos**	*they*
ella	*she, it*	**ellas**	*they*
usted	*you (form.)*	**ustedes**	*you (form.)*

> **REMEMBER:** Although the subject pronouns are not generally used, **usted** is almost always used in formal direct address. See Chapter 3, Section 3-1, for a review of the use of formal *versus* informal forms of address.

A. The plural subject

When combination subjects such as *he and I* or *you and she* are used in Spanish, there are "strong" and "weak" pronouns: **yo** is stronger than **tú**, **tú** is stronger than **él** and **ella**, and **usted** is stronger than **tú**. Study the following examples.

1. **tú + yo = nosotros, él + yo = nosotros**

   Él y yo **vamos** a ir juntos al cine.   *He and I are going to the movies together.*

2. **tú + él = vosotros** (in Spain), **tú + él = ustedes** (in Latin America)

   Tú y María **estudiáis** juntos, ¿verdad?   *You and María study together, right?*
   Tú y María **estudian** juntos, ¿verdad?   *You and María study together, right?*

3. tú + usted = ustedes

Tú y usted **siéntense** aquí, por favor.   *You and you sit here, please.*

EXERCISE 8-1:   Write in the correct present indicative form of the verb given in parentheses. Don't forget the reflexive pronoun if the verb is reflexive. See Chapter 3, Section 3-5, if you need to review the reflexive pronouns. Answers are at the end of the chapter.

1. (estudiar) Antonio y yo _____ demasiado.
2. (ser) Tú y él _____ buenos amigos, ¿verdad? *(in Spain)*
3. (casarse) Tú y yo _____ en junio.
4. (irse) ¿Cuándo _____ tú y Roberta? *(in Spain)*
5. (tener que) Usted y él _____ llegar a un acuerdo.
6. (ayudar) Tú y tu hermano _____ mucho en casa. *(in Latin America)*
7. (enfadarse) El profesor y yo _____ una vez por semana.
8. (poder) ¿A qué hora _____ salir tú y Mario? *(in Latin America)*
9. (tener que) Usted y yo _____ trabajar.
10. (callarse) Iris y yo nunca _____ .

B. The emphatic subject

The subject pronoun can be used to emphasize the participation of the subject in the action of the verb. When the subject pronoun comes after the verb, the emphasis is on the doer of the action, rather than on the action itself.

Él pinta muy bien.	*He paints very well.*
Pinta muy bien **él**.	***He** paints very well.*
¿Vas a ir?	*Are you going to go?*
¿Vas a ir **tú**?	*Are **you** going to go?*

C. The subject "it"

In Spanish, there is no impersonal subject pronoun "it." Rather, "it" is expressed by the third person singular verb form.

Llueve mucho hoy.	*It's raining a lot today.*
No **funciona**.	*It doesn't work.*
Es difícil ganarse la vida.	*It's hard to make a living.*

8-2. Prepositional Pronouns

Prepositional pronouns are used after prepositions. They are the same as the subject pronouns, with the exceptions of **mí**, **ti**, and **sí**. Study the following chart.

mí	*me*	**nosotros(-as)**	*us*
ti	*you*	**vosotros(-as)**	*you (fam. pl.)*
él	*him*	**ellos**	*them*
ella	*her*	**ellas**	*them*
usted	*you*	**ustedes**	*you (form. pl.)*

NOTE: **Sí** is used to mean *himself, herself, yourself,* and *themselves.* The written accent over **mí** and **sí** avoids confusion with **si**, *if*, and **mi**, *my*.

When the preposition **con** is used with **mí**, **ti**, or **sí**, a single word is formed by adding **-go**: **conmigo**, *with me*, **contigo**, *with you*, **consigo**, *with himself, herself,* etc.

EXERCISE 8-2:   Translate the pronouns given in parentheses into Spanish. Then read the entire sentence out loud and translate it. Answers are at the end of the chapter.

Example: Voy a ir sin (you, fam. sing.) *ti. I'm going to go without you.*
1. ¿Por qué no nos sentamos detrás de (them) _____ ?
2. Quiero que camines hacia (her) _____ .
3. Este regalo es para (you, form. sing.) _____ .

4. Quiero que almuerces con (them)_____.
5. Hay una disputa entre (her and them)_____.
6. Esteban no vive cerca de (me)_____.
7. No quiero hablar delante de (you, fam. pl., and them)_____.
8. Mi primo vive muy lejos de (you, fam. sing.)_____.
9. Compré un sombrero para (him)_____.
10. El tren salió sin (us)_____.
11. Nunca hablamos de (you, fam. pl.)_____.
12. Hay una mujer detrás de (him)_____.
13. Necesito que alguien vaya con (me)_____.
14. Quiero hablar con (you, fam. sing.)_____.
15. Puedo hacer muchas cosas sin (you, fam. sing.)_____.

8-3. Object Pronouns

Both direct and indirect object pronouns are the same except for the third person singular and plural forms. Study the following charts.

Direct object pronouns

me	*me*	**nos**	*us*
te	*you*	**os**	*you*
lo	*him, it*	**los**	*them*
la	*her, it*	**las**	*them*

Indirect object pronouns

me	*from* or *to me*	**nos**	*from* or *to us*
te	*from* or *to you*	**os**	*from* or *to you*
le	*from* or *to him, her, you*	**les**	*from* or *to them, you*

> **NOTE:** In Spain, **le** and **les** are used not just as indirect object pronouns, but also as direct object pronouns when referring to people. *I see her* may be expressed as either **la veo** or **le veo.** For our purposes, however, the use of **le** and **les** as direct object pronouns is not included in the exercises.

8-4. Use of Object Pronouns

A. **Direct object pronouns are used in place of nouns that directly receive the action of the verb.**

In Spanish, the direct object usually precedes the conjugated form of the verb. Study the following examples.

Yo rompí la silla.	*I broke the chair.*
Yo **la** rompí.	*I broke it.*
Nosotros no vimos a Manuel.	*We didn't see Manuel.*
Nosotros no **lo** vimos.	*We didn't see him.*
Raúl no encontró a las muchachas.	*Raúl didn't find the girls.*
Raúl no **las** encontró.	*Raúl didn't find them.*
Puse los huevos en la nevera.	*I put the eggs in the refrigerator.*
Los puse en la nevera.	*I put them in the refrigerator.*

EXERCISE 8-3: Rewrite the following sentences by substituting the direct object pronoun for the noun or nouns given in parentheses. Remember that some nouns that end in **a** are masculine in gender; for example, **el problema.** See Chapter 1, Section 1-2 for a review of the gender of nouns. Answers are at the end of the chapter.

Example: Corté (el césped) ayer. *Lo corté ayer.*
1. Ayer perdí (mi bolsa).

2. Nunca encontramos (la Avenida Chapultepec).

3. José y Emma buscan (a María).

4. Alguien robó (mi paraguas).

5. Todavía no tenemos (problemas).

6. Los niños terminaron (la tarea).

7. Día y noche escribo (cartas).

8. No hemos probado (la carne).

9. Vimos (a los primos) ayer.

10. Manuel no esperó (a su novia).

B. **Indirect object pronouns always refer to people and are used when the action of the verb is directed to or from the person or persons.**

A prepositional phrase, such as **a mí, a ti, a él, a ella, a usted**, etc., may be added to the basic sentence structure for emphasis or clarification. Study the following examples.

María no **le** habla.　　　　　　　*María doesn't speak to (him, her, you).*
María no **le** habla **a usted**.　　　*María doesn't speak to you.*

> **NOTE:** The prepositional phrase **a usted** clarifies the meaning of **le**.

Les quitó el tocadiscos.　　　*He took the record player.*
¿A quiénes?　　　　　　　*From whom?*
A los muchachos.　　　　　*From the boys.*

Les quitó el tocadiscos **a ellos.**⎫
Les quitó **a ellos** el tocadiscos.⎭　　*He took the record player from them.*

> **NOTE:** In this context, **a ellos** means *from them.*

Nuestro hermano no **nos** escribe.　　*Our brother doesn't write us.*
No es verdad.　　　　　　　　　　*It's not true.*
A mí me escribe pero **a ti** no.　　*He writes to me but not to you.*
A ti no **te** escribe.　　　　　　*He doesn't write to you.*

> **NOTE:** The prepositional phrase **a mí**, **a ti**, etc., is frequently placed at the beginning of the sentence to emphasize the indirect object pronoun **me**, *to me*, **te**, *to you*, etc.

¿Con cuánta frecuencia escribes a tu madre?　　*How often do you write to your mother?*

Le escribo todos los días.　　　⎫
Le escribo **a ella** todos los días.⎭　*I write her every day.*

> **NOTE:** The indirect object pronoun is frequently omitted when the indirect object is a noun: **Escribo a mi madre con frecuencia.** *I write my mother frequently.*

EXERCISE 8-4: Answer the following questions in either the affirmative or the negative as indicated, substituting the correct indirect object pronoun for the noun phrase given in parentheses. Answers are at the end of the chapter.

Examples: ¿Contaron ustedes (a Miguel) la noticia? (no) *No, no le contamos la noticia.*

¿Dio usted la invitación (a todos)? (sí) *Sí, les di la invitación.*

1. ¿Escribe Manuel (a su padre)? (no)

2. ¿Invitaron ustedes (a Ana y a Raquel)? (no)

3. ¿Pidieron permiso los obreros (al jefe)? (no)

4. ¿Oíste (al presidente) anoche en la radio? (no)

5. ¿Escuchaste (a Mariano y a Josefina)? (sí)

6. ¿Hablaron ustedes (a la doctora)? (sí)

7. ¿Escuchan ustedes (al maestro) con atención? (no)

8. ¿Prestaron ustedes el coche (a Rosa)? (sí)

9. ¿Dijo usted algo (a las muchachas)? (no)

10. ¿Diste los recados (a la secretaria)? (sí)

EXERCISE 8-5: Answer the following questions in the affirmative. Use **le** or **les** if the formal **usted** address is used. Use **te** or **os** if the informal **tú** address is used. Translate both the question and your answer into English. Answers are at the end of the chapter.

Examples: ¿Me oyó usted? *Sí, le oí. Did you hear me? Yes, I heard you.*
¿Me oíste? *Sí, te oí. Did you hear me? Yes, I heard you.*
¿Nos oyó usted? *Sí, les oí. Did you hear us? Yes, I heard you.*
¿Nos oíste? *Sí, os oí. Did you hear us? Yes, we heard you.*

1. ¿Me escuchaste anoche?

2. ¿Nos escuchaste anoche?

3. ¿Me pidió usted un favor?

4. ¿Nos pidió usted un favor?

5. ¿Me hizo usted una pregunta?

6. ¿Me hiciste una pregunta?

7. ¿Nos hiciste una pregunta?

8. ¿Nos hizo usted una pregunta?

9. ¿Me dio usted permiso?

10. ¿Nos habló usted ayer?

11. ¿Nos invitaste a la fiesta?

12. ¿Me invitó usted a la fiesta?

13. ¿Nos diste permiso?

14. ¿Me hablaste ayer?

15. ¿Me ayudó usted?

8-5. Position of Object Pronouns

A. In declarative sentences

Both direct and indirect object pronouns usually precede the conjugated form of the verb. Negatives, in turn, precede object pronouns. If there is a subject or a subject pronoun, it precedes the negative.

Subj. Pron.	Neg.	Obj. Pron.	Verb
Yo		le	he escrito.
I		*to him*	*have written.*
Yo	no	le	he escrito.
I	*not*	*to him*	*have written.*

EXERCISE 8-6: Rewrite the following sentences by substituting the correct object pronoun for the noun or noun phrase given in parentheses. Answers are at the end of the chapter.

Example: No he roto (la ventana). *No la he roto.*

1. El profesor nunca escucha (a los alumnos).

2. No perdí (mi bolsa) en el cine.

3. Ya no oyen (los ladridos de los perros).

4. No entendieron (al profesor).

5. Di un recado (al maestro).

6. El jefe no quitó el aumento de salario (a los obreros).

7. Sus hermanos no quitaron a Manuel (los discos).

8. No dimos las entradas (a mis primos).

9. No mandé (el sobre) a la maestra.

10. No mandé el sobre (a la maestra).

B. In commands

Object pronouns are attached to affirmative commands. Object pronouns precede negative commands.

Pon**lo** ahí.	*Put it there.*
No **lo** pongas ahí.	*Don't put it there.*
Escríba**le** usted a ella.	*Write to her.*
No **le** escriba usted a ella.	*Don't write to her.*

> **NOTE:** When a single object pronoun is added to a command of more than one syllable, there is a written accent on the stressed syllable of the command form: **mándalo**, *send it*, **escríbame**, *write me*, **veámosle**, *let's see him.*

EXERCISE 8-7: Rewrite the following negative commands in the affirmative and then translate them into English. Answers are at the end of the chapter.

Example: No me hables ahora. *Háblame ahora. Talk to me now.*

1. No le mandes más libros a ella.

2. No me olvides.

3. No los coma usted, por favor.

4. No le hagan ustedes preguntas.

5. No las cierre usted, por favor.

6. No me busques.

7. No lo rompan ustedes.

8. No le ayude usted.

9. No me invite usted.

10. No le escuches.

C. With infinitives and present participles

Object pronouns may be attached to infinitives and present participles, instead of preceding them.

Le tengo que escribir.
Tengo que escribir**le**. } *I have to write him, her, you.*

Lo estaremos comiendo toda la semana.
Estaremos comiéndo**lo** toda la semana. } *We will be eating it all week.*

> **NOTE:** When an object pronoun is attached to the present participle, there is a written accent over the stressed syllable of the present participle: **mandándolo**, *sending it*, **escribiéndole**, *writing him, her, you.*

EXERCISE 8-8: Rewrite the following sentences twice, substituting the correct object pronoun for the noun or noun phrase given in parentheses. First place the object pronoun before the conjugated verb form, then attach it to the infinitive or present participle. Answers are at the end of the chapter.

Example: Los niños tienen que beber (la leche). *Los niños la tienen que beber.*
Los niños tienen que beberla.

1. Debo escribir (a mi madre).

2. Estoy comiendo (el helado de chocolate).

3. Vamos a comprar (un disco de Mozart).

4. Manolo quiere beber (té).

5. No tuvimos que mandar (tarjetas).

6. Iris no está prestando atención (a Carlos).

7. Mi hermano no quiere vender (su bicicleta).

8. No hemos tenido que comer (el guisado).

9. La maestra y yo estamos leyendo (tu cuento).

10. El perro está mordiendo (un bistec).

8-6. Double Object Pronouns

When a sentence includes two object pronouns, the indirect object pronoun always precedes the direct object pronoun.

	Subj.	Neg.	Ind. Obj. Pronoun	Dir. Obj. Pronoun	Verb
I'm writing a poem.	Yo				escribo un poema.
I'm writing it.	Yo			lo	escribo.
I'm not writing to you.	Yo	no	te		escribo.
I'm not writing it to you.	Yo	no	te	lo	escribo.

A. *Se* as an indirect object pronoun

When the direct object pronouns **lo, la, los,** or **las** are used with **le** or **les**, the indirect object pronouns **le** and **les** change to **se**, in order to avoid the awkward sound of a double l. Study the following examples.

Escribo un poema.	*I'm writing a poem.*
Lo escribo.	*I'm writing it.*
Le escribo.	*I'm writing to him, her, you.*
Se lo escribo.	*I'm writing it to him, her, you.*

Escribo cartas.	*I'm writing letters.*
Las escribo.	*I'm writing them.*
Les escribo.	*I'm writing to them.*
Se las escribo.	*I'm writing them to them.*

EXERCISE 8-9: Rewrite the following sentences by substituting a direct object pronoun for the noun or noun phrase given in parentheses. Answers are at the end of the chapter.

Examples: Pepe me dio (un regalo). *Pepe me lo dio.*

Pepe le dio (un regalo) a Manolo. *Pepe se lo dio a Manolo.*

1. Yo te escribí (varias cartas).

2. Marcela les dio (su permiso) a los niños.

3. Nadie me contó (la historia de Isabel).

4. Alfredo siempre le da (galletas) al niño.

5. Alguien me manda (flores) todos los días.

6. Ya te devolví (tus discos).

7. Rafael le escuchó a María (la queja).

8. Los muchachos les pidieron (dinero) a sus padres.

9. Nadie nos dio (la noticia).

10. Alguien nos regaló (una caja de dulces).

11. Ramón y Angel le trajeron a Raúl (una bicicleta).

12. Mi hermano le dio a Laura (cinco libros).

13. Anita les prestó a los vecinos (su máquina de escribir).

14. El jefe nos negó (un día de descanso más).

15. La tía de Reynaldo nos preparó (una paella).

B. *Se* + prepositional phrase

Se is often used with a prepositional phrase: **a él, a ella, a usted, a ellos, a ellas, a ustedes**. Study the following examples.

Escribo cartas a muchas personas.	*I write letters to many people.*
Se las escribo **a él**.	*I write them to him.*
Se las escribo **a ella**.	*I write them to her.*
Se las escribo **a usted**.	*I write them to you.*
Se las escribo **a ellos**.	*I write them to them.*
Se las escribo **a ellas**.	*I write them to them.*
Se las escribo **a ustedes**.	*I write them to you.*

EXERCISE 8-10:   Answer the following questions by using an object pronoun when possible, and using a prepositional phrase with the indirect object pronoun in place of the answer cue given in parentheses. Answers are at the end of the chapter.

Example: ¿A quién prestaste la máquina de escribir? (a Manuel)
Se la presté a él.

1. ¿A quién regalaste los discos? (a los estudiantes)

2. ¿A quién escribió usted la carta? (a mi madre)

3. ¿A quién compraste la casa? (al señor Martínez)

4. ¿A quién prestó usted los libros? (a los alumnos)

5. ¿A quién vendió usted la raqueta de tenis? (a Alicia)

6. ¿A quién entregaste la fotocopia? (a la secretaria)

7. ¿A quién enviaste el telegrama? (a mis padres)

8. ¿A quién contaste la historia? (a mis amigos)

9. ¿A quién mandó usted los documentos? (al jefe)

10. ¿A quién ofreciste el trabajo? (a mi cuñada)

C. Commands

Double object pronouns are attached to affirmative commands. There is a written accent over the stressed syllable of the affirmative command form: **díganoslo**, *tell it to us*, **véndemela**, *sell it to me*. Double object pronouns precede negative commands.

REMEMBER: The indirect object pronoun always precedes the direct object pronoun.

Escriba usted una carta a Juan.	*Write a letter to Juan.*
Escríba**sela**.	*Write it to him.*
No escriba usted una carta a Juan.	*Don't write a letter to Juan.*
No **se la** escriba.	*Don't write to him.*

Dame el tocadiscos.	*Give me the record player.*
Dá**melo**.	*Give it to me.*
No me des el tocadiscos.	*Don't give me the record player.*
No **me lo** des.	*Don't give it to me.*

EXERCISE 8-11: Rewrite the following negative commands in the affirmative, substituting object pronouns for the noun or noun phrase given in parentheses. Answers are at the end of the chapter.

Examples: No me mande usted (un telegrama). *Mándemelo.*

No des (las cartas a Alicia). *Dáselas.*

1. No escribas (una carta a Pepe).

2. No me traigas (café).

3. No me entregues (el trabajo).

4. No des (helado a los niños).

5. No vendas (la casa a Justina).

6. No nos expliques (la lección).

7. No me traiga usted (las sillas).

8. No nos mande usted (los paquetes).

9. No me regale usted (el piano).

10. No muestre usted (la colección de sellos al maestro).

D. Infinitives and present participles

Double object pronouns may either precede the conjugated form of the verb, or be attached to the infinitive or present participle. Both word orders are used with equal frequency and there is no translatable difference in meaning. Study the following examples.

> **REMEMBER:** The indirect object pronoun always precedes the direct object pronoun.

Manuel no quiere dar un regalo a su abuela.	*Manuel doesn't want to give a present to his grandmother.*
Manuel no **se lo** quiere dar.⎫ Manuel no quiere dár**selo**. ⎭	*Manuel doesn't want to give it to her.*
Estamos leyendo una novela a los niños.	*We are reading a novel to the children.*
Se la estamos leyendo.⎫ Estamos leyéndo**sela**. ⎭	*We are reading it to them.*

EXERCISE 8-12: Rewrite the following sentences twice, using object pronouns where possible. First place the double object pronouns before the conjugated verb form, then attach them to the infinitive or present participle. Translate your work into English. Answers are at the end of the chapter.

Example: Voy a dar el recado al empleado. *Se lo voy a dar. Voy a dárselo. I'm going to give it to him.*

1. Me pueden arreglar la piscina.

2. Los estudiantes están presentando un manifiesto al decano.

3. No necesito mostrar mi pasaporte al aduanero.

4. No podemos prestar el dinero a Eduardo.

5. Nunca quieres divulgar al público mis opiniones.

6. No podían decir la verdad a sus padres.

7. Elena no tuvo que enviar las cajas a su prima.

8. La profesora estaba explicando el problema a sus alumnos.

9. Los niños no pudieron enseñar los juguetes al vecino.

10. La enfermera estaba ofreciendo té a los enfermos.

8-7. Reflexive Pronouns

A. Forms of reflexive pronouns

Reflexive pronouns are conjugated with reflexive verbs to indicate that the action of the verb reflects back upon the doer of the action. See Chapter 3, Section 3-4 for a review of reflexive verbs. Study the following chart of the forms of reflexive pronouns.

Subj. Pron.	Refl. Pron.	Subj. Pron.	Refl. Pron.
yo	**me**	nosotros	**nos**
tú	**te**	vosotros	**os**
él, ella, usted	**se**	ellos, ellas, ustedes	**se**

EXERCISE 8-13: Write in the correct present tense form of the reflexive verb given in parentheses. Answers are at the end of the chapter.

1. (mirarse) Los niños _____ en el espejo.
2. (peinarse) Yo _____ una vez al día.
3. (quedarse) Nadie _____ en casa.
4. (ponerse) Manolo nunca _____ la corbata azul.
5. (despedirse) Alicia y yo nunca _____ de nadie.
6. (quedarse) Raúl y Carlos no _____ a comer.
7. (acordarse) Yo no _____ de nada.
8. (comerse) Los chicos _____ todo lo que hay en la nevera.
9. (irse) Mi abuela _____ a Florida en diciembre.
10. (quitarse) Tú no _____ nunca el abrigo.

B. Reflexive pronouns with direct object pronouns

Although the reflexive pronoun is not an indirect object pronoun, it also precedes the direct object pronoun in sentences with a double object pronoun. Study the following examples.

1. Declarative sentences

Me lavo el pelo una vez por semana.	*I wash my hair once a week.*
Me lo lavo una vez por semana.	*I wash it once a week.*

2. Commands

Póngase usted los zapatos.	*Put on your shoes.*
Póngase**los**.	*Put them on.*
No **se** ponga usted los zapatos.	*Don't put on your shoes.*
No **se los** ponga usted.	*Don't put them on.*

3. Infinitives

Tú tienes que lavar**te** el pelo.	*You have to wash your hair.*
Tú **te lo** tienes que lavar.⎫ Tú tienes que lavár**telo**. ⎬	*You have to wash it.*

4. Present participles

Nosotros **nos** estamos comiendo todo el guisado.	*We are eating up all the stew.*
Nosotros **nos lo** estamos comiendo todo.⎫ Nosotros estamos comiéndo**noslo** todo. ⎬	*We are eating it all up.*

EXERCISE 8-14: Rewrite the following sentences by substituting a direct object pronoun for the noun or noun phrase given in parentheses. Remember to include the necessary written accent when the pronoun is attached to the verb. Answers are at the end of the chapter.

Example: Ayer me puse (la camisa roja).   *Ayer me la puse.*

1. Ponte (el vestido nuevo).

2. Rafael no se quita (el sombrero) nunca.

3. Tengo que quitarme (las botas).

4. Los niños se comieron (la caja de galletas).

5. No te peines (el pelo).

6. Lávate (los dientes).

7. Queremos lavarnos (las manos).

8. No estás poniéndote (la peluca).

9. Angel nunca se quita (la camisa).

10. No te pongas (los zapatos de tu hermano).

8-8. Special Uses of Indirect Object Pronouns

A. The passive *se* construction and indirect object pronouns

The passive voice is used with indirect object pronouns to express a personal involvement in a sudden or involuntary action. In English, a similar construction has the same meaning. For example, *the door opened up on me*, **se me abrió la puerta.**

Passive Construction (se + verb + subject)	Passive + Indirect Object Pronoun
Se olvidó el dinero. *The money was forgotten.*	**Se nos** olvidó el dinero. *We forgot the money. (involuntarily)*
Se quedaron en casa los billetes. *The tickets were left at home.*	**Se les** quedaron en casa los billetes. *They left the tickets at home. (involuntarily)*

NOTE: A prepositional phrase may be added to explain **le** or **les: A las muchachas se les quedaron en casa los billetes.** *The girls left the tickets at home.*

EXERCISE 8-15: Rewrite the following sentences to include the indirect object pronoun that corresponds to the prepositional phrase given in parentheses. Translate your work. Answers are at the end of the chapter.

Example: Se rompió el disco. (a mí)   *Se me rompió el disco. I broke the record.*

1. Se cayó el libro. (a mí)

2. Se rompen las copas con mucha frecuencia. (a nosotros)

3. Se cerró la puerta. (a Emilio)

4. Se descompuso la máquina de escribir. (a la secretaria)

5. Se olvidaron las cucharas y los tenedores. (a ustedes)

6. Se manchó el mantel. (a la señora White)

7. Se olvidó traer la sal. (a ti)

8. Se perdieron los apuntes. (a los estudiantes)

9. Se fueron todos los amigos. (a mí)

10. Se quebró la pluma. (a Laura)

B. Verbs used with indirect object pronouns

Many verbs are commonly used with indirect object pronouns. Study the following examples.

asustar, *to frighten*
   Me asustan los ruidos inesperados.   *Unexpected noises frighten me.*

encantar, *to delight*
   A ellos **les encanta** la música española.   *Spanish music delights them.*

importar, *to care about, to be important*
   Nos importa mucho la política. $\begin{cases}\textit{Politics is very important to us.}\\ \textit{We care a lot about politics.}\end{cases}$

fastidiar, *to be annoying*
   ¿A vosotros **os fastidian** los insectos?   *Do bugs annoy you?*

molestar, *to be bothersome*
   ¿A ustedes **les molesta** la lluvia?   *Does the rain bother you?*

sorprender, *to surprise*
   ¿**Te sorprende** la noticia?   *Does the news surprise you?*

EXERCISE 8-16: Translate the following sentences into Spanish, using the verb given in parentheses. Answers are at the end of the chapter.

1. (encantar) Baseball delights us.

2. (sorprender) The dinner surprised me.

3. (asustar) The dog frightened them.

4. (fastidiar) The noise of the birds annoys you (*fam. sing.*).

5. (importar) Poetry isn't important to her.

6. (enojar) Interruptions annoy us.

7. (molestar) Small children bother you (*form. pl.*).

8. (asustar) Do cats frighten him?

9. (importar) Is art important to them?

10. (molestar) Does the light bother you (*fam. pl.*)?

8-9. Possessive and Demonstrative Pronouns

A. Possessive pronouns

Possessive pronouns take the place of a possessive adjective + noun: **mi libro**, *my book*, **el mío**, *mine*; **mi pluma**, *my pen*, **la mía**, *mine*, etc. Study the following chart.

Possessive Adj.		Possessive Pronoun		
Singular	Plural	Singular	Plural	
mi	mis	**el mío**	**los míos**	*mine*
		la mía	**las mías**	
tu	tus	**el tuyo**	**los tuyos**	*yours (fam. sing.)*
		la tuya	**las tuyas**	
su	sus	**el suyo**	**los suyos**	*his, hers, theirs, yours*
		la suya	**las suyas**	*(form.)*
nuestro	nuestros	**el nuestro**	**los nuestros**	*ours*
nuestra	nuestras	**la nuestra**	**las nuestras**	
vuestro	vuestros	**el vuestro**	**los vuestros**	*yours (fam. pl.)*
vuestra	vuestras	**la vuestra**	**las vuestras**	

1. The possessive pronoun must agree in number and gender with the noun it replaces.

   Tengo mi **libro**.   *I have my book.*
   ¿Quién tiene **el tuyo**?   *Who has yours?*
   Alicia tiene sus **llaves**, pero Roberto   *Alicia has her keys, but Roberto doesn't*
      no tiene **las suyas**.   *have his.*

2. The definite article (**el, la, los, las**) is always used with the possessive pronoun, except after **ser**, *to be*. However, the definite article can be used after **ser** for emphasis.

   Es mi **libro**.   *It's my book.*
   Es **mío**.   *It's mine.*
   Es **el mío**.   *It's mine.*

3. For the sake of clarity, a prepositional phrase, **de** + **el**, **ella**, **usted**, **ellos(-as)**, **ustedes**, is often used with the appropriate definite article in place of **el suyo**, **la suya**, **los suyos**, **las suyas**.

   Vamos a poner mis discos y **los de María**. *We are going to play my records*
                                                  and Maria's.

   BECOMES
   Vamos a poner los míos y **los de ella**.   *We are going to play my records and*
                                                  hers.

EXERCISE 8-17: Rewrite the following sentences, substituting a possessive pronoun for the phrase given in parentheses. Answers are at the end of the chapter.

   Example: ¿Dónde están (los libros de Angel)?   *¿Dónde están los suyos?* OR *¿Dónde están los de él?*

   1. ¿Dónde están (mis flores)?

   2. Tenemos que arreglar (nuestro coche).

3. Puse los (calcetines de los niños) en la máquina de lavar.

4. No tenéis (vuestros pasaportes).

5. ¿Quién tiene (su llave)?

6. ¿Quién se llevó (mi paraguas)?

7. (Mi chaqueta) es azul.

8. ¿Dónde pusiste (tus botas)?

9. (La casa de Juan) es muy grande.

10. (La casa de Ileana) es amarilla.

11. Mario y Luisa trajeron (su radio).

12. Los señores White perdieron (sus zapatos) en la playa.

13. Emilio tiene (su guitarra).

14. Los libros azules son (mis libros).

15. Aquella casa es (mi casa).

B. Demonstrative pronouns

In English, the demonstrative pronouns are *this (one), that (one), these (ones), those (ones)*. In Spanish, the demonstrative adjectives and pronouns are identical, but the demonstrative pronouns have a written accent over the **e**: **éste, ése, aquél,** etc. Forms of **éste** are also used to mean *the latter*, and forms of **aquél** are used to mean *the former*. Study the following examples and the chart.

Éste es el zapato que me gusta pero **aquél** es mucho mejor.	*This one is the shoe that I like but that one is much better.*
Compré tomates y zanahorias. **Éstas** eran deliciosas pero **aquéllos** no sabían a nada.	*I bought tomatoes and carrots. The latter were delicious, but the former had no taste.*

	Masculine	Feminine	Neuter
this (one)	**éste**	**ésta**	**esto**
these (ones)	**éstos**	**éstas**	
that (one)	**ése**	**ésa**	**eso**
those (ones)	**ésos**	**ésas**	
that (one) (over there)	**aquél**	**aquélla**	**aquello**
those (ones) (over there)	**aquéllos**	**aquéllas**	

NOTE: The neuter demonstrative pronouns have no number, no gender, and no written accent. They are used when there is no specific reference to a noun: **Odio todo esto.** *I hate all this.*

EXERCISE 8-18: Substitute the correct demonstrative pronoun for the word or phrase given in parentheses. Remember that the difference between **ése** and **aquél** is distance from the speaker. Answers are at the end of the chapter.

Example: (those ones over there) No quiero estos zapatos, quiero *aquéllos*.
1. (this one) Aquel coche cuesta más que _____.
2. (those ones in the other room) Estos alumnos saben más que _____.
3. (these ones) Quiero comprar este libro y _____ también.
4. (that one over there) Este hombre y _____ son enemigos.
5. (this one) Cómprate aquella falda y _____ también.
6. (those ones over there) Mis discos son más viejos que _____.
7. (this) Yo no entiendo nada de _____.
8. (that) _____ fue imposible.
9. (that one over there) Esta mujer no es tan bonita como _____.
10. (the latter; the former) Mis zapatos y mis botas me duelen mucho pero _____ me duelen más que _____.
11. (that one near me) Nadie necesita ni esta camisa ni _____.
12. (this one) Ese problema no es tan importante como _____.
13. (this one) Aquel hombre es muy alto: _____ es muy bajo.
14. (these ones) Aquellos días eran más largos que _____.
15. (those ones near you) Estas plantas son caras; _____ son más baratas.

8-10. Relative Pronouns

Relative pronouns introduce subordinate clauses within the main clause: The man *who lives next door* is a good neighbor. In English, the most frequently used relative pronouns are *who, whom, that, which,* and *whose*. In Spanish, the most frequently used relative pronouns are **que, quien, cual, lo que,** and **cuyo**.

A. *que*

Que can mean *who, that,* or *which*.

Dáme los libros **que** están en la mesa.   *Give me the books that are on the table.*

Roberto no es el hombre **que** llamó ayer.   *Roberto is not the man who called yesterday.*

EXERCISE 8-19: Read each pair of sentences. Then rewrite them as one sentence, using the noun or noun phrase given in parentheses as the subject and the relative pronoun **que**. When you finish, translate the sentence into English. Answers are at the end of the chapter.

Example: Los niños perdieron (su pelota). Estaba en el jardín.
La pelota que perdieron los niños estaba en el jardín.
1. Miguel compró un (escritorio). Le costó mucho dinero.

2. Escribo (cartas). Nunca son largas.

3. El jefe pidió (ayuda). No la recibió.

4. Los niños quieren beber (leche). Es una leche deliciosa.

5. Los vecinos cortaron (un árbol). Era muy bonito.

6. Hice (un postre delicioso). Era de queso, crema, y miel.

7. Tenemos (trabajo) que hacer. Es aburrido.

8. Se rompió (el tocadiscos). Pertenecía a mi hermana.

9. Se llama Violeta (aquella mujer). Es de la Argentina.

10. Vive con nosotros (aquel hombre). Es mi tío.

B. *el que, la que, los que, las que*

El que, etc., can mean either *the one who*, or *the one that (which)*. Study the following examples.

Roberto es **el hombre que** llamó ayer.	*Roberto is the man who called yesterday.*
Roberto es **el que** llamó ayer.	*Roberto is the one who called yesterday.*
El que llamó ayer es Roberto.	*The one who called yesterday is Roberto.*
Quiero hablar con **el que** llamó ayer.	*I want to speak with the one who called yesterday.*
Éstas son **las faldas que** me ponía hace veinte años.	*These are the skirts that I wore twenty years ago.*
Éstas son **las que** me ponía hace veinte años.	*These are the ones that I used to wear twenty years ago.*
No encuentro **las que** me ponía hace veinte años.	*I can't find the ones that I wore twenty years ago.*

C. *lo que*

Lo que means *what*, *that which*, or *the thing which*. It is used to refer back to a non-specific antecedent rather than a specific one. Study the following examples.

Non-specific antecedent

Busco **lo que** perdí.	*I'm looking for that which I lost.*
No sé **lo que** quería decir Emma.	*I don't know what Emma meant.*

Specific antecedent

Busco **los zapatos que** perdí.	*I'm looking for the shoes that I lost.*
Busco **los que** perdí.	*I'm looking for the ones that I lost.*
No conozco **la canción que** Emma cantó.	*I'm not familiar with the song that Emma sang.*
No conozco **la que** Emma cantó.	*I'm not familiar with the one that Emma sang.*

EXERCISE 8-20: Complete each of the following sentences by writing in the correct relative pronoun from the following list: **que, lo que, el que, la que, los que, las que**. Then translate the sentence into English. Answers are at the end of the chapter.

Examples: La mujer ___*que*___ vive en la casa verde es mi prima.
El sombrero verde es ___*el que*___ me regalaron.
No sé ___*lo que*___ quieres decir.

1. La película que vimos no es_____queríamos ver.
2. El muchacho_____habló es mi primo.
3. Las sillas_____son blancas no son muy cómodas.
4. Siempre escuchamos_____dice el jefe.
5. Esas canciones son_____cantamos el año pasado.
6. El alumno_____ganó fue Miguel Hernández.
7. No conozco a los muchachos_____están hablando con mi tía.
8. Perdí_____compré.
9. Perdí los guantes_____compré ayer.
10. Los guantes que perdí son_____iba a regalar a mi hermana.

D. *quien* and *quienes* after prepositions

When used after a preposition, **quien** and **quienes** mean *whom*.

El hombre **con quien** trabajo es italiano.	*The man with whom I work is Italian.*
Las muchachas **a quienes** conociste anoche son mis primas.	*The girls whom you met last night are my cousins.*

E. *que* **after prepositions**

Que is used after common prepositions such as **de**, **en**, and **con**, when the antecedent referred to is a thing rather than a person. When **que** follows a preposition, it means *which*.

El aceite **con que** freímos los huevos es aceite de oliva.	*The oil with which we fry eggs is olive oil.*
BUT	
La muchacha **con quien** bailé es muy inteligente.	*The girl with whom I danced is very intelligent.*

F. *el cual, la cual, los cuales,* **and** *las cuales* **after prepositions**

These pronouns mean both *which* and *whom*. They are used most commonly after compound prepositions instead of **que** and **quien(es)**. They may be used correctly after simple prepositions as well.

El árbol **debajo del cual** lloró Cortés está en México todavía.	*The tree under which Cortes wept is still in Mexico.*
La fuente **alrededor de la cual** juegan los niños no tiene agua.	*The fountain around which the children play doesn't have water.*
La mujer **con la cual** me caso se llama Rita.	*The woman whom I am getting married to is named Rita.*
La caja **en la cual** puse mi dinero ha desaparecido.	*The box in which I put my money has disappeared.*
No conozco esos libros **de los cuales** han hablado tanto.	*I am not familiar with those books about which they have talked so much.*

NOTE: **De + el = del**: **debajo del cual**, *under which.*

EXERCISE 8-21:   Substitute **el cual, la cual, los cuales,** or **las cuales** for **que** and **quien(-es)** in the following sentences. Then translate the sentence into English. Answers are at the end of the chapter.

Example: Tú no conoces a la muchacha con quien bailaba Antonio.
   Tú no conoces a la muchacha con la cual bailaba Antonio.

1. El hombre por quien voté es joven.

2. La pluma con que escribí mi novela es roja.

3. No encuentro la casa en que vivía.

4. No conocemos a los muchachos de quienes hablas.

5. El tema de que hablas es muy importante.

6. La leche con que hice el flan no estaba fresca.

7. El maestro con quien estabas hablando es el señor Blanco.

8. Está roto el televisor en que veías los partidos de fútbol.

9. Es muy grande el armario en que guardas la ropa.

10. La prima a quien tú conoces no va a venir.

G. *Cuyo*

Cuyo, **cuya**, **cuyos**, and **cuyas**, mean *whose*. **Cuyo** must agree in number and gender with the thing being referred to, rather than the owner of the thing.

No conozco a la mujer **cuyos libros** estoy utilizando.	*I don't know the woman whose books I'm using.*
El señor Romero es el hombre **cuya casa** fue destruida por el diluvio.	*Mr. Romero is the man whose house was destroyed by the flood.*

EXERCISE 8-22: Write in the correct form of **cuyo**. Answers are at the end of the chapter.

1. La mujer _____ máquina de escribir rompiste viene ahora.
2. La mujer _____ coche fue robado no se llama Alicia.
3. No sé donde están los muchachos _____ pelota rompío los cristales de mi casa.
4. Es un perfume _____ olor me molesta muchísimo.
5. Necesito hablar con el hombre _____ paraguas tengo en casa.

SUMMARY

1. In Spanish, subject pronouns are used mainly for emphasis, except for **usted**, which is often used in formal direct address. There is no equivalent of the English subject pronoun "it." Rather, "it" is expressed by the third person singular verb form: **No es verdad**. *It isn't true.*; **Es cierto**. *It's true.*; **Llueve**. *It's raining.*
2. The subject pronouns **él**, **ella**, **usted**, **nosotros(-as)**, **vosotros(-as)**, **ellos**, **ellas**, and **ustedes** are used after prepositions. **Mí** and **ti** take the place of **yo** and **tú** after prepositions. When used with the preposition **con**, **mí** and **ti** change to **conmigo**, *with me*, and **contigo**, *with you*. The preposition **consigo** means *with yourself, herself, himself, yourselves, themselves*.
3. The first and second person object pronouns are **me**, **te**, **nos**, **os**. The third person direct object pronouns are **lo**, **la**, **los**, **las**. The third person indirect object pronouns are **le**, **les**.
4. The indirect object pronouns **le** and **les** are used when the meaning is *to* or *from him, her, you (formal), them*. Otherwise, the direct object pronouns **lo**, **las**, **los**, or **las** are used.
5. A prepositional phrase, **a** + **mí**, **ti**, **él**, **ella**, and so on, can be used to emphasize or clarify the indirect object pronouns, especially the third person **le** and **les**.
6. Object pronouns usually precede the conjugated form of the verb. Negatives precede object pronouns. If there is a subject or subject pronoun, it precedes the negative.
7. When two object pronouns are used in the same sentence, the indirect object pronoun always comes first: **Te lo doy**. *I give it to you.*
8. **Se** replaces the indirect object pronoun **le** or **les** when used with direct object pronouns **lo**, **la**, **los**, or **las**: **Se lo di**. *I gave it to him.*
9. Object pronouns are *always* attached to the affirmative command form: **Dámelo**. *Give it to me.*; **Mándesela**. *Send it to them.* There is a written accent over the stressed syllable.
10. Object pronouns may be attached to the infinitive and present participle instead of preceding the conjugated verb form: **Quiero dártelo** and **Te lo quiero dar** both mean *I want to give it to you.*
11. The reflexive pronouns are **me**, **te**, **se**, **nos**, **os**, **se**. They are used with reflexive verbs and always agree with the person and number of the verb form: **me lavo**, **te lavas**, etc.
12. Reflexive pronouns follow the same placement rules as indirect object pronouns. That is, when used with a direct object pronoun, the reflexive pronoun always comes first: **No me lo pongo nunca**. *I never wear it.*; **Póngaselos usted**. *Put them on.*
13. The passive **se** construction can be used with indirect object pronouns to indicate the effect of a sudden or involuntary action upon the person or persons: **Se rompió la silla**. *The chair was broken.*; **Se nos rompió la silla**. *The chair broke on us.*

14. The possessive pronouns take the place of possessive adjectives + noun: **mi libro**, *my book*; **el mío**, *mine*. They must agree in number and gender with the noun they replace. The definite article is always used with the possessive pronouns, except after **ser**: **es mío**, *it's mine*. The definite article can be used after **ser** for emphasis: **Es el mío.**

15. The demonstrative pronouns must agree in number and gender with the thing they refer to. When no specific reference is made, the neuter demonstrative pronouns are used: **Odio todos estos libros.** *I hate all these books.* BUT **Odio todo esto.** *I hate all this.*

16. The relative pronoun **que** means both *who* and *that (which)* when it introduces a subordinate clause modifying either a person or thing: **la mujer que ...**, *the woman who ...*; **la silla que ...**, *the chair that ....*

17. **El que, la que, los que,** and **las que** mean *the one (ones) who* when referring to a specific person, and *the one (ones) that* when referring to a specific thing: **el libro que**, *the book that* = **el que**, *the one that*; **la mujer que**, *the woman who* = **la que**, *the one who.*

18. **Lo que** means *what, that which,* or *the thing which.* It is used when the thing referred to is abstract or non-specific: **No sé lo que quieres.** *I don't know what you want.*

19. After prepositions, **que** is used to refer to things, and it means *which*: **con que**, *with which*; **de que**, *of which.*

20. After prepositions, **quien** and **quienes** are used to refer to people; **con quien**, *with whom*; **de quienes**, *about whom.*

21. After prepositions, **el cual, la cual, los cuales,** and **las cuales,** may replace **quien (-es)** and **que**: **la caja en la cual**, *the box in which*; **la mujer con la cual**, *the woman with whom.* These pronouns are almost always used with compound prepositions: **la fuente alrededor de la cual**, *the fountain around which.*

22. The relative pronouns **cuyo, cuya, cuyos, cuyas,** *whose,* indicate possession. They agree in number and gender with the thing owned, not the person who owns it: **la mujer cuyos libros**, *the woman whose books.*

RAISE YOUR GRADES

☑ **Double object pronouns** [Section 8-6]

Answer the following questions in the affirmative, substituting the appropriate direct and indirect object pronouns for the noun or noun phrases given in parentheses. Answers are at the end of the chapter.

Example: ¿Me diste (aquellas flores bonitas)? *Sí, te las di.*

1. ¿Prestaste (tu coche a Manolo)?

2. ¿Devolviste (el paraguas al señor López)?

3. ¿Escribió Andrés (una carta a su novia)?

4. ¿Pidió usted (permiso a la maestra)?

5. ¿Te devolvió Emilio (los dibujos)?

6. ¿Regalaste (la pelota a los niños)?

7. ¿Explicaste (el problema a los invitados)?

8. ¿Me vendes (tus discos de jazz)?

9. ¿Me da usted (un vaso de agua)?

10. ¿Enviaste (las muestras a Regina)?

☑ **Object pronouns after infinitives and present participles** [Section 8-6]

Rewrite the following sentences, substituting object pronouns for the nouns or noun phrases given in parentheses. Remember that the indirect object pronoun always comes first. Answers are at the end of the chapter.

Example: Te quiero vender (la casa). *Te la quiero vender.* OR *Quiero vendértela.*

1. Te voy a contar (una historia).

2. Nos pueden prestar (el coche).

3. Les quiero regalar (estas alfombras).

4. Le voy a dar (una sorpresa).

5. Os tengo que contar (un chiste).

6. Nos quiere explicar (su problema).

7. Nos iba a devolver (la máquina de coser).

8. Le tenemos que dar (los muebles viejos).

9. Me iba a cortar (el pelo).

10. Me van a quitar (los dientes).

☑ **Commands and object pronouns** [Section 8-6]

Translate the following commands into Spanish, using the command form of the verb provided, and attaching the correct object pronouns. Answers are at the end of the chapter.

Examples: Give it (*f*) to her. *Désela*.
Give it (*m*) to me. *Dámelo*.

1. Sell them (*f*) to him. Vended _____ .
2. Tell it (*m*) to them. Digan _____ .
3. Give them (*m*) to them. De _____ .
4. Promise it (*f*) to her. Prometan _____ .
5. Explain it (*m*) to us. Explique _____ .
6. Open it (*m*) for me. Abre _____ .
7. Send them (*f*) to us. Envien _____ .
8. Ask them for it (*m*). Pide _____ .
9. Look for them (*f*) for him. Busca _____ .
10. Give them (*m*) to me. Dad _____ .

☑ **Relative pronouns** [Section 8-10]

Translate the relative pronoun given in parentheses into Spanish. Answers are at the end of the chapter.

Example: Olvidé la cartera (in which) dejé los cuadernos. _____*en que*_____

1. Ha llamado la mujer (whose) libros perdí. _____
2. No están los vecinos a (whom) querías conocer. _____
3. El mapa (that) tu pediste no está en su lugar habitual. _____
4. No sabemos (what) tenemos que hacer. _____
5. Queremos hablar con el pintor (who) pintó ese cuadro. _____
6. No sé por (whom) dobla la campana. _____
7. Cortaron los árboles (whose) sombra disfrutamos tanto. _____
8. ¿Oíste (what) dijo Mario? _____
9. Es poco el dinero con (which) me mantengo. _____
10. Salieron los muchachos con (whom) viniste. _____

CHAPTER ANSWERS

EXERCISE 8-1

1. estudiamos   *Antonio and I study too much.*
2. sois   *You and he are good friends, aren't you?*
3. nos casamos   *You and I are getting married in June.*
4. os vais   *When are you and Roberta going away?*
5. tienen que   *You and he have to arrive at an agreement.*
6. ayudan   *You and your brother help out a lot at home.*
7. nos enfadamos   *The professor and I get mad (at each other) once a week.*
8. pueden   *At what time can you and Mario leave?*
9. tenemos que   *You and I have to work.*
10. nos callamos   *Iris and I never shut up.*

EXERCISE 8-2

1. ellos   *Why don't we sit down behind them?*
2. ella   *I want you to walk toward her.*
3. usted   *This gift is for you.*
4. ellos   *I want you to have lunch with them.*
5. ella y ellos   *There is a dispute between her and them.*
6. mí   *Esteban does not live near me.*
7. vosotros y ellos   *I don't want to talk in front of you and them.*
8. ti   *My cousin lives very far from you.*
9. él   *I bought a hat for him.*
10. nosotros   *The train left without us.*
11. vosotros   *We never talk about you.*
12. él   *There is a woman behind him.*
13. conmigo   *I need someone to go with me.*
14. contigo   *I want to talk with you.*
15. ti   *I can do many things without you.*

EXERCISE 8-3

1. Ayer la perdí.   *Yesterday I lost it.*
2. Nunca la encontramos.   *We never found it.*
3. José y Emma la buscan.   *José and Emma are looking for her.*
4. Alguien lo robó.   *Someone stole it.*
5. Todavía no los tenemos.   *We still don't have them.*
6. Los niños la terminaron.   *The children finished it.*
7. Día y noche las escribo.   *I write them day and night.*
8. No la hemos probado.   *We haven't tried it.*
9. Los vimos ayer.   *We saw them yesterday.*
10. Manuel no la esperó.   *Manuel didn't wait for her.*

EXERCISE 8-4

1. No, no le escribe.   *No, he doesn't write to him.*
2. No, no les invitamos.   *No, we didn't invite them.*
3. No, no le pidieron permiso.   *No, they didn't ask permission of him.*
4. No, no le oí.   *No, I didn't hear him.*
5. Sí, les escuché.   *Yes, I listened to them.*
6. Sí, le hablamos.   *Yes, we talked to her.*
7. No, no le escuchamos con atención.   *No, we don't listen attentively to him.*
8. Sí, le prestamos el coche.   *Yes, we lent her the car.*
9. No, no les dije nada.   *No, I didn't say anything to them.*
10. Sí, le di los recados.   *Yes, I gave her the messages.*

EXERCISE 8-5

1. Sí, te escuché.   *Did you listen to me last night? Yes, I listened to you.*
2. Sí, os escuché.   *Did you listen to us last night? Yes, I listened to you.*
3. Sí, le pedí un favor.   *Did you ask me for a favor? Yes, I asked you for a favor.*
4. Sí, les pedí un favor.   *Did you ask us for a favor? Yes, I asked you for a favor.*
5. Sí, le hice una pregunta.   *Did you ask me a question? Yes, I asked you a question.*
6. Sí, te hice una pregunta.   *Did you ask me a question? Yes, I asked you a question.*
7. Sí, os hice una pregunta.   *Did you ask us a question? Yes, I asked you a question.*
8. Sí, les hice una pregunta.   *Did you ask us a question? Yes, I asked you a question.*
9. Sí, le di permiso.   *Did you give me permission? Yes, I gave you permission.*
10. Sí, les hablé ayer.   *Did you talk to us yesterday? Yes, I talked to you yesterday.*
11. Sí, os invité a la fiesta.   *Did you invite us to the party? Yes, I invited you to the party.*
12. Sí, le invité a la fiesta.   *Did you invite me to the party? Yes, I invited you to the party.*
13. Sí, os di permiso.   *Did you give us permission? Yes, I gave you permission.*
14. Sí, te hablé ayer.   *Did you talk to me yesterday? Yes, I talked to you yesterday.*
15. Sí, le ayudé.   *Did you help me? Yes, I helped you.*

EXERCISE 8-6

1. El profesor nunca les escucha.   *The professor never listens to them.*
2. No la perdí en el cine.   *I didn't lose it at the movies.*

3. Ya no los oyen. *They no longer hear them.*
4. No le entendieron. *They didn't understand him.*
5. Le di un recado. *I gave him a message.*
6. El jefe no les quitó el aumento de salario. *The boss didn't take the raise away from them.*
7. Sus hermanos no los quitaron a Manuel. *His brothers didn't take them away from Manuel.*
8. No les dimos las entradas. *We didn't give them the tickets.*
9. No lo mandé a la maestra. *I didn't send it to the teacher.*
10. No le mandé el sobre. *I didn't send her the envelope.*

EXERCISE 8-7

1. Mándale más libros. *Send her more books.*
2. Olvídame. *Forget me.*
3. Cómalos usted, por favor. *Please eat them.*
4. Háganle preguntas. *Ask him or her questions.*
5. Ciérrelas usted, por favor. *Please close them.*
6. Búscame. *Look for me.*
7. Rómpanlo. *Break it.*
8. Ayúdele usted. *Help him.*
9. Invíteme usted. *Invite me.*
10. Escúchale. *Listen to him.*

EXERCISE 8-8

1. Le debo escribir. Debo escribirle. *I should write to her.*
2. Lo estoy comiendo. Estoy comiéndolo. *I'm eating it.*
3. Lo vamos a comprar. Vamos a comprarlo. *We're going to buy it.*
4. Manolo lo quiere beber. Manolo quiere beberlo. *Manolo wants to drink it.*
5. No las tuvimos que mandar. No tuvimos que mandarlas. *We didn't have to send them.*
6. Iris no le está prestando atención. Iris no está prestándole atención. *Iris isn't paying attention to him.*
7. Mi hermano no la quiere vender. Mi hermano no quiere venderla. *My brother doesn't want to sell it.*
8. No lo hemos tenido que comer. No hemos tenido que comerlo. *We haven't had to eat it.*
9. La maestra y yo lo estamos leyendo. La maestra y yo estamos leyéndolo. *The teacher and I are reading it.*
10. El perro lo está mordiendo. El perro está mordiéndolo. *The dog is chewing it.*

EXERCISE 8-9

1. Yo te las escribí. *I wrote them to you.*
2. Marcela se lo dio a los niños. *Marcela gave it to the children.*
3. Nadie me la contó. *Nobody told it to me.*
4. Alfredo siempre se las da al niño. *Alfredo always gives them to the child.*
5. Alguien me las manda todos los días. *Someone sends them to me every day.*
6. Ya te los devolví. *I already returned them to you.*
7. Rafael se la escuchó a María. *Rafael heard it from María.*
8. Los muchachos se lo pidieron a sus padres. *The boys asked their parents for it.*
9. Nadie nos la dio. *Nobody gave it to us.*
10. Alguien nos la regaló. *Somebody gave it to us (as a present).*
11. Ramón y Angel se la trajeron a Raúl. *Ramón and Angel brought it to Raúl.*
12. Mi hermano se los dio a Laura. *My brother gave them to Laura.*
13. Anita se la prestó a los vecinos. *Anita lent it to the neighbors.*
14. El jefe nos lo negó. *The boss denied it to us.*
15. La tía de Reynaldo nos la preparó. *Reynaldo's aunt fixed it for us.*

EXERCISE 8-10

1. Se los regalé a ellos. *I gave them to them.*
2. Se la escribí a ella. *I wrote it to her.*
3. Se la compré a él. *I bought it from him.*
4. Se los presté a ellos. *I lent them to them.*
5. Se la vendí a ella. *I sold it to her.*
6. Se la entregué a ella. *I handed it to her.*
7. Se lo envié a ellos. *I send it to them.*
8. Se la conté a ellos. *I told it to them.*
9. Se los mandé a él. *I sent them to him.*
10. Se lo ofrecí a ella. *I offered it to her.*

EXERCISE 8-11

1. Escríbesela. *Write it to him.*
2. Tráemelo. *Bring it to me.*
3. Entrégamelo. *Hand it in to me.*
4. Dáselo. *Give it to them.*
5. Véndesela. *Sell it to her.*
6. Explícanosla. *Explain it to us.*
7. Tráigamelas. *Bring them to me.*
8. Mándenoslos. *Send them to us.*
9. Regálemelo. *Give it to me.*
10. Muéstresela. *Show it to him.*

EXERCISE 8-12

1. Me la pueden arreglar. Pueden arreglármela. *They can fix it for me.*
2. Los estudiantes se lo están presentando. Los estudiantes están presentándoselo. *The students are presenting it to him.*
3. No se lo necesito mostrar. No necesito mostrárselo. *I don't need to show it to him.*
4. No se lo podemos prestar. No podemos prestárselo. *We can't lend it to him.*
5. Nunca se las quieres divulgar. Nunca quieres divulgárselas. *You never want to make them known to them.*

6. No se la podían decir. No podían decírsela. *They couldn't tell it to them.*
7. Elena no se las tuvo que enviar. Elena no tuvo que enviárselas. *Elena didn't have to send them to her.*
8. La profesora se lo estaba explicando. La profesora estaba explicándoselo. *The professor was explaining it to them.*
9. Los niños no se los pudieron enseñar. Los niños no pudieron enseñárselos. *The children couldn't show them to him.*
10. La enfermera se lo estaba ofreciendo. La enfermera estaba ofreciéndoselo. *The nurse was offering it to them.*

EXERCISE 8-13

1. se miran *The children look at themselves in the mirror.*
2. me peino *I comb my hair once a day.*
3. se queda *Nobody stays at home.*
4. se pone *Manolo never wears his blue tie.*
5. nos despedimos *Alicia and I never say goodbye to anyone.*
6. se quedan *Raúl and Carlos are not staying to eat.*
7. me acuerdo *I don't remember anything.*
8. se comen *The kids eat up everything there is in the refrigerator.*
9. se va *My grandmother goes away to Florida in December.*
10. te quitas *You never take your overcoat off.*

EXERCISE 8-14

1. Póntelo. *Put it on.*
2. Rafael no se lo quita nunca. *Rafael never takes it off.*
3. Tengo que quitármelas. *I have to take them off.*
4. Los niños se la comieron. *The children ate it all up.*
5. No te lo peines. *Don't comb it.*
6. Lávatelos. *Wash them.*
7. Queremos lavárnoslas. *We want to wash them.*
8. No estás poniéndotela. *You're not putting it on.*
9. Angel nunca se la quita. *Angel never takes it off.*
10. No te los pongas. *Don't put them on.*

EXERCISE 8-15

1. Se me cayó el libro. *I dropped the book (involuntarily).*
2. Se nos rompen las copas con mucha frecuencia. *The wine glasses break on us very often.*
3. Se le cerró la puerta. *The door closed on him.*
4. Se le descompuso la máquina de escribir. *The typewriter broke on her.*
5. Se les olvidaron las cucharas y los tenedores. *They forgot the spoons and the forks (involuntarily).*
6. Se le manchó el mantel. *She stained the tablecloth (involuntarily).*
7. Se te olvidó traer la sal. *You forgot to bring the salt (involuntarily).*
8. Se les perdieron los apuntes. *The notes got lost on them.*
9. Se me fueron todos los amigos. *All my friends up and went on me.*
10. Se le quebró la pluma. *The pen broke on her.*

EXERCISE 8-16

1. Nos encanta el béisbol.
2. Me sorprendió la cena.
3. El perro les asustó.
4. El ruido de los pájaros te fastidia.
5. La poesía no le importa.
6. La interrupciones nos enojan.
7. Los niños pequeños les molestan.
8. ¿Le asustan los gatos?
9. Les importa el arte?
10. ¿Os molesta la luz?

EXERCISE 8-17

1. las mías *Where are mine?*
2. el nuestro *We have to fix ours.*
3. los suyos OR los de ellos *I put theirs in the washing machine.*
4. los vuestros *You don't have your passports.*
5. la suya *Who has his (hers, yours, theirs)?*
6. el mío *Who took mine?*
7. La mía *Mine is blue.*
8. las tuyas *Where did you put yours?*
9. La suya OR La de él *His is very big.*
10. La suya OR La de ella *Hers is yellow.*
11. el suyo OR el de ellos *Mario and Luisa brought theirs.*
12. los suyos OR los de ellos *The Whites lost theirs at the beach.*
13. la suya OR la de él *Emilio has his.*
14. los míos *The blue books are mine.*
15. la mía *That house is mine.*

EXERCISE 8-18

1. éste *That car costs more than this one.*
2. aquéllos *These pupils know more than those.*
3. éstos *I want to buy this book and these too.*
4. aquél *This man and that one are enemies.*
5. ésta *Buy that skirt and this one too.*
6. aquéllos *My records are older than those.*
7. esto *I don't understand any of this.*
8. Eso *That was impossible.*
9. aquélla *This woman is not as pretty as that one.*
10. éstas, aquéllos *My shoes and my boots hurt me a lot but the latter hurt me more than the former.*

11. ésa   *Nobody needs either this shirt or that one.*
12. éste   *That problem isn't as important as this one.*
13. éste   *That man is very tall; this one is very short.*
14. éstos   *Those days were longer than these.*
15. ésas   *These plants are expensive; those are cheaper.*

EXERCISE 8-19

1. El escritorio que compró Miguel le costó mucho dinero.   *The desk that Miguel bought cost him a lot of money.*
2. Las cartas que escribo nunca son largas.   *The letters that I write are never long.*
3. La ayuda que el jefe pidió, no la recibió.   *The boss didn't receive the help that he asked for.* OR *The help the boss asked for, he didn't receive.*
4. La leche que los niños quieren beber es una leche deliciosa.   *The milk that the children want to drink is delicious milk.*
5. El árbol que cortaron los vecinos era muy bonito.   *The tree that the neighbors cut down was very pretty.*
6. El postre delicioso que hice era de queso, crema y miel.   *The delicious dessert that I made was (made) from cheese, cream, and honey.*
7. El trabajo que tenemos que hacer es aburrido.   *The work that we have to do is boring.*
8. El tocadiscos que se rompió pertenecía a mi hermana.   *The record player that broke belonged to my sister.*
9. Aquella mujer que se llama Violeta es de la Argentina.   *That woman who is named Violeta is from Argentina.*
10. Aquel hombre que vive con nosotros es mi tío.   *That man who lives with us is my uncle.*

EXERCISE 8-20

1. la que   *The movie that we saw isn't the one that we wanted to see.*
2. que   *The boy who spoke is my cousin.*
3. que   *The chairs that are white are not very comfortable.*
4. lo que   *We always listen to what the boss says.*
5. las que   *Those songs are the ones that we sang last year.*
6. que   *The pupil who won was Miguel Hernández.*
7. que   *I don't know the boys who are talking to my aunt.*
8. lo que   *I lost what I bought.*
9. que   *I lost the gloves that I bought yesterday.*
10. los que   *The gloves that I lost are the ones that I was going to give to my sister.*

EXERCISE 8-21

1. el cual   *The man for whom I voted is young.*
2. la cual   *The pen with which I wrote my novel is red.*
3. la cual·   *I can't find the house in which I lived.*
4. los cuales   *We don't know the boys of whom you speak.*
5. del cual   *The subject of which you speak is very important.*
6. la cual   *The milk with which I made the custard was not fresh.*
7. el cual   *The teacher with whom you were speaking is Mr. Blanco.*
8. el cual   *The television set on which you used to see the football games is broken.*
9. el cual   *The closet in which you keep the clothing is very large.*
10. la cual   *The cousin whom you know is not going to come.*

EXERCISE 8-22

1. cuya   *The woman whose typewriter you broke is coming now.*
2. cuyo   *The woman whose car was stolen is not named Alice.*
3. cuya   *I don't know where the boys are whose ball broke the windows in my house.*
4. cuyo   *It's a perfume whose scent bothers me a great deal.*
5. cuyo   *I need to talk to the man whose umbrella I have at home.*

RAISE YOUR GRADES

Double object pronouns

1. Sí, se lo presté.   *Yes, I lent it to him.*
2. Sí, se lo devolví.   *Yes, I returned it to him.*
3. Sí, se la escribió.   *Yes, he wrote it to her.*
4. Sí, se lo pedí.   *Yes, I asked her for it.*
5. Sí, me los devolvió.   *Yes, he returned them to me.*
6. Sí, se la regalé.   *Yes, I gave it to them.*
7. Sí, se lo expliqué.   *Yes, I explained it to them.*
8. Sí, te los vendo.   *Yes, I'll sell them to you.*
9. Sí, se lo doy.   *Yes, I'll give it to you.*
10. Sí, se las envié.   *Yes, I sent them to her.*

Object pronouns after infinitives and present participles

1. Te la voy a contar. OR Voy a contártela.   *I'm going to tell it to you.*
2. Nos lo pueden prestar. OR Pueden prestárnoslo.   *They can lend it to us.*
3. Se las quiero regalar. OR Quiero regalárselas.   *I want to lend them to you (them).*
4. Se la voy a dar. OR Voy a dársela.   *I'm going to give it to you (him, her).*
5. Os lo tengo que contar. OR Tengo que contároslo.   *I've got to tell it to you.*

6. Nos lo quiere explicar. OR Quiere explicárnoslo. *He (she) wants to explain his (her) problem to us.*

7. Nos la iba a devolver. OR Iba a devolvérnosla. *He (she) was going to return it to us.*

8. Se los tenemos que dar. OR Tenemos que dárselos. *We have to give them to you (him, her).*

9. Me lo iba a cortar. OR Iba a cortármelo. *I was going to get it cut.*

10. Me los van a quitar. OR Van a quitármelos. *They're going to take them out.*

Commands and object pronouns

1. Vendédselas.
2. Díganselo.
3. Déselos.
4. Prométansela.
5. Explíquenoslo.
6. Ábremelo.
7. Envíennoslas.
8. Pídeselo.
9. Búscaselas.
10. Dádmelos.

Relative pronouns

1. cuyos *I've called the woman whose books I lost.*

2. quienes *The neighbors whom you wanted to meet are not here.*

3. que *The map that you asked for isn't in its usual place.*

4. lo que *We don't know what we have to do.*

5. que *We want to talk to the painter who painted that painting.*

6. quien *I don't know for whom the bell tolls.*

7. cuya *They cut down the trees whose shade we enjoyed so much.*

8. lo que *Did you hear what Mario said?*

9. que *The money with which I support myself is not very much.*

10. quienes *The boys with whom you came left.*

9 PREPOSITIONS

THIS CHAPTER IS ABOUT

☑ *por* and *para*
☑ The Preposition *a*
☑ The Preposition *en*
☑ The Preposition *de*
☑ Prepositions of Place
☑ Other Important Prepositions

9-1. *por* and *para*

Por and **para** both mean *for* in Spanish; however, both **por** and **para** have a variety of other meanings that must be memorized. Study the following examples very carefully. If you concentrate on the differences in meanings of **por** and **para**, you will be less likely to confuse the two prepositions.

A. The use of *por*

1. Por means *on account of* or *because of*. Use **por** to express the cause of an action.

Lo hice **por** la lluvia.	*I did it because of the rain.*
España es famosa **por** el vino de Jerez.	*Spain is famous for sherry wine.*
Por estudiar tanto, saqué buenas notas	*Because of studying so much, I got good grades.*
No entré **por** no querer molestarle.	*I didn't go in because of not wanting to bother him.*

2. Por means *through*, *along*, *by*, *around*, or *in the area of*. When **por** is used to indicate location, the meaning is non-specific. That is, **por** refers to a general area.

Caminé **por** el río.	*I walked along (by) the river.*
Pasé **por** tu casa, pero no estabas.	*I came by your house, but you weren't there.*
Nadie viene **por** aquí.	*Nobody comes around here.*
Vagué **por** las calles de la ciudad.	*I wandered through the city streets.*

3. Por is used to refer to lengths of time and means *during* or *for*.

Vamos a viajar **por** tres meses.	*We're going to travel for three months.*
Vine **por** la mañana y no estabas pero vendré otra vez **por** la tarde.	*I came by in the morning and you weren't there, but I'll come by again in the afternoon.*
Sólo puedo quedarme **por** un ratito.	*I can only stay for a little while.*

> **NOTE:** In expressions of time duration, **durante** may be used instead of **por**: **Vamos a viajar durante tres meses.**

4. Por means *in exchange for* and is used in situations involving money and exchange.

Pagué cien dolares **por** mi abrigo.	*I paid one hundred dollars for my overcoat.*
Te doy mi guitarra **por** tu alfombra.	*I'll give you my guitar for your rug.*

5. Por means *per* or *by*. Use **por** in expressions such as *percent, per month,* and *by the pound,* or *by the minute.*

En España, se compra la carne **por** kilos y no **por** libras.	*In Spain, meat is bought by the kilo and not by the pound.*
Tengo dos semanas de vacaciones **por** año.	*I have two weeks of vacation per year.*
En el África, el cincuenta **por** cien de los niños están desnutridos.	*In Africa, fifty percent of the children are undernourished.*

> **NOTE:** When giving the price of foods sold by weight, you say **un dólar la libra,** *a dollar a pound;* **setecientas pesetas el kilo,** *seven hundred pesetas a kilo.*

6. Por means *to be in favor of.*

Luchamos **por** los derechos civiles.	*We struggle for civil rights.*
Voté **por** la señora Moreno.	*I voted for Mrs. Moreno.*
Estoy **por** comer pronto.	*I am in favor of eating soon.*

> **REMEMBER:** An infinitive after a preposition is almost always translated as a present participle (*-ing* form).

7. Por means *by means of.* Use **por** when talking about transportation.

Voy **por** avión.	*I'm going by plane.*
Haga usted el favor de enviar el paquete **por** correo aéreo.	*Please send the package by air mail.*

8. Por means *for* or *as a.*

Me tienen **por** loco.	*They think of me as crazy.*
En mi país me toman **por** extranjera.	*In my country they take me for a foreigner.*

9. Por is used with **ser** in the passive construction.

La casa **fue** construida **por** el ingeniero López.	*The house was built by the engineer López.*

10. Por is used in many colloquial expressions.

por ahora	*for now*	por lo menos	*at least*
por cierto	*by the way*	por lo tanto	*consequently*
por Dios	*my God*	por lo visto	*apparently*
por ejemplo	*for example*	por medio de	*by means of*
por eso	*therefore*	por otra parte	*on the other hand*
por fin	*finally*	por supuesto	*certainly, of course*
por favor	*please*	por teléfono	*on the telephone*
por lo general	*generally*		

B. The use of *para*

1. Para means *in order to* or *for the purpose of.*

Para freír un huevo, el aceite tiene que estar muy caliente.	*In order to fry an egg, the oil has to be very hot.*
Hago ejercicio **para** descansar de mi trabajo.	*I exercise to rest from my work.*

2. **Para** means *for the benefit of* or *directed to*.

Este regalo es **para** ti.	*This gift is for you.*
Lo hice **para** el bien de la humanidad.	*I did it for the good of humanity.*
Hay comida **para** todos.	*There's food for everyone.*

3. **Para** means *by* or *for* when referring to a specific time.

Necesito el libro **para** mañana.	*I need the book by tomorrow.*
Estamos invitados a casa de Julia **para** el fin de semana.	*We're invited to Julia's house for the weekend.*

4. **Para** means *to*, *for*, or *in the direction of* when referring to a specific place.

Me voy **para** Río Blanco mañana.	*I'm heading for Río Blanco tomorrow.*
Salgo **para** Europa en tres días.	*I'm leaving for Europe in three days.*

5. **Estar** + **para** + infinitive means *to be ready to*.

Estoy **para** volverme loco.	*I'm ready to go crazy.*
Estamos **para** salir ya.	*We're ready to leave now.*

EXERCISE 9-1: Read each sentence and think about its meaning. Then complete the sentence by filling in either **por** or **para**, using the cue given in parentheses. If you are not sure which one to use, go back and read through the examples provided. Answers are at the end of the chapter.

Example: (during) Vendré mañana _____*por*_____ la tarde.
1. (on account of) No fuimos _____ los niños, que estaban enfermos.
2. (in order to) Me levanto temprano _____ tener más tiempo libre.
3. (for) Tengo dos libros y los dos son _____ ti.
4. (by) Tenemos que terminar el trabajo _____ el mes de octubre.
5. (because of) Me caí _____ la lluvia.
6. (around) No hay nadie _____ aquí.
7. (along) Estuvimos corriendo _____ la carretera vieja.
8. (in favor of) No estoy _____ caminar mucho.
9. (in favor of) Estoy _____ comer cuanto antes.
10. (in order to) No te lo conté _____ darte una sorpresa.
11. (through) Vamos a ir _____ el atajo.
12. (in exchange for) Te doy mi coche _____ tu camioneta.
13. (for) Salimos _____ San Francisco mañana por la mañana.
14. (on account of) No asistí a la reunión _____ falta de tiempo.
15. (by the) Compro la carne _____ kilos.
16. (per) Los chicos reciben ochenta llamadas telefónicas _____ día.
17. (for the purpose of) Elena duerme mucho _____ olvidar sus penas.
18. (because of) Los niños estan peleándose _____ tu culpa.
19. (by means of) Prefiero viajar _____ tren.
20. (for) Me tomaron _____ español.

9-2. The Preposition *a*

A. The personal *a*

The preposition **a** is used to introduce direct objects that are persons. The direct object may be a noun or a pronoun.

Veo **a** Juan.	*I see Juan.*
No conozco **a** nadie aquí.	*I don't know anyone here.*

> **NOTE:** See Chapter 1, Section 1-5, for a complete discussion of the personal **a**.

B. *a* after certain verbs + infinitive

   1. Verbs of motion.

ir	**Voy a** cocinar.	*I'm going to cook.*
correr	**Corrí a** cerrar la puerta.	*I ran to close the door.*
bajar	Raúl **bajó a** verme.	*Raúl came down to see me.*

   2. Verbs of beginning.

empezar	**Empiezo a** entender lo que decías.	*I'm beginning to understand what you said.*
comenzar	**Comienzan a** trabajar mañana.	*They begin to work tomorrow.*

   3. Verbs of teaching and learning.

enseñar	María nos **enseñó a** pintar muchas cosas.	*María taught us to paint many things.*
aprender	**Aprendí a** leer a los cuatro años.	*I learned to read at the age of four.*

C. **Verbs with special meanings + *a* + infinitive**
   Certain verbs change their meaning with the use of **a** before an infinitive.

   1. Nonreflexive verbs

   volver a, *to (verb) again*

Vuelvo a leer *Don Quixote*.	*I'm reading Don Quixote again.*
Nunca **volví a** ver a Mario.	*I never saw Mario again.*

   tender a, *to tend to*

El maestro **tiende a** hablar demasiado.	*The teacher tends to talk too much.*

   obligar a, *to require, to force, to make (someone do something)*

Me **obligaron a** salir.	*They made me leave.*

   2. Reflexive verbs

   ponerse a, *to start to, to get down to*

Tengo que **ponerme a** planchar la ropa.	*I have to start ironing the clothing.*
La chica **se puso a** bailar.	*The girl started to dance.*

   echarse a reír, llorar, etc., *to burst out laughing, crying, etc.*

Los niños **se echaron a reír**.	*The children burst out laughing.*
Él **se echa a llorar** cada vez que le dices algo.	*He breaks into tears every time you say something to him.*

   echarse a perder, *to spoil*

El pescado **se echó a perder**.	*The fish spoiled.*

   negarse a, *to refuse to*

El niño **se negó a** tirarse al agua.	*The child refused to jump into the water.*

D. **Colloquial expressions with *a***

a caballo	*on horseback*	a veces	*at times*
a casa	*to go home*	al cabo de	*at the end of*
a continuación	*and then, immediately thereafter*	al día siguiente	*next day*
		al fin y al cabo	*after all*
a mano	*by hand*	al tiempo	*at room temperature*

a menudo	*often*	a la derecha	*on the right, to the right*
a pie	*on foot*	a la fuerza	*necessarily*
a tiempo	*on time*	a la izquierda	*on the left, to the left*
a todas horas	*all the time, constantly*		

E. Other uses of *a*

jugar a, *to play (a game)*
Vamos a **jugar a** las cartas.   *We are going to play cards.*
Vamos a **jugar al** béisbol.   *We are going to play baseball.*

caer a, *to fall on*
El libro **cayó al** suelo.   *The book fell on the ground.*

asomarse a, *to lean out*
La mujer **ser asomó a** la ventana.   *The woman leaned out the window.*

asistir a, *to attend*
Mi abuelo **asistió a** la universidad.   *My grandfather attended the university.*

F. *al* + infinitive

Al + infinitive means *upon (verb)-ing*.

Al salir, se me olvidó pagar la cuenta.   *Upon leaving, I forgot to pay the bill.*
Mario se cayó **al bajar**.   *Mario fell upon coming down.*

> **REMEMBER:** In Spanish, prepositions are never followed by the present participle (*-ing* form). However, the preposition followed by an infinitive is often translated into English as a present participle: **en vez de llorar**, *instead of crying*; **al abrir la puerta**, *upon opening the door*.

9-3. The Preposition *en*

A. *en* means *in*, *into*, *on*, or *upon*.

Los libros están **en** la mesa.   *The books are on the table.*
Dejaste los zapatos **en** el suelo.   *You left your shoes on the floor.*
Vamos **en** el coche.   *Let's go in the car.*
Tus camisas están **en** el armario.   *Your shirts are in the closet.*

B. *en* after certain verbs + infinitive or *que* + subjunctive

insistir en, *to insist upon*
María **insistió en** leer su poesía.   *María insisted upon reading her poetry.*
Juan **insistió en** que María no leyera su poesía.   *Juan insisted upon María not reading her poetry.*

pensar en, *to think about, to consider*
Pienso en viajar a España algún día.   *I'm thinking about traveling to Spain some day.*

quedar en, *to agree upon, to plan to*
José **quedó en** venir temprano.   *José agreed to come early.*
Hemos **quedado en** que todos traigan algo de comer.   *We've agreed that everyone will bring something to eat.*

tardar en, *to delay, to take a long time*
Julia **tardó** mucho **en** terminar su proyecto.   *Julia took a long time to finish her project.*

empeñarse en, *to insist upon*
Raimunda **se empeña en** aprender a conducir.   *Raimunda insists upon learning how to drive.*

consistir en, *to consist of*

Mi trabajo **consiste en** ayudar a la maestra.	*My work consists of helping the teacher.*

C. Colloquial expressions with *en*

en cambio	*on the other hand*	en medio de	*in the middle of*
en casa	*at home*	en seguida	*immediately*
en cuanto	*as soon as*	en todas partes	*everywhere*
en cuanto a	*as for*	en vez de	*instead of*
en fin	*after all*	en voz alta	*out loud, in a loud voice*
en lugar de	*instead of*	en voz baja	*softly, in a whisper, low voice*

9-4. The Preposition *de*

A. *de* indicates the possessive.

In English, the *apostrophe s* signals possession: *Juan's house.* In Spanish, **de** signals possession: **la casa de Juan**.

> **NOTE:** See Chapter 2, Section 2-4, for a complete discussion of the possessive.

B. *de* + noun and *de* + infinitive used as adjective

In English, nouns and present participles can be placed before other nouns to describe them: *sewing machine, paper rose.* In Spanish, nouns and infinitives used as modifiers follow the noun and are introduced by **de**: **máquina de coser, rosa de papel**. Study the following examples.

de + infinitive

la máquina de escribir	*typewriter*	la silla de montar	*saddle*
la vara de medir	*measuring stick*		

de + noun

blusa de seda	*silk blouse*	casa de ladrillo	*brick house*
jugo de naranja	*orange juice*	pista de aterrizaje	*landing strip, runway*

C. *de* + past participle

In English, the past participle is used to describe nouns: *dressed in black.* In Spanish, when the past participle modifies a noun, it is followed by *de*: **vestido de negro**. Study the following examples.

cubierto(-a) de lodo	*covered with mud*	rendido(-a) de cansancio	*exhausted*
muerto(-a) de hambre	*dying of hunger*		

D. *de* after certain verbs + infinitive

1. Nonreflexive verbs

acabar de, *to have just*

Emilio **acaba de** escribir un libro.	*Emilio has just written a book.*
Acabo de llegar.	*I have just arrived.*

dejar de, *to stop*

Ha **dejado de** llover.	*It has stopped raining.*

no dejar de, *to not fail to*

No dejes de traer los discos.	*Don't fail to bring the records.*

cesar de, *to cease, to stop*

Nunca **cesa de** hablar.	*He never stops talking.*

tratar de, *to try to, to attempt*

Traté de aprender el latín.	*I tried to learn Latin.*

terminar de, *to finish*

Por favor, **termine** usted **de** comer.	*Please, finish eating.*

2. Reflexive verbs

acordarse de, to remember
¿**Te acordaste de** traer
la ensaladilla?

*Did you remember to bring the potato
salad?*

olvidarse, *to forget*
Pedro **se olvidó de** llamarme.

Pedro forgot to call me.

alegrarse de, *to be happy about*
Me alegro de verte.

I'm happy to see you.

E. Colloquial expressions with *de*

de buena gana	*willingly*	de nada	*you're welcome*
de cuando en cuando	*from time to time*	de ninguna manera	*by no means, under no circumstances*
de día	*by day*	de noche	*at night, by night*
de enfrente	*opposite, across the way*	de nuevo	*once again*
de mala gana	*unwillingly*	de pronto	*suddenly*
de manera que + subj.	*so that, in such a way that*	de todas formas, de todos modos	*anyway*
de memoria	*by heart*	de verdad	*really*
de moda	*stylish*	de vez en cuando	*from time to time*
de modo que + subj.	*so that*		

F. Other uses of *de*

echar de menos, *to miss*
Te **eché de menos**.
Echo de menos a mis hijos.

I missed you.
I miss my children.

reírse de, *to laugh at*
No **te rías de** mí.
Manolo **se ríe de** todo.

Don't laugh at me.
Manolo laughs at everything.

cambiar de opinión, *to change one's mind*
Carlos nunca **cambiará de opinión**.

Carlos will never change his mind.

estar de pie, *to be standing up*
En mi trabajo, **estoy de pie** todo el día.
No quiero tener que **estar de pie** en la fiesta.

In my work, I stand all day.

I don't want to have to stand up at the party.

despedirse de, *to say goodbye to*
Quiero **despedirme de** Leonor.

I want to say goodbye to Leonor.

enamorarse de, *fall in love with*
Romeo **se enamoró de** Julieta.

Romeo fell in love with Julieta.

EXERCISE 9-2: Fill in the blank with the correct preposition: **a**, **en**, or **de**. Answers are at the end of the chapter.

Example: Trato ___*de*___ hablar español.
1. Ha comenzado _____ llover.
2. Voy _____ tratar _____ buscar trabajo.
3. Me alegro _____ estar aquí.
4. Mozart empezó _____ tocar el piano a una edad muy temprana.
5. No te olvides _____ traer el queso.
6. Cuando los niños vieron al payaso, se echaron _____ reír.
7. Echo _____ menos a todos mis amigos latinoamericanos.

8. Jaime y Elena quedaron _____ venir _____ ayudarnos.
9. Raúl acaba _____ entrar.
10. Mi trabajo consiste _____ hablar mucho por teléfono, salir _____ hacer recados y tratar _____ agradar al jefe.
11. Nunca dejamos _____ recordar tu visita.
12. Hablé con María pero se negó _____ venir _____ ayudarnos.
13. Bájate _____ cerrar las ventanas, por favor.
14. Si tengo tiempo, voy _____ ponerme _____ planchar.
15. Andrew se empeña _____ comer pizza _____ todas horas.
16. Los muchachos acaban _____ comer y no han tardado _____ pedir postre.
17. La maestra nos enseñó _____ leer bien.
18. Acabo _____ leer tu carta y la encontré muy divertida.
19. Cuando termine _____ leer *Don Quixote*, volveré _____ leerlo.
20. Los estudiantes van _____ volver _____ leer el libro de texto.

EXERCISE 9-3: Review the lists of colloquial expressions with **a, en,** and **de.** Then complete the following sentences by translating the word or phrase given in parentheses into Spanish. Answers are at the end of the chapter.

1. (Suddenly) la maestra empezó a hablar (out loud). _____
2. (Often) vamos (home on foot). _____
3. Me devolvieron el dinero (immediately). _____
4. (Under no circumstances) podemos trabajar con ellos. _____
5. (From time to time) me pongo a pensar en el futuro. _____
6. Descanso (by day) y trabajo (by night). _____
7. José insiste en comprar (a pearl necklace, a sewing machine, and a watchdog) para su mujer. _____
8. Lila comió sopa, ensalada, un bistec con patatas fritas, (and then) pidió postre. _____
9. Aprendí el poema (by heart), pero (at times) lo leo (anyway). _____
10. Fuimos (to the right) pero la casa estaba (on the left). _____
11. La camisa está hecha (by hand). _____
12. (From time to time) bebemos los refrescos (at room temperature). _____
13. La blusa no está muy (stylish) pero pienso comprarla (anyway). _____
14. José nunca llega (on time). _____
15. Pedro nos volvió a hablar (right away). _____
16. Yo bailo mucho. Leonor, (on the other hand), no baila nunca. _____
17. La vecina (across the way) nos ayuda (willingly). _____
18. Tenemos que irnos a la cama temprano (necessarily). _____
19. (Next day), fuimos a comer mariscos. _____
20. (In the midst of) todos los papeles, (suddenly) encontré un carta perdida.

_____

EXERCISE 9-4: Translate the following sentences into Spanish. Answers are at the end of the chapter.

1. I don't want to play cards; now I'm going to play baseball.

2. The children miss their teacher.

3. They just bought a new house.

4. I saw Raúl again in Madrid.

5. I think the meat has spoiled.

6. Elena leaned out the window and yelled at Mario.

7. Upon seeing the teacher, the students broke out laughing.

8. Why are you (fam. sing.) laughing at Adolfo?

9-5. Prepositions of Place

Prepositions, unlike adverbs, never appear by themselves in a sentence. They always introduce a phrase: **dentro de la caja,** *inside the box*; **encima de la mesa,** *on top of the table.* In Spanish, there are two kinds of prepositions, simple and compound. It is necessary to learn the entire compound preposition, paying close attention to the final words: **junto a,** *next to*; **debajo de,** *under.*

A. Simple prepositions of place

en	*in, on*	hacia	*towards*
entre	*among, between*	sobre	*on, above*

B. Compound prepositions of place

al lado de	*beside*	enfrente de	*across from, opposite*
alrededor de	*around*	en medio de	*in the midst of*
cerca de	*near*	frente a	*facing*
debajo de	*under*	fuera de	*outside of*
delante de	*in front of*	junto a	*next to*
dentro de	*inside of*	lejos de	*far from*
encima de	*on top of*	más allá de	*beyond*

EXERCISE 9-5: Translate the following sentences into Spanish. Answers are at the end of the chapter.

Example: The chair is facing the fireplace. *La silla está frente a la chimenea.*

1. I live near here.

2. The cat is sleeping under the table.

3. I put the fish inside the refrigerator.

4. He lives beyond the church of Saint Francis.

5. Last night, I slept outside the house in the garden.

6. I see spots in front of my eyes.

7. I want to sit next to you.

8. He sat down next to Pepe.

9. There are flowers around the tree.

10. There is a cafeteria opposite the school.

11. Don't talk (*fam. sing.*) in front of the children.

12. I want to put the flower vase on top of the book case.

13. It is impossible to work in the midst of chaos and noise.

14. He took the dog outside of the house.

15. Don't put (*fam. sing.*) the car under the house.

16. Put (*fam. sing.*) the milk on the table, not in the refrigerator.

17. There is always a thorn among the roses.

18. I live far from downtown.

19. Alda is coming toward us.

20. Between you and me there will always be friendship.

9-6. Other Important Prepositions

A. Simple prepositions

ante	*before*	menos	*except*
con	*with*	salvo	*except*
contra	*against*	según	*according to*
desde	*since, from*	sin	*without*
durante	*during*	sobre	*about, concerning*
excepto	*except*	tras	*after*
hasta	*until*		

B. Compound prepositions

acerca de	*about, concerning*	a través de	*through (time)*
además de	*besides, in addition to*	después de	*after*
antes de	*before (time)*	en contra de	*against*
a causa de	*because of*	en lugar de	*instead of*
a pesar de	*in spite of*	en vez de	*instead of*

C. Colloquial expressions with prepositions

contar con, *to count on*
No puedo **contar contigo**.
I can't count on you.

soñar con, *to dream about*
Anoche **soñé con** un oso gigantesco.
Last night I dreamed about a gigantic bear.

tropezar con, *to stumble into, bump against*
Al salir del cine, **tropecé con** un amigo.
On leaving the movies, I ran into a friend.

casarse con, *to get married to*
Felipe **se casa con** Isabel.
Felipe is getting married to Isabel.

con mucho gusto, *gladly*
Lo haré **con mucho gusto**.
I'll do it gladly.

sin embargo, *nevertheless*
La silla me costó cincuenta dólares. **Sin embargo**, se rompió.
The chair cost me fifty dollars. Nevertheless, it broke.

sin duda, *doubtless, without doubt*
Sin duda, España es uno de los paises más interesantes de Europa.
Without doubt, Spain is one of the most interesting countries in Europe.

desde luego, *of course, certainly*
Desde luego, tendremos que trabajar mucho.
Of course, we'll have to work a great deal.

hasta luego, *see you later*
Adiós, **hasta luego**.
Goodbye, see you later.

de antemano, *beforehand*

No tenías que decirme nada porque ya lo sabía **de antemano.**	*You didn't have to tell me anything because I already knew it beforehand.*

SUMMARY

1. **Por** means *on account of* or *because of, through, along, by, around, during, in exchange for, by* (*per*), *by means of,* or *for.*
2. **Para** means *in order to, for the purpose of, for the benefit of, by* or *for* (*a specific time*), or *to* or *for* (*a specific place*).
3. **Estar + por** + infinitive means *to be in favor of.* **Estar + para** + infinitive means *to be ready to.*
4. The preposition **a** is used to introduce objects that are persons: **Veo a Juan.** *I see Juan.*
5. The preposition **a** is used after verbs of motion, beginning, teaching, and learning to introduce an infinitive.
6. Some verbs change their meaning when used in the verb + **a** + infinitive structure; for example, **volver,** *to return,* becomes **volver a** (bailar), *to* (dance) *again.*
7. **Al** + infinitive means *upon* (*verb*)*ing*: **al salir,** *upon leaving.* In Spanish, prepositions are followed by the infinitive form of the verb, not by the present participle: **en vez de llorar,** *instead of crying.*
8. **En** means both *in* and *on.*
9. **En** is used after verbs such as **insistir en, quedar en, tardar en,** and so on, to introduce an infinitive or a dependent clause with a subjunctive.
10. **De** is used to form the possessive: **la casa de María,** *María's house.*
11. **De** + a noun or an infinitive is used as an adjective to modify another noun: **máquina de coser,** *sewing machine.* When a past participle is used to modify a noun, it is followed by **de: muerto de hambre,** *dying of hunger.*
12. **De** is used after verbs such as **olvidarse de, acordarse de, alegrarse de,** and others, to introduce an infinitive or a dependent clause with a subjunctive.
13. In Spanish, just as in English, there are simple prepositions such as **a, en, de, por,** and **para,** as well as compound prepositions such as **junto a,** *next to,* **encima de,** *on top of,* and so on.

RAISE YOUR GRADES

☑ *Por* versus *para* [Section 9-1]

Read the following sentences. Think of the logical meaning of the missing preposition and write in **por** or **para.** Then select the letter that corresponds to the correct meaning from the list below, and write it in the space provided to the left of each sentence. Answers are at the end of the chapter.

por	**para**
(*a*) on account of, because of	(*h*) in order to
(*b*) through	(*i*) for the benefit of
(*c*) around	(*j*) by (a specific time)
(*d*) during	(*k*) to (a specific place)
(*e*) in exchange for	
(*f*) by (per)	
(*g*) by means of	

Example: _e_ Pagué cinco dolares __*por*__ estos zapatos.

1. ____ Compré una esponja nueva _____ limpiar la cocina.
2. ____ Mañana salgo _____ Londres.
3. ____ Vamos a caminar _____ el parque.

4. ___ No pudimos ir _____ la lluvia.
5. ___ Fuimos a San Francisco _____ tren.
6. ___ No hay nadie _____ aquí.
7. ___ Vivimos en México _____ muchos años.
8. ___ Compré un regalo _____ mi sobrino.
9. ___ El ochenta _____ cien de mis respuestas estaban bien.
10. ___ Tenemos que terminar el trabajo _____ las ocho.
11. ___ Como mucho _____ engordar.
12. ___ Leo _____ placer.
13. ___ El me dio su bicicleta _____ mi reloj.
14. ___ El ladrón entró _____ la ventana.
15. ___ Quiero aprender el español _____ poder hablar con mi vecino.

☑ *a, de,* and *en* [Sections 9-2, 9-3, and 9-4]

These three prepositions are used frequently in colloquial expressions and after certain verbs to introduce an infinitive. Write in the missing preposition in the following sentences. Then translate your work. Answers are at the end of the chapter.

Example: __*De*__ vez __*en*__ cuando voy __*a*__ nadar.

1. Llamé _____ Adolfo y contestó _____ seguida.
2. _____ veces voy _____ casa _____ lugar _____ ir _____ jugar _____ béisbol.
3. José se empeña _____ hablar _____ voz baja.
4. Me enseñaron _____ leer _____ los cuatro años _____ casa.
5. Nunca aprendí _____ hablar bien el francés; mi hermana, _____ cambio, lo habla perfectamente.
6. _____ levantar los vasos, uno de ellos cayó _____ suelo.
7. _____ día siguiente, había nieve _____ todas partes.
8. Los niños siempre tardan _____ llegar y nunca están _____ tiempo.
9. Tenemos que ponernos _____ marcha porque Julia insiste _____ llegar temprano _____ la reunión.
10. Pienso _____ ti _____ todas horas, _____ verdad.
11. _____ cuanto _____ María, nunca pienso _____ ella.
12. Aquella mujer se asoma a la ventana _____ menudo y grita _____ voz alta _____ su vecina.
13. _____ abrir la ventana, la niña vio _____ su padre que venía _____ casa _____ caballo.
14. _____ veces voy _____ la derecha, pero _____ vez _____ cuando, voy _____ la izquierda.
15. Volví _____ ver _____ mis primos _____ cabo _____ cinco años.
16. Acabamos _____ comer y _____ todos modos, estamos pensando _____ ir _____ comer _____ nuevo.
17. No me acuerdo _____ nombre _____ la vecina _____ enfrente.
18. Me alegro _____ conocerte y de conocer _____ tu marido.
19. Isabel siempre se viste _____ seda.
20. Tenemos que descansar _____ la fuerza porque estamos rendidos _____ cansancio.

☑ **Compound prepositions** [Sections 9-5 and 9-6]

Complete the following sentences by translating the word or phrase given in parentheses into Spanish. Answers are at the end of the chapter.

Example: Vivo (opposite) la casa blanca.   *en frente de*

1. Quiero que pongas la silla (facing) el espejo.   _____
2. Me gustaría ir (beyond) la frontera.   _____
3. Tenemos que hablar (about) los problemas de los estudiantes. _____
4. Fui a nadar (in spite of) la lluvia.   _____
5. Einstein vivirá (through) los siglos.   _____
6. (Besides) ser inteligente, tiene talento.   _____

7. Ofelia siempre se sienta (beside) Jorge. _____
8. No pongas la cafetera (on top of) la mesa. _____
9. Fue (because of) mi torpeza. _____
10. Quiero dormir (instead of) comer. _____
11. Fuimos a bailar (after) cenar. _____
12. Siempre se para el autobús (in front of) mi casa. _____
13. Quiero tener una verja muy alta (around) el jardín. _____
14. Voy a tender la ropa (outside) la casa. _____
15. (In the midst of) este caos, siempre habrá un poco de
tranquilidad. _____

CHAPTER ANSWERS

EXERCISE 9-1

1. por *We didn't go on account of the children, who were sick.*
2. para *I get up early in order to have more free time.*
3. para *I have two books and the two are for you.*
4. para *We have to finish the work by the month of October.*
5. por *I fell because of the rain.*
6. por *There is nobody around here.*
7. por *We were running along the old highway.*
8. por *I'm not in favor of walking a lot.*
9. por *I'm in favor of eating as soon as possible.*
10. para *I didn't tell you about it in order to give you a surprise.*
11. por *Let's go through the shortcut.*
12. por *I'll give you my car in exchange for your pickup truck.*
13. para *We're leaving for San Francisco tomorrow morning.*
14. por *I didn't attend the meeting on account of (due to) a lack of time.*
15. por *I buy meat by the kilo.*
16. por *The kids get eighty telephone calls a day.*
17. para *Elena sleeps a lot (for the purpose of) to forget her troubles.*
18. por *The children are fighting because of you (your fault).*
19. por *I prefer to travel by (means of) train.*
20. por *They took me for a Spaniard.*

EXERCISE 9-2

1. a *It has begun to rain.*
2. a, de *I'm going to try to look for work.*
3. de *I'm happy to be here.*
4. a *Mozart began to play the piano at a very early age.*
5. de *Don't forget to bring the cheese.*
6. a *When the children saw the clown, they broke out laughing.*
7. de *I miss all my Latin American friends.*

8. en, a *Jaime and Elena agreed to come and help us.*
9. de *Raúl has just come in.*
10. en, a, de *My work consists of talking on the telephone a lot, going out and running errands, and trying to make the boss happy.*
11. de *We never stop remembering your visit.*
12. a, a *I talked with María but she refused to come and help us.*
13. a *Go down and close the windows please.*
14. a, a *If I have time, I'm going to get down to ironing.*
15. en, a *Andrew insists on eating pizza at all hours.*
16. de, en *The boys have just finished eating and have wasted no time in ordering dessert.*
17. a *The teacher taught us how to read well.*
18. de *I've just read your letter and I found it very amusing.*
19. de, a *When I finish reading* Don Quixote, *I'll read it again.*
20. a, a *The students are going to read the textbook again.*

EXERCISE 9-3

1. De repente, en voz alta *Suddenly, the teacher began talking out loud.*
2. A menudo, a casa a pie *We often go home on foot.*
3. en seguida *They returned the money to me immediately.*
4. De ninguna manera *Under no circumstances can we work with them.*
5. De vez en cuando *From time to time, I get to thinking about the future.*
6. de día, de noche *I rest by day and work by night.*
7. un collar de perlas, una máquina de coser, un perro de guardia *José insists on buying a pearl necklace, a sewing machine, and a watchdog for his wife.*
8. y a continuación *Lila had soup, salad, a steak with French fried potatoes, and then she ordered dessert.*

9. de memoria, a veces, de todas formas *I learned the poem by heart, but at times I read it anyway.*
10. a la derecha, a la izquierda *We went to the right but the house was on the left.*
11. a mano *The shirt is handmade.*
12. De vez en cuando, al tiempo *From time to time, we drink soda pop at room temperature.*
13. de moda, de todas formas *The blouse isn't very stylish but I intend to buy it anyway.*
14. a tiempo *José never arrives on time.*
15. en seguida *Pedro talked to us again (got back to us) right away.*
16. en cambio *I dance a lot. Leonor, on the other hand, never dances.*
17. de enfrente, de buena gana *The neighbor across the way helps us willingly.*
18. a la fuerza *We necessarily have to go to bed early.*
19. Al día siguiente *Next day, we went and ate seafood.*
20. En medio, de repente *In the midst of all the papers, I suddenly found a lost letter.*

EXERCISE 9-4

1. No quiero jugar a las cartas; ahora voy a jugar al béisbol.
2. Los niños echan de menos a su maestra.
3. Acaban de comprar una casa nueva.
4. Volví a ver a Raúl en Madrid.
5. Pienso (creo) que la carne se ha echado a perder.
6. Elena se asomó a la ventana y gritó a Mario.
7. Al ver a la maestra, los estudiantes se echaron a reír.
8. ¿Por qué te ríes de Adolfo?

EXERCISE 9-5

1. Vivo cerca de aquí.
2. El gato está durmiendo debajo de la mesa.
3. Puse el pescado en la nevera.
4. El vive más allá de la iglesia de San Francisco
5. Anoche, dormí fuera de casa en el jardín.
6. Veo manchas delante de los ojos.
7. Quiero sentarme junto a ti.
8. El se sentó junto a Pepe.
9. Hay flores alrededor del árbol.
10. Hay una cafetería en frente de la escuela.
11. No hables delante de los niños.
12. Quiero poner el florero encima de la librería.
13. Es imposible trabajar en medio del caos y del ruido.
14. Sacó al perro fuera de la casa.
15. No pongas el coche debajo de la casa.
16. Pon la leche en la mesa, no en la nevera.
17. Siempre hay una espina entre las rosas.
18. Vivo lejos del centro de la ciudad.
19. Alda viene hacia nosotros.
20. Entre tú y yo siempre habrá una amistad.

RAISE YOUR GRADES

Por versus *para*

1. h, para *I bought a new sponge in order to clean the kitchen.*
2. k, para *I leave for London tomorrow.*
3. b OR c, por *We are going to walk (around or through) the park.*
4. a, por *We couldn't go because of the rain.*
5. g, por *We went to San Francisco by train.*
6. c, por *There's nobody around here.*
7. d, por *We lived in Mexico for many years.*
8. i, para *I bought a present for my nephew.*
9. f, por *Eighty percent of my answers were all right.*
10. j, para *We have to finish the work by eight o'clock.*
11. h, para *I eat a lot in order to get fat.*
12. a, por *I read for pleasure. (because it gives me pleasure)*
13. e, por *He gave me his bicycle in exchange for my watch.*
14. b, por *The thief came in through the window.*
15. h, para *I want to learn Spanish in order to be able to talk with my neighbor.*

a, de, and *en*

1. a, en *I called Adolfo and he answered immediately.*
2. A, a, en, de, a, al *Sometimes I go home instead of going to play baseball.*
3. en, en *José insists on speaking in a low voice.*
4. a, a, en *They taught me to read at age four at home.*
5. a, en *I never learned to speak French well; my sister, on the other hand, speaks it perfectly.*
6. Al, al *Upon lifting up one of the glasses, one of them fell to the floor.*
7. Al, en *On the next day, there was snow everywhere.*
8. en, a *The children always arrive late and are never on time.*
9. en, en, a *We've got to get moving because Julia insists on arriving early at the meeting.*
10. en, a, de *I think of you all the time, really.*
11. En, a, en *As for María, I never think of her.*
12. a, en, a *That woman often leans out the window and yells in a loud voice to her neighbor.*
13. Al, a, a, a *Upon opening the window, the girl saw her father who was coming home on horseback.*
14. A, a, de, en, a *At times I go to the right, but from time to time I go to the left.*
15. a, a, al, de *I saw my cousins again after five years.*
16. de, de, en, a, de *We've just eaten and in any event, we're thinking about going to eat again.*

17. del, de, de *I don't remember the name of the neighbor across the way.*
18. de, a *I'm glad to meet you and to meet your husband.*
19. de *Isabel always dresses in silk.*
20. a, de *We necessarily have to rest because we're exhausted.*

Compound prepositions

1. frente al *I want you to put the chair facing the mirror.*
2. más allá de *I'd like to go beyond the border.*
3. acerca de *We have to talk about the students' problems.*
4. a pesar de *I went swimming in spite of the rain.*
5. a través de *Einstein will live through the centuries.*
6. Además de *Besides being intelligent, he (she) is talented.*
7. junto a *Ofelia always sits beside Jorge.*
8. encima de *Don't put the coffee pot on top of the table.*
9. a causa de *It was (happened) because of my clumsiness.*
10. en vez de *I want to sleep instead of eating.*
11. después de *We went dancing after dinner.*
12. delante de *The bus always stops in front of my house.*
13. alrededor del *I want to have a very high fence around my garden.*
14. fuera de *I'm going to hang the clothes outside the house.*
15. En medio de *In the midst of this chaos, there will always be a little calm.*

10 SPECIAL VERBS AND IDIOMS

10-1. *gustar* and Similar Verbs

Certain verbs such as **gustar**, *to be pleasing*, and **faltar**, *to be lacking*, are almost always used with the indirect object pronouns, **me**, **te**, **le**, **nos**, **os**, and **les**. In the following examples, note that the subject of the sentence is either third person singular or plural and is placed *after* the verb.

A. *gustar*, to be pleasing

The literal translation of **gustar** is *to be pleasing*, but the English meaning is *to like*. Study the following sentence constructions carefully.

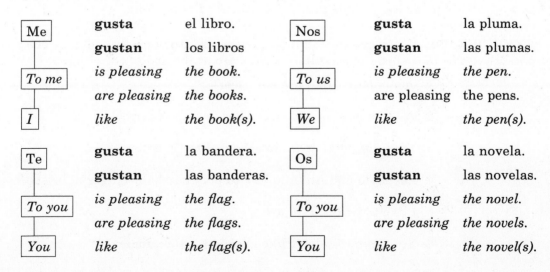

Me	**gusta**	el libro.	Nos	**gusta**	la pluma.
	gustan	los libros		**gustan**	las plumas.
To me	*is pleasing*	*the book.*	To us	*is pleasing*	*the pen.*
	are pleasing	*the books.*		are pleasing	the pens.
I	*like*	*the book(s).*	We	*like*	*the pen(s).*
Te	**gusta**	la bandera.	Os	**gusta**	la novela.
	gustan	las banderas.		**gustan**	las novelas.
To you	*is pleasing*	*the flag.*	To you	*is pleasing*	*the novel.*
	are pleasing	*the flags.*		*are pleasing*	*the novels.*
You	*like*	*the flag(s).*	You	*like*	*the novel(s).*

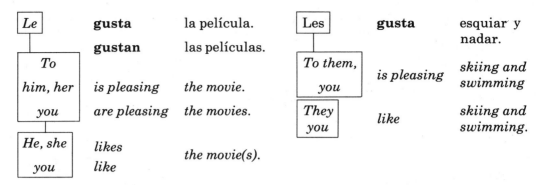

NOTE: When the subject is an infinitive, the verb is always singular even if more than one infinitive is included: **Les gusta esquiar y nadar.**

B. *gustar* + **prepositional phrase**

1. The prepositional phrases, **a él, a ella, a usted, a ellos, a ellas,** or **a ustedes** are used to clarify **le** and **les.**

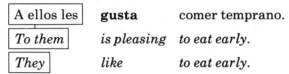

2. If the object is a noun, the indirect object pronoun must still be used.

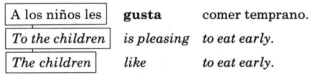

3. In *all* cases, the negative immediately precedes the indirect object pronoun.

A los niños	**nunca**	**les**	**gusta**	acostarse temprano.
To the children	never		is pleasing	to go to bed early.
Children	never		like	to go to bed early.

4. The prepositional phrases, **a mí, a ti, a nosotros,** or **a vosotros** may be used for emphasis.

¿A ti te gusta bailar?	*Do you like to dance?*
No, a mí no me gusta bailar.	*No, I don't like to dance.*

EXERCISE 10-1: Translate the following sentences into Spanish, using the cue given in parentheses as the subject of **gustar.** Answers are at the end of the chapter.

1. Juan doesn't like to read. (leer)

2. We like flowers and trees. (las flores y los árboles)

3. They don't like to go to school. (ir a la escuela)

4. Reynaldo and Antonio like to play baseball. (jugar al béisbol)

5. I like to travel. (viajar)

6. You (*vosotros*) don't like chemistry. (la química)

7. Nobody likes difficult questions. (las preguntas difíciles)

8. They (*ellos*) like romantic novels. (las novelas románticas)

9. Children never like to wash their face. (lavarse la cara)

10. Everybody likes popcorn. (las palomitas)

11. Laura doesn't like vegetables. (las verduras)

12. We like Spanish and French. (el español y el francés)

13. You (*tú*) don't like to do your biology homework. (tu tarea de biología)

14. They (*ellas*) like to play cards. (jugar a las cartas)

15. Juan and Leonor like Spanish food. (la comida española)

C. *faltar*, *hacer falta*, **and** *quedar*

1. Faltar, *to lack*

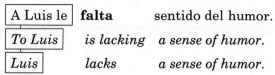

A Luis le	**falta**	sentido del humor.
To Luis	*is lacking*	*a sense of humor.*
Luis	*lacks*	*a sense of humor.*

2. Hacer falta, *to be needed*

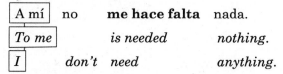

A mí	no	**me hace falta**	nada.
To me		*is needed*	*nothing.*
I	*don't*	*need*	*anything.*

> **NOTE:** **Hacer falta** emphasizes the need for something.
> **Faltar** emphasizes the lack or absence of something.

3. quedar, *to have left, remain*

Nos	**quedan**	tres horas.
To us	*remain*	*three hours.*
We	*have*	*three hours left.*

EXERCISE 10-2: Study the examples carefully. Then rewrite the following sentences by using the verb given in parentheses and changing the basic sentence structure as required. Translate your work into English. Answers are at the end of the chapter.

Examples: José necesita una silla. (hacer falta) *A José le hace falta una silla. José needs a chair*
No tenemos interés en el proyecto. (faltar) *Nos falta interés en el proyecto. We lack interest in the project.*
Tengo cinco minutos. (quedar) *Me quedan cinco minutos. I have five minutes left.*

1. Los estudiantes necesitan estudiar. (hacer falta)

2. No necesito un reloj nuevo. (no hacer falta)

3. No hay ni sal ni mostaza. (faltar)

4. Los estudiantes no tienen ganas de hablar. (faltar)

5. Raimundo no tiene dinero. (no quedar)

6. Necesitamos más tiempo. (hacer falta)

7. ¿Tienes gasolina? (quedar)

8. Tengo tres camisas de seda. (quedar)

9. Los vecinos no tienen más comida. (no quedar)

10. No tengo ganas de comer. (faltar)

11. Necesitamos hablar con Rubén. (hacer falta)

12. No hay que escribir nada. (no hacer falta)

13. No hay suficiente espacio. (faltar)

14. Los muchachos no necesitan postre. (no hacer falta)

15. Alicia no tiene tiempo para ayudarnos. (faltar)

10-2. Idiomatic Expressions with *hacer*

A. *hace* + measurable time + *que* + present tense

In English, the phrase *for* + *measurable time* (five minutes, two hours, many years, etc.) is used to express the amount of time during which an action has been taking place: *I've been studying for two hours.* In Spanish, the third person singular **hace** is used with expressions of measurable time: **hace cinco minutos**, *for five minutes.* In the following examples, note that Spanish uses the present tense rather than the present perfect to express an action begun in the past and still continuing in the present.

Hace un año que vivimos en California.	*We've been living in California for a year.*
Hace cinco años que no veo a Juanita.	*I haven't seen Juanita for five years.*
¿Cuánto tiempo **hace que viven** ustedes en Hawaii?	*How long have you been living in Hawaii?*
¿Cuántos años **hace que estudias** francés?	*How many years have you been studying French?*

EXERCISE 10-3: Answer the following questions, using the cue given in parentheses. When you finish, translate your work into English. Answers are at the end of the chapter.

Example: ¿Cuánto tiempo hace que estudias química? (un semestre) *Hace un semestre que estudio química. I've been studying chemistry for a semester.*

1. ¿Cuántos meses hace que Linda juega al tenis? (dos meses)

2. ¿Cuánto tiempo hace que usas gafas? (un año)

3. ¿Cuánto tiempo hace que usted no toca el piano? (diez años)

4. ¿Cuántos meses hace que usted estudia biología? (tres meses)

5. ¿Cuántos minutos hace que ladra el perro? (veinte minutos)

6. ¿Cuánto tiempo hace que conoces a Antonio? (mucho tiempo)

7. ¿Cuánto tiempo hace que tus abuelos no vienen? (bastante tiempo)

8. ¿Cuántos días hace que tienes catarro? (ocho días)

9. ¿Cuántos días hace que el motor no funciona? (sólo un día)

10. ¿Cuántos minutos hace que hierven los huevos? (tres minutos)

B. *hacía* + **measurable time** + *que* + **imperfect tense**

Hacía + measurable time is used with the imperfect to describe an action that began in the past and is still happening in the past. The main verb is usually translated into English using the past perfect.

Hacía mucho tiempo que Jorge no **nadaba**.   *Jorge hadn't been swimming for a long time.*

Hacía una hora que dormíamos.   *We had been sleeping for an hour.*

¿Cuánto tiempo **hacía que** ustedes **tocaban** el piano juntos?   *How long had you been playing the piano together?*

EXERCISE 10-4: Translate the following sentences into Spanish. Answers are at the end of the chapter.

1. The students had been studying for two weeks.

2. I've been playing the piano for many years.

3. Their parents had lived in Mexico for a year.

4. How long had Rafael been smoking?

5. How long have you (*tú*) been living in Seattle?

6. We've been reading this newspaper for many years.

7. How long has Jaime been sick?

8. I haven't seen my friends for a long time.

9. I had been sick for a week.

10. We had lived in Madrid for two years.

C. **Preterite** + *hace* + **measurable time**

When the preterite tense is used with the **hace** + time construction, the meaning is (*measurable time*) *ago*. Note that **hace** + time follows the main clause. Therefore, the connective, **que**, is not needed.

Viví en San Diego **hace dos años**.   *I lived in San Diego two years ago.*

Se descompuso el coche **hace mucho tiempo**.   *The car broke down a long time ago.*

Todo eso pasó **hace siglos**.   *All that happened centuries ago.*

EXERCISE 10-5: Answer the following questions, using the cue given in parentheses. When you have finished, translate your work into English. Answers are at the end of the chapter.

Example: ¿Cuándo viajaste a México? (hace tres años)   *Viajé a México hace tres años. I traveled to Mexico three years ago.*

1. ¿Cuándo estuviste en Nueva York? (hace solamente un mes)

2. ¿Cuándo se rompió el dedo David? (hace una semana)

3. ¿Cuándo salieron tus padres? (hace cinco minutos)

4. ¿Cuándo se murio el perro? (hace mucho tiempo)

5. ¿Cuándo terminaste la carrera? (hace poco tiempo)

D. **Present tense +** *desde* **+** *hace* **+ measurable time**

When **hace** + time follows the present tense, it is introduced by **desde**.

Vivo en San Diego desde **hace dos años**.	*I've been living in San Diego for two years.*
Me siento enfermo desde **hace una hora**.	*I've been feeling sick for an hour.*

When the time referred to is a specific moment or date rather than a length of time, use **desde** + the specific moment or date.

Mi madre nos visita **desde el primero de enero**.	*My mother has been visiting us since the first of January.*
Toco la guitarra **desde el verano pasado**.	*I've been playing the guitar since last summer.*

EXERCISE 10-6: Answer the following questions, using the cue given in parentheses. When you finish, translate your work into English. Answers are at the end of the chapter.

Example: ¿Desde cuándo tienes una motocicleta? (hace un año) *Tengo una motocicleta desde hace un año. I've had a motorcycle for a year.*

1. ¿Desde cuándo vive Irene con sus padres? (hace seis meses)

2. ¿Desde cuándo juega al béisbol tu padre? (el verano pasado)

3. ¿Desde cuándo asistes al Liceo Francés? (el catorce de julio)

4. ¿Desde cuándo se acuesta temprano Carlos? (hace un año)

5. ¿Desde cuándo te levantas temprano? (ayer)

6. ¿Desde cuándo estás enferma? (la semana pasada)

7. ¿Desde cuándo estás de vuelta? (hace dos semanas)

8. ¿Desde cuándo saben ustedes la verdad? (hace mucho tiempo)

9. ¿Desde cuándo escribe Sara poesía? (hace dos días)

10. ¿Desde cuándo conoce Susan a Bill? (el primero de mayo)

E. *hacer* **and the weather**

The verb **hacer** is used to discuss the weather. Study the following examples.

¿Qué tiempo **hace**?	*How's the weather?*
Hace frío, calor, sol, viento, fresco.	*It's cold, hot, sunny, windy, cool.*
¿**Hace** buen tiempo? ¿**Hace** mal tiempo?	*Is the weather good? Is the weather bad?*
Hace buen tiempo. **Hace** mal tiempo.	*The weather's good. The weather's bad.*

F. **Other idiomatic expressions with** *hacer*

hacer una pregunta, *to ask a question*

Los estudiantes me hicieron una buena pregunta.	*The students asked me a good question.*

hacer la maleta, *to pack a suitcase*

Tenemos que hacer las maletas.	*We have to pack the suitcases.*

hacer caso, *to pay attention*
Nadie me hace caso.   *No one pays attention to me.*

hacer daño, *to hurt*; **hacerse daño**, *to hurt oneself*
Al caerme del árbol, me hice daño.   *On falling from the tree, I hurt myself.*

hacerse, *to become (through one's own efforts)*
Mi hermano mayor se hizo millonario.   *My older brother became a millionaire.*

10-3. Idiomatic Expressions with *tener*

A. *Tener*, to be, is often used instead of *ser* or *estar* when refering to certain physical and mental states or to a person's age.

tener . . . años, *to be . . . years old*
¿Cuántos años tienes?   *How old are you?*
Tengo diez años.   *I'm ten years old.*

tener calor, frío, *to be hot, cold*
Nunca tengo calor.   *I'm never hot.*
Vivian siempre tiene frío.   *Vivian is always cold.*

tener hambre, sed, sueño, *to be hungry, thirsty, sleepy*
Tengo mucha hambre.   *I'm very hungry.*
No tengo sed.   *I'm not thirsty.*
Los chicos nunca tienen sueño.   *The kids are never sleepy.*

tener prisa, *to be in a hurry*
El jefe siempre tiene prisa.   *The boss is always in a hurry.*

tener miedo a + noun, *to be afraid of*
Tengo miedo a los insectos.   *I'm afraid of bugs.*

tener miedo de + infinitive, *to be afraid to*
Tengo miedo de hablar en público.   *I'm afraid to speak in public.*

tener cuidado con, *to be careful of*
Ten cuidado con el coche.   *Be careful with the car.*
no tener cuidado, *to not worry*
No tengas cuidado.   *Don't worry.*

tener razón, *to be right*
El jefe nunca tiene razón.   *The boss is never right.*

tener la culpa, *to be guilty*
Tú no tienes la culpa de nada.   *You are not guilty of anything.*

B. **Other idiomatic expressions with *tener***

tener lugar, *to take place*
La reunión tiene lugar en casa de Laura.   *The meeting is taking place at Laura's house.*

tener ganas de + infinitive, *to feel like*
No tengo ganas de comer ahora.   *I don't feel like eating now.*

tener en cuenta, *to take into account, to keep in mind*
Tendré en cuenta lo que me has dicho. *I'll keep what you've said to me in mind.*

EXERCISE 10-7: Review the idiomatic expressions with **hacer** and **tener**. Then translate the phrases given in parentheses into Spanish. Answers are at the end of the chapter.

Example: Este verano, (it's very hot).   *Este verano, hace mucho calor.*
1. Los niños (are very thirsty).

2. Por favor, (be careful) (*tú*) con el perro.

3. Emilio (is always in a hurry).

4. (I am afraid of) caerme.

5. Mi tía (is afraid of) todo.

6. Tengo que (pack the suitcases).

7. (We're not thirsty) porque (it's not hot).

8. (I'm in a hurry) porque tengo que llegar pronto.

9. Los chicos (feel like) jugar al béisbol.

10. Yo, en cambio, (don't feel like) hacer nada.

11. Ayer (it was very cold).

12. ¿Dónde (is taking place) la fiesta?

13. Rita siempre (asks a lot of questions).

14. ¿Quién (is to blame) del accidente?

15. ¿(How old is) la hermana de Raquel?

16. Estoy enojado porque (I'm sleepy).

17. Después de terminar los estudios, Manolo (became) maestro.

18. Nadie (pays attention to) lo que dicen los jóvenes.

19. Tenemos que (keep in mind) la escasez de agua.

20. Mi hermano (is older) que tu hermano.

10-4. Idiomatic Expressions with *dar*, *echar*, and *poner*

A. *dar*

darse cuenta de, *to realize, to be aware of*
Ayer no nos dimos cuenta de que no había agua caliente.

Yesterday we didn't realize that there wasn't any hot water.

dar miedo, *to be afraid of*
A Fernando le dan miedo los túneles.

Fernando is afraid of tunnels.

dar verguenza, *to be embarrassed*
Me da verguenza hablar en público.

I am embarrassed to speak in public.

dar de comer a, *to feed*
Tengo que dar de comer al niño.

I have to feed the baby.

dar la mano a, *to shake hands with*
Jaime, dale la mano a tu tío Joaquín.

Jaime, shake hands with your uncle Joaquín.

dar las gracias, *to thank*
Antes de despedirme, quiero darte las gracias.

Before saying goodbye, I want to thank you.

dar un paseo, *to take a walk*
Vamos a dar un paseo por el parque.

Let's take a walk through the park.

Special Verbs and Idioms 223

B. *echar*

echar una siesta, *to take a nap*
Carlos echa una siesta después del almuerzo. — *Carlos takes a nap after lunch.*

echar una carta, *to mail a letter*
Tengo que ir a correos a echar unas cartas. — *I have to go to the post office to mail some letters.*

echar de menos, *to miss (a person, a thing)*
Echo de menos la lluvia. — *I miss the rain.*
Echamos de menos a Janet. — *We miss Janet.*

echar una mano, *to help, to give a hand*
¿Te puedo echar una mano con la mudanza de los muebles? — *Can I give you a hand with the furniture moving?*

C. *poner*

ponerse, *to put on (clothing), to wear*
Luisa se puso un sombrero de paja. — *Luisa wore a straw hat.*

ponerse, *to become (a temporary physical or emotional state)*
El señor Rivera se ha puesto enfermo. — *Mr. Rivera has become ill.*
Mike se puso triste cuando oyó la noticia. — *Mike became sad when he heard the news.*

ponerse colorado, *to blush*
El muchacho se puso colorado cuando tuvo que hablar en clase. — *The boy blushed when he had to talk in class.*

ponerse el sol, *to set (the sun)*
Hoy, el sol se puso a las siete y media. — *Today, the sun set at seven thirty.*

ponerse a + infinitive, *to begin to, to get down to*
Tengo que ponerme a estudiar. — *I have to begin to study (get down to studying).*

ponerse en marcha, *to get started, to get going*
Nos pondremos en marcha en seguida. — *We'll get started immediately.*

poner la mesa, *to set the table*
Jane, pon la mesa, por favor. — *Jane, please set the table.*

10-5. Other Important Idiomatic Expressions

llegar a ser, *to become (after a period of time)*
Un amigo mío llegó a ser novelista. — *A friend of mine became a novelist.*

volverse, *to become (unexpectedly), to turn into*
El pobre se volvió loco de tristeza. — *The poor man went crazy from sadness.*

querer decir, *to mean*
No sé lo que quieres decir. — *I don't know what you mean.*

prestar atención, *to pay attention*
Por favor, presta atención a lo que te estoy diciendo. — *Please, pay attention to what I'm telling you.*

fijarse en, *to notice, to look at*
Fíjate en lo que está haciendo el gato. — *Look at what the cat's doing.*

> **NOTE:** **Fíjate** or **fíjese usted** is often used as a way of getting the listener's attention: **Fíjate que voy a comprar un coche.** *You know, I'm going to buy a car.*

hoy día, hoy en día, *nowadays, these days*
Hoy día, la gente come menos carne.   *These days, people eat less meat.*

actualmente, *at present, right now*
Actualmente, mis padres viven en Maine.   *Right now, my parents live in Maine.*

hecho, *fact*; **de hecho**, *in fact*
De hecho, la primera guerra mundial terminó en 1918.   *In fact, the first World War ended in 1918.*

pensar + infinitive, *to plan to*
Pienso trasladarme a Madrid.   *I am planning to move to Madrid.*

pensar en, *to think about*
Nunca pienso en ti.   *I never think about you.*

pensar de, *to have an opinion about, to think about*
¿Qué piensa usted del arte moderno?   *What do you think about modern art?*

llevar a cabo, *to carry out*
Quisiera llevar a cabo mi proyecto.   *I would like to carry out my project.*

al fin y al cabo, *when all is said and done, after all*
Al fin y al cabo, no es para tanto.   *After all, it's not such a big deal.*

ahora mismo, *right away, right now*
Tengo que salir ahora mismo.   *I have to leave right now.*

EXERCISE 10-8:   Translate the following sentences into Spanish, using the correct idiomatic expressions. Answers are at the end of the chapter.

1. I have to feed the dog.
2. The children miss their grandfather.
3. Sara left to take a walk.
4. Upon leaving, the children became sad.
5. Nowadays, children think about becoming astronauts.
6. I want to become a movie star someday.
7. Raúl can't talk in public because he gets nervous.
8. The children get sick when they eat strawberries.
9. My brother became a millionaire.
10. Paco, pay attention (*tú*) to your work.
11. At present, I am not planning to retire.
12. I want you (*tú*) to help me.
13. Carlos wants to take a nap.
14. I would like to shake hands with Fred Astaire.
15. I would like to thank John's teacher.
16. Pablo always blushes when he sees Doris.

17. Evelyn Waugh became a Catholic.

18. As a matter of fact, I am thinking about retiring.

19. What does she mean?

20. I'm not afraid of mice.

10-6. Cardinal Numbers

The cardinal numbers are used to count things: **cuatro tazas**, *four cups*; **trece niños**, *thirteen children*.

A. Cardinal numbers 1–15

1	uno(-a)	6	seis	11	once
2	dos	7	siete	12	doce
3	tres	8	ocho	13	trece
4	cuatro	9	nueve	14	catorce
5	cinco	10	diez	15	quince

Only **uno(-a)** changes to agree in gender with the noun it modifies. The other numbers do not change. **Uno** becomes **un** before a masculine noun, and **una** before a feminine noun. When **uno** does not modify a noun, it remains unchanged.

Hay **una** taza y **un** plato en la mesa.   *There is a cup and a plate on the table.*

B. Cardinal numbers 16–99

16	dieciséis *or* diez y seis	29	veintinueve *or* veinte y nueve
17	diecisiete *or* diez y siete	30	treinta
18	dieciocho *or* diez y ocho	31	treinta y uno(-a)
19	diecinueve *or* diez y nueve	32	treinta y dos
20	veinte	40	cuarenta
21	veintiuno(-a) *or* veinte y uno(-a)	50	cincuenta
22	veintidós *or* veinte y dos	60	sesenta
23	veintitrés *or* veinte y tres	70	setenta
24	veinticuatro *or* veinte y cuatro	80	ochenta
25	veinticinco *or* veinte y cinco	90	noventa
26	veintiséis *or* veinte y seis	91	noventa y uno(-a)
27	veintisiete *or* veinte y siete	92	noventa y dos
28	veintiocho *or* veinte y ocho	99	noventa y nueve

> **NOTE:** **Dieciséis**, **veintidós**, **veintitrés**, and **veintiséis** have a written accent.

Numbers from 16 through 29 may be written in either a one-word connected form, or in an unconnected form using **y**: 16 = **dieciséis** or **diez y seis**. Only the unconnected form with **y** is used in numbers from 31 through 99.

C. Cardinal numbers 100–999

100	ciento *(cien before all nouns)*	300	trescientos(-as)
101	ciento uno(-a)	400	cuatrocientos(-as)
102	ciento dos	500	quinientos(-as)
116	ciento dieciséis *or* diez y seis	600	seiscientos(-as)
120	ciento veinte	700	setecientos(-as)
121	ciento veintiuno(-a) *or* veinte y uno(-a)	800	ochocientos(-as)
200	doscientos(-as)	900	novecientos(-as)
201	doscientos(-as) uno(-a)	901	novecientos(-as) uno(-a)
202	doscientos(-as) dos	999	novecientos(-as) noventa y nueve

Ciento changes to **cien** before all nouns, both masculine and feminine: **cien hombres**, *one hundred men*; **cien mujeres**, *one hundred women*. Multiples of 100 (200, 300, etc.) are plural and change according to the gender of the noun they modify. Remember that **uno(-a)** is never plural.

doscient**as** lámparas	*two hundred lamps*
doscient**os** un libros	*two hundred and one books*
doscient**as** dieciséis banderas	*two hundred and sixteen flags*
doscient**os** treinta y un estudiantes	*two hundred thirty one students*
novecient**as** noventa y nueve botellas	*nine hundred ninety nine bottles*

D. **Cardinal numbers 1,000–1,000,000,000**

1,000	mil	3,000	tres mil
1,001	mil uno(-a)	100,000	cien mil
1,984	mil novecientos ochenta y cuatro	1,000,000	un millón
2,000	dos mil	2,000,000	dos millones
2,210	dos mil doscientos(-as) diez	1,000,000,000	mil millones

1. **Mil** is never pluralized, except when it is an indeterminate number equivalent to the English "thousands." **Ciento** is shortened to **cien** before **mil**.

mil obreros	*a thousand workers*
dos mil obreros	*two thousand workers*
cien mil obreros	*one hundred thousand workers*
miles y **miles** de obreros	*thousands and thousands of workers*

2. **Millón** has a plural form, **millones**. **Un** is used before **millón**, and **de** follows **millón** to introduce the noun that is being modified.

un millón de obreros	*a million workers*
dos millones de obreros	*two million workers*

E. **Mathematical terms**

+	**y**	*plus*	dos **y** dos son cuatro
−	**menos**	*minus*	cuatro **menos** dos son dos
×	**por**	*times*	dos **por** cuatro son ocho
÷	**dividido por**	*divided by*	ocho **dividido por** cuatro son dos
=	**son**	*equals*	dos y dos **son** cuatro

EXERCISE 10-9: Translate the following into Arabic numerals. Answers are at the end of the chapter.

1. _____ mil setecientos ochenta y tres
2. _____ quinientos veintidós
3. _____ catorce
4. _____ sesenta y nueve
5. _____ cuatro mil uno
6. _____ diez mil trescientos doce
7. _____ cien mil dos
8. _____ cuarenta y siete
9. _____ ciento catorce
10. _____ diez y ocho

EXERCISE 10-10: In the space provided, translate the following numbers and phrases into Spanish. Answers are at the end of the chapter.

1. _____ seventy six trombones
2. _____ one rose
3. _____ one hundred one opportunities
4. _____ three thousand things to do
5. _____ sixteen years old

6. _____ a million dollars
7. _____ two shoes
8. _____ twenty four hours
9. _____ two thousand two hundred one years
10. _____ ninety nine bottles of beer
11. _____ thirty one pages
12. _____ seventy one trees
13. _____ one hundred twenty one pounds
14. _____ a temperature of one hundred one degrees
15. _____ thirty eight degrees centigrade

10-7. Ordinal Numbers

The ordinal numbers are used to put things in order: **primero(-a)**, *first*; **segundo(-a)**, *second*; **tercero(-a)**, *third*.

A. Ordinal numbers 1st–10th

1st	primero(-a)	6th	sexto(-a)
2nd	segundo(-a)	7th	séptimo(-a)
3rd	tercero(-a)	8th	octavo(-a)
4th	cuarto(-a)	9th	noveno(-a)
5th	quinto(-a)	10th	décimo(-a)

> **NOTE:** There is a written accent over the **é** of **séptimo** and **décimo**.

1. Ordinal numbers agree in gender with the noun they modify. The **-o** masculine ending of **primero** and **tercero** is dropped before a masculine singular noun.

el séptim**o** día	*the seventh day*
la séptim**a** persona	*the seventh person*
el prime**r** libro	*the first book*
la primer**a** pregunta	*the first question*

2. Ordinal numbers from 1st through 10th usually precede the noun they modify, except if the noun is a person or a street. In Spanish, royal names are written with Roman numerals.

la calle sexta	*Sixth Street*
BUT	
la quinta avenida	*Fifth Avenue*
Juan III (tercero)	*Juan the Third*
BUT	
el tercer hombre	*the third man*

B. Ordinal numbers above 10th

Ordinal numbers above 10th are the same as cardinal numbers. They follow the noun they modify.

el día **once**	*the eleventh day*
Pío XII (**doce**)	*Pius the Twelfth*
la calle **cuarenta y dos**	*Forty Second Street*
la avenida **dieciséis**	*Sixteenth Avenue*

EXERCISE 10-11: In the space provided, translate the following phrases into Spanish. Answers are at the end of the chapter.

1. _____ the third circle
2. _____ the fourth day
3. _____ the first president

4. _____ Fourth Street
5. _____ Pius the Ninth
6. _____ the twentieth century
7. _____ the second row
8. _____ Napoleon the Third
9. _____ the tenth page
10. _____ the third car

10-8. Days, Months, Seasons, and Dates

A. The days of the week

el domingo	*Sunday*	el jueves	*Thursday*
el lunes	*Monday*	el viernes	*Friday*
el martes	*Tuesday*	el sábado	*Saturday*
el miércoles	*Wednesday*		

> **NOTE:** Days of the week ending in **s** do not have a plural form: **Me gustan los viernes.** *I like Fridays.* There is a written accent over **miércoles** and **sábado**.

B. The months of the year

enero	*January*	julio	*July*
febrero	*February*	agosto	*August*
marzo	*March*	septiembre	*September*
abril	*April*	octubre	*October*
mayo	*May*	noviembre	*November*
junio	*June*	diciembre	*December*

> **NOTE:** In Spanish, days and months are not capitalized.

C. The seasons

el invierno	*winter*	el verano	*summer*
la primavera	*spring*	el otoño	*autumn*

D. Dates

1. In English, it is possible to divide a four-digit date such as *1984* into two multiples of ten: *nineteen eighty four*. This is not done in Spanish. The basic units are tens, hundreds, and thousands. Thus, *1984* in Spanish reads **mil novecientos ochenta y cuatro**.

1492	mil cuatrocientos noventa y dos
1776	mil setecientos setenta y seis
1901	mil novecientos uno

   > **NOTE:** The Spanish term for B.C. is **antes de Cristo, a.C.**
   > The term for A.D. is **después de Cristo, d.C.**

2. In Spanish, cardinal numbers are used for the days of the month, not ordinal numbers. The one exception is **primero**. The preposition **de** separates day, month, and year. The day of the month always precedes the month.

el **primero de** mayo	*the first of May*
el **cuatro de** julio **de** mil setecientos setenta y seis	*July 4, 1776*

3. When writing the date in numerals, the day of the month always precedes the month, and the month is always written in Roman numerals: 4/VII/76. In English, the month precedes the day, and both are written in Arabic numerals: 7/4/76.

EXERCISE 10-12: Write out the following dates in Spanish, including the year. Answers are at the end of the chapter.

1. April 14, 1931

2. March 1, 1868

3. December 25, 1474

4. May 1, 1808

5. September 15, 1957

6. January 30, 1939

7. October 23, 1981

8. February 3, 1755

9. November 20, 1601

10. June 30, 1521

E. **How to ask the date**

The date of the month, **la fecha**, tells you what day of the month it is: first, second, etc. Since **día** is masculine, the date, **el (día) cuatro de julio**, is always masculine singular. There are two ways to ask the date.

1. Use **estar**.

¿A cuántos **estamos**?	*What's the date?*
Estamos al quince de septiembre.	*It's September 15.*

2. Use **ser**.

¿Cuál **es la** fecha de hoy?	*What's today's date?*
Hoy **es** el quince de septiembre.	*Today is September 15.*

3. Use **el** for *on* before days and dates.

Empiezo a trabajar **el** lunes.	*I begin work on Monday.*
Nací **el** primero de mayo.	*I was born on May 1.*

EXERCISE 10-13: Answer the following questions in Spanish, using complete sentences. Answers are at the end of the chapter.

1. ¿Cuáles son los días de la semana laboral?
2. ¿Cuál es la fecha del primer día del año?
3. ¿En qué fecha se celebra la independencia de los Estados Unidos?
4. ¿Qué día es la fiesta de la Navidad?
5. ¿En qué año descubrió América Cristóbal Colón?

10-9. How to Tell Time

A. *Ser* **is used to express time.**

The singular **es** is used when referring to one o'clock, plus or minus the number of minutes up to 30. The plural **son** is used for the rest of the hours. When expressing time in the past tense, the imperfect of **ser**, **era** or **eran**, is used.

Es la una.	*It's one o'clock.*
Son las dos.	*It's two o'clock*
Eran las seis de la mañana.	*It was six o'clock in the morning.*

B. **Minutes are added from the hour up to the half hour, using *y*.**

Es la una **y** cinco.	*It's five minutes after one.*
Es la una **y** cuarto. (y quince)	*It's a quarter after one. (fifteen after)*
Es la una **y** media. (y treinta)	*It's half past one. (one thirty)*
Son las dos **y** cinco.	*It's five minutes after two.*

C. **After half past the hour, minutes are subtracted from the following hour, using *menos*.**

Es la una **menos** veinticino.	*It's twenty five minutes to one.*
Es la una **menos** cuarto.	*It's a quarter to one.*
Es la una **menos** cinco.	*It's five minutes to one.*
Son las dos **menos** diez.	*It's ten minutes to two.*
Son las tres **menos** veinte.	*Its twenty minutes to three.*

D. **The feminine article (*la* or *las*) always precedes time expressions of minutes and hours.**

The feminine article is not used before the words **mediodía**, *noon*, and **medianoche**, *midnight*.

Son **las** doce del día.	*It's twelve o'clock noon.*
BUT	
Es mediodía.	*It's noon.*
Son **las** doce de la noche.	*It's twelve o'clock midnight.*
BUT	
Es medianoche.	*It's midnight.*

E. **Useful time expressions**

1. *Phrases.*

a mediodía	*at noon*	de la noche	*in the evening*
a la medianoche	*at midnight*	por la noche	*at night, during the evening*
anoche	*last night*		
ayer	*yesterday*	de día	*days*
mañana	*tomorrow*	durante el día	*during the day*
alrededor de	*around*	anteayer	*the day before yesterday*
de la mañana	*in the morning*	a tiempo	*on time*
de la tarde	*in the afternoon*	en punto	*exactly, on the dot, sharp*
de noche	*nights*	tarde	*late*
		temprano	*early*

2. *Questions and statements concerning time.* In the following examples, pay close attention to the use of the prepositions **a**, **de**, **por**, and **alrededor de**.

¿Qué hora es?	*What time is it?*
Es la una.	*It's one o'clock.*
¿A qué hora es la clase?	*What time is the class?*
Es a la una.	*It's at one o'clock.*
Es la hora de comer.	*It's time to eat.*
¿Cuándo trabajas?	*When do you work?*
Trabajo de noche.	*I work nights.*
Voy a la escuela de día.	*I go to school during the day (days).*
Quiero estar en casa alrededor de las once.	*I want to be home around eleven o'clock.*
Llego a las nueve en punto.	*I arrive at nine o'clock sharp.*
Mi madre llega mañana por la mañana.	*My mother arrives tomorrow morning.*
Necesitamos llegar a tiempo.	*We need to arrive on time.*
El avión sale a las once y media.	*The plane leaves at eleven thirty.*
¿A qué hora tenemos que estar?	*What time do we have to be there?*

EXERCISE 10-14: Review the list of time expressions. Then complete the following translations by writing in the correct word or phrase. Answers are at the end of the chapter.

1. What time is it? ¿_____ es?
2. It's 2:00 PM. Son _____ dos _____.
3. Classes begin at 8:15 AM. Las clases empiezan _____ ocho _____.
4. I want to arrive on time. Quiero llegar _____.
5. The train leaves at ten to three. El tren sale a las _____.
6. He left last night at 10:00 PM. Salió _____ a _____ diez de _____.
7. I leave at midnight. Salgo _____.
8. It's midnight. Es _____.
9. She gets up at 7:00 sharp. Ella se levanta _____ siete _____.
10. When she left, it was 6:00 PM. Cuando salió, _____ las seis _____.
11. Yesterday I got up late. _____ me levanté _____.
12. What time does the movie start? ¿_____ empieza la película?
13. It's exactly 5:00 PM. _____ cinco _____ punto _____ tarde.
14. It's 8:40 AM. Son _____ ocho _____ de la _____.
15. It was 1:00 AM when she called _____ la una _____ mañana cuando llamó.
16. I always work days. Siempre trabajo _____.
17. I don't like to work nights. No me gusta trabajar _____.
18. I take a nap in the afternoon. Echo la siesta _____ la _____.
19. It's time to eat. Es _____ comer.
20. I come back around 5:00. Regreso _____ las cinco.

F. Idiomatic expressions of time using *vez*

In English, the word *time* is used to refer to clock time, moments in time (e.g., *the time I went to Paris*), and durations of time not measured by the clock (e.g., *a lot of time on my hands*). Spanish uses **hora** to refer to clock time, **tiempo** to refer to lengths of time not measured by the clock, and **vez** to refer to moments in time: **la vez que fui a París**. Study the following expressions using **vez**.

la vez, *the time*
La vez que fui a París, no hacía calor. — *The time I went to Paris, it wasn't hot.*

una vez, *once, one time*
Lo he hecho solamente una vez. — *I've only done it once.*

dos veces, *twice, two times*
Manolo se cayó dos veces. — *Manolo fell twice.*

a veces, *at times*
A veces, no duermo bien. — *At times, I don't sleep well.*

algunas veces, *sometimes, a few times, occasionally*
Hemos comido fuera algunas veces este verano. — *We've eaten out occasionally this summer.*

a la vez, *at the same time, at once*
No me gusta hacer dos cosas a la vez. — *I don't like to do two things at once.*

de vez en cuando, *from time to time*
Voy al cine de vez en cuando. — *I go to the movies from time to time.*

la última vez, *the last time*
La última vez que estuve en México, hubo un terremoto. — *The last time I was in Mexico, there was an earthquake.*

otra vez, *again*
Queremos ir a México otra vez. — *We want to go to Mexico again.*

rara vez, *seldom, rarely*
Rara vez enciendo el televisor. — *I seldom turn on the television.*

tal vez, *perhaps, maybe*
Tal vez vaya a México el año que viene.   *Maybe I'll go to Mexico next year.*

varias veces, *several times*
Hemos visto a Pepe varias veces esta semana.   *We've seen Pepe several times this week.*

G. Other idiomatic expressions concerning time

pasarlo bien, *to have a good time*
Los pasamos muy bien en España el año pasado.   *We had a good time in Spain last year.*

con el paso del tiempo, *as time goes by*
Con el paso del tiempo, las cosas mejoran.   *As time goes by, things get better.*

un buen momento para, *a good time to*
Este es un buen momento para descansar.   *This is a good time to rest.*

EXERCISE 10-15: Write in the Spanish word or phrase that corresponds to the English cue given in parentheses. Answers are at the end of the chapter.

         Example: (once) Lo hice solamenta ___una vez___ .
1. (again) No quiero comer hamburguesas_____.
2. (the time) _____ que Norma vino a visitarnos, hizo mal tiempo.
3. (perhaps) Queríamos ir a España pero_____no vayamos.
4. (from time to time) _____, pienso en ustedes.
5. (seldom) _____van a la playa los muchachos.
6. (at times) _____ me dan ganas de gritar.
7. (once) Vimos a Alda y a Ricardo_____la semana pasada.
8. (the last time)_____ que vi a María, estaba muy feliz.
9. (at the same time) A Adolfo no le gusta comer y conversar_____.
10. (twice) He ido a Chicago_____.

SUMMARY

1. The verb **gustar**, *to be pleasing*, means *to like* in English. **Gustar** is always used with indirect object pronouns: **Me gusta**, *I like it* (it is pleasing to me).
2. The indirect object pronouns are always used with **gustar**, **faltar**, and similar verbs even when a noun object is present in the sentence: **A los estudiantes les gustó la novela.** *The students liked the novel.*
3. If the subject of **gustar** is one or more infinitives, the third person singular is used: **Nos gusta leer y escuchar música.** *We like to read and listen to music.*
4. **Faltar**, *to lack*, **hacer falta**, *to need*, and **quedar**, *to have left*, all function like **gustar**.
5. The preposition *for* + *time* is expressed in Spanish as **hace** + time: **hace un año**, *for a year.*
6. When **hace** + time precedes the verb, it is connected to the main clause by **que**: **Hace un año que no veo a Isabel.** *I haven't seen Isabel for a year.* When **hace** + time follows the verb, the phrase is introduced by **desde**: **No veo a Isabel desde hace un año.** *I haven't seen Isabel for a year.*
7. When **hace** + time is used with a verb in the preterite tense, the meaning is *ago*. In this case, **hace** + time usually follows the verb and requires no connective: **Viví en México hace un año.** *I lived in Mexico a year ago.*
8. **Hace** + time is used with verbs in the present tense. The present tense is translated into the present perfect in English: **Hace un año que vivo en Nueva York.** *I've been living in New York for a year.* **Hacía** + time is used with verbs in the imperfect tense. This usage translates into the past perfect in English: **Hacía dos días que caminábamos.** *We had been walking for two days.*

9. The verb **hacer** is used in discussing the weather and in many other important idiomatic expressions.

10. The verb **tener** is used with the meaning *to be* in idiomatic expressions such as **tengo sed**, *I'm thirsty*, **tengo prisa**, *I'm in a hurry*, **tengo ocho años**, *I'm eight years old*, and many others.

11. **Ponerse, hacerse, volverse,** and **llegar a ser** all mean *to become*, but they are used in different contexts.

12. The cardinal numbers are the counting numbers: **uno, dos, tres**, and so on. All cardinal numbers have only one form except (1) **uno** is shortened to **un** before masculine nouns, and is changed to **una** before feminine nouns; (2) numbers from 16 through 29 may be written as one word or three words using **y**—**dieciséis** or **diez y seis**; (3) **ciento** is shortened to **cien** before all masculine and feminine nouns and before **mil**; (4) multiples of 100 such as 200, 300, etc., have both a masculine plural and a feminine plural ending—**doscientos, doscientas**, etc.; (5) **mil** has a plural form, **miles**, which is only used when referring to an indeterminate number of thousands— **muchos miles**, *many thousands*; and (6) **millón** has a plural form, **millones. Millón** is always preceded by **un** and followed by **de** when modifying a noun: **un millón de dólares**, *a million dollars*.

13. In Spanish, the ordinal numbers from first to tenth have a masculine and feminine form: **primero, primera; segundo, segunda**, etc. Ordinal numbers from first to tenth precede the noun they modify, except when the noun is a person or a street. **Primero** and **tercero** are shortened to **primer** and **tercer** before masculine nouns.

14. Ordinal numbers above tenth are the same as cardinal numbers. Ordinal numbers above tenth always follow the noun they modify. Thus, they cannot be confused with the cardinal numbers, which always precede the noun: **las doce páginas**, *the twelve pages*; **la página doce**, *the twelfth page*.

15. In Spanish, the days of the week, the months, and the seasons are not capitalized.

16. Spanish uses cardinal numbers to write the date, except for the first, **el primero**. The day, month, and year are introduced by **el** and are separated by the preposition **de**: **el dos de mayo de 1808**, *May 2, 1808*.

17. The verb **ser** is used to express clock time. Because clock time is referred to as **la hora**, it is always feminine: **Es la una**. *It's one o'clock*; **Son las dos**. *It's two o'clock*.

18. Minutes are added from the hour up to the half hour, using **y**. After half past the hour, minutes are subtracted from the following hour, using **menos**.

19. Spanish uses **hora** to refer to clock time, **tiempo** to refer to lengths of time not measured by the clock, and **vez** to refer to moments in time.

RAISE YOUR GRADES

☑ *Gustar* **and similar verbs** [Section 10-1]

Fill in the correct singular or plural form of the verb given in parentheses, and write in the indirect object pronoun that corresponds to the prepositional phrase, **a** + pronoun. Translate each sentence after completion. Answers are at the end of the chapter.

Example: (gustar) A Jorge ___*le gusta*___ la música. *Jorge likes music.*

    1. (gustar) A nosotros no_____ tener que salir temprano.

    2. (faltar) A mí_____ tiempo para hacer todo lo que tengo que hacer.

    3. (gustar) ¿A vosotros_____ las pirámides de Egipto?

    4. (quedar) ¿Cuántos días de vacaciones_____ a ustedes?

    5. (gustar) ¿A ti_____ la carne or prefieres el pescado?

    6. (hacer falta) A Vivian_____ un buen abrigo.

7. (hacer falta) A los enfermos _____ varios medicamentos.

8. (quedar) ¿Cuánto tiempo _____ a ti?

9. (gustar) ¿A quién no _____ el champán?

10. (faltar) A todos _____ dinero y tiempo para gastarlo.

✓ **Verbs meaning *to be*** [Sections 10-2 and 10-3]

Review the uses of **ser** and **estar** in Chapter 4. Then review the idiomatic uses of **hacer** and **tener** in this chapter. Read each of the following sentences carefully and write in the infinitive form of the correct verb, **ser, estar, tener,** or **hacer**. Then translate the entire sentence into Spanish. Answers are at the end of the chapter.

Examples: ___estar___ How are you (*tú*)? ¿Cómo estas?
___tener___ How old are you (*tú*)? ¿Cuántos años tienes?

1. _____ Are you (*tú*) sick?
2. _____ Is Lucía cold?
3. _____ I'm very tired.
4. _____ The children are thirsty.
5. _____ He's not here.
6. _____ Kathy is very nervous today.
7. _____ I'm afraid to sit down.
8. _____ Is the weather good?
9. _____ Where's my hat?
10. _____ Was it cold yesterday?
11. _____ Diane is a lawyer.
12. _____ We're always in a hurry.
13. _____ Please, don't be afraid (*usted*).
14. _____ It's hot in Florida.
15. _____ You're right (*tú*).
16. _____ He was a handsome man.
17. _____ I'm sad.
18. _____ I'm sleepy.
19. _____ The milk is warm.
20. _____ They're afraid of the dog.

✓ **Verbs meaning *to become*** [Sections 10-4 and 10-5]

Translate the following sentences into Spanish, using the verb given in parentheses. Answers are at the end of the chapter.

1. (ponerse) Emilio gets sad when he listens to music.

2. (volverse) She believes that she's going crazy.

3. (llegar a ser) After many years, she became president of the bank.

4. (hacerse) Juan became rich in a short time.

5. (ponerse) Don't be nervous, Joan.

6. (hacerse) Do you (*tú*) want to become a doctor?

7. (llegar a ser) I am going to become a professor of Spanish.

8. (ponerse) Raúl got furious.

9. (volverse) Francisco turned into a snob.

10. (ponerse) Pepe gets happy when he goes on vacation.

✓ **Cardinal and ordinal numbers** [Section 10-6 and 10-7]

Complete the following sentences by translating the phrases given in parentheses into Spanish. Answers are at the end of the chaper.

Example: (50 pages) He leído *cincuenta páginas* de tu novela.

1. (December 31, 1911) Mi padre nació _____ .
2. (the thirteenth) Andrés llega _____ .
3. (six pairs of shoes) Mi hermano compró _____ .
4. (eighteen girls and eleven boys) Hay _____ en mi clase.
5. (the third red bird) Es _____ que he visto hoy.
6. (the first time) _____ que lo vi, estaba bailando.
7. (one pine tree) Solamente queda _____ en el bosque.
8. (the fifth day) _____ de la semana laboral es el viernes.
9. (eleven days) Mi suegra estuvo con nosotros _____ .
10. (one hundred one) Hay _____ maneras de construir una casa.

CHAPTER ANSWERS

EXERCISE 10-1

1. A Juan no le gusta leer.
2. Nos gustan las flores y los árboles.
3. No les gusta ir a la escuela.
4. A Reynaldo y a Antonio les gusta jugar al béisbol.
5. Me gusta viajar.
6. A vosotros no os gusta la química.
7. A nadie le gustan las preguntas difíciles.
8. A ellos les gustan las novelas románticas.
9. A los niños nunca les gusta lavarse la cara.
10. A todo el mundo le gustan las palomitas.
11. A Laura no le gustan las verduras.
12. Nos gustan el español y el francés.
13. No te gusta hacer tu tarea de biología.
14. A ellas les gusta jugar a las cartas.
15. A Juan y a Leonor les gusta la comida española.

EXERCISE 10-2

1. A los estudiantes les hace falta estudiar. *The students need to study.*
2. No me hace falta un reloj nuevo. *I don't need a new watch.*
3. Faltan sal y mostaza. *Salt and mustard are lacking.*
4. A los estudiantes les faltan ganas de hablar. *The students don't feel like talking*
5. A Raimundo no le queda dinero. *Raimundo has no money left.*
6. Nos hace falta más tiempo. *We need more time.*
7. ¿Te queda gasolina? *Do you have any gasoline left?*
8. Me quedan tres camisas de seda. *I have three silk shirts left.*
9. A los vecinos no les queda más comida. *The neighbors don't have any food left.*
10. Me faltan ganas de comer. *I don't feel like eating.*

11. Nos hace falta hablar con Rubén. *We need to talk to Rubén.*
12. No hace falta escribir nada. *There's no need to write anything.*
13. Falta suficiente espacio. *There's a lack of sufficient space.*
14. A los muchachos no les hace falta postre. *The boys don't need dessert.*
15. A Alicia le falta tiempo para ayudarnos. *Alicia is lacking time to help us.*

EXERCISE 10-3

1. Hace dos meses que Linda juega al tenis. *Linda has been playing tennis for two months.*
2. Hace un año que uso gafas. *I've been using glasses for a year.*
3. Hace diez años que no toco el piano. *I haven't played the piano for ten years.*
4. Hace tres meses que estudio biología. *I've been studying biology for three months.*
5. Hace veinte minutos que ladra el perro. *The dog has been barking for twenty minutes.*
6. Hace mucho tiempo que conozco a Antonio. *I've known Antonio for a long time.*
7. Hace bastante tiempo que mis abuelos no vienen. *My grandparents haven't come for quite a while.*
8. Hace ocho días que tengo catarro. *I've had a cold for eight days.*
9. Hace sólo un día que el motor no funciona. *The motor hasn't worked for just one day.*
10. Hace tres minutos que hierven los huevos. *The eggs have been boiling for three minutes.*

EXERCISE 10-4

1. Hacía dos semanas que los estudiantes estudiaban.
2. Hace muchos años que toco el piano.

3. Hacía un año que sus padres vivían en México.
4. ¿Cuánto tiempo hacía que fumaba Rafael?
5. ¿Cuánto tiempo hace que vives en Seattle?
6. Hace muchos años que leemos este periódico.
7. ¿Cuánto tiempo hace que Jaime está enfermo?
8. Hace mucho tiempo que no veo a mis amigos.
9. Hacía una semana que yo estaba enfermo.
10. Hacía dos años que vivíamos en Madrid.

EXERCISE 10-5

1. Estuve en Nueva York hace solamente un mes. *I was in New York just a month ago.*
2. David se rompió el dedo hace una semana. *David broke his finger a week ago.*
3. Mis padres salieron hace cinco minutos. *My parents left five minutes ago.*
4. Se murió el perro hace mucho tiempo. *The dog died a long time ago.*
5. Terminé la carrera hace poco tiempo. *I finished my studies a short time ago.*

EXERCISE 10-6

1. Irene vive con sus padres desde hace seis meses. *Irene has lived with her parents for six months.*
2. Mi padre juega al béisbol desde el verano pasado. *My father has played baseball since last summer.*
3. Asisto al Liceo Francés desde el catorce de julio. *I've gone to the French High School since July 14.*
4. Carlos se acuesta temprano desde hace un año. *Carlos has gone to bed early for a year.*
5. Me levanto temprano desde ayer. *I've been getting up early since yesterday.*
6. Estoy enferma desde la semana pasada. *I've been sick since last week.*
7. Estoy de vuelta desde hace dos semanas. *I've been back for two weeks.*
8. Sabemos la verdad desde hace mucho tiempo. *We've known the truth for a long time.*
9. Sara escribe poesía desde hace dos días. *Sara has been writing poetry for two days.*
10. Susan conoce a Bill desde el primero de mayo. *Susan has known Bill since the first of May.*

EXERCISE 10-7

1. Los niños tienen mucha sed. *The children are very thirsty.*
2. Por favor, ten cuidado con el perro. *Please be careful with the dog.*
3. Emilio siempre tiene prisa. *Emilio is always in a hurry.*
4. Tengo miedo de caerme. *I'm afraid of falling.*

5. Mi tía tiene miedo a todo. *My aunt is afraid of everything.*
6. Tengo que hacer las maletas. *I have to pack the suitcases.*
7. No tenemos sed porque no hace calor. *We're not thirsty because it's not hot.*
8. Tengo prisa porque tengo que llegar pronto. *I'm in a hurry because I have to get there soon.*
9. Los chicos tienen ganas de jugar al béisbol. *The kids feel like playing baseball.*
10. Yo, en cambio, no tengo ganas de hacer nada. *I, on the other hand, don't feel like doing anything.*
11. Ayer hacía mucho frío. *Yesterday it was very cold.*
12. ¿Dónde tiene lugar la fiesta? *Where is the party taking place?*
13. Rita siempre hace muchas preguntas. *Rita always asks a lot of questions.*
14. ¿Quién tiene la culpa del accidente? *Who's to blame for the accident?*
15. ¿Cuántos años tiene la hermana de Raquel? *How old is Raquel's sister?*
16. Estoy enojado porque tengo sueño. *I'm angry because I'm sleepy.*
17. Después de terminar los estudios, Manolo se hizo maestro. *After finishing his studies, Manolo became a teacher.*
18. Nadie presta atención a lo que dicen los jóvenes. *Nobody pays attention to what young people say.*
19. Tenemos que tener en cuenta la escasez de agua. *We have to keep the water shortage in mind.*
20. Mi hermano tiene más años que tu hermano. *My brother is older than your brother.*

EXERCISE 10-8

1. Tengo que dar de comer al perro.
2. Los niños echan de menos a su abuelo.
3. Sara salió a dar un paseo.
4. Al salir, los niños se pusieron tristes.
5. Hoy día, los niños piensan en hacerse astronautas.
6. Quiero llegar a ser estrella de cine algún día.
7. Raúl no puede hablar en público porque se pone nervioso.
8. Los niños se ponen enfermos cuando comen fresas.
9. Mi hermano se hizo millonario.
10. Paco, presta atención a tu trabajo.
11. De momento, no pienso jubilarme.
12. Quiero que me eches una mano.
13. Carlos quiere echar la siesta.
14. Me gustaría darle la mano a Fred Astaire.
15. Me gustaría darle las gracias al maestro de John.
16. Pablo siempre se pone colorado cuando ve a Doris.

17. Evelyn Waugh se hizo católico.
18. De hecho, pienso en jubilarme.
19. ¿Qué quiere decir ella?
20. No me dan miedo los ratones.

EXERCISE 10-9

1. 1,783
2. 522
3. 14
4. 69
5. 4,001
6. 10,312
7. 100,002
8. 47
9. 114
10. 18

EXERCISE 10-10

1. setenta y seis trombones
2. una rosa
3. ciento una oportunidades
4. tres mil cosas que hacer
5. dieciséis (diez y seis) años
6. un millón de dólares
7. dos zapatos
8. veinticuatro (veinte y cuatro) horas
9. dos mil doscientos un años
10. noventa y nueve botellas de cerveza
11. treinta y una páginas
12. setenta y un árboles
13. ciento veintiuna (veinte y una) libras
14. una temperatura de ciento un grados
15. treinta y ocho grados centígrados

EXERCISE 10-11

1. el tercer círculo
2. el cuarto día
3. el primer presidente
4. la calle cuarta
5. Pío IX (noveno)
6. el siglo veinte (XX)
7. la segunda fila
8. Napoleón III (tercero)
9. la décima página
10. el tercer coche

EXERCISE 10-12

1. el catorce de abril de mil novecientos treinta y uno
2. el primero de marzo de mil ochocientos sesenta y ocho
3. el veinticinco (veinte y cinco) de diciembre de mil cuatrocientos setenta y cuatro
4. el primero de mayo de mil ochocientos ocho
5. el quince de septiembre de mil novecientos cincuenta y siete
6. el treinta de enero de mil novecientos treinta y nueve
7. el veintitres (veinte y tres) de octubre de mil novecientos ochenta y uno
8. el tres de febrero de mil setecientos cincuenta y cinco
9. el veinte de noviembre de mil seiscientos uno
10. el treinta de junio de mil quinientos veintiuno (veinte y uno)

EXERCISE 10-13

1. Los días de la semana laboral son lunes, martes, miércoles, jueves, y viernes. *The days of the work week are Monday, Tuesday, Wednesday, Thursday, and Friday.*
2. La fecha del primer día del año es el primero de enero. *The date of the first day of the year is January 1.*
3. La independencia de los Estados Unidos se celebra el cuatro julio. *The independence of the United States is celebrated on the fourth of July.*
4. La fiesta de la Navidad es el veinticinco de diciembre. *Christmas in on December 25.*
5. Colón descubrió América en mil cuatrocientos noventa y dos. *Colombus discovered America in 1492.*

EXERCISE 10-14

1. ¿Qué hora es?
2. Son las dos de la tarde.
3. Las clases empiezan a las ocho y cuarto de la mañana.
4. Quiero llegar a tiempo.
5. El tren sale a las tres menos diez.
6. Salió anoche a las diez de la noche.
7. Salgo a la medianoche.
8. Es medianoche.
9. Ella se levanta a las siete en punto.
10. Cuando salió, eran las seis de la tarde.
11. Ayer me levanté tarde.
12. ¿A qué hora empieza la película?
13. Son las cinco en punto de la tarde.
14. Son las ocho y cuarenta de la mañana.
15. Era la una de la mañana cuando llamó.
16. Siempre trabajo de día.
17. No me gusta trabajar de noche.
18. Echo la siesta por la tarde.
19. Es la hora de comer.
20. Regreso alrededor de las cinco.

EXERCISE 10-15

1. otra vez *I don't want to eat hamburgers again.*
2. La vez *The time that Norma came to visit us, the weather was bad.*
3. tal vez *We wanted to go to Spain, but maybe we won't go.*
4. De vez en cuando *From time to time, I think about you.*
5. rara vez *The boys seldom go to the beach.*
6. A veces *At times, I feel like yelling.*
7. una vez *We saw Alda and Ricardo once last week.*

8. La última vez   *The last time I saw María, she was very happy.*
9. a la vez   *Adolfo doesn't like to eat and converse at the same time.*
10. dos veces   *I've gone to Chicago twice.*

RAISE YOUR GRADES

Gustar and similar verbs

1. nos gusta   *We don't like to have to leave early.*
2. me falta   *I'm short of (I lack) time to do all that I have to do.*
3. os gustan   *Do you like the pyramids of Egypt?*
4. les quedan   *How many days of vacation do you have left?*
5. te gusta   *Do you like meat or do you prefer fish?*
6. le hace falta   *Vivian needs a good coat.*
7. les hacen falta   *The patients need various medicines.*
8. te queda   *How much time do you have left?*
9. le gusta   *Who doesn't like champagne?*
10. nos falta   *We are all short of (lacking) money and time to spend it.*

Verbs meaning *to be*

1. estar   ¿Estás enfermo?
2. tener   ¿Tiene frío Lucía?
3. estar   Estoy muy cansado.
4. tener   Los niños tienen sed.
5. estar   No está aqui.
6. estar   Kathy está muy nerviosa hoy.
7. tener   Tengo miedo de sentarme.
8. hacer   ¿Hace buen tiempo?
9. estar   ¿Dónde está mi sombrero?
10. hacer   ¿Hacía frío ayer?
11. ser   Diane es abogada.
12. tener   Siempre tenemos prisa.
13. tener   Por favor, no tenga usted miedo.
14. hacer   Hace calor en Florida.
15. tener   Tienes razón.
16. ser   Era un hombre guapo.
17. estar   Estoy triste.
18. tener   Tengo sueño.
19. estar   La leche está caliente.
20. tener   Tienen miedo al perro.

Verbs meaning *to become*

1. Emilio se pone triste cuando escucha música.
2. Ella cree que se vuelve loca.
3. Después de muchos años, ella llegó a ser presidente del banco.
4. Juan se hizo rico en poco tiempo.
5. No te pongas nerviosa, Joan.
6. ¿Quiéres hacerte médico?
7. Voy a llegar a ser profesor de español.
8. Raúl se puso furioso.
9. Francisco se volvió snob.
10. Pepe se pone contento cuando se va de vacaciones.

Cardinal and ordinal numbers.

1. el treinta y uno de diciembre de mil novecientos once   *My father was born on December 31, 1911.*
2. el trece   *Andrés arrives on the thirteenth.*
3. seis pares de zapatos   *My brother bought six pairs of shoes.*
4. dieciocho muchachas y once muchachos   *There are eighteen girls and eleven boys in my class.*
5. el tercer pájaro rojo   *It's the third red bird that I've seen today.*
6. La primera vez   *The first time I saw him, he was dancing.*
7. un pino   *There's only one pine tree left in the forest.*
8. El quinto día   *The fifth day of the work week is Friday.*
9. once días   *My mother-in-law was with us for eleven days.*
10. ciento una   *There are a hundred and one ways to build a house.*

APPENDIX A
Rules of Accentuation

1. All words that end in a consonant, except **-n** and **-s**, are stressed on the last syllable.

canci**ller**	proximi**dad**
embaja**dor**	ra**paz**
espa**ñol**	vi**vir**

2. All words that end in **-n**, **-s**, or a vowel are stressed on the next to the last syllable.

ad**ver**bio	**su**man
medios	**Te**re
Paco	Zara**go**za

3. All other words have a written accent on the vowel of the stressed syllable.

ca**tá**logo	ha**bló**
declara**ción**	**mán**dalo
fran**cés**	pi**rá**mide

APPENDIX B
How to Use the Dictionary

The Spanish alphabet contains all twenty six letters of the English alphabet. In addition, **ch**, **ll**, **ñ**, and **rr** are letters of the Spanish alphabet. In the dictionary, **ch** follows **c**, **ll** follows **l**, and **ñ** follows **n**. In Spanish, no word begins with **rr**, so it does not have a separate heading in the dictionary. However, when you are looking up words, **rr** follows **r**, so that **parra**, *grape vine*, comes after **para**, *for*.

APPENDIX C
Verb Charts

REGULAR VERBS

Infinitive	mirar	beber	vivir
	to look	*to drink*	*to live*
Present participle	mirando	bebiendo	viviendo
Past participle	mirado	bebido	vivido

Simple Tenses

Indicative:

Present	miro	bebo	vivo
	miras	bebes	vives
	mira	bebe	vive
	miramos	bebemos	vivimos
	miráis	bebéis	vivís
	miran	beben	viven

Preterite	miré	bebí	viví
	miraste	bebiste	viviste
	miró	bebió	vivió
	miramos	bebimos	vivimos
	mirasteis	bebisteis	vivisteis
	miraron	bebieron	vivieron
Imperfect	miraba	bebía	vivía
	mirabas	bebías	vivías
	miraba	bebía	vivía
	mirábamos	bebíamos	vivíamos
	mirabais	bebíais	vivíais
	miraban	bebían	vivían
Future	miraré	beberé	viviré
	mirarás	beberás	vivirás
	mirará	beberá	vivirá
	miraremos	beberemos	viviremos
	miraréis	beberéis	viviréis
	mirarán	beberán	vivirán
Conditional	miraría	bebería	viviría
	mirarías	beberías	vivirías
	miraría	bebería	viviría
	miraríamos	beberíamos	viviríamos
	miraríais	beberíais	viviríais
	mirarían	beberían	vivirían

Subjunctive:

Present	mire	beba	viva
	mires	bebas	vivas
	mire	beba	viva
	miremos	bebamos	vivamos
	miréis	bebáis	viváis
	miren	beban	vivan
Imperfect	mirara (-se)	bebiera (-se)	viviera (-se)
	miraras	bebieras	vivieras
	mirara	bebiera	viviera
	miráramos	bebiéramos	viviéramos
	mirarais	bebierais	vivierais
	miraran	bebieran	vivieran

Compound Tenses

Indicative:

Present perfect	he has ha hemos habéis han	mirado	bebido	vivido
Pluperfect	había habías había habíamos habíais habían	mirado	bebido	vivido

Future perfect	habré habrás habrá habremos habréis habrán	mirado	bebido	vivido
Conditional perfect	habría habrías habría habríamos habríais habrían	mirado	bebido	vivido

Subjunctive:

Present perfect	haya hayas haya hayamos hayáis hayan	mirado	bebido	vivido
Pluperfect	hubiera (-se) hubieras hubiera hubiéramos hubierais hubieran	mirado	bebido	vivido

Commands

Familiar aff.	mira (tú) mirad	bebe (tú) bebed	vive (tú) vivid
Familiar neg.	no mires no miréis	no bebas no bebáis	no vivas no viváis
Formal	mire Ud. miren Uds.	beba Ud. beban Uds.	viva Ud. vivan Uds.

STEM-CHANGING VERBS

Class I: -ar and -er Verbs

	-ar verbs		**-er verbs**	
	e—ie	o—ue	e—ie	o—ou
Infinitive	gobernar *to govern*	encontrar *to find*	entender *to understand*	volver *to return*
Past participle	gobernado	encontrado	entendido	vuelto
Present indicative	gobierno gobiernas gobierna gobernamos gobernáis gobiernan	encuentro encuentras encuentra encontramos encontráis encuentran	entiendo entiendes entiende entendemos entendéis entienden	vuelvo vuelves vuelve volvemos volvéis vuelven

Present subjunctive	gobierne	encuentre	entienda	vuelva
	gobiernes	encuentres	entiendas	vuelvas
	gobierne	encuentre	entienda	vuelva
	gobernemos	encontremos	entendamos	volvamos
	gobernéis	encontréis	entendáis	volváis
	gobiernen	encuentren	entiendan	vuelvan

Commands:

Familiar aff.	gobierna	encuentra	entiende	vuelve
	gobernad	encontrad	entended	volved
Familiar neg.	no gobiernes	no encuentres	no entiendas	no vuelvas
	no gobernéis	no encontréis	no entendáis	no volváis
Formal	gobierne Ud.	encuentre Ud.	entienda Ud.	vuelva Ud.
	gobiernen Uds.	encuentren Uds.	entiendan Uds.	vuelvan Uds.

Class II and Class III: -ir Verbs

	Class II		Class III
	e—ie, i	o—ue, u	e—i
Infinitive	mentir	dormir	pedir
	to lie	*to sleep*	*to ask for, request*
Present participle	mintiendo	durmiendo	pidiendo
Present indicative	miento	duermo	pido
	mientes	duermes	pides
	miente	duerme	pide
	mentimos	dormimos	pedimos
	mentís	dormís	pedís
	mienten	duermen	piden
Preterite	mentí	dormí	pedí
	mentiste	dormiste	pediste
	mintió	durmió	pidió
	mentimos	dormimos	pedimos
	mentisteis	dormisteis	pedisteis
	mintieron	durmieron	pidieron
Present subjunctive	mienta	duerma	pida
	mientas	duermas	pidas
	mienta	duerma	pida
	mintamos	durmamos	pidamos
	mintáis	durmáis	pidáis
	mientan	duerman	pidan
Imperfect subjunctive	mintiera	durmiera	pidiera
	mintieras	durmieras	pidieras
	mintiera	durmiera	pidiera
	mintiéramos	durmiéramos	pidiéramos
	mintierais	durmierais	pidierais
	mintieran	durmieran	pidieran

Commands:

Familiar aff.	miente	duerme	pide
	mentid	dormid	pedid
Familiar neg.	no mientas	no duermas	no pidas
	no mintáis	no durmáis	no pidáis
Formal	mienta Ud.	duerma Ud.	pida Ud.
	mientan Uds.	duerman Uds.	pidan Uds.

IRREGULAR VERBS

almorzar, *to have lunch*
Present indicative	almuerzo, almuerzas, almuerza, almorzamos, almorzáis, almuerzan
Preterite	almorcé, almorzaste, etc.
Present subjunctive	almuerce, almuerces, almuerce, almorcemos, almorcéis, almuercen
Formal command	almuerce Ud., almuercen Uds.

andar, *to walk*
Preterite	anduve, anduviste, anduvo, anduvimos, anduvisteis, anduvieron
Imperfect subjunctive	anduviera (-se), anduvieras, anduviera, anduviéramos, anduvierais, anduvieran

buscar, *to look for*
Preterite	busqué, buscaste, etc.
Present subjunctive	busque, busques, busque, busquemos, busquéis, busquen
Formal command	busque Ud., busquen Uds.

caber, *to fit*
Present indicative	quepo, cabes, etc.
Preterite	cupe, cupiste, cupo, cupimos, cupisteis, cupieron
Future	cabré, cabrás, cabrá, cabremos, cabréis, cabrán
Present subjunctive	quepa, quepas, quepa, quepamos, quepáis, quepan
Imperfect subjunctive	cupiera (-se), cupieras, cupiera, cupiéramos, cupierais, cupieran
Formal command	quepa Ud., quepan Uds.

caer, *to fall*
Present participle	cayendo
Past participle	caído
Present indicative	caigo, caes, etc.
Preterite	caí, caíste, cayó, caímos, caísteis, cayeron
Present subjunctive	caiga, caigas, caiga, caigamos, caigáis, caigan
Imperfect subjunctive	cayera (-se), cayeras, cayera, cayéramos, cayerais, cayeran
Formal command	caiga Ud., caigan Uds.

conocer, *to know*
Present indicative	conozco, conoces, etc.
Present subjunctive	conozca, conozcas, conozca, conozcamos, conozcáis, conozcan
Formal command	conozca Ud., conozcan Uds.

creer, *to believe*
Present participle	creyendo
Past participle	creído
Preterite	creí, creíste, creyó, creímos, creísteis, creyeron
Imperfect subjunctive	creyera (-se), creyeras, creyera, creyéramos, creyerais, creyeran

dar, *to give*
Present indicative	doy, das, da, damos, dais, dan
Preterite	di, diste, dio, dimos, disteis, dieron
Present subjunctive	dé, des, dé, demos, deis, den
Imperfect subjunctive	diera (-se), dieras, diera, diéramos, dierais, dieran
Formal command	dé Ud., den Uds.

decir, *to say*
Present participle	diciendo
Past participle	dicho
Present indicative	digo, dices, dice, decimos, decís, dicen
Preterite	dije, dijiste, dijo, dijimos, dijisteis, dijeron
Future	diré, dirás, dirá, diremos, diréis, dirán
Present subjunctive	diga, digas, diga, digamos, digáis, digan
Imperfect subjunctive	dijera (-se), dijeras, dijera, dijéramos, dijerais, dijeran
Familiar command	di, decid; no digas, no digáis
Formal command	diga Ud., digan Uds.

elegir, *to choose, to elect*
Present participle	eligiendo
Past participle	elegido
Present indicative	elijo, eliges, elige, elegimos, elegís, eligen
Preterite	elegí, elegiste, eligió, elegimos, elegisteis, eligieron
Present subjunctive	elija, elijas, elija, elijamos, elijáis, elijan
Imperfect subjunctive	eligiera (-se), eligieras, eligiera, eligiéramos, eligierais, eligieran
Familiar command	elige, elegid; no elijas, no elijáis
Formal command	elija Ud., elijan Uds.

empezar, *to begin*
Present indicative	empiezo, empiezas, empieza, empezamos, empezáis, empiezan
Preterite	empecé, empezaste, etc.
Present subjunctive	empiece, empieces, empiece, empecemos, empecéis, empiecen
Familiar command	empieza, empezad; no empieces, no empecéis
Formal command	empiece, empiecen

estar, *to be*
Present indicative	estoy, estás, está, estamos, estáis, están
Preterite	estuve, estuviste, estuvo, estuvimos, estuvisteis, estuvieron
Present subjunctive	esté, estés, esté, estemos, estéis, estén
Imperfect subjunctive	estuviera (-se), estuvieras, estuviera, estuviéramos, estuvierais, estuvieran
Familiar command	está, estad; no estés, no estéis
Formal command	esté, esten

haber, *to have (auxiliary verb)*
Present indicative	he, has, ha, hemos, habéis, han
Preterite	hube, hubiste, hubo, hubimos, hubisteis, hubieron
Future	habré, habrás, habrá, habremos, habréis, habrán
Present subjunctive	haya, hayas, haya, hayamos, hayáis, hayan
Imperfect subjunctive	hubiera (-se), hubieras, hubiera, hubiéramos, hubierais, hubieran

hacer, *to do, to make*
Present participle	haciendo
Past participle	hecho
Present indicative	hago, haces, etc.
Preterite	hice, hiciste, hizo, hicimos, hicisteis, hicieron
Future	haré, harás, hará, haremos, haréis, harán
Present subjunctive	haga, hagas, haga, hagamos, hagáis, hagan
Imperfect subjunctive	hiciera (-se), hicieras, hiciera, hiciéramos, hicierais, hicieran
Familiar command	haz, haced; no hagas, no hagáis
Formal command	haga, hagan

huir, *to flee*
Present participle	huyendo
Past participle	huido

Present indicative	huyo, huyes, huye, huimos, huís, huyen
Preterite	huí, huiste, huyó, huimos, huisteis, huyeron
Present subjunctive	huya, huyas, huya, huyamos, huyáis, huyan
Imperfect subjunctive	huyera (-se), huyeras, huyera, huyéramos, huyerais, huyeran
Familiar command	huye, huid; no huyas, no huyáis
Formal command	huya, huyan

ir, *to go*
Present participle	yendo
Past participle	ido
Present indicative	voy, vas, va, vamos, vais, van
Preterite	fui, fuiste, fue, fuimos, fuisteis, fueron
Present subjunctive	vaya, vayas, vaya, vayamos, vayáis, vayan
Imperfect subjunctive	fuera (-se), fueras, fuera, fuéramos, fuerais, fueran
Familiar command	ve, id; no vayas, no vayáis
Formal command	vaya, vayan

llegar, *to arrive*
Preterite	llegué, llegaste, etc.
Present subjunctive	llegue, llegues, llegue, lleguemos, lleguéis, lleguen

oír, *to hear*
Present participle	oyendo
Past participle	oído
Present indicative	oigo, oyes, oye, oímos, oís, oyen
Preterite	oí, oíste, oyó, oímos, oísteis, oyeron
Future	oiré, oirás, oirá, oiremos, oiréis, oirán
Present subjunctive	oiga, oigas, oiga, oigamos, oigáis, oigan
Imperfect subjunctive	oyera (-se), oyeras, oyera, oyéramos, oyerais, oyeran
Familiar command	oye, oíd; no oigas, no oigáis
Formal command	oiga, oigan

oler, *to smell*
Present indicative	huelo, hueles, huele, olemos, oléis, huelen
Present subjunctive	huela, huelas, huela, olamos, oláis, huelan

poder, *to be able*
Present participle	pudiendo
Past participle	podido
Present indicative	puedo, puedes, puede, podemos, podéis, pueden
Preterite	pude, pudiste, pudo, pudimos, pudisteis, pudieron
Future	podré, podrás, podrá, podremos, podréis, podrán
Present subjunctive	pueda, puedas, pueda, podamos, podáis, puedan
Imperfect subjunctive	pudiera (-se), pudieras, pudiera, pudiéramos, pudierais, pudieran
Familiar command	puede, poded; no puedas, no podáis
Formal command	pueda, puedan

poner, *to put*
Present participle	poniendo
Past participle	puesto
Present indicative	pongo, pones, etc.
Preterite	puse, pusiste, puso, pusimos, pusisteis, pusieron
Future	pondré, pondrás, pondrá, pondremos, pondréis, pondrán
Present subjunctive	ponga, pongas, ponga, pongamos, pongáis, pongan
Imperfect subjunctive	pusiera (-se), pusieras, pusiera, pusiéramos, pusierais, pusieran
Familiar command	pon, poned; no pongas, no pongáis
Formal command	ponga, pongan

querer, *to want, to love*
Present indicative	quiero, quieres, quiere, queremos, queréis, quieren
Preterite	quise, quisiste, quiso, quisimos, quisisteis, quisieron
Future	querré, querrás, querrá, querremos, querréis, querrán
Present subjunctive	quiera, quieras, quiera, queramos, queráis, quieran
Imperfect subjunctive	quisiera (-se), quisieras, quisiera, quisiéramos, quisierais, quisieran
Familiar command	quiere, quered; no quieras, no queráis
Formal command	quiera, quieran

reír, *to laugh*
Present participle	riendo
Past participle	reído
Present indicative	río, ríes, ríe, reímos, reís, ríen
Preterite	reí, reíste, rió, reímos, reísteis, rieron
Future	reiré, reirás, reirá, reiremos, reiréis, reirán
Present subjunctive	ría, rías, ría, riamos, riáis, rían
Imperfect subjunctive	riera (-se), rieras, riera, riéramos, rierais, rieran
Familiar command	ríe, reid; no rías, no riáis
Formal command	ría, rían

saber, *to know*
Present indicative	sé, sabes, etc.
Preterite	supe, supiste, supo, supimos, supisteis, supieron
Future	sabré, sabrás, sabrá, sabremos, sabréis, sabrán
Present subjunctive	sepa, sepas, sepa, sepamos, sepáis, sepan
Imperfect subjunctive	supiera (-se), supieras, supiera, supiéramos, supierais, supieran

salir, *to leave*
Present indicative	salgo, sales, etc.
Future	saldré, saldrás, saldrá, saldremos, saldréis, saldrán
Present subjunctive	salga, salgas, salga, salgamos, salgáis, salgan
Familiar command	sal, salid; no salgas, no salgáis
Formal command	salga, salgan

seguir, *to follow*
Present participle	siguiendo
Past participle	seguido
Present indicative	sigo, sigues, sigue, seguimos, seguís, siguen
Preterite	seguí, seguiste, siguió, seguimos, seguisteis, siguieron
Present subjunctive	siga, sigas, siga, sigamos, sigáis, sigan
Imperfect subjunctive	siguiera (-se), siguieras, siguiera, siguiéramos, siguierais, siguieran
Familiar command	sigue, seguid; no sigas, no sigáis
Formal command	siga, sigan

ser, *to be*
Present indicative	soy, eres, es, somos, sois, son
Preterite	fui, fuiste, fue, fuimos, fuisteis, fueron
Present subjunctive	sea, seas, sea, seamos, seáis, sean
Imperfect subjunctive	fuera (-se), fueras, fuera, fuéramos, fuerais, fueran
Familiar command	se, sed; no seas, no seáis
Formal command	sea, sean

tener, *to have*
Present indicative	tengo, tienes, tiene, tenemos, tenéis, tienen
Preterite	tuve, tuviste, tuvo, tuvimos, tuvisteis, tuvieron
Future	tendré, tendrás, tendrá, tendremos, tendréis, tendrán
Present subjunctive	tenga, tengas, tenga, tengamos, tengáis, tengan

Imperfect subjunctive	tuviera (-se), tuvieras, tuviera, tuviéramos, tuvierais, tuvieran
Familiar command	ten, tened; no tengas, no tengáis
Formal command	tenga, tengan

traer, *to bring*

Present participle	trayendo
Past participle	traído
Present indicative	traigo, traes, etc.
Preterite	traje, trajiste, trajo, trajimos, trajisteis, trajeron
Present subjunctive	traiga, traigas, traiga, traigamos, traigáis, traigan
Imperfect subjunctive	trajera (-se), trajeras, trajera, trajéramos, trajerais, trajeran
Familiar command	trae, traed; no traigas, no traigáis
Formal command	traiga, traigan

venir, *to come*

Present participle	viniendo
Past participle	venido
Present indicative	vengo, vienes, viene, venimos, venís, vienen
Preterite	vine, viniste, vino, vinimos, vinisteis, vinieron
Present subjunctive	venga, vengas, venga, vengamos, vengáis, vengan
Imperfect subjunctive	viniera (-se), vinieras, viniera, viniéramos, vinierais, vinieran
Familiar command	ven, venid; no vengas, no vengáis
Formal command	venga, vengan

ver, *to see*

Past participle	visto
Present indicative	veo, ves, etc.
Present subjunctive	vea, veas, vea, veamos, veáis, vean

INDEX